THE COMPLETE WORKS OF
CHRISTOPHER MARLOWE
VOLUME 1

Verso and recto of manuscript leaf of Scene xviii, lines 806–20, of *The Massacre at Paris*, believed to be the only preserved example of Marlowe's hand. Reproduced by kind permission of the Folger Shakespeare Library, Washington. (Approximately half-size.)

THE COMPLETE WORKS OF
Christopher Marlowe

EDITED BY
FREDSON BOWERS

LINDEN KENT MEMORIAL PROFESSOR OF ENGLISH LITERATURE
UNIVERSITY OF VIRGINIA

VOLUME I

DIDO, QUEENE OF CARTHAGE
TAMBURLAINE
THE JEW OF MALTA
THE MASSACRE AT PARIS

CAMBRIDGE
AT THE UNIVERSITY PRESS
1973

106549

PUBLISHED BY THE SYNDICS OF THE CAMBRIDGE UNIVERSITY PRESS
BENTLEY HOUSE, 200 EUSTON ROAD, LONDON NWI 2DB
AMERICAN BRANCH: 32 EAST 57TH STREET, NEW YORK, N.Y.10022

© CAMBRIDGE UNIVERSITY PRESS 1973

LIBRARY OF CONGRESS CATALOGUE CARD NUMBER: 67–10016

ISBN: 0 521 20031 8

PRINTED IN GREAT BRITAIN
AT THE UNIVERSITY PRINTING HOUSE, CAMBRIDGE
(BROOKE CRUTCHLEY, UNIVERSITY PRINTER)

ERRATA

page 76, line 1, *for* (1862) *read* (1962)

I. *Tamburlaine*
Prologue, line 8, *for* if *read* as
II. iii. 36, for *Usumcansae* read *Usumcasane*
IV. iii. 42, *for* ferae *read* feare

II. *Tamburlaine*
I. iii. 21, *for* me thks irinthe *read* me thinks their
III. v, *lines 152 and 153 should be transposed*

The Massacre at Paris
v. 281, 283, for *Getes* read *Retes*
v. 282, 284, for *Ruise* read *Guise*
p. 98, *note, 5 lines from the foot*, for *Guire* read *Guise*

CONTENTS

VOLUME I

VOLUME II

FOREWORD

This is a critically edited, old-spelling edition of the preserved works of Christopher Marlowe that can be identified with confidence. Through a choice of copy-texts that stand nearest in direct line to the lost manuscripts, these plays and poems are presented in as close a form to the original inscription as can be recovered from the printed editions both in respect to the texture of spelling, punctuation, capitalization and word-division and in respect to the words that Marlowe wrote. In addition to footnotes that detail all substantive emendations from the copy-text and their earliest source (the editor is responsible for all unassigned emendations), the apparatus consists of a record of press-variants in collated copies of the first edition; a series of textual notes that discuss various emendations or failure to emend; a separate record of all emendations to the accidentals of the copy-text, with their earliest source when drawn from some sixteenth- or seventeenth-century edition; and finally a historical collation of all substantive variants from the edited text not only in the early editions but also in a series of edited texts of historical or textual interest, including all complete editions of Marlowe and a selection of texts of individual plays and poems. From this apparatus a reader may reconstruct the original copy-text in almost complete detail save for the conventional silent alterations of details of purely typographical interest. The editing of critical old-spelling Elizabethan texts seems to have been sufficiently codified as not to require here an extended description. A concerned reader may find a full account of the methods and procedures in the Textual Introduction to the editor's *Dramatic Works in the Beaumont and Fletcher Canon*, vol. 1 (1968), with especial reference on pp. xiv–xviii to the range of silent alterations.

Despite the various admirable modernized editions of Marlowe that are presently available, room may be made for a more specialized edition that attempts to provide a reading text in critical old-spelling form yet with the means furnished to enable the scholar to recover the copy-text originals in convenient manner. Over sixty years have passed since the standard old-spelling Marlowe was put out by Tucker Brooke in 1910. For its date this edition cannot be sufficiently praised, for it is amazingly accurate, with but a few trifling differences, from the spellings of the first editions. But in the interval concepts of editing early texts have developed in sophistication. The Tucker Brooke edition is only partly a reading text and is unduly faithful to the defects of its copy-texts; yet very oddly it combines a conservatism in emendation of substantives with a certain amount of unsuspected silent alteration of the punctuation, so that one can never be entirely sure of the original readings in these respects. The collations are sometimes slightly erratic, so that the historical record of the readings of editions after the first, both early and in edited form, is not entirely adequate for exact scholarly use. Also, the number of identified early editions has increased since 1910.

Moreover, in the past sixty years a few more materials have become available. The present edition is fortunate in being able to include in the *Hero and Leander* collations the previously unrecorded readings of the unique perfect copy of Q5 of 1609, owned by Mr Allerton Hickmott of West Hartford, Connecticut, to whom the editor's thanks are due for his generosity. The Garrett copy of the unique 1619 B2 quarto of *Doctor Faustus* is now publicly available in the Princeton University Library so that Sir Walter Greg's records of its substantive variants have been rechecked (a superfluous operation, of course), but in addition such of its accidental variants as are needed for emendation can be correctly assigned. The order of the undated editions of the *Elegies* is now demonstrable and a complete record of their substantive variation is provided for the first time. Together with Professor Millar MacLure's Revels edition of the Poems (1968), this edition has escaped attributing to Marlowe the lyric 'I walkt along a stream for pureness rare' which the late Mr John Crow correctly assigned to Gervase Markham's *Devoreux* (1597). Through the researches of Professor Mark Eccles this edition also joins the Revels in adding two of Marlowe's Latin works previously rejected, and one of these – the epitaph on Sir Roger Manwood – has had the two manuscript copies in the Folger Shakespeare Library given a full collation and assignment of order not previously available.

It would be pretentious to claim that the present edition has done very much more than, by a fresh survey, to offer fuller records of the textual transmission and the edited tradition, and in some respects, perhaps, to refine the wording. When a dramatist and poet like Marlowe has been edited so many times by scholars, startling upsets and illuminations are likely to be rare indeed. As with Shakespeare, an editor can but re-order a few details in the presentation of the text and occasionally glean a new reading after the gathering of the sheaves, or, as in *Hero and Leander*, remove a persistent corruption or two in the several texts. On the other hand, in one or two works a fresh investigation of the textual bases has resulted in information that has been put to editorial use. The transmission of the *Elegies* had not heretofore been fully investigated, but the order of the two undated editions of the *Certain Elegies* can now be demonstrated, so that the printing closest to the lost manuscript can be used for the first time as copy-text for these particular elegies. In addition, the information that this edition of the *Certain Elegies* is physically linked with the first of the complete editions and thus exercised an influence on it has had a specific effect on the estimate of the authority of the readings of this complete edition which hitherto have been perhaps too uncritically accepted. More confidence can now be placed in the 1594 *Edward II* since a demonstration is possible that it is the true first edition.

A more comprehensive analysis of the transmission of 'The Passionate Shepherd to his Love' has advanced by a step our knowledge of the authoritative readings of this poem. The one novelty, however, is the investigation of the notorious problem of *Doctor Faustus* with the simplifying conclusion that the older normal view is correct that the 1602 Rowley–Birde additions and revisions are present in the 1616 B1 text. It would seem that scholarship of the past twenty years has been led into labyrinthine courses by rejecting this view on what turns out to be insufficient and ambiguous evidence. The problem of the contamination of the text of the tragic action by the use of the 1613 A3 quarto in putting together the printer's copy for the new 1616 edition remains. In this matter editorial decision is made slightly easier from time to time in dealing with changes that are mystifying if performed direct from printed copy by the compositor, or from annotation of the leaves of the A3 quarto by the B1 editor, but are somewhat less so if they are the result of a manuscript transcript to serve as printer's copy for these parts of the play inscribed by this editor using both the basic manuscript and the A3 quarto as his authorities. Critical views of the play may be clarified, perhaps, by the new account of the contents of the original play and of its revised 1602 version, which has some bearing also on the authorship of previously debated parts of the comic and farcical sections and also of the concluding scene.

The editor wishes to express his gratitude to the various libraries which permitted the use of their books and manuscripts, including the British Museum, the Bodleian Library, the Dyce Collection of the Victoria and Albert Museum, the Pepys Collection of Magdalen College Cambridge, Lincoln College Oxford, the Folger Shakespeare Library, the Henry E. Huntington Library, the Chapin Collection in the Williams College Library, the Carl H. Pforzheimer Library, and the libraries of Harvard and of Princeton Universities. The editor is particularly grateful to Mr Allerton Hickmott for xeroxes of his unique perfect copy of the 1609 *Hero and Leander* and for permission to print the collation. Professor Arthur F. Stocker of the Department of Classics in the University of Virginia most kindly made a translation of the Latin epitaph on Sir Roger Manwood, and Professor Mark Eccles of the University of Wisconsin gave permission for the use of his translation of the dedicatory Latin epistle to the Countess of Pembroke in *Amintæ Gaudia Authore Thoma Watsono*. Professor H. J. Oliver generously assisted with problems of the Oxberry editions, which he was the first to discover. Mr Eugene Lyman of the University of Virginia School of Graduate Studies devoted much time to checking the collations of *Tamburlaine* and the *Elegies*, and Miss Carolinda Hales those of *Edward II*. Mr Desmond Neill of the Bodleian Library, Mr R. J. Roberts of the British Museum, Miss Dorothy Mason of the Folger Shakespeare Library, Miss May Isabel Fry of the Huntington Library, Miss Carolyn Jakeman of the Houghton Library in Harvard University, and Miss Gillian G. M. Kyles of Charlottesville kindly answered queries and assisted in the collection of materials, as did Professor Robert Fehrenbach in the Department of English of the College of William and Mary, who is preparing a computer concordance of Marlowe based on the present text. The scrupulous attention of the Cambridge University Press has weeded out various inconsistencies and errors that would otherwise have been overlooked. Grants for photographic expenses and a semester of research leave of absence from the University of Virginia have materially assisted the completion of this edition.

F. B.

Charlottesville, Virginia
15 July 1971

DIDO, QUEENE OF CARTHAGE

TEXTUAL INTRODUCTION

The Tragedy of Dido, Queene of Carthage was not entered in the Stationers' Register before its publication in quarto, 1594, printed by the Widow Orwin for Thomas Woodcock (Greg, *Bibliography*, no. 128). Since Woodcock died on 22 April 1594, the quarto is generally taken as having been printed before that date (Greg, *Bibliography*, IV, 1669). No other early edition is known, although on 9 February 1596 Woodcock's widow transferred her right to Paul Linley, and on 26 June 1600 Linley his right to John Flasket. Two perhaps untrustworthy witnesses reported in mid-eighteenth century a copy with an elegy by Nashe to Marlowe inserted, probably after the title. This copy, if it ever existed, has not been found. Only three examples of the 1594 quarto are known: the Bodleian Library (Mal. 133), the Folger Shakespeare Library, and the Henry E. Huntington Library. Collation discloses no press-variants in these copies.

The date of composition, and the share of Nashe, are uncertain. The titlepage advertises the play as acted by the Children of Her Majesty's Chapel, and names both Marlowe and Nashe as authors. The titlepage also includes a cast of characters, names only.[1]

The quarto collates A–F⁴ G², its leaves unnumbered. In his type-script dissertation *The Printing of the Early Editions of Marlowe's Plays* (University Microfilms, 1964), Dr Robert F. Welsh makes a bibliographical analysis of the quarto (pp. 73–84) that discloses it was machined with only one skeleton-forme throughout, that sheet A (the text begins on sig. A2) was printed after half-sheet G, and that in sheet E the outer forme preceded the inner through the press. Only a single compositor set the play, casting off his copy and setting by formes. In sheets D–F the outer forme was first on the press, and presumably first composed. The evidence of identifiable types, however, discloses that although sheets B and C were set by formes, the order of setting was B(o), C(o), B(i), C(i). Sheet A

---

[1] The cast can have little authority, of course, but it is complete. In it *Mercurie* is listed, succeeded by *or Hermes*, and *Cloanthus* is spelled 'Cloanthes'.

was also set by formes, but in this case the inner was first. Dr Welsh has been unable to identify the compositor in other plays from Orwin's shop.

The present editor agrees with H. J. Oliver's conclusions (Revels edition, pp. xxii–xxv) that the compositorial characteristics are in general so even as to conceal any evidence that might have been available in the printer's copy as to the assignment of authorship. The same relative uniformity prevents any guesses about the nature of the manuscript that underlies the print, whether holograph papers of one or of both authors, or else a transcript. Despite the surface smoothness, however, the text for its length has a relatively large number of substantive errors, chiefly misreadings that may go back to a difficulty with the handwriting. For some reason, III.ii is particularly corrupt.

So far as is known, J. Chappell did not publish an edition of Dido,[1] so that the earliest observed edition after Q of 1594 is that by William Oxberry in 1818. In 1825 the play appeared in volume II of *The Old English Drama*, published by Hurst, Robinson, & Co., and generally taken to be edited by Hurst. Thereafter *Dido* was included in the 1826 Pickering edition of Marlowe's *Works*, probably edited by George Robinson, in Alexander Dyce's *Works* of 1850, revised in 1858, in Francis Cunningham's *Works* (1870), in Bullen's *Works* (1884–5), in the C. F. Tucker Brooke *Works* for Clarendon (1910), again edited by Tucker Brooke for the Methuen edition (1930), by Irving Ribner for *Plays* (1963), and by H. J. Oliver for the Revels edition (1968). It was also included in the Alexander Grosart *Works of Thomas Nashe*, volume VI of 1885 and the *Works of Nashe* edited by R. B. McKerrow, volume II of 1904. The variant substantive readings from these editions have been recorded, as have the manuscript readings in James Broughton's copy of Robinson now in the British Museum, and the John Payne Collier notes in the 1850 Dyce in the British Museum. The 1594 quarto is, of course, the copy-text.

On 3 January 1598 Henslowe lent twenty-nine shillings for

[1] Although the Hurst edition does not follow the Oxberry omissions, except for one example, its substantive variants from Q almost invariably agree with Oxberry. This anomaly could be explained if both Hurst and Oxberry derived from an unknown Chappell edition in 1818.

costuming 'the littell boye...A geanst the playe of dido & enevs'; on 10 March 'j tome of Dido' appears in an inventory of the properties of the Admiral's Men, and later in the same inventory 'Cupedes bowe, & quiver; the clothe of the Sone & Mone' and in another inventory on 13 March 'Dides robe'.[1] The item for Cupid's bow, Greg believes, was more likely for *Five Plays in One* than for the 1597 production of the play *Dido and Aeneas*. But no critic is at all certain that this Henslowe play was the Marlowe and Nashe *Dido* or some other.

[1] *Henslowe's Diary*, ed. Foakes and Rickert (1961), pp. 86, 319, 320, 323.

[DRAMATIS PERSONÆ

JUPITER
GANYMEDE
MERCURY, or HERMES } Gods
CUPID

VENUS } Goddesses
JUNO

ÆNEAS
ASCANIUS, his son
ACHATES
ILIONEUS } Trojans
CLOANTHUS
SERGESTUS

IARBAS, King of Gaetulia
DIDO, Queen of Carthage
ANNA, her sister
Nurse
Trojan soldiers, Cathaginian Lords, servants.]

The Tragedie of *Dido*, Queene of *Carthage*

Here the Curtaines draw, there is discovered Jupiter *dandling*   [I.i]
Ganimed *upon his knee, and* Mercury
lying asleepe.

Jupiter.   Come gentle *Ganimed* and play with me,
  I love thee well, say *Juno* what she will.
Ganimed.   I am much better for your worthles love,
  That will not shield me from her shrewish blowes:
  To day when as I fild into your cups,
  And held the cloath of pleasance whiles you dranke,
  She reacht me such a rap for that I spilde,
  As made the bloud run downe about mine eares.
Jupiter.   What? dares she strike the darling of my thoughts?
  By *Saturnes* soule, and this earth threatning haire,   10
  That shaken thrise, makes Natures buildings quake,
  I vow, if she but once frowne on thee more,
  To hang her meteor like twixt heaven and earth,
  And bind her hand and foote with golden cordes,
  As once I did for harming *Hercules*.
Ganimed.   Might I but see that pretie sport a foote,
  O how would I with *Helens* brother laugh,
  And bring the Gods to wonder at the game:
  Sweet *Jupiter*, if ere I pleasde thine eye,
  Or seemed faire walde in with Egles wings,   20
  Grace my immortall beautie with this boone,
  And I will spend my time in thy bright armes.
Jupiter.   What ist sweet wagge I should deny thy youth?
  Whose face reflects such pleasure to mine eyes,
  As I exhal'd with thy fire darting beames,
  Have oft driven backe the horses of the night,
  When as they would have hal'd thee from my sight:
  Sit on my knee, and call for thy content,

*10 haire] Dyce; aire Q

Controule proud Fate, and cut the thred of time.
Why, are not all the Gods at thy commaund,   30
And heaven and earth the bounds of thy delight?
Vulcan shall daunce to make thee laughing sport,
And my nine Daughters sing when thou art sad,
From *Junos* bird Ile pluck her spotted pride,
To make thee fannes wherewith to coole thy face,
And *Venus* Swannes shall shed their silver downe,
To sweeten out the slumbers of thy bed:
Hermes no more shall shew the world his wings,
If that thy fancie in his feathers dwell,
But as this one Ile teare them all from him,   40

                  [*Plucks a feather from* Mercuries *wings.*]

Doe thou but say their colour pleaseth me.
Hold here my little love: these linked gems,   [*Gives jewells.*]
My *Juno* ware upon her marriage day,
Put thou about thy necke my owne sweet heart,
And tricke thy armes and shoulders with my theft.
Ganimed.   I would have a jewell for mine eare,
And a fine brouch to put in my hat,
And then Ile hugge with you an hundred times.
Jupiter.   And shall have *Ganimed,* if thou wilt be my love.

                  Enter Venus.

Venus.   I, this is it, you can sit toying there,   50
And playing with that female wanton boy,
Whiles my *Æneas* wanders on the Seas,
And rests a pray to every billowes pride.
Juno, false *Juno* in her Chariots pompe,
Drawne through the heavens by Steedes of *Boreas* brood,
Made *Hebe* to direct her ayrie wheeles
Into the windie countrie of the clowdes,
Where finding *Æolus* intrencht with stormes,
And guarded with a thousand grislie ghosts,
She humbly did beseech him for our bane,   60
And charg'd him drowne my sonne with all his traine.

42 love:] Dyce (~ ;); ~ ∧ Q

Then gan the windes breake ope their brazen doores,
And all *Æolia* to be up in armes:
Poore *Troy* must now be sackt upon the Sea,
And *Neptunes* waves be envious men of warre,
Epeus horse, to *Ætnas* hill transformd,
Prepared stands to wracke their woodden walles,
And *Æolus* like *Agamemnon* sounds
The surges, his fierce souldiers, to the spoyle:
See how the night *Ulysses*-like comes forth,   70
And intercepts the day as *Dolon* erst:
Ay me! the Starres supprisde like *Rhesus* Steedes,
Are drawne by darknes forth *Astræus* tents.
What shall I doe to save thee my sweet boy?
When as the waves doe threat our Chrystall world,
And *Proteus* raising hils of flouds on high,
Entends ere long to sport him in the skie.
False *Jupiter*, rewardst thou vertue so?
What? is not pietie exempt from woe?
Then dye *Æneas* in thine innocence,   80
Since that religion hath no recompence.
Jupiter.   Content thee *Cytherea* in thy care,
Since thy *Æneas* wandring fate is firme,
Whose wearie lims shall shortly make repose,
In those faire walles I promist him of yore:
But first in bloud must his good fortune bud,
Before he be the Lord of *Turnus* towne,
Or force her smile that hetherto hath frownd:
Three winters shall he with the Rutiles warre,
And in the end subdue them with his sword,   90
And full three Sommers likewise shall he waste,
In mannaging those fierce barbarian mindes:
Which once performd, poore *Troy* so long supprest,
From forth her ashes shall advance her head,
And flourish once againe that erst was dead:
But bright *Ascanius*, beauties better worke,
Who with the Sunne devides one radiant shape,

96 *Ascanius*, beauties] Broughton MS; ~ ∧ ~ Q

Shall build his throne amidst those starrie towers,
That earth-borne *Atlas* groning underprops:
No bounds but heaven shall bound his Emperie,   100
Whose azured gates enchased with his name,
Shall make the morning hast her gray uprise,
To feede her eyes with his engraven fame.
Thus in stoute *Hectors* race three hundred yeares,
The Romane Scepter royall shall remaine,
Till that a Princesse priest conceav'd by *Mars*,
Shall yeeld to dignitie a dubble birth,
Who will eternish *Troy* in their attempts.
Venus. How may I credite these thy flattering termes,
When yet both sea and sands beset their ships,   110
And *Phœbus* as in Stygian pooles, refraines
To taint his tresses in the Tyrrhen maine?
Jupiter. I will take order for that presently:
Hermes awake, and haste to *Neptunes* realme,
Whereas the Wind-god warring now with Fate,
Besiege the ofspring of our kingly loynes,
Charge him from me to turne his stormie powers,
And fetter them in *Vulcans* sturdie brasse,
That durst thus proudly wrong our kinsmans peace.

                        [*Exit* Mercury.]

Venus farewell, thy sonne shall be our care: 120
Come *Ganimed*, we must about this geare.

                  Exeunt Jupiter *cum* Ganimed.

Venus. Disquiet Seas lay downe your swelling lookes,
And court *Æneas* with your calmie cheere,
Whose beautious burden well might make you proude,
Had not the heavens conceav'd with hel-borne clowdes,
Vaild his resplendant glorie from your view.
For my sake pitie him *Oceanus*,
That erst-while issued from thy watrie loynes,
And had my being from thy bubling froth:
Triton I know hath fild his trumpe with *Troy*,   130

---

106 Princesse priest] *i.e.*, Princesse-   *115 Whereas] *stet* Q
    priest

And therefore will take pitie on his toyle,
And call both *Thetis* and *Cimothoe*,
To succour him in this extremitie.

Enter Æneas with Ascanius [*and* Achates], *with one or two more.*

What? doe I see my sonne now come on shoare:
Venus, how art thou compast with content,
The while thine eyes attract their sought for joyes:
Great *Jupiter*, still honourd maist thou be,
For this so friendly ayde in time of neede.
Here in this bush disguised will I stand,
Whiles my *Æneas* spends himselfe in plaints,   140
And heaven and earth with his unrest acquaints.
Æneas.   You sonnes of care, companions of my course,
Priams misfortune followes us by sea,
And *Helens* rape doth haunt ye at the heeles.
How many dangers have we over past?
Both barking *Scilla*, and the sounding Rocks,
The *Cyclops* shelves, and grim *Ceranias* seate
Have you oregone, and yet remaine alive?
Pluck up your hearts, since fate still rests our friend,
And chaunging heavens may those good daies returne,   150
Which *Pergama* did vaunt in all her pride.
Achates.   Brave Prince of *Troy*, thou onely art our God,
That by thy vertues freest us from annoy,
And makes our hopes survive to coming joyes:
Doe thou but smile, and clowdie heaven will cleare,
Whose night and day descendeth from thy browes:
Though we be now in extreame miserie,
And rest the map of weatherbeaten woe:
Yet shall the aged Sunne shed forth his haire,
To make us live unto our former heate,   160
And every beast the forrest doth send forth,
Bequeath her young ones to our scanted foode.

132 *Cimothoe*] Dyce (*qy*) (Cymothoe);   *147 *Ceranias*] stet Q
    Cimodoæ Q   *154 coming] Dyce; cunning Q
*144 ye] Dyce; thee Q   159 haire] Broughton MS; aire Q

Ascanius. Father I faint, good father give me meate.
Æneas. Alas sweet boy, thou must be still a while,
Till we have fire to dresse the meate we kild:
Gentle *Achates,* reach the Tinder boxe,
That we may make a fire to warme us with,
And rost our new found victuals on this shoare.
Venus. See what strange arts necessitie findes out, [*Aside.*]
How neere my sweet *Æneas* art thou driven? 170
Æneas. Hold, take this candle and goe light a fire,
You shall have leaves and windfall bowes enow
Neere to these woods, to rost your meate withall:
Ascanius, goe and drie thy drenched lims,
Whiles I with my *Achates* roave abroad,
To know what coast the winde hath driven us on,
Or whether men or beasts inhabite it.
[*Exit* Ascanius *with others.*]
Achates. The ayre is pleasant, and the soyle most fit
For Cities, and societies supports:
Yet much I marvell that I cannot finde, 180
No steps of men imprinted in the earth.
Venus. Now is the time for me to play my part:
Hoe yong men, saw you as you came
Any of all my Sisters wandring here?
Having a quiver girded to her side,
And cloathed in a spotted Leopards skin.
Æneas. I neither saw nor heard of any such:
But what may I faire Virgin call your name?
Whose lookes set forth no mortall forme to view,
Nor speech bewraies ought humaine in thy birth, 190
Thou art a Goddesse that delud'st our eyes,
And shrowdes thy beautie in this borrowd shape:
But whether thou the Sunnes bright Sister be,
Or one of chast *Dianas* fellow Nimphs,
Live happie in the height of all content,
And lighten our extreames with this one boone,
As to instruct us under what good heaven
We breathe as now, and what this world is calde,

On which by tempests furie we are cast.
Tell us, O tell us that are ignorant,   200
And this right hand shall make thy Altars crack
With mountaine heapes of milke white Sacrifize.
Venus.   Such honour, stranger, doe I not affect:
It is the use for Tirien maides to weare
Their bowe and quiver in this modest sort,
And suite themselves in purple for the nonce,
That they may trip more lightly ore the lawndes,
And overtake the tusked Bore in chase.
But for the land whereof thou doest enquire,
It is the Punick kingdome rich and strong,   210
Adjoyning on *Agenors* stately towne,
The kingly seate of Southerne *Libia,*
Whereas Sidonian *Dido* rules as Queene.
But what are you that aske of me these things?
Whence may you come, or whither will you goe?
Æneas.   Of *Troy* am I, *Æneas* is my name,
Who driven by warre from forth my native world,
Put sailes to sea to seeke out *Italy,*
And my divine descent from sceptred *Jove*:
With twise twelve Phrigian ships I plowed the deepe,   220
And made that way my mother *Venus* led:
But of them all scarce seven doe anchor safe,
And they so wrackt and weltred by the waves,
As every tide tilts twixt their oken sides:
And all of them unburdened of their loade,
Are ballassed with billowes watrie weight.
But haples I, God wot, poore and unknowne,
Doe trace these Libian deserts all despisde,
Exild forth *Europe* and wide *Asia* both,
And have not any coverture but heaven.   230
Venus.   Fortune hath favord thee what ere thou be,
In sending thee unto this curteous Coast:
A Gods name on and hast thee to the Court,
Where *Dido* will receive ye with her smiles:

204 Tirien] Oxbury (Tyrian); Turen Q

13

And for thy ships which thou supposest lost,
Not one of them hath perisht in the storme,
But are arived safe not farre from hence:
And so I leave thee to thy fortunes lot,
Wishing good lucke unto thy wandring steps.   *Exit.*
Æneas.   *Achates,* tis my mother that is fled,   240
I know her by the movings of her feete:
Stay gentle *Venus,* flye not from thy sonne,
Too cruell, why wilt thou forsake me thus?
Or in these shades deceiv'st mine eye so oft?
Why talke we not together hand in hand?
And tell our griefes in more familiar termes:
But thou art gone and leav'st me here alone,
To dull the ayre with my discoursive moane.

                                        Exeunt.

          Enter [Iarbus, *with*] Illioneus, *and* Cloanthus   [I.ii]
                    [*and* Sergestus].

Illioneus.   Follow ye Troians, follow this brave Lord,
  And plaine to him the summe of your distresse.
Iarbus.   Why, what are you, or wherefore doe you sewe?
Illioneus.   Wretches of *Troy,* envied of the windes,
  That crave such favour at your honors feete,
  As poore distressed miserie may pleade:
  Save, save, O save our ships from cruell fire,
  That doe complaine the wounds of thousand waves,
  And spare our lives whom every spite pursues.
  We come not we to wrong your Libian Gods,   10
  Or steale your houshold lares from their shrines:
  Our hands are not prepar'd to lawles spoyle,
  Nor armed to offend in any kind:
  Such force is farre from our unweaponed thoughts,
  Whose fading weale of victorie forsooke,
  Forbids all hope to harbour neere our hearts.
Iarbus.   But tell me Troians, Troians if you be,

*1 Troians] *stet* Q

14

Unto what fruitfull quarters were ye bound,
Before that *Boreas* buckled with your sailes?
Cloanthus.   There is a place *Hesperia* term'd by us,   20
An ancient Empire, famoused for armes,
And fertile in faire *Ceres* furrowed wealth,
Which now we call *Italia* of his name,
That in such peace long time did rule the same:
Thither made we,
When suddenly gloomie *Orion* rose,
And led our ships into the shallow sands,
Whereas the Southerne winde with brackish breath,
Disperst them all amongst the wrackfull Rockes:
From thence a fewe of us escapt to land,   30
The rest we feare are foulded in the flouds.
Iarbus.   Brave men at armes, abandon fruitles feares,
Since *Carthage* knowes to entertaine distresse.
Sergestus.   I but the barbarous sort doe threat our ships,
And will not let us lodge upon the sands:
In multitudes they swarme unto the shoare,
And from the first earth interdict our feete.
Iarbus.   My selfe will see they shall not trouble ye,
Your men and you shall banquet in our Court,
And every Troian be as welcome here,   40
As *Jupiter* to sillie *Baucis* house:
Come in with me, Ile bring you to my Queene,
Who shall confirme my words with further deedes.
Sergestus.   Thankes gentle Lord for such unlookt for grace.
Might we but once more see *Æneas* face,
Then would we hope to quite such friendly turnes,
As shall surpasse the wonder of our speech.

            [*Exeunt.*]

    Enter Æneas, Achates, and Ascanius [*attended*].   II.i

Æneas.   Where am I now? these should be *Carthage* walles.
Achates.   Why stands my sweete *Æneas* thus amazde?

41 *Baucis*] Oxberry; *Vausis* Q

Æneas. O my *Achates*, Theban *Niobe*,
Who for her sonnes death wept out life and breath,
And drie with griefe was turnd into a stone,
Had not such passions in her head as I.   [*Sees* Priams *statue.*]
Me thinkes that towne there should be *Troy*, yon *Idas* hill,
There *Zanthus* streame, because here's *Priamus*,
And when I know it is not, then I dye.
Achates.   And in this humor is *Achates* to,   10
I cannot choose but fall upon my knees,
And kisse his hand: O where is *Hecuba*?
Here she was wont to sit, but saving ayre
Is nothing here, and what is this but stone?
Æneas.   O yet this stone doth make *Æneas* weepe,
And would my prayers (as *Pigmalions* did)
Could give it life, that under his conduct
We might saile backe to *Troy*, and be revengde
On these hard harted Grecians, which rejoyce
That nothing now is left of *Priamus*:   20
O *Priamus* is left and this is he,
Come, come abourd, pursue the hatefull Greekes.
Achates.   What meanes *Æneas*?
Æneas.   *Achates* though mine eyes say this is stone,
Yet thinkes my minde that this is *Priamus*:
And when my grieved heart sighes and sayes no,
Then would it leape out to give *Priam* life:
O were I not at all so thou mightst be.
Achates, see King *Priam* wags his hand,
He is alive, *Troy* is not overcome.   30
Achates.   Thy mind *Æneas* that would have it so
Deludes thy eye sight, *Priamus* is dead.
Æneas.   Ah *Troy* is sackt, and *Priamus* is dead,
And why should poore *Æneas* be alive?
Ascanius.   Sweete father leave to weepe, this is not hè:
For were it *Priam* he would smile on me.
Achates.   *Æneas* see, here come the Citizens,
Leave to lament lest they laugh at our feares.

Enter Cloanthus, Sergestus, Illioneus [*and others*].

Æneas.   Lords of this towne, or whatsoever stile
Belongs unto your name, vouchsafe of ruth   40
To tell us who inhabits this faire towne,
What kind of people, and who governes them:
For we are strangers driven on this shore,
And scarcely know within what Clime we are.
Illioneus.   I heare *Æneas* voyce, but see him not,
For none of these can be our Generall.
Achates.   Like *Illioneus* speakes this Noble man,
But *Illioneus* goes not in such robes.
Sergestus.   You are *Achates*, or I am deciv'd.
Achates.   *Æneas* see, *Sergestus* or his ghost.   50
Illioneus.   He names *Æneas*, let us kisse his feete.
Cloanthus.   It is our Captaine, see *Ascanius*.
Sergestus.   Live long *Æneas* and *Ascanius*.
Æneas.   *Achates*, speake, for I am overjoyed.
Achates.   O *Illioneus*, art thou yet alive?
Illioneus.   Blest be the time I see *Achates* face.
Cloanthus.   Why turnes *Æneas* from his trustie friends?
Æneas.   *Sergestus*, *Illioneus* and the rest,
Your sight amazde me, O what destinies
Have brought my sweete companions in such plight?   60
O tell me, for I long to be resolv'd.
Illioneus.   Lovely *Æneas*, these are *Carthage* walles,
And here Queene *Dido* weares th'imperiall Crowne,
Who for *Troyes* sake hath entertaind us all,
And clad us in these wealthie robes we weare.
Oft hath she askt us under whom we serv'd,
And when we told her she would weepe for griefe,
Thinking the sea had swallowed up thy ships,
And now she sees thee how will she rejoyce?
Sergestus.   See where her servitors passe through the hall   70
Bearing a banket, *Dido* is not farre.

49 am] Broughton (*qy*); *omit* Q   51 names] Oxberry; means Q

2   17   B C D

Illioneus.   Looke where she comes: *Æneas* view her well.
Æneas.   Well may I view her, but she sees not me.

           Enter Dido [*with* Anna *and* Iarbus] *and her traine.*

Dido.   What stranger art thou that doest eye me thus?
Æneas.   Sometime I was a Troian, mightie Queene:
  But *Troy* is not, what shall I say I am?
Illioneus.   Renowmed *Dido,* tis our Generall:
  Warlike *Æneas.*
Dido.   Warlike *Æneas,* and in these base robes?
  Goe fetch the garment which *Sicheus* ware:
                    [*Exit servant.*] 80
  Brave Prince, welcome to *Carthage* and to me,
  Both happie that *Æneas* is our guest:
  Sit in this chaire and banquet with a Queene,
  Æneas is *Æneas,* were he clad
  In weedes as bad as ever *Irus* ware.
Æneas.   This is no seate for one thats comfortles,
  May it please your grace to let *Æneas* waite:
  For though my birth be great, my fortunes meane,
  Too meane to be companion to a Queene.
Dido.   Thy fortune may be greater then thy birth,   90
  Sit downe *Æneas,* sit in *Didos* place,
  And if this be thy sonne as I suppose,
  Here let him sit, be merrie lovely child.
Æneas.   This place beseemes me not, O pardon me.
Dido.   Ile have it so, *Æneas* be content.

        [*Enter servant with robe and* Æneas *puts it on.*]

Ascanius.   Madame, you shall be my mother.
Dido.   And so I will sweete child: be merrie man,
  Heres to thy better fortune and good starres.   [*Drinks.*]
Æneas.   In all humilitie I thanke your grace.
Dido.   Remember who thou art, speake like thy selfe,   100
  Humilitie belongs to common groomes.
Æneas.   And who so miserable as *Æneas* is?

72 view] Oxberry; viewd Q   **88, 235** fortunes] *i.e.* fortune is

Dido.   Lyes it in *Didos* hands to make thee blest,
Then be assured thou art not miserable.
Æneas.   O *Priamus*, O *Troy*, oh *Hecuba*!
Dido.   May I entreate thee to discourse at large,
And truely to, how *Troy* was overcome:
For many tales goe of that Cities fall,
And scarcely doe agree upon one poynt:
Some say *Antenor* did betray the towne,   110
Others report twas *Sinons* perjurie:
But all in this that *Troy* is overcome,
And *Priam* dead, yet how we heare no newes.
Æneas.   A wofull tale bids *Dido* to unfould,
Whose memorie like pale deaths stony mace,
Beates forth my senses from this troubled soule,
And makes *Æneas* sinke at *Didos* feete.
Dido.   What, faints *Æneas* to remember *Troy*?
In whose defence he fought so valiantly:
Looke up and speake.   120
Æneas.   Then speake *Æneas* with *Achilles* tongue,
And *Dido* and you Carthaginian Peeres
Heare me, but yet with *Mirmidons* harsh eares,
Daily inur'd to broyles and Massacres,
Lest you be mov'd too much with my sad tale.
The Grecian souldiers tired with ten yeares warre,
Began to crye, let us unto our ships,
Troy is invincible, why stay we here?
With whose outcryes *Atrides* being apal'd,
Summoned the Captaines to his princely tent,   130
Who looking on the scarres we Troians gave,
Seeing the number of their men decreast,
And the remainder weake and out of heart,
Gave up their voyces to dislodge the Campe,
And so in troopes all marcht to *Tenedos*:
Where when they came, *Ulysses* on the sand
Assayd with honey words to turne them backe:
And as he spoke, to further his entent

*138 spoke,...intent᷄] Oxbury (~, ...~,); ~ ᵥ...~, Q

The windes did drive huge billowes to the shoare,
And heaven was darkned with tempestuous clowdes: 140
Then he alleag'd the Gods would have them stay,
And prophecied *Troy* should be overcome:
And therewithall he calde false *Sinon* forth,
A man compact of craft and perjurie,
Whose ticing tongue was made of *Hermes* pipe,
To force an hundred watchfull eyes to sleepe:
And him, *Epeus* having made the horse,
With sacrificing wreathes upon his head,
Ulysses sent to our unhappie towne:
Who groveling in the mire of *Zanthus* bankes, 150
His hands bound at his backe, and both his eyes
Turnd up to heaven as one resolv'd to dye,
Our Phrigian shepherds haled within the gates,
And brought unto the Court of *Priamus*:
To whom he used action so pitifull,
Lookes so remorcefull, vowes so forcible,
As therewithall the old man overcome,
Kist him, imbrast him, and unloosde his bands,
And then—O *Dido*, pardon me.
Dido. Nay leave not here, resolve me of the rest. 160
Æneas. O th'inchaunting words of that base slave,
Made him to thinke *Epeus* pine-tree Horse
A sacrifize t'appease *Minervas* wrath:
The rather for that one *Laocoon*
Breaking a speare upon his hollow breast,
Was with two winged Serpents stung to death.
Whereat agast, we were commanded straight
With reverence to draw it into *Troy*.
In which unhappie worke was I employd,
These hands did helpe to hale it to the gates, 170
Through which it could not enter twas so huge.
O had it never entred, *Troy* had stood.
But *Priamus* impatient of delay,
Inforst a wide breach in that rampierd wall,

153 shepherds] Oxberry; shepherd Q

Which thousand battering Rams could never pierce,
And so came in this fatall instrument:
At whose accursed feete as overjoyed,
We banquetted till overcome with wine,
Some surfetted, and others soundly slept.
Which *Sinon* viewing, causde the Greekish spyes   180
To hast to *Tenedos* and tell the Campe:
Then he unlockt the Horse, and suddenly
From out his entrailes, *Neoptolemus*
Setting his speare upon the ground, leapt forth,
And after him a thousand Grecians more,
In whose sterne faces shin'd the quenchles fire,
That after burnt the pride of *Asia*.
By this the Campe was come unto the walles,
And through the breach did march into the streetes,
Where meeting with the rest, kill kill they cryed.   190
Frighted with this confused noyse, I rose,
And looking from a turret, might behold
Yong infants swimming in their parents bloud,
Headles carkasses piled up in heapes,
Virgins halfe dead dragged by their golden haire,
And with maine force flung on a ring of pikes,
Old men with swords thrust through their aged sides,
Kneeling for mercie to a Greekish lad,
Who with steele Pol-axes dasht out their braines.
Then buckled I mine armour, drew my sword,   200
And thinking to goe downe, came *Hectors* ghost
With ashie visage, blewish sulphure eyes,
His armes torne from his shoulders, and his breast
Furrowd with wounds, and that which made me weepe,
Thongs at his heeles, by which *Achilles* horse
Drew him in triumph through the Greekish Campe,
Burst from the earth, crying, *Æneas* flye,
Troy is a fire, the Grecians have the towne.
Dido.   O *Hector* who weepes not to heare thy name?
Æneas.   Yet flung I forth, and desperate of my life,   210
Ran in the thickest throngs, and with this sword

Sent many of their savadge ghosts to hell.
At last came *Pirrhus* fell and full of ire,
IIis harnesse dropping bloud, and on his speare
The mangled head of *Priams* yongest sonne,
And after him his band of Mirmidons,
With balles of wilde fire in their murdering pawes,
Which made the funerall flame that burnt faire *Troy*:
All which hemd me about, crying, this is he.
Dido.   Ah, how could poore *Æneas* scape their hands?   220
Æneas.   My mother *Venus* jealous of my health,
Convaid me from their crooked nets and bands:
So I escapt the furious *Pirrhus* wrath:
Who then ran to the pallace of the King,
And at *Joves* Altar finding *Priamus*,
About whose withered necke hung *Hecuba*,
Foulding his hand in hers, and joyntly both
Beating their breasts and falling on the ground,
He with his faulchions poynt raisde up at once,
And with *Megeras* eyes stared in their face,   230
Threatning a thousand deaths at every glaunce.
To whom the aged King thus trembling spoke:
Achilles sonne, remember what I was,
Father of fiftie sonnes, but they are slaine,
Lord of my fortune, but my fortunes turnd,
King of this Citie, but my *Troy* is fired,
And now am neither father, Lord, nor King:
Yet who so wretched but desires to live?
O let me live, great *Neoptolemus*.
Not mov'd at all, but smiling at his teares,   240
This butcher whil'st his hands were yet held up,
Treading upon his breast, strooke off his hands.
Dido.   O end *Æneas*, I can heare no more.
Æneas.   At which the franticke Queene leapt on his face,
And in his eyelids hanging by the nayles,
A little while prolong'd her husbands life:
At last the souldiers puld her by the heeles,
And swong her howling in the emptie ayre,

Which sent an eccho to the wounded King:
Whereat he lifted up his bedred lims,   250
And would have grappeld with *Achilles* sonne,
Forgetting both his want of strength and hands,
Which he disdaining whiskt his sword about,
And with the wind thereof the King fell downe:
Then from the navell to the throat at once,
He ript old *Priam*: at whose latter gaspe
Joves marble statue gan to bend the brow,
As lothing *Pirrhus* for this wicked act:
Yet he undaunted tooke his fathers flagge,
And dipt it in the old Kings chill cold bloud,   260
And then in triumph ran into the streetes,
Through which he could not passe for slaughtred men:
So leaning on his sword he stood stone still,
Viewing the fire wherewith rich *Ilion* burnt.
By this I got my father on my backe,
This young boy in mine armes, and by the hand
Led faire *Creusa* my beloved wife,
When thou *Achates* with thy sword mad'st way,
And we were round inviron'd with the Greekes:
O there I lost my wife: and had not we   270
Fought manfully, I had not told this tale:
Yet manhood would not serve, of force we fled,
And as we went unto our ships, thou knowest
We sawe *Cassandra* sprauling in the streetes,
Whom *Ajax* ravisht in *Dianas* Fane,
Her cheekes swolne with sighes, her haire all rent,
Whom I tooke up to beare unto our ships:
But suddenly the Grecians followed us,
And I alas, was forst to let her lye.
Then got we to our ships, and being abourd,   280
Polixena cryed out, *Æneas* stay,
The Greekes pursue me, stay and take me in.
Moved with her voyce, I lept into the sea,

---

*254 wind] Coll (qy) (*History of English*   275 Fane] Oxberry; Fawne Q
   Dramatic Poetry, 1831, vol. III,
   p. 226); wound Q

Thinking to beare her on my backe abourd,
For all our ships were launcht into the deepe:
And as I swomme, she standing on the shoare,
Was by the cruell Mirmidons surprizd,
And after by that *Pirrhus* sacrifizde.
Dido. I dye with melting ruth, *Æneas* leave.
Anna. O what became of aged *Hecuba?* 290
Iarbus. How got *Æneas* to the fleete againe?
Dido. But how scapt *Helen*, she that causde this warre?
Æneas. *Achates* speake, sorrow hath tired me quite.
Achates. What happened to the Queene we cannot shewe,
We heare they led her captive into *Greece*.
As for *Æneas* he swomme quickly backe,
And *Helena* betraied *Deiphobus*,
Her Lover after *Alexander* dyed,
And so was reconcil'd to *Menelaus*.
Dido. O had that ticing strumpet nere been borne: 300
Troian, thy ruthfull tale hath made me sad:
Come let us thinke upon some pleasing sport,
To rid me from these melancholly thoughts. *Exeunt omnes.*

Enter Venus [*with* Cupid] *at another doore, and takes*
Ascanius *by the sleeve [as he is going off].*

Venus. Faire child stay thou with *Didos* waiting maide,
Ile give thee Sugar-almonds, sweete Conserves,
A silver girdle, and a golden purse,
And this yong Prince shall be thy playfellow.
Ascanius. Are you Queene *Didos* sonne?
Cupid. I, and my mother gave me this fine bow. 310
Ascanius. Shall I have such a quiver and a bow?
Venus. Such bow, such quiver, and such golden shafts,
Will *Dido* give to sweete *Ascanius*:
For *Didos* sake I take thee in my armes,
And sticke these spangled feathers in thy hat,
Eate Comfites in mine armes, and I will sing. [*Song.*]

298 Alexander] *i.e.,* Paris

Now is he fast asleepe, and in this grove
Amongst greene brakes Ile lay *Ascanius*,
And strewe him with sweete smelling Violets,
Blushing Roses, purple *Hyacinthe*:
These milke white Doves shall be his Centronels: 320
Who if that any seeke to doe him hurt,
Will quickly flye to *Cithereas* fist.
Now *Cupid* turne thee to *Ascanius* shape,
And goe to *Dido,* who in stead of him
Will set thee on her lap and play with thee:
Then touch her white breast with this arrow head,
That she may dote upon *Æneas* love:
And by that meanes repaire his broken ships,
Victuall his Souldiers, give him wealthie gifts,
And he at last depart to *Italy,*   330
Or els in *Carthage* make his kingly throne.
Cupid.   I will faire mother, and so play my part,
As every touch shall wound Queene *Didos* heart.   [*Exit.*]
Venus.   Sleepe my sweete nephew in these cooling shades,
Free from the murmure of these running streames,
The crye of beasts, the ratling of the windes,
Or whisking of these leaves, all shall be still,
And nothing interrupt thy quiet sleepe,
Till I returne and take thee hence againe.

Exit.

Enter Cupid *solus* [*for* Ascanius].   III.i

Cupid.   Now *Cupid* cause the Carthaginian Queene,
To be inamourd of thy brothers lookes,
Convey this golden arrowe in thy sleeve,
Lest she imagine thou art *Venus* sonne:
And when she strokes thee softly on the head,
Then shall I touch her breast and conquer her.

322 *Cithereas*] Oxberry; *Citheidas* Q

Enter Iarbus, Anna, *and* Dido.

Iarbus.   How long faire *Dido* shall I pine for thee?
Tis not enough that thou doest graunt me love,
But that I may enjoy what I desire:
That love is childish which consists in words.   10
Dido.   *Iarbus,* know that thou of all my wooers
(And yet have I had many mightier Kings)
Hast had the greatest favours I could give:
I feare me *Dido* hath been counted light,
In being too familiar with *Iarbus*:
Albeit the Gods doe know no wanton thought
Had ever residence in *Didos* breast.
Iarbus.   But *Dido* is the favour I request.
Dido.   Feare not *Iarbus, Dido* may be thine.
Anna.   Looke sister how *Æneas* little sonne   20
Playes with your garments and imbraceth you.
Cupid.   No *Dido* will not take me in her armes,
I shall not be her sonne, she loves me not.
Dido.   Weepe not sweet boy, thou shalt be *Didos* sonne,
Sit in my lap and let me heare thee sing.

                                         [Cupid *sings.*]

No more my child, now talke another while,
And tell me where learndst thou this pretie song?
Cupid.   My cosin *Helen* taught it me in *Troy.*
Dido.   How lovely is *Ascanius* when he smiles?
Cupid.   Will *Dido* let me hang about her necke?   30
Dido.   I wagge, and give thee leave to kisse her to.
Cupid.   What will you give me now? Ile have this Fanne.
Dido.   Take it *Ascanius,* for thy fathers sake.
Iarbus.   Come *Dido,* leave *Ascanius,* let us walke.
Dido.   Goe thou away, *Ascanius* shall stay.
Iarbus.   Ungentle Queene, is this thy love to me?
Dido.   O stay *Iarbus,* and Ile goe with thee.
Cupid.   And if my mother goe, Ile follow her.
Dido.   Why staiest thou here? thou art no love of mine.

27 learndst] Dyce; learnst Q   32 me‸ now?] Dyce; ~ ? ~ ‸

Iarbus.   *Iarbus* dye, seeing she abandons thee.   40
Dido.   No, live *Iarbus,* what hast thou deserv'd,
  That I should say thou art no love of mine?
  Something thou hast deserv'd.—— Away I say,
  Depart from *Carthage,* come not in my sight.
Iarbus.   Am I not King of rich *Getulia?*
Dido.   *Iarbus* pardon me, and stay a while.
Cupid.   Mother, looke here.
Dido.   What telst thou me of rich *Getulia?*
  Am not I Queen of *Libia?* then depart.
Iarbus.   I goe to feed the humour of my Love,   50
  Yet not from *Carthage* for a thousand worlds.
Dido.   *Iarbus.*
Iarbus.   Doth *Dido* call me backe?
Dido.   No, but I charge thee never looke on me.
Iarbus.   Then pull out both mine eyes, or let me dye.

                                        Exit Iarbus.

Anna.   Wherefore doth *Dido* bid *Iarbus* goe?
Dido.   Because his lothsome sight offends mine eye,
  And in my thoughts is shrin'd another love:
  O *Anna,* didst thou know how sweet love were,
  Full soone wouldst thou abjure this single life.   60
Anna.   Poore soule I know too well the sower of love, [*Aside.*]
  O that *Iarbus* could but fancie me.
Dido.   Is not *Æneas* faire and beautifull?
Anna.   Yes, and *Iarbus* foule and favourles.
Dido.   Is he not eloquent in all his speech?
Anna.   Yes, and *Iarbus* rude and rusticall.
Dido.   Name not *Iarbus,* but sweete *Anna* say,
  Is not *Æneas* worthie *Didos* love?
Anna.   O sister, were you Empresse of the world,
  Æneas well deserves to be your love,   70
  So lovely is he that where ere he goes,
  The people swarme to gaze him in the face.
Dido.   But tell them none shall gaze on him but I,
  Lest their grosse eye-beames taint my lovers cheekes:

*48 What_] *stet* Q   58 love] Dyce; Ioue Q

Anna, good sister *Anna* goe for him,
Lest with these sweete thoughts I melt cleane away.
Anna.   Then sister youle abjure *Iarbus* love?
Dido.   Yet must I heare that lothsome name againe?
Runne for *Æneas,* or Ile flye to him.   *Exit* Anna.
Cupid.   You shall not hurt my father when he comes.   80
Dido.   No, for thy sake Ile love thy father well.
O dull conceipted *Dido,* that till now
Didst never thinke *Æneas* beautifull:
But now for quittance of this oversight,
Ile make me bracelets of his golden haire,
His glistering eyes shall be my looking glasse,
His lips an altar, where Ile offer up
As many kisses as the Sea hath sands,
In stead of musicke I will heare him speake,
His lookes shall be my only Librarie,   90
And thou *Æneas, Didos* treasurie,
In whose faire bosome I will locke more wealth,
Then twentie thousand *Indiaes* can affoord:
O here he comes, love, love, give *Dido* leave
To be more modest then her thoughts admit,
Lest I be made a wonder to the world.

[*Enter* Æneas, Achates, Sergestus, Illioneus, *and* Cloanthus.]

Achates, how doth *Carthage* please your Lord?
Achates.   That will *Æneas* shewe your majestie.
Dido.   *Æneas,* art thou there?
Æneas.   I understand your highnesse sent for me.   100
Dido.   No, but now thou art here, tell me in sooth
In what might *Dido* highly pleasure thee.
Æneas.   So much have I receiv'd at *Didos* hands,
As without blushing I can aske no more:
Yet Queene of *Affricke,* are my ships unrigd,
My Sailes all rent in sunder with the winde,
My Oares broken, and my Tackling lost,
Yea all my Navie split with Rockes and Shelfes:
Nor Sterne nor Anchor have our maimed Fleete,

Our Masts the furious windes strooke over bourd: 110
Which piteous wants if *Dido* will supplie,
We will account her author of our lives.
Dido.   *Æneas*, Ile repaire thy Troian ships,
Conditionally that thou wilt stay with me,
And let *Achates* saile to *Italy*:
Ile give thee tackling made of riveld gold,
Wound on the barkes of odoriferous trees,
Oares of massie Ivorie full of holes,
Through which the water shall delight to play:
Thy Anchors shall be hewed from Christall Rockes,   120
Which if thou lose shall shine above the waves:
The Masts whereon thy swelling sailes shall hang,
Hollow Pyramides of silver plate:
The sailes of foulded Lawne, where shall be wrought
The warres of *Troy*, but not *Troyes* overthrow:
For ballace, emptie *Didos* treasurie,
Take what ye will, but leave *Æneas* here.
Achates, thou shalt be so meanly clad,
As Seaborne Nymphes shall swarme about thy ships,
And wanton Mermaides court thee with sweete songs,   130
Flinging in favours of more soveraigne worth,
Then *Thetis* hangs about *Apolloes* necke,
So that *Æneas* may but stay with me.
Æneas.   Wherefore would *Dido* have *Æneas* stay?
Dido.   To warre against my bordering enemies:
Æneas, thinke not *Dido* is in love:
For if that any man could conquer me,
I had been wedded ere *Æneas* came:
See where the pictures of my suiters hang,
And are not these as faire as faire may be?   140
Achates.   I saw this man at *Troy* ere *Troy* was sackt.
Æneas.   I this in *Greece* when *Paris* stole faire *Helen*.
Illioneus.   This man and I were at *Olympus* games.
Sergestus.   I know this face, he is a Persian borne,
I traveld with him to *Ætolia*.

*128 meanly] *stet* Q

Cloanthus.   And I in *Athens* with this gentleman,
Unlesse I be deceiv'd disputed once.
Dido.   But speake *Æneas*, know you none of these?
Æneas.   No Madame, but it seemes that these are Kings.
Dido.   All these and others which I never sawe,   150
Have been most urgent suiters for my love,
Some came in person, others sent their Legats:
Yet none obtaind me, I am free from all.——
And yet God knowes intangled unto one.——   [*Aside.*]
This was an Orator, and thought by words
To compasse me, but yet he was deceiv'd:
And this a Spartan Courtier vaine and wilde,
But his fantastick humours pleasde not me:
This was *Alcion*, a Musition,
But playd he nere so sweet, I let him goe: 160
This was the wealthie King of *Thessaly*,
But I had gold enough and cast him off:
This *Meleagers* sonne, a warlike Prince,
But weapons gree not with my tender yeares:
The rest are such as all the world well knowes,
Yet how I sweare by heaven and him I love,
I was as farre from love, as they from hate.
Æneas.   O happie shall he be whom *Dido* loves.
Dido.   Then never say that thou art miserable,
Because it may be thou shalt be my love: 170
Yet boast not of it, for I love thee not,
And yet I hate thee not:—— O if I speake
I shall betray my selfe:—— *Æneas* speake,
We two will goe a hunting in the woods,
But not so much for thee, thou art but one,
As for *Achates*, and his followers.

Exeunt.

*166 how] *stet* Q

Enter Juno *to* Ascanius *asleepe.*   [III.ii]

Juno.   Here lyes my hate, *Æneas* cursed brat,
The boy wherein false destinie delights,
The heire of fame, the favorite of the fates,
That ugly impe that shall outweare my wrath,
And wrong my deitie with high disgrace:
But I will take another order now,
And race th'eternall Register of time:
Troy shall no more call him her second hope,
Nor *Venus* triumph in his tender youth:
For here in spight of heaven Ile murder him,   10
And feede infection with his let out life:
Say *Paris*, now shall *Venus* have the ball?
Say vengeance, now shall her *Ascanius* dye?
O no God wot, I cannot watch my time,
Nor quit good turnes with double fee downe told:
Tut, I am simple, without minde to hurt,
And have no gall at all to grieve my foes:
But lustfull *Jove* and his adulterous child,
Shall finde it written on confusions front,
That onely *Juno* rules in *Rhamnuse* towne.   20

Enter Venus.

Venus.   What should this meane? my Doves are back returnd,
Who warne me of such daunger prest at hand,
To harme my sweete *Ascanius* lovely life.
Juno, my mortall foe, what make you here?
Avaunt old witch and trouble not my wits.
Juno.   Fie *Venus*, that such causeles words of wrath,
Should ere defile so faire a mouth as thine:
Are not we both sprong of celestiall rase,
And banquet as two Sisters with the Gods?
Why is it then displeasure should disjoyne,   30
Whom kindred and acquaintance counites?

---

3 fame] Broughton (*qy*); furie Q   11 let out] Oxberry (let-out); left out Q
3 fates] Oxberry; face Q   16 minde] Dyce; made Q

Venus.   Out hatefull hag, thou wouldst have slaine my sonne,
Had not my Doves discov'rd thy entent:
But I will teare thy eyes fro forth thy head,
And feast the birds with their bloud-shotten balles,
If thou but lay thy fingers on my boy.
Juno.   Is this then all the thankes that I shall have,
For saving him from Snakes and Serpents stings,
That would have kild him sleeping as he lay?
What though I was offended with thy sonne,   40
And wrought him mickle woe on sea and land,
When for the hate of Troian *Ganimed,*
That was advanced by my *Hebes* shame,
And *Paris* judgement of the heavenly ball,
I mustred all the windes unto his wracke,
And urg'd each Element to his annoy:
Yet now I doe repent me of his ruth,
And wish that I had never wrongd him so:
Bootles I sawe it was to warre with fate,
That hath so many unresisted friends: 50
Wherefore I chaungd my counsell with the time,
And planted love where envie erst had sprong.
Venus.   Sister of *Jove,* if that thy love be such,
As these thy protestations doe paint forth,
We two as friends one fortune will devide:
Cupid shall lay his arrowes in thy lap,
And to a Scepter chaunge his golden shafts,
Fancie and modestie shall live as mates,
And thy faire peacockes by my pigeons pearch:
Love my *Æneas,* and desire is thine,   60
The day, the night, my Swannes, my sweetes are thine.
Juno.   More then melodious are these words to me,
That overcloy my soule with their content:
Venus, sweete *Venus,* how may I deserve
Such amourous favours at thy beautious hand?
But that thou maist more easilie perceive,
How highly I doe prize this amitie,

51 chaungd] Dyce; chaunge Q

Harke to a motion of eternall league,
Which I will make in quittance of thy love:
Thy sonne thou knowest with *Dido* now remaines,   70
And feedes his eyes with favours of her Court,
She likewise in admyring spends her time,
And cannot talke nor thinke of ought but him:
Why should not they then joyne in marriage,
And bring forth mightie Kings to *Carthage* towne,
Whom casualtie of sea hath made such friends?
And *Venus*, let there be a match confirmd
Betwixt these two, whose loves are so alike,
And both our Deities conjoynd in one,
Shall chaine felicitie unto their throne.   80
Venus.   Well could I like this reconcilements meanes,
But much I feare my sonne will nere consent,
Whose armed soule alreadie on the sea,
Darts forth her light to *Lavinias* shoare.
Juno.   Faire Queene of love, I will devorce these doubts,
And finde the way to wearie such fond thoughts:
This day they both a hunting forth will ride
Into these woods, adjoyning to these walles,
When in the midst of all their gamesome sports,   90
Ile make the Clowdes dissolve their watrie workes,
And drench *Silvanus* dwellings with their shewers,
Then in one Cave the Queene and he shall meete,
And interchangeably discourse their thoughts,
Whose short conclusion will seale up their hearts,
Unto the purpose which we now propound.
Venus.   Sister, I see you savour of my wiles,
Be it as you will have it for this once,
Meane time, *Ascanius* shall be my charge,
Whom I will beare to *Ida* in mine armes,
And couch him in *Adonis* purple downe.   100

                                        Exeunt.

97 have it] Oxberry; have Q

Enter Dido, Æneas, Anna, Iarbus, Achates, [Cupid   [III.iii]
        for Ascanius,] *and followers.*

Dido.   *Æneas*, thinke not but I honor thee,
  That thus in person goe with thee to hunt:
  My princely robes thou seest are layd aside,
  Whose glittering pompe *Dianas* shrowdes supplies,
  All fellowes now, disposde alike to sporte,
  The woods are wide, and we have store of game:
  Faire Troian, hold my golden bowe awhile,
  Untill I gird my quiver to my side:
  Lords goe before, we two must talke alone.
Iarbus.   Ungentle, can she wrong *Iarbus* so?   10
  Ile dye before a stranger have that grace:
  We two will talke alone, what words be these?
Dido.   What makes *Iarbus* here of all the rest?
  We could have gone without your companie.
Æneas.   But love and duetie led him on perhaps,
  To presse beyond acceptance to your sight.
Iarbus.   Why, man of *Troy*, doe I offend thine eyes?
  Or art thou grievde thy betters presse so nye?
Dido.   How now Getulian, are ye growne so brave,
  To challenge us with your comparisons?   20
  Pesant, goe seeke companions like thy selfe,
  And meddle not with any that I love:
  Æneas, be not movde at what he sayes,
  For otherwhile he will be out of joynt.
Iarbus.   Women may wrong by priviledge of love:
  But should that man of men (*Dido* except)
  Have taunted me in these opprobrious termes,
  I would have either drunke his dying bloud,
  Or els I would have given my life in gage.
Dido.   Huntsmen, why pitch you not your toyles apace,   30
  And rowse the light foote Deere from forth their laire?
Anna.   Sister, see see *Ascanius* in his pompe,
  Bearing his huntspeare bravely in his hand.
Dido.   Yea little sonne, are you so forward now?

34

Cupid.   I mother, I shall one day be a man,
And better able unto other armes.
Meane time these wanton weapons serve my warre,
Which I will breake betwixt a Lyons jawes.
Dido.   What, darest thou looke a Lyon in the face?
Cupid.   I, and outface him to, doe what he can.   40
Anna.   How like his father speaketh he in all?
Æneas.   And mought I live to see him sacke rich *Thebes*,
And loade his speare with Grecian Princes heads,
Then would I wish me with *Anchises* Tombe,
And dead to honour that hath brought me up.
Iarbus.   And might I live to see thee shipt away,
And hoyst aloft on *Neptunes* hideous hilles,
Then would I wish me in faire *Didos* armes,
And dead to scorne that hath pursued me so.
Æneas.   Stoute friend *Achates*, doest thou know this wood?   50
Achates.   As I remember, here you shot the Deere,
That sav'd your famisht souldiers lives from death,
When first you set your foote upon the shoare,
And here we met faire *Venus* virgine like,
Bearing her bowe and quiver at her backe.
Æneas.   O how these irksome labours now delight,
And overjoy my thoughts with their escape:
Who would not undergoe all kind of toyle,
To be well stor'd with such a winters tale?
Dido.   *Æneas*, leave these dumpes and lets away,   60
Some to the mountaines, some unto the soyle,
You to the vallies, thou unto the house.   [*To* Iarbus.]
                          Exeunt omnes: manet [Iarbus].
Iarbus.   I, this it is which wounds me to the death,
To see a Phrigian far fet on the sea,
Preferd before a man of majestie:
O love, O hate, O cruell womens hearts,
That imitate the Moone in every chaunge,
And like the Planets ever love to raunge:
What shall I doe thus wronged with disdaine?

*64 far fet on] far fet to Q

35   3-2

Revenge me on *Æneas*, or on her: 70
On her? fond man, that were to warre gainst heaven,
And with one shaft provoke ten thousand darts:
This Troians end will be thy envies aime,
Whose bloud will reconcile thee to content,
And make love drunken with thy sweete desire:
But *Dido* that now holdeth him so deare,
Will dye with very tidings of his death:
But time will discontinue her content,
And mould her minde unto newe fancies shapes:
O God of heaven, turne the hand of fate 80
Unto that happie day of my delight,
And then, what then? *Iarbus* shall but love:
So doth he now, though not with equall gaine,
That resteth in the rivall of thy paine,
Who nere will cease to soare till he be slaine.

Exit.

The storme. Enter Æneas and Dido in the Cave [III.iv]
at severall times.

Dido.   *Æneas.*
Æneas.   *Dido.*
Dido.   Tell me deare love, how found you out this Cave?
Æneas.   By chance sweete Queene, as *Mars* and *Venus* met.
Dido.   Why, that was in a net, where we are loose,
  And yet I am not free, oh would I were.
Æneas.   Why, what is it that *Dido* may desire
  And not obtaine, be it in humaine power?
Dido.   The thing that I will dye before I aske,
  And yet desire to have before I dye. 10
Æneas.   It is not ought *Æneas* may atchieve?
Dido.   *Æneas* no, although his eyes doe pearce.
Æneas.   What, hath *Iarbus* angred her in ought?
  And will she be avenged on his life?
Dido.   Not angred me, except in angring thee.
Æneas.   Who then of all so cruell may he be,
  That should detaine thy eye in his defects?

Dido.   The man that I doe eye where ere I am,
Whose amorous face like *Pean* sparkles fire,
When as he buts his beames on *Floras* bed,   20
Prometheus hath put on *Cupids* shape,
And I must perish in his burning armes.
Æneas, O *Æneas*, quench these flames.
Æneas.   What ailes my Queene, is she falne sicke of late?
Dido.   Not sicke my love, but sicke:—— I must conceale
The torment, that it bootes me not reveale,
And yet Ile speake, and yet Ile hold my peace,
Doe shame her worst, I will disclose my griefe:——
Æneas, thou art he, what did I say?
Something it was that now I have forgot.   30
Æneas.   What meanes faire *Dido* by this doubtfull speech?
Dido.   Nay, nothing, but *Æneas* loves me not.
Æneas.   *Æneas* thoughts dare not ascend so high
As *Didos* heart, which Monarkes might not scale.
Dido.   It was because I sawe no King like thee,
Whose golden Crowne might ballance my content:
But now that I have found what to effect,
I followe one that loveth fame for me,
And rather had seeme faire to *Sirens* eyes,
Then to the *Carthage* Queene that dyes for him.   40
Æneas.   If that your majestie can looke so lowe,
As my despised worths, that shun all praise,
With this my hand I give to you my heart,
And vow by all the Gods of Hospitalitie,
By heaven and earth, and my faire brothers bowe,
By *Paphos*, *Capys*, and the purple Sea,
From whence my radiant mother did descend,
And by this Sword that saved me from the Greekes,
Never to leave these newe upreared walles,
Whiles *Dido* lives and rules in *Junos* towne,   10
Never to like or love any but her.
Dido.   What more then Delian musicke doe I heare,
That calles my soule from forth his living seate,

*25 sicke: ——I] ~, ~ Q   *47 descend] *stet* Q

37

To move unto the measures of delight:
Kind clowdes that sent forth such a curteous storme,
As made disdaine to flye to fancies lap:
Stoute love in mine armes make thy *Italy*,
Whose Crowne and kingdome rests at thy commande:
Sicheus, not *Æneas* be thou calde:
The King of *Carthage*, not *Anchises* sonne: 60
Hold, take these Jewels at thy Lovers hand,
These golden bracelets, and this wedding ring,
Wherewith my husband woo'd me yet a maide,
And be thou king of *Libia*, by my guift.

                                          Exeunt to the Cave.

            Enter Achates, [Cupid *for*] Ascanius, Iarbus, *and* Anna.   IV.i

Achates.   Did ever men see such a sudden storme?
   Or day so cleere so suddenly orecast?
Iarbus.   I thinke some fell Inchantresse dwelleth here,
   That can call them forth when as she please,
   And dive into blacke tempests treasurie,
   When as she meanes to maske the world with clowdes.
Anna.   In all my life I never knew the like,
   It haild, it snowde, it lightned all at once.
Achates.   I thinke it was the divels revelling night,
   There was such hurly burly in the heavens: 10
   Doubtles *Apollos* Axeltree is crackt,
   Or aged *Atlas* shoulder out of joynt,
   The motion was so over violent.
Iarbus.   In all this coyle, where have ye left the Queene?
Cupid.   Nay, where is my warlike father, can you tell?
Anna.   Behold where both of them come forth the Cave.
Iarbus.   Come forth the Cave: can heaven endure this sight?
   Iarbus, curse that unrevenging *Jove*,
   Whose flintie darts slept in *Tipheus* den,
   Whiles these adulterors surfetted with sinne: 20
   Nature, why mad'st me not some poysonous beast,
   That with the sharpnes of my edged sting,

I might have stakte them both unto the earth,
Whil'st they were sporting in this darksome Cave?

[*Enter Æneas and* Dido.]

Æneas.   The ayre is cleere, and Southerne windes are whist,
  Come *Dido*, let us hasten to the towne,
  Since gloomie *Æolus* doth cease to frowne.
Dido.   *Achates* and *Ascanius*, well met.
Æneas.   Faire *Anna*, how escapt you from the shower?
Anna.   As others did, by running to the wood.   30
Dido.   But where were you *Iarbus* all this while?
Iarbus.   Not with *Æneas* in the ugly Cave.
Dido.   I see *Æneas* sticketh in your minde,
  But I will soone put by that stumbling blocke,
  And quell those hopes that thus employ your cares.

                                            Exeunt.

                Enters Iarbus *to Sacrifize.*   [IV.ii]

Iarbus.   Come servants, come bring forth the Sacrifize,
  That I may pacifie that gloomie *Jove*,
  Whose emptie Altars have enlarg'd our illes.
  Eternall *Jove*, great master of the Clowdes,
  Father of gladnesse, and all frollicke thoughts,
  That with thy gloomie hand corrects the heaven,
  When ayrie creatures warre amongst themselves:
  Heare, heare, O heare *Iarbus* plaining prayers,
  Whose hideous ecchoes make the welkin howle,
  And all the woods *Eliza* to resound: 10
  The woman that thou wild us entertaine,
  Where straying in our borders up and downe,
  She crav'd a hide of ground to build a towne,
  With whom we did devide both lawes and land,
  And all the fruites that plentie els sends forth,
  Scorning our loves and royall marriage rites,
  Yeelds up her beautie to a strangers bed,

35 cares] Oxbery; eares Q   *10 *Eliza*] stet Q

39

Who having wrought her shame, is straight way fled:
Now if thou beest a pitying God of power,
On whom ruth and compassion ever waites,   20
Redresse these wrongs, and warne him to his ships,
That now afflicts me with his flattering eyes.

Enter Anna.

Anna. How now *Iarbus*, at your prayers so hard?
Iarbus. I *Anna*, is there ought you would with me?
Anna. Nay, no such waightie busines of import,
 But may be slackt untill another time:
 Yet if you would partake with me the cause
 Of this devotion that detaineth you,
 I would be thankfull for such curtesie.
Iarbus. *Anna*, against this Troian doe I pray,   30
 Who seekes to rob me of thy Sisters love,
 And dive into her heart by coloured lookes.
Anna. Alas poore King that labours so in vaine,
 For her that so delighteth in thy paine:
 Be rul'd by me, and seeke some other love,
 Whose yeelding heart may yeeld thee more reliefe.
Iarbus. Mine eye is fixt where fancie cannot start,
 O leave me, leave me to my silent thoughts,
 That register the numbers of my ruth,
 And I will either move the thoughtles flint,   40
 Or drop out both mine eyes in drisling teares,
 Before my sorrowes tide have any stint.
Anna. I will not leave *Iarbus* whom I love,
 In this delight of dying pensivenes:
 Away with *Dido*, *Anna* be thy song,
 Anna that doth admire thee more then heaven.
Iarbus. I may nor will list to such loathsome chaunge,
 That intercepts the course of my desire:
 Servants, come fetch these emptie vessels here,
 For I will flye from these alluring eyes,   50
 That doe pursue my peace where ere it goes. *Exit.*
Anna. *Iarbus* stay, loving *Iarbus* stay,

For I have honey to present thee with:
Hard hearted, wilt not deigne to heare me speake?
Ile follow thee with outcryes nere the lesse,
And strewe thy walkes with my discheveld haire.

Exit.

Enter Æneas alone.   [IV.iii]

Æneas.   *Carthage,* my friendly host adue,
Since destinie doth call me from thy shoare:
Hermes this night descending in a dreame,
Hath summond me to fruitfull *Italy:*
Jove wils it so, my mother wils it so:
Let my Phenissa graunt, and then I goe:
Graunt she or no, *Æneas* must away,
Whose golden fortunes clogd with courtly ease,
Cannot ascend to Fames immortall house,
Or banquet in bright honors burnisht hall,   10
Till he hath furrowed *Neptunes* glassie fieldes,
And cut a passage through his toples hilles:
Achates come forth, *Sergestus, Illioneus,*
Cloanthus, haste away, *Æneas* calles.

Enter Achates, Cloanthus, Sergestus, *and* Illioneus.

Achates.   What willes our Lord, or wherefore did he call?
Æneas.   The dreames (brave mates) that did beset my bed,
When sleepe but newly had imbrast the night,
Commaunds me leave these unrenowmed reames,
Whereas Nobilitie abhors to stay,
And none but base *Æneas* will abide: 20
Abourd, abourd, since Fates doe bid abourd,
And slice the Sea with sable coloured ships,
On whom the nimble windes may all day waight,
And follow them as footemen through the deepe:
Yet *Dido* casts her eyes like anchors out,
To stay my Fleete from loosing forth the Bay:

2 thy] Oxberry; the Q   18 reames] Dyce (*i.e.,* realmes *as in* Dyce²); beames Q

Come backe, come backe, I heare her crye a farre,
And let me linke thy bodie to my lips,
That tyed together by the striving tongues,
We may as one saile into *Italy*.   30
Achates.   Banish that ticing dame from forth your mouth,
And follow your foreseeing starres in all;
This is no life for men at armes to live,
Where daliance doth consume a Souldiers strength,
And wanton motions of alluring eyes,
Effeminate our mindes inur'd to warre.
Illioneus.   Why, let us build a Citie of our owne,
And not stand lingering here for amorous lookes:
Will *Dido* raise old *Priam* forth his grave,
And build the towne againe the Greekes did burne?   40
No no, she cares not how we sinke or swimme,
So she may have *Æneas* in her armes.
Cloanthus.   To *Italy*, sweete friends to *Italy*,
We will not stay a minute longer here.
Æneas.   Troians abourd, and I will follow you,
                              [*Exeunt omnes, manet Æneas.*]
I faine would goe, yet beautie calles me backe:
To leave her so and not once say farewell,
Were to transgresse against all lawes of love:
But if I use such ceremonious thankes,
As parting friends accustome on the shoare,   50
Her silver armes will coll me round about,
And teares of pearle, crye stay, *Æneas*, stay:
Each word she sayes will then containe a Crowne,
And every speech be ended with a kisse:
I may not dure this female drudgerie,
To sea *Æneas*, finde out *Italy*.

                                            Exit.

*28 thy bodie to my lips] Dyce; my . . . my Q

42

Enter Dido *and* Anna [*with traine*].   [IV.iv]

Dido.   O *Anna*, runne unto the water side,
They say *Æneas* men are going abourd,
It may be he will steale away with them:
Stay not to answere me, runne *Anna* runne.   [*Exit* Anna.]
O foolish Troians that would steale from hence,
And not let *Dido* understand their drift:
I would have given *Achates* store of gold,
And *Illioneus* gum and Libian spice,
The common souldiers rich imbrodered coates,
And silver whistles to controule the windes,   10
Which *Circes* sent *Sicheus* when he lived:
Unworthie are they of a Queenes reward:
See where they come, how might I doe to chide?

Enter Anna, *with* Æneas, Achates, Illioneus, *and*
Sergestus.

Anna.   Twas time to runne, *Æneas* had been gone,
The sailes were hoysing up, and he abourd.
Dido.   Is this thy love to me?
Æneas.   O princely *Dido*, give me leave to speake,
I went to take my farewell of *Achates*.
Dido.   How haps *Achates* bid me not farewell?
Achates.   Because I feard your grace would keepe me here.   20
Dido.   To rid thee of that doubt, abourd againe,
I charge thee put to sea and stay not here.
Achates.   Then let *Æneas* goe abourd with us.
Dido.   Get you abourd, *Æneas* meanes to stay.
Æneas.   The sea is rough, the windes blow to the shoare.
Dido.   O false *Æneas*, now the sea is rough,
But when you were abourd twas calme enough,
Thou and *Achates* ment to saile away.
Æneas.   Hath not the *Carthage* Queene mine onely sonne?
Thinkes *Dido* I will goe and leave him here?   30
Dido.   *Æneas* pardon me, for I forgot
That yong *Ascanius* lay with me this night:

Love made me jealous, but to make amends,
Weare the emperiall Crowne of *Libia*,
Sway thou the Punike Scepter in my steede,
And punish me *Æneas* for this crime.

                                  [*Gives him crowne and scepter.*]

Æneas.   This kisse shall be faire *Didos* punishment.
Dido.   O how a Crowne becomes *Æneas* head!
Stay here *Æneas*, and commaund as King.
Æneas.   How vaine am I to weare this Diadem,   40
And beare this golden Scepter in my hand?
A Burgonet of steele, and not a Crowne,
A Sword, and not a Scepter fits *Æneas*.
Dido.   O keepe them still, and let me gaze my fill:
Now lookes *Æneas* like immortall *Jove*,
O where is *Ganimed* to hold his cup,
And *Mercury* to flye for what he calles?
Ten thousand *Cupids* hover in the ayre,
And fanne it in *Æneas* lovely face,
O that the Clowdes were here wherein thou fledst,   50
That thou and I unseene might sport our selves:
Heavens envious of our joyes is waxen pale,
And when we whisper, then the starres fall downe,
To be partakers of our honey talke.
Æneas.   O *Dido*, patronesse of all our lives,
When I leave thee, death be my punishment,
Swell raging seas, frowne wayward destinies,
Blow windes, threaten ye Rockes and sandie shelfes,
This is the harbour that *Æneas* seekes,
Lets see what tempests can anoy me now.   60
Dido.   Not all the world can take thee from mine armes,
Æneas may commaund as many Moores,
As in the Sea are little water drops:
And now to make experience of my love,
Faire sister *Anna* leade my lover forth,
And seated on my Gennet, let him ride
As *Didos* husband through the Punicke streetes,

50 fledst] Dyce; fleest Q

44

And will my guard with Mauritanian darts,
To waite upon him as their soveraigne Lord.
Anna.   What if the Citizens repine thereat?   70
Dido.   Those that dislike what *Dido* gives in charge,
Commaund my guard to slay for their offence:
Shall vulgar pesants storme at what I doe?
The ground is mine that gives them sustenance,
The ayre wherein they breathe, the water, fire,
All that they have, their lands, their goods, their lives,
And I the Goddesse of all these, commaund
Æneas ride as Carthaginian King.
Achates.   *Æneas* for his parentage deserves
As large a kingdome as is *Libia*.   80
Æneas.   I, and unlesse the destinies be false,
I shall be planted in as rich a land.
Dido.   Speake of no other land, this land is thine,
Dido is thine, henceforth Ile call thee Lord:
Doe as I bid thee sister, leade the way,
And from a turret Ile behold my love.
Æneas.   Then here in me shall flourish *Priams* race,
And thou and I *Achates,* for revenge,
For *Troy,* for *Priam,* for his fiftie sonnes,
Our kinsmens lives, and thousand guiltles soules,   90
Will leade an hoste against the hatefull Greekes,
And fire proude *Lacedemon* ore their heads.

                                   Exit [*with Troians*].

Dido.   Speakes not *Æneas* like a Conqueror?
O blessed tempests that did drive him in,
O happie sand that made him runne aground:
Henceforth you shall be our *Carthage* Gods:
I, but it may be he will leave my love,
And seeke a forraine land calde *Italy:*
O that I had a charme to keepe the windes
Within the closure of a golden ball,   100
Or that the Tyrrhen sea were in mine armes,
That he might suffer shipwracke on my breast,

90 lives] Dyce; loves Q

As oft as he attempts to hoyst up saile:
I must prevent him, wishing will not serve:
Goe, bid my Nurse take yong *Ascanius*,
And beare him in the countrey to her house,
Æneas will not goe without his sonne:
Yet lest he should, for I am full of feare,
Bring me his oares, his tackling, and his sailes: [*Exit a Lord.*]
What if I sinke his ships? O heele frowne: 110
Better he frowne, then I should dye for griefe:
I cannot see him frowne, it may not be:
Armies of foes resolv'd to winne this towne,
Or impious traitors vowde to have my life,
Affright me not, onely *Æneas* frowne
Is that which terrifies poore *Didos* heart:
Not bloudie speares appearing in the ayre,
Presage the downfall of my Emperie,
Nor blazing Commets threatens *Didos* death,
It is *Æneas* frowne that ends my daies: 120
If he forsake me not, I never dye,
For in his lookes I see eternitie,
And heele make me immortall with a kisse.

Enter a Lord.

Lord.   Your Nurse is gone with yong *Ascanius*,
   And heres *Æneas* tackling, oares and sailes.
Dido.   Are these the sailes that in despight of me,
   Packt with the windes to beare *Æneas* hence?
   Ile hang ye in the chamber where I lye,
   Drive if you can my house to *Italy*:
   Ile set the casement open that the windes   130
   May enter in, and once againe conspire
   Against the life of me poore *Carthage* Queene:
   But though he goe, he stayes in *Carthage* still,
   And let rich *Carthage* fleete upon the seas,
   So I may have *Æneas* in mine armes.
   Is this the wood that grew in *Carthage* plaines,
   And would be toyling in the watrie billowes,

To rob their mistresse of her Troian guest?
O cursed tree, hadst thou but wit or sense,
To measure how I prize *Æneas* love,   140
Thou wouldst have leapt from out the Sailers hands,
And told me that *Æneas* ment to goe:
And yet I blame thee not, thou art but wood.
The water which our Poets terme a Nimph,
Why did it suffer thee to touch her breast,
And shrunke not backe, knowing my love was there?
The water is an Element, no Nimph,
Why should I blame *Æneas* for his flight?
O *Dido*, blame not him, but breake his oares,
These were the instruments that launcht him forth,   150
Theres not so much as this base tackling too,
But dares to heape up sorrowe to my heart:
Was it not you that hoysed up these sailes?
Why burst you not, and they fell in the seas?
For this will *Dido* tye ye full of knots,
And sheere ye all asunder with her hands:
Now serve to chastize shipboyes for their faults,
Ye shall no more offend the *Carthage* Queene.
Now let him hang my favours on his masts,
And see if those will serve in steed of sailes: 160
For tackling, let him take the chaines of gold,
Which I bestowd upon his followers:
In steed of oares, let him use his hands,
And swim to *Italy*, Ile keepe these sure:
Come beare them in.

                       Exeunt [*attended*].

       Enter the Nurse *with* Cupid *for* Ascanius.   **[IV.v]**

Nurse.   My Lord *Ascanius*, ye must goe with me.
Cupid.   Whither must I goe? Ile stay with my mother.
Nurse.   No, thou shalt goe with me unto my house,
  I have an Orchard that hath store of plums,
  Browne Almonds, Servises, ripe Figs and Dates,

Dewberries, Apples, yellow Orenges,
A garden where are Bee hives full of honey,
Musk-roses, and a thousand sort of flowers,
And in the midst doth run a silver streame,
Where thou shalt see the red gild fishes leape, 10
White Swannes, and many lovely water fowles:
Now speake *Ascanius*, will ye goe or no?
Cupid. Come come, Ile goe, how farre hence is your house?
Nurse. But hereby child, we shall get thither straight.
Cupid. Nurse I am wearie, will you carrie me?
Nurse. I, so youle dwell with me and call me mother.
Cupid. So youle love me, I care not if I doe.
Nurse. That I might live to see this boy a man,
How pretilie he laughs, goe ye wagge,
Youle be a twigger when you come to age. 20
Say *Dido* what she will I am not old,
Ile be no more a widowe, I am young,
Ile have a husband, or els a lover.
Cupid. A husband and no teeth!
Nurse. O what meane I to have such foolish thoughts!
Foolish is love, a toy.—— O sacred love,
If there be any heaven in earth, tis love:
Especially in women of our yeares.——
Blush blush for shame, why shouldst thou thinke of love?
A grave, and not a lover fits thy age:—— 30
A grave? why, I may live a hundred yeares,
Fourescore is but a girles age, love is sweete:——
My vaines are withered, and my sinewes drie,
Why doe I thinke of love now I should dye?
Cupid. Come Nurse.
Nurse. Well, if he come a wooing he shall speede,
O how unwise was I to say him nay!

            Exeunt.

*28 our] Deighton (*Old Dramatists:* 31 grave? why,] Dyce (grave! why,);
 Conjectural Readings, 1896);   ~, ~? Q
 your Q

48

Enter Æneas with a paper in his hand, drawing the platforme of V.i
the citie, with him Achates, [Sergestus,] Cloanthus, *and* Illioneus.

Æneas. Triumph, my mates, our travels are at end,
Here will *Æneas* build a statelier *Troy,*
Then that which grim *Atrides* overthrew:
Carthage shall vaunt her pettie walles no more,
For I will grace them with a fairer frame,
And clad her in a Chrystall liverie,
Wherein the day may evermore delight:
From golden *India Ganges* will I fetch,
Whose wealthie streames may waite upon her towers,
And triple wise intrench her round about: 10
The Sunne from *Egypt* shall rich odors bring,
Wherewith his burning beames like labouring Bees,
That loade their thighes with *Hyblas* honeys spoyles,
Shall here unburden their exhaled sweetes,
And plant our pleasant suburbes with her fumes.
Achates. What length or bredth shal this brave towne containe?
Æneas. Not past foure thousand paces at the most.
Illioneus. But what shall it be calde, *Troy* as before?
Æneas. That have I not determinde with my selfe.
Cloanthus. Let it be term'd *Ænea* by your name.   20
Sergestus. Rather *Ascania* by your little sonne.
Æneas. Nay, I will haue it calde *Anchisæon,*
Of my old fathers name.

Enter Hermes *with* Ascanius.

Hermes. *Æneas* stay, *Joves* Herald bids thee stay.
Æneas. Whom doe I see, *Joves* winged messenger?
Welcome to *Carthage* new erected towne.
Hermes. Why cosin, stand you building Cities here,
And beautifying the Empire of this Queene,
While *Italy* is cleane out of thy minde?
To too forgetfull of thine owne affayres,   30
Why wilt thou so betray thy sonnes good hap?

30, 185 To too] *i.e.,* too, too (*as in* Oxberry)

The king of Gods sent me from highest heaven,
To sound this angrie message in thine eares.
Vaine man, what Monarky expectst thou here?
Or with what thought sleepst thou in *Libia* shoare?
If that all glorie hath forsaken thee,
And thou despise the praise of such attempts:
Yet thinke upon *Ascanius* prophesie,
And yong *Iulus* more then thousand yeares,
Whom I have brought from *Ida* where he slept,   40
And bore yong *Cupid* unto *Cypresse* Ile.
Æneas.   This was my mother that beguild the Queene,
And made me take my brother for my sonne:
No marvell *Dido* though thou be in love,
That daylie dandlest *Cupid* in thy armes:
Welcome sweet child, where hast thou been this long?
Ascanius.   Eating sweet Comfites with Queene *Didos* maide,
Who ever since hath luld me in her armes.
Æneas.   *Sergestus,* beare him hence unto our ships,
Lest *Dido* spying him keepe him for a pledge.   50
                          [*Exit* Sergestus *with* Ascanius.]
Hermes.   Spendst thou thy time about this little boy,
And givest not eare unto the charge I bring?
I tell thee thou must straight to *Italy,*
Or els abide the wrath of frowning *Jove.*   [*Exit.*]
Æneas.   How should I put into the raging deepe,
Who have no sailes nor tackling for my ships?
What, would the Gods have me, *Deucalion* like,
Flote up and downe where ere the billowes drive?
Though she repairde my fleete and gave me ships,
Yet hath she tane away my oares and masts,   60
And left me neither saile nor sterne abourd.

Enter to them Iarbus.

Iarbus.   How now *Æneas,* sad, what meanes these dumpes?
Æneas.   *Iarbus,* I am cleane besides my selfe,
Jove hath heapt on me such a desperate charge,

39 *Iulus*] *i.e., Iulus'* (*as in* Dyce)

Which neither art nor reason may atchieve,
Nor I devise by what meanes to contrive.
Iarbus.   As how I pray, may I entreate you tell.
Æneas.   With speede he bids me saile to *Italy*,
When as I want both rigging for my fleete,
And also furniture for these my men.   70
Iarbus.   If that be all, then cheare thy drooping lookes,
For I will furnish thee with such supplies:
Let some of those thy followers goe with me,
And they shall have what thing so ere thou needst.
Æneas.   Thankes good *Iarbus* for thy friendly ayde,
Achates and the rest shall waite on thee,
Whil'st I rest thankfull for this curtesie.

                        Exit Iarbus *and* Æneas *traine.*

Now will I haste unto *Lavinian* shoare,
And raise a new foundation to old *Troy*,
Witnes the Gods, and witnes heaven and earth,   80
How loth I am to leave these *Libian* bounds,
But that eternall *Jupiter* commands.

      Enter Dido [*attended*] *to* Æneas.

Dido.   I feare I sawe *Æneas* little sonne,
Led by *Achates* to the Troian fleete:
If it be so, his father meanes to flye:
But here he is, now *Dido* trie thy wit.
Æneas, wherefore goe thy men abourd?
Why are thy ships new rigd? or to what end
Launcht from the haven, lye they in the Rhode?
Pardon me though I aske, love makes me aske.   90
Æneas.   O pardon me, if I resolve thee why:
Æneas will not faine with his deare love,
I must from hence: this day swift *Mercury*
When I was laying a platforme for these walles,
Sent from his father *Jove*, appeard to me,
And in his name rebukt me bitterly,
For lingering here, neglecting *Italy*.

*82.1 *to*] Revels; *and* Q

Dido.   But yet *Æneas* will not leave his love?

Æneas.   I am commaunded by immortall *Jove*,

To leave this towne and passe to *Italy*,   100

And therefore must of force.

Dido.   These words proceed not from *Æneas* heart.

Æneas.   Not from my heart, for I can hardly goe,

And yet I may not stay, *Dido* farewell.

Dido.   Farewell: is this the mends for *Didos* love?

Doe Troians use to quit their Lovers thus?

Fare well may *Dido*, so *Æneas* stay,

I dye, if my *Æneas* say farewell.

Æneas.   Then let me goe and never say farewell?

Dido.   Let me goe, farewell, I must from hence,   110

These words are poyson to poore *Didos* soule,

O speake like my *Æneas*, like my love:

Why look'st thou toward the sea? the time hath been

When *Didos* beautie chaind thine eyes to her:

Am I lesse faire then when thou sawest me first?

O then *Æneas*, tis for griefe of thee:

Say thou wilt stay in *Carthage* with thy Queene,

And *Didos* beautie will returne againe:

Æneas, say, how canst thou take thy leave?

Wilt thou kisse *Dido*? O thy lips have sworne   120

To stay with *Dido*: canst thou take her hand?

Thy hand and mine have plighted mutuall faith,

Therefore unkind *Æneas*, must thou say,

Then let me goe, and never say farewell?

Æneas.   O Queene of *Carthage*, wert thou ugly blacke,

Æneas could not choose but hold thee deare,

Yet must he not gainsay the Gods behest.

Dido.   The Gods, what Gods be those that seeke my death?

Wherein have I offended *Jupiter*,

That he should take *Æneas* from mine armes?   130

O no, the Gods wey not what Lovers doe,

It is *Æneas* calles *Æneas* hence,

110 *Dido.*] McKerrow (*qy*); Q *places*   114 chaind] Robinson; chaungd Q
  before line 111   117 thy] Oxberry; my Q

And wofull *Dido* by these blubbred cheekes,
By this right hand, and by our spousall rites,
Desires *Æneas* to remaine with her:
Si bene quid de te merui, fuit aut tibi quidquam
Dulce meum, miserere domus labentis: et istam
Oro, si quis adhuc precibus locus, exue mentem.
Æneas.   Desine meque tuis incendere teque querelis,
Italiam non sponte sequor.   140
Dido.   Hast thou forgot how many neighbour kings
Were up in armes, for making thee my love?
How *Carthage* did rebell, *Iarbus* storme,
And all the world calles me a second *Helen*,
For being intangled by a strangers lookes:
So thou wouldst prove as true as *Paris* did,
Would, as faire *Troy* was, *Carthage* might be sackt,
And I be calde a second *Helena*.
Had I a sonne by thee, the griefe were lesse,
That I might see *Æneas* in his face: 150
Now if thou goest, what canst thou leave behind,
But rather will augment then ease my woe?
Æneas.   In vaine my love thou spendst thy fainting breath,
If words might move me I were overcome.
Dido.   And wilt thou not be mov'd with *Didos* words?
Thy mother was no Goddesse perjurd man,
Nor *Dardanus* the author of thy stocke:
But thou art sprung from *Scythian Caucasus*,
And Tygers of *Hircania* gave thee sucke:
Ah foolish *Dido* to forbeare this long!   160
Wast thou not wrackt upon this *Libian* shoare,
And cam'st to *Dido* like a Fisher swaine?
Repairde not I thy ships, made thee a King,
And all thy needie followers Noblemen?
O Serpent that came creeping from the shoare,
And I for pitie harbord in my bosome,
Wilt thou now slay me with thy venomed sting,
And hisse at *Dido* for preserving thee?

138 *adhuc*] Oxberry; *ad hæc* Q

Goe goe and spare not, seeke out *Italy*,
I hope that that which love forbids me doe,   170
The Rockes and Sea-gulfes will performe at large,
And thou shalt perish in the billowes waies,
To whom poore *Dido* doth bequeath revenge.
I traytor, and the waves shall cast thee up,
Where thou and false *Achates* first set foote:
Which if it chaunce, Ile give ye buriall,
And weepe upon your liveles carcases,
Though thou nor he will pitie me a whit.
Why star'st thou in my face? if thou wilt stay,
Leape in mine armes, mine armes are open wide: 180
If not, turne from me, and Ile turne from thee:
For though thou hast the heart to say farewell,
I have not power to stay thee: is he gone?   [*Exit* Æneas.]
I but heele come againe, he cannot goe,
He loves me to too well to serve me so:
Yet he that in my sight would not relent,
Will, being absent, be obdurate still.
By this is he got to the water side,
And, see the Sailers take him by the hand,
But he shrinkes backe, and now remembring me,   190
Returnes amaine: welcome, welcome my love:
But wheres *Æneas*? ah hees gone hees gone!

[*Enter* Anna.]

Anna.   What meanes my sister thus to rave and crye?
Dido.   O *Anna*, my *Æneas* is abourd,
And leaving me will saile to *Italy*.
Once didst thou goe, and he came backe againe,
Now bring him backe, and thou shalt be a Queene,
And I will live a private life with him.
Anna.   Wicked *Æneas*.
Dido.   Call him not wicked, sister, speake him faire,   200
And looke upon him with a Mermaides eye,
Tell him, I never vow'd at *Aulis* gulfe
The desolation of his native *Troy*,

Nor sent a thousand ships unto the walles,
Nor ever violated faith to him:
Request him gently (*Anna*) to returne,
I crave but this, he stay a tide or two,
That I may learne to beare it patiently,
If he depart thus suddenly, I dye:
Run *Anna*, run, stay not to answere me.   210
Anna.   I goe faire sister, heavens graunt good successe.

Exit Anna.

Enter the Nurse.

Nurse.   O *Dido*, your little sonne *Ascanius*
Is gone! he lay with me last night,
And in the morning he was stolne from me,
I thinke some Fairies have beguiled me.
Dido.   O cursed hagge and false dissembling wretch!
That slayest me with thy harsh and hellish tale,
Thou for some pettie guift hast let him goe,
And I am thus deluded of my boy:
Away with her to prison presently,   220
Traytoresse too keene and cursed Sorceresse.
Nurse.   I know not what you meane by treason, I,
I am as true as any one of yours.
Dido.   Away with her, suffer her not to speake.

Exeunt the Nurse [*and Attendants*].

My sister comes, I like not her sad lookes.

Enter Anna.

Anna.   Before I came, *Æneas* was abourd,
And spying me, hoyst up the sailes amaine:
But I cride out, *Æneas*, false *Æneas* stay.
Then gan he wagge his hand, which yet held up,
Made me suppose he would have heard me speake: 230
Then gan they drive into the Ocean,
Which when I viewd, I cride, *Æneas* stay,

221 keene] Oxberry; keend Q

Dido, faire *Dido* wils *Æneas* stay:
Yet he whose hearts of adamant or flint,
My teares nor plaints could mollifie a whit:
Then carelesly I rent my haire for griefe,
Which seene to all, though he beheld me not,
They gan to move him to redresse my ruth,
And stay a while to heare what I could say,
But he clapt under hatches saild away. 240
Dido. O *Anna, Anna,* I will follow him.
Anna. How can ye goe when he hath all your fleete?
Dido. Ile frame me wings of waxe like *Icarus,*
And ore his ships will soare unto the Sunne,
That they may melt and I fall in his armes:
Or els Ile make a prayer unto the waves,
That I may swim to him like *Tritons* neece:
O *Anna,* fetch *Arions* Harpe,
That I may tice a Dolphin to the shoare,
And ride upon his backe unto my love: 250
Looke sister, looke lovely *Æneas* ships,
See see, the billowes heave him up to heaven,
And now downe falles the keeles into the deepe:
O sister, sister, take away the Rockes,
Theile breake his ships, O *Proteus, Neptune, Jove,*
Save, save *Æneas, Didos* leefest love!
Now is he come on shoare safe without hurt:
But see, *Achates* wils him put to sea,
And all the Sailers merrie make for joy,
But he remembring me shrinkes backe againe: 260
See where he comes, welcome, welcome my love.
Anna. Ah sister, leave these idle fantasies,
Sweet sister cease, remember who you are.
Dido. *Dido* I am, unlesse I be deceiv'd,
And must I rave thus for a runnagate?
Must I make ships for him to saile away?
Nothing can beare me to him but a ship,

*234 hearts] Oxberry (*i.e.,* heart's);   248 *Arions*] Dyce (*i.e.,* Arion's); *Orions*
    heart Q   Q

And he hath all my fleete, what shall I doe
But dye in furie of this oversight?
I, I must be the murderer of my selfe: 270
No but I am not, yet I will be straight.
Anna be glad, now have I found a meane
To rid me from these thoughts of Lunacie:
Not farre from hence
There is a woman famoused for arts,
Daughter unto the Nimphs *Hesperides*,
Who wild me sacrifize his ticing relliques:
Goe *Anna*, bid my servants bring me fire.   *Exit* Anna.

Enter Iarbus.

Iarbus.   How long will *Dido* mourne a strangers flight,
That hath dishonord her and *Carthage* both?   280
How long shall I with griefe consume my daies,
And reape no guerdon for my truest love?

[*Enter Attendants with wood and fire.*]

Dido.   *Iarbus*, talke not of *Æneas*, let him goe,
Lay to thy hands and helpe me make a fire,
That shall consume all that this stranger left,
For I entend a private Sacrifize,
To cure my minde that melts for unkind love.
Iarbus.   But afterwards will *Dido* graunt me love?
Dido.   I, I, *Iarbus*, after this is done,
None in the world shall have my love but thou: 290
So, leave me now, let none approach this place.   *Exit* Iarbus.
Now *Dido*, with these reliques burne thy selfe,
And make *Æneas* famous through the world,
For perjurie and slaughter of a Queene:
Here lye the Sword that in the darksome Cave
He drew, and swore by to be true to me,
Thou shalt burne first, thy crime is worse then his;
Here lye the garment which I cloath'd him in,
When first he came on shoare, perish thou to:

268 my] Oxberry; thy Q   270 I, I] *i.e.*, Aye, I (*as in* Oxberry)

These letters, lines, and perjurd papers all,   300
Shall burne to cinders in this pretious flame.
And now ye gods that guide the starrie frame,
And order all things at your high dispose,
Graunt, though the traytors land in *Italy*,
They may be still tormented with unrest,
And from mine ashes let a Conquerour rise,
That may revenge this treason to a Queene,
By plowing up his Countries with the Sword:
Betwixt this land and that be never league,
Littora littoribus contraria, fluctibus undas   310
Imprecor: arma armis: pugnent ipsíque nepotes:
Live false *Æneas*, truest *Dido* dyes,
Sic sic juvat ire sub umbras.

                                     [Throws herself into the flames.]

Enter Anna.

Anna.   O helpe *Iarbus*, *Dido* in these flames
Hath burnt her selfe, aye me, unhappie me!

Enter Iarbus *running.*

Iarbus.   Cursed *Iarbus*, dye to expiate
The griefe that tires upon thine inward soule.
Dido I come to thee, aye me *Æneas.*   *[Kills himself.]*
Anna.   What can my teares or cryes prevaile me now?
Dido is dead,   320
Iarbus slaine, *Iarbus* my deare love,
O sweet *Iarbus*, *Annas* sole delight,
What fatall destinie envies me thus,
To see my sweet *Iarbus* slay himselfe?
But *Anna* now shall honor thee in death,
And mixe her bloud with thine, this shall I doe,
That Gods and men may pitie this my death,
And rue our ends senceles of life or breath:
Now sweet *Iarbus* stay, I come to thee.

                                      [Kills herself.]

        FINIS

TEXTUAL NOTES

I.i

10 haire] Q makes the same error 'aire' at I.i.159. It is worth note that the conventional Q spelling, when correctly used, is 'ayre', as at I.i.178, II.i.13, IV.i.25, IV.ii.7, IV.iv.48, 75.

115 Whereas] As Oliver points out in the Revels edition, 'whereas' here means what it says, not *where*. The subjunctive 'Besiege' in line 116 indicates that this is the reading, which means that the comma after 'realme' in line 114 should represent a strong stop. If 'whereas' were to mean *where*, as some editors believe, 'Besiege' would need to be emended to 'Besieges'.

144 ye] Q's singular 'thee' is clearly impossible. The change to 'us' as in Oxberry and a few others is well enough but the word would not readily be mistaken for 'thee'. Dyce's emendation 'ye' is most plausible paleographically although 'you' would make the pronoun consistent with that in lines 142, 148. On the other hand, although the distinction between singular *you* and plural *ye* is observed at I.ii.38 and probably at IV.i.14–15, and 'ye' is plural at III.i.127 and V.i.176, yet 'ye' is singular at III.iii.19 and V.i.242, and there is a 'ye'–'you' confusion in IV.v.19. Hence 'ye' is possible in line 144.

147 Ceranias] This is properly 'Ceraunia's' as in Oxberry. On the evidence of the *Elegies* II.xi.19 Marlowe spelled the mountains as 'Cerania', however.

154 coming joyes] Given the frequent confusion of *cunning–coming* in Elizabethan texts, Dyce's emendation to 'coming' of Q 'cunning' must be taken seriously. The Revels edition, alone among modern texts, retains Q 'cunning', and explains *cunning joys* as 'subtle, to be eagerly appreciated because they have to be contrived'. Unfortunately, *O.E.D.* seems to furnish no basis for this interpretation. The *O.E.D.* definition that comes closest to the text may be 1.*b.*, 'Of things: Characterized by or full of knowledge or learning; learned', with an illustration from Tindale's translation of the New Testament 1534 I Cor. ii. 13, 'Which thinges also we speake, not in the conyinge wordes of mannes wysdome, but with the connyinge wordes of the holy goost.' This application to learning or to wisdom is found in Shakespeare's *Taming of the Shrew*, 'for to cunning men, | I will be very kinde and liberall, | To mine owne children, in good bringing up' (I.i.97–9, TLN 401–3), and again in the same play, 'he tooke some care | To get her cunning Schoolemasters to instruct her' (I.i.191–2, TLN 489–90), or 'Cunning in Musicke, and the Mathematickes' (II.i.56, TLN 917). With some strain, perhaps, this sense of learned or of wise might stem from Aeneas's 'vertues' in line 153 and thus be transferred to 'joys' to distinguish them from thoughtless or idle pleasures. Or, since 'cunning' can mean *artful* (in a good sense), something of the same distinction could be made. One may compare 'set downe with as much modestie, as cunning' (*Hamlet*, II.ii.461, TLN 1481–2), or 'in our sports my better cunning faints, | Under his chance' (*Antony and Cleopatra*, II.iii.34–5, TLN 1001–2). Or, with a stronger sense of

59

wisdom again, 'Virtue and cunning were endowments greater | Than nobleness and riches' (*Pericles*, III.ii.27–8). Yet all these illustrations really show how different is the *Dido* use, and how much strain is required to attempt to justify the Q reading. One may appeal, perhaps, to 'sought for joyes' (I.i.136) spoken by Venus. But the context itself would seem to be sufficient. In the preceding speech Aeneas has heartened his companions with the promise, 'Pluck up your hearts, since fate still rests our friend, | And chaunging heavens may those good daies returne, | Which *Pergama* did vaunt in all her pride' (I.i.149–51). Achates does little more than echo this sentiment by praising Aeneas for making 'our hopes survive', to which 'coming' (not 'cunning') joys is the natural object since Aeneas' promise has been of future good to come; and Achates reverts to this promise in lines 157–62, still with the bright future as against the gloomy present as his theme.

I.ii

1 Troians]   In the Methuen edition Tucker Brooke stated that the invariable Q spelling 'Troians' indicated the pronunciation. However, Oliver in the Revels edition objects that Q nowhere used *j* medially but instead the conventional *i* and hence it could be *Trojans* since *O.E.D.* is uncertain at what date the spelling with *i* represents the modern pronunciation. For what it is worth, *Tamburlaine* consistently uses the form 'Troyans', about which there can be no question of pronunciation; it may be possible in *Dido*, then, to view the *i* as a form of *y*, not of *j*, and to agree with Tucker Brooke.

II.i

138 spoke, to further his entent,]   Editors since Oxberry have added a comma after 'spoke' to emend the lack of punctuation in Q; and although they have retained the Q comma after 'entent', thus making the phrase parenthetical, their interpretation has seemed clear that it was the action of the winds in driving the billows to the shore that furthered Ulysses' intent, and 'to further his entent' did not modify Ulysses' 'honey words'. However, Oliver disagrees, remarking, 'Surely Aeneas' point is that Ulysses' opportunism led him to claim that the Gods were intervening on his side.' Oliver's estimate of Ulysses' use of the wind as a divine omen is accurate, as shown by lines 141–2, but his argument has no bearing on the question of Q's modification. If line 138 is a mere repetition of line 137, it is not only otiose but the word 'further' is inapposite. Although Aeneas does not specifically assign the action of the wind to supernatural intervention, such an assumption is a natural one in view of the comments at the start of IV.i on the storm raised by Juno. The error in Q is readily explicable and would seem to be in need of repair.

254 wind]   Oliver is the only editor to challenge Collier's ingenious emendation 'wind' for Q 'wound' made as early as 1831 (*History of English Dramatic Poetry*, vol. III, p. 226) citing *Hamlet*, II.ii.472ff. Perhaps the chief argument in favor of 'wound' has not been sufficiently emphasized, which is that it is simpler to suppose that Shakespeare drew his *Hamlet* speech from Q, the most readily available source, where he would have read 'wound', instead of his hypothetical memory of 'wind' from seeing the 1598 revival of *Dido* (if it was this play) for which Henslowe lent

the Admiral's Men money for costumes. The Q 'wound' is appropriate enough, for Pyrrhus does not make an enraged thrust that goes wide of the mark, as in Shakespeare, but lightly flirts his sword about, disdaining the weakness of Priam's attack. Priam falls wounded, not killed as he would have been by a serious lunge, and then in the next two lines Pyrrhus gets down to his butchery. All this is reasonable enough, for if there had been only Marlowe and Shakespeare, then 'wind' as Shakespeare's hyperbolic invention to match the extreme violence of his scene would have been probable. What convinces the present editor that Collier was right, however, is the fact that it is not just Marlowe and Shakespeare, and that the idea of an opponent being felled by the wind of a sword appears to have been something of a commonplace. McKerrow's notes point out the passage in Nashe's *Strange News at Intercepting Certain Letters*, printed in 1592, 'I feare-blast thee nowe but with the winde of my weapon' (*Works*, I, 321.29–30). F. P. Wilson in his note in the revised 1958 McKerrow *Nashe* calls attention to Spenser's *Faerie Queene* (1590), I.vii.xii, in which the weak and helpless Red Cross Knight leaps from under the descending club of Orgoglio 'Yet so exceeding was the villeins powre, | That with the wind it did him ouerthrowe, | And all his sences stound, that still he lay full low.' Oliver adds Shakespeare's *Troilus and Cressida*, V.iii.40–2, where Troilus reproves Hector, 'When many times the captive Grecian falls, | Even in the fan and wind of your fair sword, | You bid them rise and live.' If this is, then, a somewhat conventional image, it makes no difference whether Shakespeare read 'wound' in the *Dido* Q or 'wind' in Spenser. The *Hamlet* passage is only one part of the total evidence that leads to the belief that Marlowe was more likely to write 'wind' than 'wound' and that it was the Q compositor who misread or misunderstood the word. In this case there is a particular appropriateness to Marlowe's choice of 'whisk about', which *O.E.D.* defines as a 'light sweeping motion'. In its own way it is as hyperbolic as the *Hamlet* image, for the aged Priam, attempting to grapple Pyrrhus with his bleeding stumps, is so feeble that he falls from the wind even of a disdainful lightly swept sword.

III.i

48 What,] Perhaps this should be punctuated with a comma as 'What,' (in modern terms 'What!'), an ejaculation; but one cannot be sure. The ejaculation so often went unpointed in Elizabethan play-texts that only the sense can usually act as evidence. Here it is quite ambiguous.

128 meanly clad] The present editor is not convinced that the Q reading 'meanly' has now been justified beyond doubt by J. C. Maxwell and F. P. Wilson (see the revision of McKerrow's *Nashe*, v, 42). No matter how strong the sense of *suitable*, without the pejorative, the implication is always *in the middle and without extreme*. On the contrary, Dido's speech here is lavish in its imagery throughout, even hyperbolic, and the sense of *suitable* possible for 'meanly' cannot be stretched under any circumstances to take in the rich brilliance of Achates's proposed costume that would attract mermaids to swarm about his ship. His glorious clothing might be that which would be *suitable* to attract mermaids, but not in any sense of 'meanly' that has been remarked. This caveat applies also to Tucker Brooke's unsupported rationalization (p. 172) in the Methuen edition: 'The only interpretation that seems to me reasonably intelligible is to take *meanly* as "normally": "even your normal

dress shall be such that sea-born nymphs," *etc.*' The present editor shares McKerrow's own conclusion: 'I have allowed this reading to stand simply because none of the emendations proposed seems at all satisfactory.'

166 how] Early editors emended to 'here', which makes more sense and is paleo-graphically slightly superior to Dyce and later editors (save Oliver) 'now', which if correct would make 'how' a compositor's memorial error. The Q reading can be defended as a suspension, the sense being roughly, *Yet how I was as far from love as they from hate, I swear* . . .

III.iii

64 far fet on the sea] Ingenious as was Broughton's suggestion (adopted by Revels) of 'forfeit to the sea' for Q 'far fet to', there are at least two objections. One is Marlowe's use of 'far fet' for *far-fetched* in his translation of Lucan, line 94. The other is the naturalness of 'far fet' for a seafaring stranger as compared with the somewhat strained sense, in context, of *forfeit to*. In addition, the consistent use of *fetch* as a nautical term encourages a wordplay here that is appropriate. If these considerations are valid, it is not 'far fet' that is the error in Q but 'to', since *O.E.D.* gives no idiom that would encourage its retention. The error seems to be less paleographic than memorial, in which case recovery of the exact reading of the manuscript is impossible: it might be *on*, *ore*, *by*, *o*', or any other appropriate word. Under these circumstances, 'on', as earlier in the scene at line 47, is as good as any suggestion such as 'o'er' or 'of' and may be supported by the *Elegies* I.xiii.1, in O 1-2, which is a literal translation of *super mare*. The collected edition (O 3) of the *Elegies* reads 'ore', but this O 3 text sometimes sophisticates O 1.

III.iv

25 sicke:——— I] Broughton's conjecture that Q 'sicke, I' should read 'sicke I', with *sicke* as the adjective modifying *I*, is accepted by Revels and is somewhat tempting. However, the question of the modification does not alter the essential fact that an aside is present in the speech; this being so, the only question is where the aside begins. The present editor takes it that Dido is about to play on *sick* in two senses (as not physically sick yet sick for love) when she halts, conscious that the elaboration would reveal her passion. An editorial dash, thus, is inserted at this point, with the conclusion of the aside noted by another dash in line 28.

47 descend] Early editors' emendation 'ascend' is unnecessary. As pointed out by the Revels editor, the meaning is *takes her descent* as in I.i.127-9. It may be remarked that I.i.119 (drawn from *Aeneid* I.380) is also pertinent.

IV.ii

10 Eliza] This is *Elissa*, Dido's original name, forming a parallel, of course, to Spenser's *Epithalamium* and its references to Queen Elizabeth.

IV.iii

28 thy bodie to my lips]   Q's 'my bodie to my lips' exhibits memorial error, but whether an original 'my' in the manuscript contaminated a following 'thy', or the reverse, is mechanically a complete tossup. The first hypothesis was held by the earliest editors (followed by the Methuen edition), the second by the more recent. It may be thought better to adopt 'thy...my' on the belief that in the passage it is Dido who thinks of herself as the operative force and hence it will be by the suction of her lips that she will link Aeneas's body to hers in union.

IV.v

28 our]   The Q reading 'women of your years' has been followed by all editors, presumably in the belief that the Nurse is here addressing herself as in the next lines 29–30. Although it is clear that the whole speech represents a form of dialogue between the Nurse in her normal mind and in the inflamed state created by her carrying Cupid in her arms, the exact demarcations have not always been established. However, they may be clearly marked off by the pronouns. Starting with line 21, when Cupid's influence is in the ascendant the Nurse speaks in the first person. On the other hand, except for lines 25 and the first half of 26 when she is responding to Cupid's line 24, her self-reproaches in lines 29–30 are addressed to herself as *thou*. It would seem, then, that in line 28 Q 'your' is wrong on two counts: it does not agree with the familiar *thy* which the Nurse elsewhere appropriately uses to herself (*your* is far too formal); and it clashes with the first-person address that is elsewhere invariable for the Nurse in her Cupid-intoxicated state. Although Deighton's proposed emendations of Marlowe are mostly shallow sophistications, not worth recording, it would appear that he hit the mark in the present example.

V.i

82.1 *Enter* Dido *to* Aeneas.]   Oliver's emendation of Q '*and*' to '*to*' is almost demonstrably correct. Earlier editors adopted the distasteful expedient of adding an exit for Aeneas after line 82, for which there is no Q warrant, emending 82.1 to exclude Aeneas, and inventing an entrance direction from him at 86.1. In the Methuen edition Tucker Brooke in fact anticipated the Revels editor by keeping Aeneas onstage and printing the simple direction, '*Enter* Dido' but it is unaccountable why he did not think of retaining the complete Q direction with the simple emendation of '*and*' to '*to*'.

234 hearts]   Starting with Oxberry, editors adopted the easy emendation of 'heart's' for Q 'heart', which makes 'he' the ungrammatical object of the verb 'mollifie' instead of 'heart'. Conscious of this difficulty, Tucker Brooke in the Methuen edition placed a dash after 'whit' in line 235 and suggested: 'there is no great difficulty in understanding the text as it stands in the Quarto as an example of anacoluthon or ellipsis. Either Anna breaks off her sentence purposely after *whit*, leaving the obvious sequel of Aeneas' indifference to be guessed, or else in her emotion she loses track of the logical relation to her words.' The present editor is

not convinced that this break is viable after 'whit' and he does not see any parallelism in the other example of anacoluthon at II.i.201 cited by Brooke as evidence. Nor is the editor impressed by the strain on the syntax imposed by Oliver's conclusion that 'Yet he' means *even he*, in apposition with '*Aeneas*'. The truth may be, as McKerrow guessed, that a line is missing after 235 'signifying that Aeneas turned his back upon Anna or went below', the subject continuing to be 'he'. That this would be the only line known to be skipped in the play is not evidence against such a hypothesis, but a close reading of the passage may perhaps disclose some difficulties in the content of such a missing line. Line 237 'though he beheld me not' could agree well enough with Aeneas having turned away, but it does not help with the mysterious 'he clapt under hatches' of line 240. On the other hand, if the missing material were to describe how the crew clapped Aeneas under hatches to prevent his being affected by Anna's siren song, then (*a*) more than one line is missing and (*b*) there is trouble adjusting the crew's action with Anna's statement in lines 238–9 (which would follow the lost line[s]) that the crew 'gan to move him to redresse my ruth' unless we are to suppose that they addressed him as a prisoner below decks, he refused their offer to release him so that he could make redress, and in confinement he sailed away. If this question of a missing line were more certain – and 'he clapt under hatches' is its best evidence, for otherwise no explanation for this detail exists – an editor would be correct in leaving the error and not attempting to patch it up by creating another departure from manuscript in the emendation of manuscript 'heart' to 'hearts'. On the other hand, to rear a hypothesis about missing text on a question of grammar in Elizabethan times is dangerous, and it is by no means certain that, in the structure of this particular sentence, 'he' as the object of 'mollifie' would have raised an Elizabethan eyebrow. Since the case is, then, a tossup as to where the corruption lies in the text, the conventional emendation may be adopted in lieu of a better with something of a clear conscience.

EMENDATIONS OF ACCIDENTALS

I.i

29 time.] ~ ,
30 Why,] ~ ∧
41 me.] ~ :
50 I,] ~ ∧
66 horse,] ~ ∧
69 souldiers,] ~ ∧

111 Stygian] stygian
126 view.] ~ ,
199 cast.] ~ ,
210 Punick] punick
218–19 *Italy,...Jove:*] ~ :...~ ,
248.1 *Exeunt.*] *Exit.*

I.ii

0.1 Cloanthus] *Cloanthes*

44 grace.] ~ ,

II.i

0 II.i] Actus 2.
1, 62, 81 *Carthage*] Carthage
12 *Hecuba?*] ~ ,
37, 50 see,] ~ ∧
77–8 *One line in* Q
107 to,] ~ ∧
118 What,] ~ ∧

147 him,] ~ ∧
159 then—] ~ ,
239 *Neoptolemus.*] ~ ,
284–5 abourd,...deepe:] ~ :...~ ,
295 *Greece.*] Greece,
297 *Deiphobus,*] *Diiphobus* ∧
298 Lover∧] ~ ,

III.i

0 III.i] Actus 3. Scene 1.
39 mine.] ~ ?
43 deserv'd.—— Away] ~ , away
93 *Indiaes*] Indiaes

153–4 all. —— ...one.——] ~ , ∧...
~ . ∧
172–3 not: —— ...selfe:——] ~ :
∧... ~ . ∧

III.ii

13 dye?] ~ .
16 simple,] ~ ∧

31 counites?] ~ .
75 *Carthage*] Carthage

III.iii

5 now,] ~ ∧
17 Why,] ~ ∧
29 gage.] ~ ?
31 laire?] ~ .

35 *Cupid.*] Q *speech-prefix in this scene*
is Asca.
36 armes.] ~ ,
62.1 *manet*] *manent*

III.iv

25 sicke:—— I] ~ , ˄ ~
28 griefe:——] ~ : ˄

40 *Carthage*] Carthage
52 Delian] delian

IV.i

0 IV.i] Actus 4. Scene 1.
15 *Cupid.*] *Asca.*

19 *Tipheus*] *Typhous*

IV.ii

54 speake?] ~ ,

IV.iv

29 *et seq. this scene Carthage*] Carthage
47 calles?] ~ ,
67 Punicke] punicke

85 thee˄ sister,] ~ , ~ ˄
123.1 *Lord.*] *omit* Q
165.1 *Exeunt.*] *Exit.*

IV.v

26 toy.——] ~ , ˄
28 yeares.——] ~ . ˄

30 age:——] ~ : ˄
32 sweete:——] ~ : ˄

V.i

0 V.i] Actus 5.
11 *Egypt*] Egypt
45 dandlest] danlest
57 What,] ~ ˄
98 love?] ~ .
109 farewell.] ~ ,
110 hence,] ~ .

124 farewell?] ~ .
187 obdurate] abdurate
200 sister,] ~ ˄
224.1 *Exeunt....*] Q *places after line* 223
274–5 *One line in* Q
317 soule.] ~ ,
320–1 *One line in* Q

HISTORICAL COLLATION

[NOTE: The following editions are herein collated: Q (1594), Ox (edited Oxberry, 1818), H (*Old English Drama*, vol. II, published by Hurst, Robinson & Co., 1825), R (*Works*, ed. Robinson, 1826), D¹ (*Works*, ed. Dyce, 1850), D² (*Works*, rev. 1858), C (*Works*, ed. Cunningham, 1870), B (*Works*, ed. Bullen, 1884–5), G (*Works of Nashe*, ed. Grosart, vol. VI, 1885), McK (*Works of Nashe*, vol. II, 1904), TB (*Works*, ed. Tucker Brooke, 1910), M (Methuen, ed. Tucker Brooke, 1930) Ri (*Plays*, ed. Ribner, 1963), Rv (Revels, ed. Oliver, 1968). Reference is made to Br (MS notes by Broughton in BM copy of Robinson) and Coll (MS notes by Collier in BM copy of 1850 Dyce).]

I.i

10 earth] earth's Ox
10 haire] aire Q, Ox, H, R
42 love:] ~ ᴧ Q; ~ , Ox, H, R, C, G, McK, TB; ~ ; D, B, M; ~ . Ri, Rv
46 have] have too D (*qy*)
47 in] into Ox, H, R, C, B.
48 an] a Ox, H, R, D, C
49 shall] shalt Ox, H, R, D, C, M
52 Whiles] While Ox, H, R
59 ghosts] gusts Coll MS
72 Ay] Ah Ox, H, R, C
73 *Astræus*] Astræa's Ox, H, R, C
76 floods] flood Ox
80 thine] thy Ox, H, R, C
96 *Ascanius*, beauties] Ascanius' beauties Ox, H, R
106 Princesse priest conceav'd] princess, priest-conceiv'd Ox, H, R
110 sands] sand Ox, H, R
115 Wind-god] wind-gods Br MS, C
116 Besiege] Besieges D, B, G, M

132 *Cimothoe*] *Cimodoæ* Q; Cymodoce Ox, H, R, D, C
134 What?...see ᴧ] What ᴧ...see? D (*qy*), C, B
136 attract] attrect G (*qy*)
144 ye] thee Q, Ri, Rv; us Ox, H, R, B
153 annoy] annoys D (*qy*)
154 coming] cunning Q, Ox, H, R, Rv
159 aged...shed] azur'd...spread Coll MS
159 haire] aire Q, Ox, H, R
175 roave] roam Ox, H, R, C
183 came] came along D (*qy*), C
190 bewraies] betrays C
198 as] us Coll MS, G
204 Tirien] Turen Q
233 A] In Ox, H, R, C
241 I...feete:] *omit* Ox
244 shades] shapes C (*qy*)
244 deceiv'st] deceive C
245 talke] walk C

I.ii

9 spite] fate Ox
41 *Baucis*] *Vausis* Q
42 you] ye B

46 would] should Ox
47 shall] all D² (*qy*); still McK (*qy*)

5-2

II.i

37 come] comes C
38 feares] tears Coll MS, B (*qy*)
49 am] *omit* Q, Ox, H, R, Ri
51 names] meanes Q
53 Live long] Long live Ox
66 hath] has C
72 view] viewd Q
103 blest,] ~ ? Ox, H, R, D, C, B
138 spoke,] ~ ∧ Q, TB, Ri, Rv
153 shepherds] shepherd Q
166 stung] put Ox

189 streetes] street Ox
204 wounds] wound Ox
220 Ah] Ha? Ox, H, R, C
254 wind] wound Q, Ox, H, R, Rv
275 Fane] Fawne Q
288 by that] that, by D¹ (*qy*), D², B, G
319 Blushing] With blushing C (*after* Mitford)
319 *Hyacinthe*] hyacinths D, C
322 *Cithereas*] *Citheidas* Q
338 And...sleepe,] *omit* Ox

III.i

5 the] thy Ox
27 learndst] learnst Q, Ox, H, R, G, McK, TB
32 me∧ now?] ~ ? ~ ∧ Q, Ox, H, R, C, G, McK, TB, Rv
57 eye] eyes C
58 love] Iove Q, Ox, H, R, G
61 sower] power Ox, H, R
86 glistering] glist'ning Ox
121 lose] loose C

128 meanly] seemly D (*but qy* meetly), B; newly Coll MS, C
142 *Æneas.*] Serg. D²; *A Lord.* G
143 *Olympus*] Olympia's D, C, B, M
164 gree] greed G
166 how] here Ox, H, R, C; now D, B, TB, M, Ri
173 *Æneas* speake] Æneas come *or* hark D¹ (*qy*); Æneas come D², B; Æneas—— | *Æn.* Speake! | *Dido.* We two McK (*qy*)

III.ii

3 fame] furie Q, Ox, H, R, D, B, TB, McK, Ri; Troy C; furies G
3 the fates] the face Q; fate Rv
11 let out] left out Q
16 without] with ought made McK (*qy*)
16 minde] made Q; might Ox, H, R
22 such] some C (*qy*)
51 chaungd] chaunge Q, Ox, H, R, TB
84 light to] light unto Br MS, C, B;

lightning to *or* light unto D (*qy*); light to the G
84 *Lavinias*] Lavinian D (*qy*); the *Lavinian* G (*but qy* unto *Lavinium's*)
88 these woods] the woods D, C, B, G, McK
93–5 And...propound] *omit* Ox, H, R
97 have it] have Q, D¹ (*but qy* it), M, Rv

III.iii

4 shrowdes] shroud Ox, S, R, D, C, B
5 fellowes] follow us C
14 could] would Ox, S, R
19 ye] you D, B
50 thou] *omit* Ox

64 far fet] far set Ox, H, R; forfeit Ri, Rv, Br MS
64 on] to Q, Ox, H, R, Ri, Rv; o'er D, C, B, G, McK; o' TB, M
79 fancies] fancies' Ox, H, R, D¹, C, G; fancy's D², B, M, Ri, Rv

III.iv

5 where] here Ox, H, R, C
7 it] *omit* Ox, H, R, C
19 *Pean*] *Pæan's* Ox, H, R
21 hath] now hath G
38 for] 'fore Br, D, C, B, G
39 seeme] seen Ox, H, R

39 faire to] faire Q, Ox, H, R; foreign Coll MS; fair in D, B, G, Ri
47 descend] ascend Br, B
54 delight] delights Ox
58 rests] rest Ox, H, R, C

IV.i

4 That] One that G (*after* Mitford)
4 them forth] forth the winds B (*qy*)
17 this] the Ox, H, R

19 darts] dart B
35 cares] eares Q, Rv

IV.ii

12 Where] When Coll MS
22 eyes] lips Coll MS
39 numbers] number Ox, H, R

42 have] has Ox, H, R, C
51 goes] flies Coll MS

IV.iii

2 thy] the Q, McK, TB, M, Ri, Rv
8 fortunes] fortune Ox, H, R, C
16 dreames] dream Ox, H, R, D, C
18 reames] beames Q, Ox, H, R
26 loosing] losing Ox

28 thy...my] my...my Q; my...thy Ox, H, R, M
32 starres] star Ox, S, R
51 coll] coil Ox, H, R, C (*qy* coll)

IV.iv

11 *Circes*] Circe Ox, H, R, D, C, B, TB
25 windes blow] wind blows Ox, H, R, C
50 fledst] fleest Q, Ox, H, R, C, G, McK
52 Heavens] Heaven Ox, H, R, D, C, B, G, M

61 thee] that R, C
90 lives] loves Q, Ox, H, R, TB, Rv
96 our] 'mong our D (*qy*); of our B, G
119 threatens] threaten Ox, H, R, D, C, B, Ri
124 is] has Ox
133 he goe] ye go D, C, B

IV.v

1 ye] you Ox, D, B
8 sort] sorts Ox, H, R
12 ye] you D, B
19 goe] go to B (*after Athenæum*, no. 2977)
19 ye] you D
20 twigger] trigger Coll MS
26 Foolish ∧...toy.] ~ !...~ ? Coll MS

28 Especially] *Cupid.* Especially Coll MS
28 our] your Q, Ox, H, R, D, C, B, G, McK, TB, M, Ri, Rv
31 A grave] *Nurse.* A grave Coll MS
31 grave? why,] ~ , ~ ? Q, Ox, H, R, G, McK, TB; ~ ! ~ , D, C, B, M; ~ ? ~ ? Ri, Rv
37 was I] I was Ox

V.i

6 clad] clothe Ox, H, R
7 evermore] overcome Ox
13 honeys spoyles] honey-spoils Ox,
    H, R, D, C, B
15 her] their D¹ (*qy*), D², B
19 have I] I have Ox
35 in *Libia*] on Libia's Ox, H, R, C
39 *Iulus*ₐ] ~ , Ox, H, R, G
50 spying him] spying Ox, H, R
62 meanes] mean Ox, H, R, D, C
63 besides] beside Ox, H, R, C
69 When as] Whereas Ox, H, R
82.1 *to*] *and* Q, Ox, H, G, TB
84 *Achates*] Sergestus D (*qy*)
86.1 *omit*] *Enter Æneas.* Ox, H, R, C
110 *Dido.*] *assigned to line* 111 Q, Ox, H,
    R, D, C, B, G, McK
110 Let] O let G
110 goe] go is C
110 farewell] farewell none D²; farewell
    or none G (*qy*)
114 chaind] chaungd Q, Ox, H; charm'd
    TB (*qy*)
114 eyes] eye Ox, H, R, C
117 thy] my Q, G (*qy*)

138 *adhuc*] *ad hæc* Q
144 calles] call'd Ox, H, R, D, C
145 by] with Ox
151 Now] Nor M
155 thou not] not thou Ox
160 this] thus Ox, H, R
171 Sea-gulfes] sea-gulls Ox, H, R, C
182 heart] power Ox, H, R
211 heavens] heaven Ox, H, R
221 keene] keend Q, D, G, McK, TB;
    kind Coll MS, M, Ri; kenn'd D
    (*qy*), C, B; too, keendₐ G
234 hearts] heart Q, TB, Ri, Rv
242 ye] you D, B
244 ships] ship Ox, H, R, C
248 *Anna*] Anna, Anna D (*qy*), C, B, G
248 *Arions*] Orions Q, Ox, H, R
252 him] 'em D²; them C
253 falles] fall Ox, H, R, D, C
268 my] thy Q
276 Daughter] Guardian B (*qy*)
295, 298 lye] lies Ox, H, R, D
298 I] *omit* Ox, H, R
315, 318 aye] ah Ox, H, R, C

TAMBURLAINE

Part i

TEXTUAL INTRODUCTION

Richard Jones entered for his copy in the Stationers' Register on 14 August 1590, 'the twooe commicall discourses of Tomberlein the Cithian Shepparde'. The book was published as an octavo, in 1590, with the imprint: 'London. Printed by Richard Ihones: at the signe of the Rose and Crowne neere Holborne Bridge. 1590' (Greg, no. 94.95). The printer is not known but may have been Thomas Orwin, who printed various books for Jones in 1589–91.[1] The octavo collates A–K⁸ L², the first part ending on sig. F2. A woodcut of a bust of a man in armor, titled (in type) 'Tamburlaine, the great.'[2] occupies sig. F2^v, and part II begins with a headtitle on sig. F3.

The fact that the spelling is generally uniform and that only one pair of cases was used suggests that a single compositor set the whole of the two parts, probably composing by formes from cast-off copy.[3] The punctuation system, also, is relatively uniform in certain eccentricities. That is, the compositor with some frequency placed a full stop before the second part of a compound sentence beginning with 'and' or 'or', before a relative clause, and sometimes even before participial clauses. As much of this special punctuation has been preserved in this edition as possible when the sense is not thereby made too difficult to follow. Whether or not it was part of his system, the compositor often transposed colons and periods at the ends of two consecutive lines but this peculiarity has been emended. Just possibly some of the completely erroneous full stops may represent foul case. Various of these types are so broken as almost to

---

[1] See the discussion in Robert Ford Welsh, *The Printing of the Early Editions of Marlowe's Plays* (University Microfilms, 1964), pp. 9–16.

[2] The late Mr John Crow identified for me the woodcut as that on the titlepage of *A Short Admonition or Warning, Upon the detestable Treason wherewith Sir William Stanley and Rowland Yorke have Betraied and Delivered Monie unto the Spaniards . . . At London printed by Richard Iones . . . 1587*.' This title, not in the *S.T.C.*, was licensed to Jones on 9 April 1587.

[3] For an analysis, see Welsh, pp. 16–31. A new group of running-titles was set for Part II, but this section, like Part I, was printed from only one skeleton-forme and hence the compositor was somewhat behind the press in his speed of composition.

defy positive identification, particularly since only two copies of the first edition have been preserved. However, the editor has attempted to follow the more difficult sorts through setting and distribution, and somewhere in the process the inking was usually clear enough to serve for identification.

The plays were reprinted in 1593, again supposedly by Jones but no doubt by another printer, and once more for Jones in 1597. The third edition returns for its copy to the 1590 text, so that 1592 is terminal. In 1605 (no transfer of copy being preserved) Edward White published the last of the early editions, Edward Allde being the printer. Part I is dated 1605 and Part II, with its own titlepage and independent collation, 1606.[1] This edition was printed from that of 1597. These last three editions are simple reprints. The edition of 1590, therefore, becomes not only the copy-text but also the sole authority.

The conventional date for Part I is the winter of 1587–8, with Part II following in the summer of 1588, but this early dating (at least for Part II) involves the hypothesis that Marlowe saw in manuscript Paul Ive's *Practice of Fortification* (1589) from which some details are drawn in Part II.[2] Little is known of the stage-history except that Henslowe's Diary records a performance by the Admiral's men (listed as the players on the 1590 titlepage) at the end of August 1594, that fourteen performances of the first part followed before 12 November 1595, and that there were seven performances of the second part between 19 December 1594 and 13 November 1595. In 1598 a Henslowe inventory mentions various costumes and properties, including a cage.

The copy behind the 1590 edition was very likely Marlowe's own papers, though whether his foul papers or the fair copy he would normally have made himself for sale to the company, or commissioned, is uncertain. Except for a few notable cruxes, the copy seems to have been relatively clean, and thus a fair copy, whether holograph or scribal, would seem to be the best hypothesis.

---

[1] It is probable that no real interval separated the publication of the two parts; very likely the second came out near the end of 1605 and so was pre-dated.

[2] The question is discussed thoroughly by Una Ellis-Fermor in her introduction to the Methuen edition (1930), pp. 6–10.

Theatrical origin is not likely, in part owing to the erratic scene numberings, which – especially in Part II – may veer towards the French system from time to time. Moreover, Jones's dedication to the Gentlemen Readers may have a pertinence. He writes that he has 'purposely' omitted what seem to have been comic or farcical scenes that were acted on the stage. The language is not, perhaps, to be taken too literally. By 'purposely' Jones implies that he could have printed these scenes if he had wished, in which case the copy would almost necessarily have been theatrical in origin.[1] But since it bears no signs of the playhouse, it is much more likely that Jones's copy did not contain this material; hence his virtuous defense of the omission of unsuitable scenes may very possibly be an attempt to anticipate criticism that they were not present, though acted. If so, the material would not have been available to him in the papers he acquired, which as a consequence would most probably have had an authorial provenience.

In the preparation of the present edition the two preserved copies of the 1590 edition, one in the Henry E. Huntington Library and the other in the Bodleian (sig. K3 wanting),[2] have been collated, the press-variants recorded, and doubtful types identified insofar as possible. For the Historical Collation the 1592 edition in the British Museum (C.34.a.4), the 1597 edition in the Huntington Library, and the 1605–6 edition in the British Museum (644.e.67[a–b]) have been used. So far as is known, Chappell Jr did not print this play. Thus the earliest recorded modern edition is that by William Oxberry in 1820, followed in the Historical Collation selection by the *Works*, edited by Robinson (1826), *Works*, edited by Alexander Dyce (1850; revised 1858), *Works*, edited by Francis Cunningham (1870), *Works*, edited by A. H. Bullen (1884), I *Tamburlaine*, edited by Albrecht Wagner (1885), *Works*, edited by Tucker Brooke (1910), *Tamburlaine*, edited by Una Ellis-Fermor (Methuen, 1930),

---

[1] This is to take it that Marlowe would not have written such material for inclusion in an already lengthy play.

[2] In the Bodleian copy the lower few lines of sig. D6 have been torn off, affecting Part I, IV.iii.43–6 and IV.iv.0.1–2. In Part II, the absence of sig. K3 means that for V.i.56–112 the Huntington copy is the only authority. Sigs. A1–2 of a third copy of 1590 have been preserved prefixed to the Huntington (Bridgewater) copy of 1605, and these two leaves have been collated.

Plays, edited by Leo Kirschbaum (1862), *Plays*, edited by Irving Ribner (1963), and *Tamburlaine*, edited by John D. Jump (Regents, 1967). Broughton's notes in the British Museum copy of Robinson, and Collier's notes in the British Museum copy of the 1850 Dyce edition have also been consulted.

To the Gentlemen Readers: and others that take pleasure in reading Histories

Gentlemen, and curteous Readers whosoever: I have here published in print for your sakes, the two tragical Discourses of the Scythian Shepheard, Tamburlaine, *that became so great a Conquerour, and so mightie a Monarque: My hope is, that they wil be now no lesse acceptable unto you to read after your serious affaires and studies, then they have bene (lately) delightfull for many of you to see, when the same were shewed in* London *upon stages: I have (purposely) omitted and left out some fond and frivolous Jestures, digressing (and in my poore opinion) far unmeet for the matter, which I thought, might seeme more tedious unto the wise, than any way els to be regarded, though (happly) they have bene of some vaine conceited fondlings greatly gaped at, what times they were shewed upon the stage in their graced deformities: nevertheles now, to be mixtured in print with such matter of worth, it wuld proove a great disgrace to so honorable and stately a historie: Great folly were it in me, to commend unto your wisedomes, either the eloquence of the Authour that writ them, or the worthinesse of the matter it selfe; I therefore leave unto your learned censures, both the one and the other, and my selfe the poore printer of them unto your most curteous and favourable protection; which if you vouchsafe to accept, you shall ever more binde mee to imploy what travell and service I can, to the advauncing and pleasuring of your excellent degree.*

Yours, most humble at commaundement,

R. J. Printer

[DRAMATIS PERSONÆ

MYCETES, King of Persia

COSROE, his brother

MEANDER
THERIDAMAS
ORTYGIUS } Persian lords
CENEUS
MENAPHON

TAMBURLAINE, a Scythian shepherd

TECHELLES } his followers
USUMCASANE

BAJAZETH, emperor of the Turks

KING OF FEZ

KING OF MOROCCO

KING OF ARGIER

KING OF ARABIA

SOLDAN OF EGYPT

GOVERNOR OF DAMASCUS

AGYDAS } Median lords
MAGNETESY

CAPOLIN, an Egyptian

PHILEMUS, a Messenger

Bassoes, Lords, Citizens, Moors, Soldiers, and Attendants

ZENOCRATE, daughter to the Soldan of Egypt

ANIPPE, her maid

ZABINA, wife to Bajazeth

EBEA, her maid

Virgins of Damascus]

The two tragicall Discourses of mighty Tamburlaine, *the Scythian Shepheard, &c.*

The Prologue.

From jygging vaines of riming mother wits,
And such conceits as clownage keepes in pay,
Weele leade you to the stately tent of War:
Where you shall heare the Scythian Tamburlaine,
Threatning the world with high astounding tearms
And scourging kingdoms with his conquering sword.
View but his picture in this tragicke glasse,
And then applaud his fortunes if you please.

[*Enter*] Mycetes, Cosroe, Meander, Theridamas, Ortygius, Ceneus, I. i
[Menaphon,] *with others.*

Mycetes.   Brother *Cosroe*, I find my selfe agreev'd,
  Yet insufficient to expresse the same:
  For it requires a great and thundring speech:
  Good brother tell the cause unto my Lords,
  I know you have a better wit than I.
Cosroe.   Unhappie *Persea*, that in former age
  Hast bene the seat of mightie Conquerors,
  That in their prowesse and their pollicies,
  Have triumpht over *Affrike*, and the bounds
  Of *Europe* wher the Sun dares scarce appeare,   10
  For freezing meteors and conjealed colde:
  Now to be rulde and governed by a man,
  At whose byrth-day *Cynthia* with *Saturne* joinde,
  And *Jove*, the Sun, and *Mercurie* denied
  To shed their influence in his fickle braine,
  Now Turkes and Tartars shake their swords at thee,
  Meaning to mangle all thy Provinces.
Mycetes.   Brother, I see your meaning well enough.
  And thorough your Planets I perceive you thinke,
  I am not wise enough to be a kinge,   20
  But I refer me to my noble men,
  That knowe my wit, and can be witnesses:
  I might command you to be slaine for this,
  Meander, might I not?
Meander.   Not for so small a fault my soveraigne Lord.
Mycetes.   I meane it not, but yet I know I might,
  Yet live, yea, live, *Mycetes* wils it so:
  Meander, thou my faithfull Counsellor,
  Declare the cause of my conceived griefe,

15 their] Oxberry; his O 1–4

Which is (God knowes) about that *Tamburlaine*,   30
That like a Foxe in midst of harvest time,
Dooth pray uppon my flockes of Passengers,
And as I heare, doth meane to pull my plumes.
Therefore tis good and meete for to be wise.

Meander.   Oft have I heard your Majestie complain,
Of *Tamburlaine*, that sturdie Scythian thiefe,
That robs your merchants of *Persepolis*,
Trading by land unto the Westerne Isles,
And in your confines with his lawlesse traine,
Daily commits incivill outrages,   40
Hoping (misled by dreaming prophesies)
To raigne in *Asia*, and with barbarous Armes,
To make himselfe the Monarch of the East:
But ere he march in *Asia*, or display
His vagrant Ensigne in the Persean fields,
Your Grace hath taken order by *Theridamas*,
Chardg'd with a thousand horse, to apprehend
And bring him Captive to your Highnesse throne.

Mycetes.   Ful true thou speakst, and like thy selfe my lord,
Whom I may tearme a *Damon* for thy love.   50
Therefore tis best, if so it lik you all,
To send my thousand horse incontinent,
To apprehend that paltrie Scythian.
How like you this, my honorable Lords?
Is it not a kingly resolution?

Cosroe.   It cannot choose, because it comes from you.

Mycetes.   Then heare thy charge, valiant *Theridamas*,
The chiefest Captaine of *Mycetes* hoste,
The hope of *Persea*, and the verie legges
Whereon our state doth leane, as on a staffe,   60
That holds us up, and foiles our neighbour foes.
Thou shalt be leader of this thousand horse,
Whose foming galle with rage and high disdaine,
Have sworne the death of wicked *Tamburlaine*.
Go frowning foorth, but come thou smyling home,

38 Trading] O 2; Treading O 1

As did Sir *Paris* with the Grecian Dame:
Returne with speed, time passeth swift away,
Our life is fraile, and we may die to day.
Theridamas. Before the Moone renew her borrowed light,
Doubt not my Lord and gratious Soveraigne, 70
But *Tamburlaine*, and that Tartarian rout,
Shall either perish by our warlike hands,
Or plead for mercie at your highnesse feet.
Mycetes. Go, stout *Theridamas*, thy words are swords,
And with thy lookes thou conquerest all thy foes:
I long to see thee backe returne from thence,
That I may view these milk-white steeds of mine,
All loden with the heads of killed men.
And from their knees, even to their hoofes below,
Besmer'd with blood, that makes a dainty show. 80
Theridamas. Then now my Lord, I humbly take my leave.

Exit.

Mycetes. *Theridamas*, farewel ten thousand times.
Ah, *Menaphon*, why staiest thou thus behind,
When other men prease forward for renowne:
Go *Menaphon*, go into *Scythia*,
And foot by foot follow *Theridamas*.
Cosroe. Nay, pray you let him stay, a greater task
Fits *Menaphon*, than warring with a Thiefe:
Create him Prorex of *Assiria*,
That he may win the Babylonians hearts, 90
Which will revolt from Persean government,
Unlesse they have a wiser king than you.
Mycetes. Unlesse they have a wiser king than you?
These are his words, *Meander* set them downe.
Cosroe. And ad this to them, that all *Asia*
Lament to see the follie of their King.
Mycetes. Well here I sweare by this my royal seat——
Cosroe. You may doe well to kisse it then.
Mycetes. Embost with silke as best beseemes my state,
To be reveng'd for these contemptuous words. 100

87 task] Ox; *omit* O1-4   *89 *Assiria*] Van Dam; *Affrica* O1-3; all *Affrica* O4

O where is dutie and allegeance now?
Fled to the Caspean or the Ocean maine?
What, shall I call thee brother? No, a foe,
Monster of Nature, shame unto thy stocke,
That dar'st presume thy Soveraigne for to mocke.
Meander come, I am abus'd *Meander*.   *Exeunt.*
                              Manent Cosroe *and* Menaphon.
Menaphon.   How now my Lord, what, mated and amaz'd
  To heare the king thus threaten like himselfe?
Cosroe.   Ah *Menaphon,* I passe not for his threates,
  The plot is laid by Persean Noble men,   110
  And Captaines of the Medean garrisons,
  To crowne me Emperour of *Asia.*
  But this it is that doth excruciate
  The verie substance of my vexed soule:
  To see our neighbours that were woont to quake
  And tremble at the Persean Monarkes name,
  Now sits and laughs our regiment to scorne:
  And that which might resolve me into teares,
  Men from the farthest Equinoctiall line,
  Have swarm'd in troopes into the Easterne *India*:   120
  Lading their shippes with golde and pretious stones:
  And made their spoiles from all our provinces.
Menaphon.   This should intreat your highnesse to rejoice,
  Since Fortune gives you opportunity,
  To gaine the tytle of a Conquerour,
  By curing of this maimed Emperie.
  Affrike and *Europe* bordering on your land,
  And continent to your Dominions:
  How easely may you with a mightie hoste,
  Passe into *Græcia,* as did *Cyrus* once.   130
  And cause them to withdraw their forces home,
  Least you subdue the pride of Christendome?
Cosroe.   But *Menaphon,* what means this trumpets sound?
Menaphon.   Behold, my Lord, *Ortigius* and the rest,
  Bringing the Crowne to make you Emperour.

134 Lord, *Ortigius*ᴧ] Oxberry; ~ ᴧ ~,   135.1 Ceneus] Oxberry; Conerus O 1–4
    O 1–4

6-2

Enter Ortigius *and* Ceneus *bearing a Crowne, with others.*

Ortygius.   Magnificent and mightie Prince *Cosroe,*
We in the name of other Persean states,
And commons of this mightie Monarchie,
Present thee with th'Emperiall Diadem.
Ceneus.   The warlike Souldiers, and the Gentlemen,   140
That heretofore have fild *Persepolis*
With *Affrike* Captaines, taken in the field:
Whose ransome made them martch in coates of gold,
With costlie jewels hanging at their eares,
And shining stones upon their loftie Crestes:
Now living idle in the walled townes,
Wanting both pay and martiall discipline,
Begin in troopes to threaten civill warre,
And openly exclaime against the King.
Therefore to stay all sodaine mutinies,   150
We will invest your Highnesse Emperour:
Whereat the Souldiers will conceive more joy,
Then did the Macedonians at the spoile
Of great *Darius* and his wealthy hoast.
Cosroe.   Wel, since I see the state of *Persea* droope,
And languish in my brothers government:
I willingly receive th'emperiall crowne,
And vow to weare it for my countries good:
In spight of them shall malice my estate.
Ortygius.   And in assurance of desir'd successe,   160
We here doo crowne thee Monarch of the East,
Emperour of *Asia,* and of *Persea,*
Great Lord of *Medea* and *Armenia*:
Duke of *Assiria* and *Albania,*
Mesopotamia and of *Parthia,*
East *India* and the late discovered Isles,
Chiefe Lord of all the wide vast *Euxine* sea,
And of the ever raging Caspian Lake:
Long live *Cosroe* mighty Emperour.

*164 *Assiria*] Van Dam; *Affrica* O 1–4.   *169 Long live] *stet* O 1

Cosroe.   And *Jove* may never let me longer live,   170
  Then I may seeke to gratifie your love,
  And cause the souldiers that thus honour me,
  To triumph over many Provinces.
  By whose desires of discipline in Armes,
  I doubt not shortly but to raigne sole king,
  And with the Armie of *Theridamas*,
  Whether we presently will flie (my Lords)
  To rest secure against my brothers force.
Ortygius.   We knew my Lord, before we brought the crowne,
  Intending your investion so neere   180
  The residence of your dispised brother,
  The Lords would not be too exasperate,
  To injure or suppresse your woorthy tytle.
  Or if they would, there are in readines
  Ten thousand horse to carie you from hence,
  In spite of all suspected enemies.
Cosroe.   I know it wel my Lord, and thanke you all.
Ortygius.   Sound up the trumpets then, God save the King.
Exeunt [attended].

[*Enter*] Tamburlaine *leading* Zenocrate: Techelles, Usumcasane, I.ii
other Lords [,Magnetes, Agidas,] *and Souldiers loden with treasure.*

Tamburlaine.   Come lady, let not this appal your thoughts.
  The jewels and the treasure we have tane
  Shall be reserv'd, and you in better state,
  Than if you were arriv'd in *Siria*,
  Even in the circle of your Fathers armes:
  The mightie Souldan of *Egyptia*.
Zenocrate.   Ah Shepheard, pity my distressed plight,
  (If as thou seem'st, thou art so meane a man)
  And seeke not to inrich thy followers,
  By lawlesse rapine from a silly maide.   10
  Who traveiling with these Medean Lords
  To *Memphis*, from my uncles country of *Medea*,

Where all my youth I have bene governed,
Have past the armie of the mightie Turke:
Bearing his privie signet and his hand:
To safe conduct us thorow *Affrica*.
Magnetes.   And since we have arriv'd in *Scythia*,
Besides rich presents from the puisant Cham,
We have his highnesse letters to command
Aide and assistance if we stand in need.   20
Tamburlaine.   But now you see these letters and commandes,
Are countermanded by a greater man:
And through my provinces you must expect
Letters of conduct from my mightinesse,
If you intend to keep your treasure safe.
But since I love to live at liberty,
As easely may you get the Souldans crowne,
As any prizes out of my precinct.
For they are friends that help to weane my state,
Till men and kingdomes help to strengthen it: 30
And must maintaine my life exempt from servitude.
But tell me Maddam, is your grace betroth'd?
Zenocrate.   I am (my Lord,) for so you do import.
Tamburlaine.   I am a Lord, for so my deeds shall proove,
And yet a shepheard by my Parentage:
But Lady, this faire face and heavenly hew,
Must grace his bed that conquers *Asia*:
And meanes to be a terrour to the world,
Measuring the limits of his Emperie
By East and west, as *Phœbus* doth his course: 40
Lie here ye weedes that I disdaine to weare,

[Takes off shepheards cloak.]

This compleat armor, and this curtle-axe
Are adjuncts more beseeming *Tamburlaine*.
And Maddam, whatsoever you esteeme
Of this successe, and losse unvallued,
Both may invest you Empresse of the East:
And these that seeme but silly country Swaines,

May have the leading of so great an host,
As with their waight shall make the mountains quake,
Even as when windy exhalations,   50
Fighting for passage, tilt within the earth.
Techelles.   As princely Lions when they rouse themselves,
Stretching their pawes, and threatning heardes of Beastes,
So in his Armour looketh *Tamburlaine*:
Me thinks I see kings kneeling at his feet,
And he with frowning browes and fiery lookes,
Spurning their crownes from off their captive heads.
Usumcasane.   And making thee and me *Techelles,* kinges,
That even to death will follow *Tamburlaine.*
Tamburlaine.   Nobly resolv'd, sweet friends and followers.   60
These Lords (perhaps) do scorne our estimates,
And thinke we prattle with distempered spirits:
But since they measure our deserts so meane,
That in conceit bear Empires on our speares,
Affecting thoughts coequall with the cloudes,
They shall be kept our forced followers,
Till with their eies they view us Emperours.
Zenocrate.   The Gods, defenders of the innocent,
Will never prosper your intended driftes,
That thus oppresse poore friendles passengers.   70
Therefore at least admit us libertie,
Even as thou hop'st to be eternized,
By living *Asias* mightie Emperour.
Agidas.   I hope our Ladies treasure and our owne,
May serve for ransome to our liberties:
Returne our Mules and emptie Camels backe,
That we may traveile into *Siria,*
Where her betrothed Lord *Alcidamus,*
Expects th'arrivall of her highnesse person.
Magnetes.   And wheresoever we repose our selves,   80
We will report but well of *Tamburlaine.*
Tamburlaine.   Disdaines *Zenocrate* to live with me?
Or you my Lordes to be my followers?

67 they] O2; thee O1

Thinke you I way this treasure more than you?
Not all the Gold in *Indias* welthy armes,
Shall buy the meanest souldier in my traine.
Zenocrate, lovelier than the Love of *Jove*,
Brighter than is the silver Rhodope.
Fairer than whitest snow on Scythian hils,
Thy person is more woorth to *Tamburlaine*,   90
Than the possession of the Persean Crowne,
Which gratious starres have promist at my birth.
A hundreth Tartars shall attend on thee,
Mounted on Steeds, swifter than *Pegasus*.
Thy Garments shall be made of Medean silke,
Enchast with precious juelles of mine owne:
More rich and valurous than *Zenocrates*.
With milke-white Hartes upon an Ivorie sled,
Thou shalt be drawen amidst the frosen Pooles,
And scale the ysie mountaines lofty tops: 100
Which with thy beautie will be soone resolv'd.
My martiall prises with five hundred men,
Wun on the fiftie headed *Vuolgas* waves,
Shall all we offer to *Zenocrate*,
And then my selfe to faire *Zenocrate*.
Techelles.   What now? In love?   [*Aside.*]
Tamburlaine.   *Techelles*, women must be flatered.   [*Aside.*]
But this is she with whom I am in love.

            Enter a Souldier.

Souldier.   Newes, newes.
Tamburlaine.   How now, what's the matter?   110
Souldier.   A thousand Persean horsmen are at hand,
Sent from the King to overcome us all.
Tamburlaine.   How now my Lords of *Egypt* and *Zenocrate*?
Now must your jewels be restor'd againe:
And I that triumpht so be overcome.
How say you Lordings, Is not this your hope?
Agidas.   We hope your selfe wil willingly restore them.

88 Rhodope] Oxberry; Rhodolfe O 1–4

Tamburlaine.   Such hope, such fortune have the thousand horse.
Soft ye my Lords and sweet *Zenocrate*.
You must be forced from me ere you goe: 120
A thousand horsmen? We five hundred foote?
An ods too great, for us to stand against:
But are they rich? And is their armour good?
Souldier.   Their plumed helmes are wrought with beaten golde.
Their swords enameld, and about their neckes
Hangs massie chaines of golde downe to the waste,
In every part exceeding brave and rich.
Tamburlaine.   Then shall we fight couragiously with them.
Or looke you, I should play the Orator?
Techelles.   No: cowards and fainthearted runawaies,   130
Looke for orations when the foe is neere.
Our swordes shall play the Orators for us.
Usumcasane.   Come let us meet them at the mountain foot,
And with a sodaine and an hot alarme
Drive all their horses headlong down the hill.
Techelles.   Come let us martch.
Tamburlaine.   Stay *Techelles*, aske a parlee first.

                                   The Souldiers enter.

Open the Males, yet guard the treasure sure,
Lay out our golden wedges to the view,
That their reflexions may amaze the Perseans.   140
And looke we friendly on them when they come:
But if they offer word or violence,
Weele fight five hundred men at armes to one,
Before we part with our possession.
And gainst the Generall we will lift our swords,
And either lanch his greedy thirsting throat,
Or take him prisoner, and his chaine shall serve
For Manackles, till he be ransom'd home.
Techelles.   I heare them come, shal we encounter them?
Tamburlaine.   Keep all your standings, and not stir a foote,   150
My selfe will bide the danger of the brunt.

138 Males] *i.e.,* mails, *or* trunks

Enter Theridamas *with others.*

Theridamas. Where is this Scythian *Tamburlaine?*
Tamburlaine. Whom seekst thou Persean? I am *Tamburlain.*
Theridamas. Tamburlaine? [*Aside.*]
A Scythian Shepheard, so imbellished
With Natures pride, and richest furniture?
His looks do menace heaven and dare the Gods,
His fierie eies are fixt upon the earth,
As if he now devis'd some Stratageme:
Or meant to pierce *Avernus* darksome vaults, 160
And pull the triple headed dog from hell.
Tamburlaine. Noble and milde this Persean seemes to be,
[*To* Techelles.]
If outward habit judge the inward man.
Techelles. His deep affections make him passionate.
Tamburlaine. With what a majesty he rears his looks:——
In thee (thou valiant man of *Persea*) [*To* Theridamas.]
I see the folly of thy Emperour:
Art thou but Captaine of a thousand horse,
That by Characters graven in thy browes,
And by thy martiall face and stout aspect, 170
Deserv'st to have the leading of an hoste?
Forsake thy king and do but joine with me
And we will triumph over all the world.
I hold the Fates bound fast in yron chaines,
And with my hand turne Fortunes wheel about,
And sooner shall the Sun fall from his Spheare,
Than *Tamburlaine* be slaine or overcome.
Draw foorth thy sword, thou mighty man at Armes,
Intending but to rase my charmed skin:
And *Jove* himselfe will stretch his hand from heaven, 180
To ward the blow, and shield me safe from harme.
See how he raines down heaps of gold in showers,
As if he meant to give my Souldiers pay,
And as a sure and grounded argument,

*161 And] O 1 *catchword*; To O 1–4 *text*

That I shall be the Monark of the East,
He sends this Souldans daughter rich and brave,
To be my Queen and portly Emperesse.
If thou wilt stay with me, renowmed man,
And lead thy thousand horse with my conduct,
Besides thy share of this Egyptian prise,   190
Those thousand horse shall sweat with martiall spoile
Of conquered kingdomes, and of Cities sackt.
Both we wil walke upon the lofty clifts,
And Christian Merchants that with Russian stems
Plow up huge furrowes in the Caspian sea,
Shall vaile to us, as Lords of all the Lake.
Both we will raigne as Consuls of the earth,
And mightie kings shall be our Senators.
Jove sometime masked in a Shepheards weed,
And by those steps that he hath scal'd the heavens,   200
May we become immortall like the Gods.
Joine with me now in this my meane estate,
(I cal it meane, because being yet obscure,
The Nations far remoov'd admyre me not)
And when my name and honor shall be spread,
As far as *Boreas* claps his brazen wings,
Or faire *Boötes* sends his cheerefull light,
Then shalt thou be Competitor with me,
And sit with *Tamburlaine* in all his majestie.
Theridamas.   Not *Hermes* Prolocutor to the Gods,   210
Could use perswasions more patheticall.
Tamburlaine.   Nor are *Apollos* Oracles more true,
Then thou shalt find my vaunts substantiall.
Techelles.   We are his friends, and if the Persean king
Should offer present Dukedomes to our state,
We thinke it losse to make exchange for that
We are assured of by our friends successe.
Usumcasane.   And kingdomes at the least we all expect,
Besides the honor in assured conquestes:
Where kings shall crouch unto our conquering swords,   220
And hostes of souldiers stand amaz'd at us,

When with their fearfull tongues they shall confesse
Theise are the men that all the world admires.
Theridamas. What stronge enchantments tice my yeelding soule?
Are these resolved noble Scythians?
But shall I proove a Traitor to my King?
Tamburlaine. No, but the trustie friend of *Tamburlaine.*
Theridamas. Won with thy words, and conquered with thy looks,
I yeeld my selfe, my men and horse to thee:
To be partaker of thy good or ill,   230
As long as life maintaines *Theridamas.*
Tamburlaine. *Theridamas* my friend, take here my hand,
Which is as much as if I swore by heaven,
And call'd the Gods to witnesse of my vow,
Thus shall my heart be still combinde with thine,
Untill our bodies turne to Elements:
And both our soules aspire celestiall thrones.
Techelles, and *Casane*, welcome him.
Techelles. Welcome renowmed Persean to us all.
Usumcasane. Long may *Theridamas* remaine with us.   240
Tamburlaine. These are my friends in whom I more rejoice,
Than dooth the King of *Persea* in his Crowne:
And by the love of *Pyllades* and *Orestes*,
Whose statutes we adore in *Scythia*,
Thy selfe and them shall never part from me,
Before I crowne you kings in *Asia*.
Make much of them gentle *Theridamas*,
And they will never leave thee till the death.
Theridamas. Nor thee, nor them, thrice noble *Tamburlain*,
Shal want my heart to be with gladnes pierc'd   250
To do you honor and securitie.
Tamburlaine. A thousand thankes worthy *Theridamas*:
And now faire Madam, and my noble Lords,
If you will willingly remaine with me,
You shall have honors, as your merits be:
Or els you shall be forc'd with slaverie.
Agidas. We yeeld unto thee happie *Tamburlaine*.

---

*225 Are] *stet* O1   244 statutes] *i.e.*, statues *as in* O3–4

Tamburlaine.   For you then Maddam, I am out of doubt.
Zenocrate.   I must be pleasde perforce, wretched *Zenocrate.*

                                                      Exeunt.

[*Enter*] Cosroe, Menaphon, Ortygius, Ceneus, *with other Souldiers.* II.i

Cosroe.   Thus farre are we towards *Theridamas,*
  And valiant *Tamburlaine,* the man of fame,
  The man that in the forhead of his fortune,
  Beares figures of renowne and myracle:
  But tell me, that hast seene him, *Menaphon,*
  What stature wields he, and what personage?
Menaphon.   Of stature tall, and straightly fashioned,
  Like his desire, lift upwards and divine,
  So large of lims, his joints so strongly knit,
  Such breadth of shoulders as might mainely beare   10
  Olde *Atlas* burthen. Twixt his manly pitch,
  A pearle more worth, then all the world is plaste:
  Wherein by curious soveraintie of Art,
  Are fixt his piercing instruments of sight:
  Whose fiery cyrcles beare encompassed
  A heaven of heavenly bodies in their Spheares
  That guides his steps and actions to the throne,
  Where honor sits invested royally:
  Pale of complexion: wrought in him with passion,
  Thirsting with soveraity, with love of armes: 20
  His lofty browes in foldes, do figure death,
  And in their smoothnesse, amitie and life:
  About them hangs a knot of Amber heire,
  Wrapped in curles, as fierce *Achilles* was,
  On which the breath of heaven delights to play,
  Making it daunce with wanton majestie:
  His armes and fingers long and sinowy,
  Betokening valour and excesse of strength:
  In every part proportioned like the man,
  Should make the world subdued to *Tamburlaine.*   30

27 sinowy] Dyce; snowy O 1–3; snowy-white O 4

Cosroe.   Wel hast thou pourtraid in thy tearms of life,
The face and personage of a woondrous man:
Nature doth strive with Fortune and his stars,
To make him famous in accomplisht woorth:
And well his merits show him to be made
His Fortunes maister, and the king of men,
That could perswade at such a sodaine pinch,
With reasons of his valour and his life,
A thousand sworne and overmatching foes:
Then when our powers in points of swords are join'd,   40
And closde in compasse of the killing bullet,
Though straight the passage and the port be made,
That leads to Pallace of my brothers life,
Proud is his fortune if we pierce it not.
And when the princely Persean Diadem,
Shall overway his wearie witlesse head,
And fall like mellowed fruit, with shakes of death,
In faire *Persea* noble *Tamburlaine*
Shall be my Regent, and remaine as King.
Ortygius.   In happy hower we have set the Crowne   50
Upon your kingly head, that seeks our honor,
In joyning with the man, ordain'd by heaven
To further every action to the best.
Ceneus.   He that with Shepheards and a litle spoile,
Durst in disdaine of wrong and tyrannie,
Defend his freedome gainst a Monarchie:
What will he doe supported by a king?
Leading a troope of Gentlemen and Lords,
And stuft with treasure for his highest thoughts?
Cosroe.   And such shall wait on worthy *Tamburlaine*.   60
Our army will be forty thousand strong,
When *Tamburlain* and brave *Theridamas*
Have met us by the river *Araris*:
And all conjoin'd to meet the witlesse King,
That now is marching neer to *Parthia*:
And with unwilling souldiers faintly arm'd,
To seeke revenge on me and *Tamburlaine*.

To whom sweet *Menaphon*, direct me straight.
Menaphon.   I will my Lord.

Exeunt.

[*Enter*] Mycetes, Meander, *with other Lords and Souldiers*.   II.ii

Mycetes.   Come my *Meander*, let us to this geere,
I tel you true my heart is swolne with wrath,
On this same theevish villaine *Tamburlaine*.
And of that false *Cosroe*, my traiterous brother.
Would it not grieve a King to be so abusde,
And have a thousand horsmen tane away?
And which is worst to have his Diadem
Sought for by such scalde knaves as love him not?
I thinke it would: wel then, by heavens I sweare,
Aurora shall not peepe out of her doores,   10
But I will have *Cosroe* by the head,
And kill proud *Tamburlaine* with point of sword.
Tell you the rest (*Meander*) I have said.
Meander.   Then having past Armenian desarts now,
And pitcht our tents under the Georgean hilles,
Whose tops are covered with Tartarian thieves,
That lie in ambush, waiting for a pray:
What should we doe but bid them battaile straight,
And rid the world of those detested troopes?
Least if we let them lynger here a while,   20
They gather strength by power of fresh supplies.
This countrie swarmes with vile outragious men,
That live by rapine and by lawlesse spoile,
Fit Souldiers for the wicked *Tamburlaine*.
And he that could with giftes and promises
Inveigle him that lead a thousand horse,
And make him false his faith unto his King,
Will quickly win such as are like himselfe.
Therefore cheere up your mindes, prepare to fight,
He that can take or slaughter *Tamburlaine*,   30

15 pitcht] O2; pitch O1

Shall rule the Province of *Albania*.
Who brings that Traitors head *Theridamas*,
Shal have a government in *Medea*:
Beside the spoile of him and all his traine:
But if *Cosroe* (as our Spials say,
And as we know) remaines with *Tamburlaine*,
His Highnesse pleasure is that he should live,
And be reclaim'd with princely lenitie.

[*Enter a* Spy.]

A Spy.   An hundred horsmen of my company
Scowting abroad upon these champion plaines,   40
Have view'd the army of the Scythians,
Which make reports it far exceeds the Kings.
Meander.   Suppose they be in number infinit,
Yet being void of Martiall discipline,
All running headlong after greedy spoiles:
And more regarding gaine than victory:
Like to the cruell brothers of the earth,
Sprong of the teeth of Dragons venomous,
Their carelesse swords shal lanch their fellowes throats
And make us triumph in their overthrow.   50
Mycetes.   Was there such brethren, sweet *Meander*, say,
That sprong of teeth of Dragons venomous?
Meander.   So Poets say, my Lord.
Mycetes.   And tis a pretty toy to be a Poet.
Wel, wel (*Meander*) thou art deeply read:
And having thee, I have a jewell sure:
Go on my Lord, and give your charge I say,
Thy wit will make us Conquerors to day.
Meander.   Then noble souldiors, to intrap these theeves,
That live confounded in disordered troopes,   60
If wealth or riches may prevaile with them,
We have our Cammels laden all with gold:
Which you that be but common souldiers,
Shall fling in every corner of the field:
And while the base borne Tartars take it up,

96

You fighting more for honor than for gold,
Shall massacre those greedy minded slaves.
And when their scattered armie is subdu'd,
And you march on their slaughtered carkasses:
Share equally the gold that bought their lives,   70
And live like Gentlemen in *Persea*.
Strike up the Drum and martch corragiously,
Fortune her selfe dooth sit upon our Crests.
Mycetes.   He tells you true, my maisters, so he does.
Drums, why sound ye not when *Meander* speaks.

                                        Exeunt.

[*Enter*] Cosroe, Tamburlaine, Theridamas, Techelles, Usumcasane, II.iii
                Ortygius, *with others*.

Cosroe.   Now worthy *Tamburlaine*, have I reposde,
In thy approoved Fortunes all my hope,
What thinkst thou man, shal come of our attemptes?
For even as from assured oracle,
I take thy doome for satisfaction.
Tamburlaine.   And so mistake you not a whit my Lord.
For Fates and Oracles of heaven have sworne,
To roialise the deedes of *Tamburlaine*:
And make them blest that share in his attemptes.
And doubt you not, but if you favour me,   10
And let my Fortunes and my valour sway,
To some direction in your martiall deeds,
The world will strive with hostes of men at armes,
To swarme unto the Ensigne I support.
The host of *Xerxes*, which by fame is said
To drinke the mightie Parthian *Araris*,
Was but a handful to that we will have.
Our quivering Lances shaking in the aire,
And bullets like *Joves* dreadfull Thunderbolts,
Enrolde in flames and fiery smoldering mistes,   20
Shall threat the Gods more than Cyclopian warres,

7 Oracles of heaven] Oxberry; oracles, heaven O 1-4

And with our Sun-bright armour as we march,
Weel chase the Stars from heaven, and dim their eies
That stand and muse at our admyred armes.
Theridamas.   You see my Lord, what woorking woordes he hath.
But when you see his actions top his speech,
Your speech will stay, or so extol his worth,
As I shall be commended and excusde
For turning my poore charge to his direction.
And these his two renowmed friends my Lord,   30
Would make one thrust and strive to be retain'd
In such a great degree of amitie.
Techelles.   With dutie and with amitie we yeeld
Our utmost service to the faire *Cosroe.*
Cosroe.   Which I esteeme as portion of my crown.
Usumcansae and *Techelles* both,
When she that rules in *Rhamnis* golden gates,
And makes a passage for all prosperous Armes,
Shall make me solely Emperour of *Asia:*
Then shall your meeds and vallours be advaunst   40
To roomes of honour and Nobilitie.
Tamburlaine.   Then haste *Cosroe* to be king alone,
That I with these my friends and all my men,
May triumph in our long expected Fate.
The King your Brother is now hard at hand,
Meete with the foole, and rid your royall shoulders
Of such a burthen, as outwaies the sands
And all the craggie rockes of Caspea.

[*Enter a* Messenger.]

Messenger.   My Lord, we have discovered the enemie
Ready to chardge you with a mighty armie.   50
Cosroe.   Come, *Tamburlain*, now whet thy winged sword
And lift thy lofty arme into the cloudes,
That it may reach the King of *Perseas* crowne,
And set it safe on my victorious head.

26 top] Oxberry (*qy*), Dyce; stop   33 and] O4; not O1–3
   O1–4

Tamburlaine.　　See where it is, the keenest Cutle-axe,
　That ere made passage thorow Persean Armes.
　These are the wings shall make it flie as swift,
　As dooth the lightening, or the breath of heaven:
　And kill as sure as it swiftly flies.
Cosroe.　　Thy words assure me of kind successe:　　　　　　60
　Go valiant Souldier, go before and charge
　The fainting army of that foolish King.
Tamburlaine.　　*Usumcasane* and *Techelles* come,
　We are enough to scarre the enemy,
　And more than needes to make an Emperour.

　　　[*Exeunt*] *To the Battaile, and* Mycetes *comes out alone with*　　[II.iv]
　　　　　　his Crowne in his hand, offering to hide it.

Mycetes.　　Accurst be he that first invented war,
　They knew not, ah, they knew not simple men,
　How those were hit by pelting Cannon shot,
　Stand staggering like a quivering Aspen leafe,
　Fearing the force of *Boreas* boistrous blasts.
　In what a lamentable case were I,
　If Nature had not given me wisedomes lore?
　For Kings are clouts that every man shoots at,
　Our Crowne the pin that thousands seeke to cleave.
　Therefore in pollicie I thinke it good　　　　　　　　　　10
　To hide it close: a goodly Stratagem,
　And far from any man that is a foole.
　So shall not I be knowen, or if I bee,
　They cannot take away my crowne from me.
　Here will I hide it in this simple hole.

　　　　　　　Enter Tamburlain.

Tamburlaine.　　What, fearful coward, stragling from the camp
　When Kings themselves are present in the field?
Mycetes.　　Thou liest.
Tamburlaine.　　Base villaine, darst thou give the lie?

*55 Cutle-axe] *stet* O1–2　　　　　　64 scarre] *i.e.,* scare

Mycetes.   Away, I am the King: go, touch me not.   20
Thou breakst the law of Armes unlesse thou kneele,
And cry me mercie, noble King.
Tamburlaine.   Are you the witty King of *Persea?*
Mycetes.   I marie am I: have you any suite to me?
Tamburlaine.   I would intreat you to speak but three wise wordes.
Mycetes.   So I can when I see my time.
Tamburlaine.   Is this your Crowne?
Mycetes.   I, Didst thou ever see a fairer?
Tamburlaine.   You will not sell it, wil ye?
Mycetes.   Such another word, and I will have thee executed.   30
Come give it me.
Tamburlaine.   No, I tooke it prisoner.
Mycetes.   You lie, I gave it you.
Tamburlaine.   Then tis mine.
Mycetes.   No, I meane, I let you keep it.
Tamburlaine.   Wel, I meane you shall have it againe.
Here take it for a while, I lend it thee,
Till I may see thee hem'd with armed men.
Then shalt thou see me pull it from thy head:
Thou art no match for mightie *Tamburlaine.*   [*Exit.*] 40
Mycetes.   O Gods, is this *Tamburlaine* the thiefe,
I marveile much he stole it not away.

Sound trumpets to the battell, and he runs in.

[*Enter*] Cosroe, Tamburlaine, Theridamas, Menaphon, Meander, [II.v]
Ortygius, Techelles, Usumcasane, *with others.*

Tamburlaine.   Holde thee *Cosroe*, weare two imperiall Crownes.
Thinke thee invested now as royally,
Even by the mighty hand of *Tamburlaine,*
As if as many kinges as could encompasse thee,
With greatest pompe had crown'd thee Emperour.
Cosroe.   So do I thrice renowmed man at armes,
And none shall keepe the crowne but *Tamburlaine*:
Thee doo I make my Regent of *Persea,*

100

And Generall Lieftenant of my Armies.
Meander, you that were our brothers Guide,   10
And chiefest Counsailor in all his acts,
Since he is yeelded to the stroke of War,
On your submission we with thanks excuse,
And give you equall place in our affaires.
Meander.   Most happy Emperour in humblest tearms
I vow my service to your Majestie,
With utmost vertue of my faith and dutie.
Cosroe.   Thanks good *Meander*, then *Cosroe* raign
And governe *Persea* in her former pomp:
Now send Ambassage to thy neighbor Kings,   20
And let them know the Persean King is chang'd:
From one that knew not what a King should do,
To one that can commaund what longs thereto:
And now we will to faire *Persepolis*,
With twenty thousand expert souldiers.
The Lords and Captaines of my brothers campe,
With litle slaughter take *Meanders* course,
And gladly yeeld them to my gracious rule:
Ortigius and *Menaphon*, my trustie friendes,
Now will I gratify your former good,   30
And grace your calling with a greater sway.
Ortygius.   And as we ever aim'd at your behoofe,
And sought your state all honor it deserv'd,
So will we with our powers and our lives,
Indevor to preserve and prosper it.
Cosroe.   I will not thank thee (sweet *Ortigius*)
Better replies shall proove my purposes.
And now Lord *Tamburlaine*, my brothers Campe
I leave to thee, and to *Theridamas*,
To follow me to faire *Persepolis*.   40
Then will we march to all those Indian Mines,
My witlesse brother to the Christians lost:
And ransome them with fame and usurie.
And till thou overtake me *Tamburlaine*,

32 aim'd] O3; and O1–2

(Staying to order all the scattered troopes)
Farewell Lord Regent, and his happie friends,
I long to sit upon my brothers throne.
Menaphon. Your Majestie shall shortly have your wish,
And ride in triumph through *Persepolis.* *Exeunt.*

Manent Tamburlaine, Techelles, Theridamas, Usumcasane.

Tamburlaine. And ride in triumph through *Persepolis?* 50
Is it not brave to be a King, *Techelles?*
Usumcasane and *Theridamas,*
Is it not passing brave to be a King,
And ride in triumph through *Persepolis?*
Techelles. O my Lord, tis sweet and full of pompe.
Usumcasane. To be a King, is halfe to be a God.
Theridamas. A God is not so glorious as a King,
I thinke the pleasure they enjoy in heaven
Can not compare with kingly joyes in earth.
To weare a Crowne enchac'd with pearle and golde, 60
Whose vertues carie with it life and death.
To aske, and have: commaund, and be obeied.
When looks breed love, with lookes to gaine the prize.
Such power attractive shines in princes eies.
Tamburlaine. Why say *Theridamas,* wilt thou be a king?
Theridamas. Nay, though I praise it, I can live without it.
Tamburlaine. What saies my other friends, wil you be kings?
Techelles. I, if I could with all my heart my Lord.
Tamburlaine. Why, that's wel said *Techelles,* so would I,
And so would you my maisters, would you not? 70
Usumcasane. What then my Lord?
Tamburlaine. Why then *Casane,* shall we wish for ought
The world affoords in greatest noveltie,
And rest attemplesse, faint and destitute?
Me thinks we should not, I am strongly moov'd,
That if I should desire the Persean Crowne,
I could attaine it with a woondrous ease,
And would not all our souldiers soone consent,
If we should aime at such a dignitie?

Theridamas.   I know they would with our perswasions.   80
Tamburlaine.   Why then *Theridamas*, Ile first assay,
  To get the Persean Kingdome to my selfe:
  Then thou for *Parthia*, they for *Scythia* and *Medea*.
  And if I prosper, all shall be as sure,
  As if the Turke, the Pope, *Affrike* and *Greece*,
  Came creeping to us with their crownes apace.
Techelles.   Then shall we send to this triumphing King,
  And bid him battell for his novell Crowne?
Usumcasane.   Nay quickly then, before his roome be hot.
Tamburlaine.   Twil proove a pretie jest (in faith) my friends.   90
Theridamas.   A jest to chardge on twenty thousand men?
  I judge the purchase more important far.
Tamburlaine.   Judge by thy selfe *Theridamas*, not me,
  For presently *Techelles* here shal haste,
  To bid him battaile ere he passe too farre,
  And lose more labor than the gaine will quight.
  Then shalt thou see the Scythian *Tamburlaine*,
  Make but a jest to win the Persean crowne.
  Techelles, take a thousand horse with thee,
  And bid him turne him back to war with us,   100
  That onely made him King to make us sport.
  We will not steale upon him cowardly,
  But give him warning and more warriours.
  Haste thee *Techelles*, we will follow thee.
  What saith *Theridamas*?
Theridamas.   Goe on for me.

                       Exeunt.

    [*Enter*] Cosroe, Meander, Ortygius, Menaphon, *with other*   II.vi
                      Souldiers.

Cosroe.   What means this divelish shepheard to aspire
  With such a Giantly presumption,
  To cast up hils against the face of heaven:
  And dare the force of angrie *Jupiter*.

100 him] Robinson; his O 1–4

But as he thrust them underneath the hils,
And prest out fire from their burning jawes:
So will I send this monstrous slave to hell,
Where flames shall ever feed upon his soule.
Meander.   Some powers divine, or els infernall, mixt
Their angry seeds at his conception: 10
For he was never sprong of humaine race,
Since with the spirit of his fearefull pride,
He dares so doubtlesly resolve of rule,
And by profession be ambitious.
Ortygius.   What God or Feend, or spirit of the earth,
Or Monster turned to a manly shape,
Or of what mould or mettel he be made,
What star or state soever governe him,
Let us put on our meet incountring mindes,
And in detesting such a divelish Thiefe,   20
In love of honor and defence of right,
Be arm'd against the hate of such a foe,
Whether from earth, or hell, or heaven he grow.
Cosroe.   Nobly resolv'd, my good *Ortygius.*
And since we all have suckt one wholsome aire,
And with the same proportion of Elements
Resolve, I hope we are resembled,
Vowing our loves to equall death and life.
Let's cheere our souldiers to incounter him,
That grievous image of ingratitude: 30
That fiery thirster after Soveraigntie:
And burne him in the fury of that flame,
That none can quence but blood and Emperie.
Resolve my Lords and loving souldiers now,
To save your King and country from decay:
Then strike up Drum, and all the Starres that make
The loathsome Circle of my dated life,
Direct my weapon to his barbarous heart,
That thus opposeth him against the Gods,
And scornes the Powers that governe *Persea.*   40

Exeunt to the Battell, and after the battell, enter Cosroe   [II.vii]
wounded, Theridamas, Tamburlaine, Techelles,
Usumcasane, *with others.*

Cosroe.   Barbarous and bloody *Tamburlaine,*
Thus to deprive me of my crowne and life.
Treacherous and false *Theridamas,*
Even at the morning of my happy state,
Scarce being seated in my royall throne,
To worke my downfall and untimely end.
An uncouth paine torments my grieved soule,
And death arrests the organe of my voice,
Who entring at the breach thy sword hath made,
Sackes every vaine and artier of my heart.   10
Bloody and insatiate *Tamburlain.*
Tamburlaine.   The thirst of raigne and sweetnes of a crown,
That causde the eldest sonne of heavenly *Ops,*
To thrust his doting father from his chaire,
And place himselfe in the Emperiall heaven,
Moov'd me to manage armes against thy state.
What better president than mightie *Jove?*
Nature that fram'd us of foure Elements,
Warring within our breasts for regiment,
Doth teach us all to have aspyring minds: 20
Our soules, whose faculties can comprehend
The wondrous Architecture of the world:
And measure every wandring plannets course:
Still climing after knowledge infinite,
And alwaies mooving as the restles Spheares,
Wils us to weare our selves and never rest,
Untill we reach the ripest fruit of all,
That perfect blisse and sole felicitie,
The sweet fruition of an earthly crowne.
Theridamas.   And that made me to joine with *Tamburlain,*   30
For he is grosse and like the massie earth,
That mooves not upwards, nor by princely deeds

0.1 *Exeunt*] Oxberry (*All go out*); *Enter* O 1–4

105

Doth meane to soare above the highest sort.
Techelles.   And that made us, the friends of *Tamburlaine*,
 To lift our swords against the Persean King.
Usumcasane.   For as when *Jove* did thrust old *Saturn* down,
 Neptune and *Dis* gain'd each of them a Crowne,
 So do we hope to raign in *Asia*,
 If *Tamburlain* be plac'd in *Persea*.
Cosroe.   The strangest men that ever nature made,   40
 I know not how to take their tyrannies.
 My bloodlesse body waxeth chill and colde,
 And with my blood my life slides through my wound,
 My soule begins to take her flight to hell:
 And sommons all my sences to depart.
 The heat and moisture which did feed each other,
 For want of nourishment to feed them both,
 Is drie and cold, and now dooth gastly death
 With greedy tallents gripe my bleeding hart,
 And like a Harpyr tires on my life.   50
 Theridamas and *Tamburlaine*, I die,
 And fearefull vengeance light upon you both.   [*Dies*.]

                    He takes the Crowne and puts it on.

Tamburlaine.   Not all the curses which the furies breathe,
 Shall make me leave so rich a prize as this:
 Theridamas, *Techelles*, and the rest,
 Who thinke you now is king of *Persea*?
All. *Tamburlaine*, *Tamburlaine*.
Tamburlaine.   Though *Mars* himselfe the angrie God of armes,
 And all the earthly Potentates conspire,
 To dispossesse me of this Diadem: 60
 Yet will I weare it in despight of them,
 As great commander of this Easterne world,
 If you but say that *Tamburlaine* shall raigne.
All.   Long live *Tamburlaine*, and raigne in *Asia*.
Tamburlaine.   So, now it is more surer on my head,

50 Harpyr] *i.e.,* Harpy *as in* O 2

Than if the Gods had held a Parliament:
And all pronounst me king of *Persea*.

[*Exeunt.*]

[*Enter*] Bajazeth, *the kings of* Fesse, Moroco, *and* Argier, *with*   III.i
others, in great pompe.

Bajaʒeth.   Great Kings of *Barbary*, and my portly Bassoes,
We heare, the Tartars and the Easterne theeves
Under the conduct of one *Tamburlaine*,
Presume a bickering with your Emperour:
And thinks to rouse us from our dreadful siege
Of the famous Grecian *Constantinople*.
You know our Armie is invincible:
As many circumcised Turkes we have,
And warlike bands of Christians renied,
As hath the Ocean or the Terrene sea   10
Small drops of water, when the Moon begins
To joine in one her semi-circled hornes:
Yet would we not be brav'd with forrain power,
Nor raise our siege before the Gretians yeeld,
Or breathles lie before the citie walles.
Fesse.   Renowmed Emperour, and mighty Generall,
What if you sent the Bassoes of your guard,
To charge him to remaine in *Asia*.
Or els to threaten death and deadly armes,
As from the mouth of mighty *Bajaʒeth*.   20
Bajaʒeth.   Hie thee my Bassoe fast to *Persea*,
Tell him thy Lord the Turkish Emperour,
Dread Lord of *Affrike, Europe* and *Asia*,
Great King and conquerour of *Grecia*,
The Ocean, Terrene, and the cole-blacke sea,
The high and highest Monarke of the world,
Wils and commands (for say not I intreat)
Not once to set his foot in *Affrica*,
Or spread his collours in *Grecia*,
Least he incurre the furie of my wrath.   30
Tell him, I am content to take a truce,

Because I heare he beares a valiant mind.
But if presuming on his silly power,
He be so mad to manage Armes with me,
Then stay thou with him, say I bid thee so.
And if before the Sun have measured heaven
With triple circuit thou regreet us not,
We meane to take his mornings next arise
For messenger, he will not be reclaim'd,
And meane to fetch thee in despight of him. 40

Bassoe. Most great and puisant Monarke of the earth,
Your Bassoe will accomplish your behest:
And show your pleasure to the Persean,
As fits the Legate of the stately Turk. *Exit* Bassoe.

Argier. They say he is the King of *Persea.*
But if he dare attempt to stir your siege,
Twere requisite he should be ten times more,
For all flesh quakes at your magnificence.

Bajazeth. True (*Argier*) and tremble at my lookes.

Morocus. The spring is hindred by your smoothering host, 50
For neither rain can fall upon the earth,
Nor Sun reflexe his vertuous beames thereon,
The ground is mantled with such multitudes.

Bajazeth. All this is true as holy *Mahomet,*
And all the trees are blasted with our breathes.

Fesse. What thinks your greatnes best to be atchiev'd
In pursuit of the Cities overthrow?

Bajazeth. I wil the captive Pioners of *Argier,*
Cut of the water, that by leaden pipes
Runs to the citie from the mountain *Carnon.* 60
Two thousand horse shall forrage up and downe,
That no reliefe or succour come by Land.
And all the sea my Gallies countermaund.
Then shall our footmen lie within the trench,
And with their Cannons mouth'd like *Orcus* gulfe
Batter the walles, and we will enter in:
And thus the Grecians shall be conquered.

Exeunt.

[*Enter*] Agidas, Zenocrate, Anippe, *with others*.   III.ii

Agidas.   Madame *Zenocrate*, may I presume
   To know the cause of these unquiet fits:
   That worke such trouble to your woonted rest:
   Tis more then pitty such a heavenly face
   Should by hearts sorrow wax so wan and pale,
   When your offensive rape by *Tamburlaine*,
   (Which of your whole displeasures should be most)
   Hath seem'd to be digested long agoe.
Zenocrate.   Although it be digested long agoe,
   As his exceding favours have deserv'd,   10
   And might content the Queene of heaven as well,
   As it hath chang'd my first conceiv'd disdaine.
   Yet since a farther passion feeds my thoughts,
   With ceaselesse and disconsolate conceits,
   Which dies my lookes so livelesse as they are.
   And might, if my extreams had full events,
   Make me the gastly counterfeit of death.
Agidas.   Eternall heaven sooner be dissolv'd,
   And all that pierceth *Phœbes* silver eie,
   Before such hap fall to *Zenocrate*.   20
Zenocrate.   Ah, life and soule still hover in his Breast,
   And leave my body sencelesse as the earth.
   Or els unite you to his life and soule,
   That I may live and die with *Tamburlaine*.

      Enter [*aloofe*] Tamburlaine *with* Techelles *and others*.

Agidas.   With *Tamburlaine?* Ah faire *Zenocrate*,
   Let not a man so vile and barbarous,
   That holds you from your father in despight,
   And keeps you from the honors of a Queene,
   Being supposde his worthlesse Concubine,
   Be honored with your love, but for necessity.   30
   So now the mighty Souldan heares of you,
   Your Highnesse needs not doubt but in short time,
   He will with *Tamburlaines* destruction

                              109

Redeeme you from this deadly servitude.

Zenocrate.   *Agidas*, leave to wound me with these words:
And speake of *Tamburlaine* as he deserves.
The entertainment we have had of him,
Is far from villanie or servitude.
And might in noble minds be counted princely.

Agidas.   How can you fancie one that lookes so fierce,   40
Onelie disposed to martiall Stratagems?
Who when he shall embrace you in his armes,
Will tell how many thousand men he slew.
And when you looke for amorous discourse,
Will rattle foorth his facts of war and blood.
Too harsh a subject for your dainty eares.

Zenocrate.   As looks the sun through *Nilus* flowing stream,
Or when the morning holds him in her armes:
So lookes my Lordly love, faire *Tamburlaine*.
His talke much sweeter than the Muses song,   50
They sung for honor gainst *Pierides*,
Or when *Minerva* did with *Neptune* strive.
And higher would I reare my estimate,
Than *Juno* sister to the highest God,
If I were matcht with mightie *Tamburlaine*.

Agidas.   Yet be not so inconstant in your love,
But let the yong Arabian live in hope,
After your rescue to enjoy his choise.
You see though first the King of *Persea*
(Being a Shepheard) seem'd to love you much,   60
Now in his majesty he leaves those lookes,
Those words of favour, and those comfortings,
And gives no more than common courtesies.

Zenocrate.   Thence rise the tears that so distain my cheeks,
Fearing his love through my unworthynesse.

35 *Agidas*,] Dyce; *omit* O 1–4

Tamburlaine *goes to her, and takes her away lovingly by the hand,*
looking wrathfully on Agidas, *and sayes nothing.*

[*Exeunt. Manet* Agidas.]

Agidas.   Betraide by fortune and suspitious love,
  Threatned with frowning wrath and jealousie,
  Surpriz'd with feare of hideous revenge,
  I stand agast: but most astonied
  To see his choller shut in secrete thoughtes,   70
  And wrapt in silence of his angry soule.
  Upon his browes was pourtraid ugly death,
  And in his eies the furie of his hart,
  That shine as Comets, menacing revenge,
  And casts a pale complexion on his cheeks.
  As when the Sea-man sees the *Hyades*
  Gather an armye of Cemerian clouds,
  (*Auster* and *Aquilon* with winged Steads
  All sweating, tilt about the watery heavens,
  With shivering speares enforcing thunderclaps,   80
  And from their shieldes strike flames of lightening)
  All fearefull foldes his sailes, and sounds the maine,
  Lifting his prayers to the heavens for aid,
  Against the terrour of the winds and waves.
  So fares *Agydas* for the late felt frownes
  That sent a tempest to my daunted thoughtes,
  And makes my soule devine her overthrow.

Enter Techelles *with a naked dagger.*

Techelles.   See you *Agidas* how the King salutes you.
  He bids you prophesie what it imports.   *Exit.*
Agidas.   I prophecied before and now I proove,   90
  The killing frownes of jealousie and love.
  He needed not with words confirme my feare,
  For words are vaine where working tooles present
  The naked action of my threatned end.
  It saies, *Agydas,* thou shalt surely die,
  And of extremities elect the least.

III

More honor and lesse paine it may procure,
To dy by this resolved hand of thine,
Than stay the torments he and heaven have sworne.
Then haste *Agydas*, and prevent the plagues: 100
Which thy prolonged Fates may draw on thee:
Go wander free from feare of Tyrants rage,
Remooved from the Torments and the hell:
Wherewith he may excruciate thy soule.
And let *Agidas* by *Agidas* die,
And with this stab slumber eternally. [*Dies.*]

[*Enter* Techelles *and* Usumcasane.]

Techelles. *Usumcasane*, see how right the man
Hath hit the meaning of my Lord the King.
Usumcasane. Faith, and *Techelles*, it was manly done:
And since he was so wise and honorable, 110
Let us affoord him now the bearing hence.
And crave his triple worthy buriall.
Techelles. Agreed *Casane*, we wil honor him.
[*Exeunt with body.*]

[*Enter*] Tamburlain, Techelles, Usumcasane, Theridamas, III.iii
Bassoe, Zenocrate, [Anippe,] *with others*.

Tamburlaine. Bassoe, by this thy Lord and maister knowes,
I meane to meet him in *Bithynia*:
See how he comes? Tush. Turkes are ful of brags
And menace more than they can wel performe:
He meet me in the field and fetch thee hence?
Alas (poore Turke) his fortune is to weake,
T'incounter with the strength of *Tamburlaine*.
View well my Camp, and speake indifferently,
Doo not my captaines and my souldiers looke
As if they meant to conquer *Affrica*. 10
Bassoe. Your men are valiant but their number few,
And cannot terrefie his mightie hoste.
My Lord, the great Commander of the worlde,

Besides fifteene contributorie kings,
Hath now in armes ten thousand Janisaries,
Mounted on lusty Mauritanian Steeds,
Brought to the war by men of *Tripoly*:
Two hundred thousand footmen that have serv'd
In two set battels fought in *Grecia*:
And for the expedition of this war,   20
If he think good, can from his garrisons,
Withdraw as many more to follow him.

Techelles.   The more he brings, the greater is the spoile,
For when they perish by our warlike hands,
We meane to seate our footmen on their Steeds,
And rifle all those stately Janisars.

Tamburlaine.   But wil those Kings accompany your Lord?

Bassoe.   Such as his Highnesse please, but some must stay
To rule the provinces he late subdude.

Tamburlaine.   Then fight couragiously, their crowns are yours.   30
This hand shal set them on your conquering heads:
That made me Emperour of *Asia*.

Usumcasane.   Let him bring millions infinite of men,
Unpeopling Westerne *Affrica* and *Greece*:
Yet we assure us of the victorie.

Theridamas.   Even he that in a trice vanquisht two kings,
More mighty than the Turkish Emperour:
Shall rouse him out of *Europe*, and pursue
His scattered armie til they yeeld or die.

Tamburlaine.   Wel said *Theridamas*, speake in that mood,   40
For Wil and Shall best fitteth *Tamburlain*,
Whose smiling stars gives him assured hope
Of martiall triumph, ere he meete his foes:
I that am tearm'd the Scourge and Wrath of God,
The onely feare and terrour of the world,
Wil first subdue the Turke, and then inlarge
Those Christian Captives, which you keep as slaves,
Burdening their bodies with your heavie chaines,
And feeding them with thin and slender fare,
That naked rowe about the Terrene sea.   50

And when they chance to breath and rest a space,
Are punisht with Bastones so grievously,
That they lie panting on the Gallies side,
And strive for life at every stroke they give.
These are the cruell priates of *Argeire*,
That damned traine, the scum of *Affrica*,
Inhabited with stragling Runnagates,
That make quick havock of the Christian blood.
But as I live that towne shall curse the time
That *Tamburlaine* set foot in *Affrica*.   60

   Enter Bajazeth *with his Bassoes and contributorie*
     Kinges [*and* Zabina *and* Ebea].

Baja{eth. Bassoes and Janisaries of my Guard,
 Attend upon the person of your Lord,
 The greatest Potentate of *Affrica*.
Tamburlaine. *Techelles*, and the rest prepare your swordes,
 I meane t'incounter with that *Baja{eth*.
Baja{eth. Kings of *Fesse*, *Moroccus* and *Argier*,
 He cals me *Baja{eth*, whom you call Lord.
 Note the presumption of this Scythian slave:
 I tell thee villaine, those that lead my horse
 Have to their names tytles of dignity,   70
 And dar'st thou bluntly call me *Baja{eth*?
Tamburlaine. And know thou Turke, that those which lead my
  horse,
 Shall lead thee Captive thorow *Affrica*.
 And dar'st thou bluntly call me *Tamburlaine*?
Baja{eth. By *Mahomet*, my Kinsmans sepulcher,
 And by the holy *Alcaron* I sweare,
 He shall be made a chast and lustlesse Eunuke,
 And in my Sarell tend my Concubines:
 And all his Captaines that thus stoutly stand,   80
 Shall draw the chariot of my Emperesse,
 Whom I have brought to see their overthrow.
Tamburlaine. By this my sword that conquer'd *Persea*,
 Thy fall shall make me famous through the world:

I will not tell thee how Ile handle thee,
But every common souldier of my Camp
Shall smile to see thy miserable state.
Fesse.   What meanes the mighty Turkish Emperor
  To talk with one so base as *Tamburlaine?*
Morocus.   Ye Moores and valiant men of *Barbary,*
  How can ye suffer these indignities?   90
Argier.   Leave words and let them feele your lances pointes,
  Which glided through the bowels of the Greekes.
Bajazeth.   Wel said my stout contributory kings,
  Your threefold armie and my hugie hoste,
  Shall swallow up these base borne Perseans.
Techelles.   Puissant, renowmed and mighty *Tamburlain,*
  Why stay we thus prolonging all their lives?
Theridamas.   I long to see those crownes won by our swords,
  That we may raigne as kings of *Affrica.*
Usumcasane.   What Coward wold not fight for such a prize?   100
Tamburlaine.   Fight all couragiously and be you kings.
  I speake it, and my words are oracles.
Bajazeth.   *Zabina,* mother of three braver boies,
  Than *Hercules,* that in his infancie
  Did pash the jawes of Serpents venomous:
  Whose hands are made to gripe a warlike Lance,
  Their shoulders broad, for complet armour fit,
  Their lims more large and of a bigger size
  Than all the brats ysprong from *Typhons* loins:
  Who, when they come unto their fathers age,   110
  Will batter Turrets with their manly fists.
  Sit here upon this royal chaire of state,
  And on thy head weare my Emperiall crowne,
  Untill I bring this sturdy *Tamburlain,*
  And all his Captains bound in captive chaines.
Zabina.   Such good successe happen to *Bajazeth.*
Tamburlaine.   *Zenocrate,* the loveliest Maide alive,
  Fairer than rockes of pearle and pretious stone,
  The onely Paragon of *Tamburlaine,*
  Whose eies are brighter than the Lamps of heaven,   120

And speech more pleasant than sweet harmony:
That with thy lookes canst cleare the darkened Sky:
And calme the rage of thundring *Jupiter*:
Sit downe by her: adorned with my Crowne,
As if thou wert the Empresse of the world.
Stir not *Zenocrate* untill thou see
Me martch victoriously with all my men,
Triumphing over him and these his kings,
Which I will bring as Vassals to thy feete.
Til then take thou my crowne, vaunt of my worth,   130
And manage words with her as we will armes.

Zenocrate.   And may my Love, the king of *Persea*,
Returne with victorie, and free from wound.

Bajazeth.   Now shalt thou feel the force of Turkish arms,
Which lately made all *Europe* quake for feare:
I have of Turkes, Arabians, Moores and Jewes
Enough to cover all *Bythinia*.
Let thousands die, their slaughtered Carkasses
Shall serve for walles and bulwarkes to the rest:
And as the heads of *Hydra*, so my power   140
Subdued, shall stand as mighty as before:
If they should yeeld their necks unto the sword,
Thy souldiers armes could not endure to strike
So many blowes as I have heads for thee.
Thou knowest not (foolish hardy *Tamburlaine*)
What tis to meet me in the open field,
That leave no ground for thee to martch upon.

Tamburlaine.   Our conquering swords shall marshal us the way
We use to march upon the slaughtered foe:
Trampling their bowels with our horses hooffes: 150
Brave horses, bred on the white Tartarian hils:
My Campe is like to *Julius Cæsars* Hoste,
That never fought but had the victorie:
Nor in *Pharsalia* was there such hot war,
As these my followers willingly would have:
Legions of Spirits fleeting in the aire,

*158 aire] Dyce (*qy*), Tucker Brooke; lure O1, 3–4; lute O2

116

Direct our Bullets and our weapons pointes
And make our strokes to wound the sencelesse aire.
And when she sees our bloody Collours spread,
Then Victorie begins to take her flight,   160
Resting her selfe upon my milk-white Tent:
But come my Lords, to weapons let us fall.
The field is ours, the Turk, his wife and all.

Exit, with his followers.

Bajazeth.   Come Kings and Bassoes, let us glut our swords
That thirst to drinke the feble Perseans blood.

Exit, with his followers.

Zabina.   Base Concubine, must thou be plac'd by me
That am the Empresse of the mighty Turke?
Zenocrate.   Disdainful Turkesse and unreverend Bosse,
Cal'st thou me Concubine that am betroath'd
Unto the great and mighty *Tamburlaine?*   170
Zabina.   To *Tamburlaine* the great Tartarian thiefe?
Zenocrate.   Thou wilt repent these lavish words of thine,
When thy great Bassoe-maister and thy selfe,
Must plead for mercie at his kingly feet,
And sue to me to be your Advocates.
Zabina.   And sue to thee? I tell thee shamelesse girle,
Thou shalt be Landresse to my waiting maid.
How lik'st thou her *Ebea,* will she serve?
Ebea.   Madame, she thinks perhaps she is too fine.
But I shall turne her into other weedes,   180
And make her daintie fingers fall to woorke.
Zenocrate.   Hearst thou *Anippe,* how thy drudge doth talk,
And how my slave, her mistresse menaceth.
Both for their sausinesse shall be employed,
To dresse the common souldiers meat and drink.
For we will scorne they should come nere our selves.
Anippe.   Yet somtimes let your highnesse send for them
To do the work my chamber maid disdaines.

They sound to the battell within, and stay.

Zenocrate.   Ye Gods and powers that governe *Persea*,
And made my lordly Love her worthy King: 190
Now strengthen him against the Turkish *Bajazeth*,
And let his foes like flockes of fearfull Roes,
Pursude by hunters, flie his angrie lookes,
That I may see him issue Conquerour.
Zabina.   Now *Mahomet*, solicit God himselfe,
And make him raine down murthering shot from heaven
To dash the Scythians braines, and strike them dead,
That dare to manage armes with him,
That offered jewels to thy sacred shrine,
When first he war'd against the Christians.   200

To the battell againe.

Zenocrate.   By this the Turks lie weltring in their blood
And *Tamburlaine* is Lord of *Affrica*.
Zabina.   Thou art deceiv'd, I heard the Trumpets sound,
As when my Emperour overthrew the Greeks:
And led them Captive into *Affrica*.
Straight will I use thee as thy pride deserves:
Prepare thy selfe to live and die my slave.
Zenocrate.   If *Mahomet* should come from heaven and sweare,
My royall Lord is slaine or conquered,
Yet should he not perswade me otherwise,   210
But that he lives and will be Conquerour.

Bajazeth *flies* [*over the stage*], *and he pursues him.*
The battell short, and they enter, Bajazeth *is overcome.*

Tamburlaine.   Now king of Bassoes, who is Conqueror?
Bajazeth.   Thou, by the fortune of this damned foile.
Tamburlaine.   Where are your stout contributorie kings?

188.1 *to*] O3; *omit* O1–2   213 foile] Dyce²; soile O1–4

Enter Techelles, Theridamas, Usumcasane.

Techelles.   We have their crownes, their bodies strowe the fielde.
Tamburlaine.   Each man a crown? why kingly fought ifaith.
  Deliver them into my treasurie.
Zenocrate.   Now let me offer to my gracious Lord,
  His royall Crowne againe, so highly won.
Tamburlaine.   Nay take the Turkish Crown from her, *Zenocrate,* 220
  And crowne me Emperour of *Affrica.*
Zabina.   No *Tamburlain,* though now thou gat the best,
  Thou shalt not yet be Lord of *Affrica.*
Theridamas.   Give her the Crowne Turkesse, you wer best.
                    He takes it from her, and gives it Zenocrate.
Zabina.   Injurious villaines, thieves, runnagates,
  How dare you thus abuse my Majesty?
Theridamas.   Here Madam, you are Empresse, she is none.
Tamburlaine.   Not now *Theridamas,* her time is past:
  The pillers that have bolstered up those tearmes,
  Are falne in clusters at my conquering feet.   230
Zabina.   Though he be prisoner, he may be ransomed.
Tamburlaine.   Not all the world shall ransom *Bajazeth.*
Bajazeth.   Ah faire *Zabina,* we have lost the field.
  And never had the Turkish Emperour
  So great a foile by any forraine foe.
  Now will the Christian miscreants be glad,
  Ringing with joy their superstitious belles:
  And making bonfires for my overthrow.
  But ere I die those foule Idolaters
  Shall make me bonfires with their filthy bones,   240
  For though the glorie of this day be lost,
  Affrik and *Greece* have garrisons enough
  To make me Soveraigne of the earth againe.
Tamburlaine.   Those walled garrisons wil I subdue,
  And write my selfe great Lord of *Affrica:*
  So from the East unto the furthest West,
  Shall *Tamburlain* extend his puisant arme.
  The Galles and those pilling Briggandines,

That yeerely saile to the Venetian gulfe,
And hover in the straightes for Christians wracke, 250
Shall lie at anchor in the Isle *Asant,*
Untill the Persean Fleete and men of war,
Sailing along the Orientall sea,
Have fetcht about the Indian continent:
Even from *Persepolis* to *Mexico,*
And thence unto the straightes of *Jubalter:*
Where they shall meete, and joine their force in one,
Keeping in aw the Bay of *Portingale:*
And all the Ocean by the British shore.
And by this meanes Ile win the world at last. 260
Bajazeth. Yet set a ransome on me *Tamburlaine.*
Tamburlaine. What, thinkst thou *Tamburlain* esteems thy gold?
Ile make the kings of *India* ere I die,
Offer their mines (to sew for peace) to me,
And dig for treasure to appease my wrath:
Come bind them both and one lead in the Turke.
The Turkesse let my Loves maid lead away.
                                    They bind them.
Bajazeth. Ah villaines, dare ye touch my sacred armes?
O *Mahomet,* Oh sleepie *Mahomet.*
Zabina. O cursed *Mahomet* that makest us thus 270
The slaves to Scythians rude and barbarous.
Tamburlaine. Come bring them in, and for this happy conquest
Triumph, and solemnize a martiall feast.
                                    Exeunt.

[*Enter*] Souldan *of* Egipt *with three or four Lords,* IV.i
Capolin [*, and a* Messenger.]

Souldan. Awake ye men of *Memphis,* heare the clange
Of Scythian trumpets, heare the Basiliskes,
That roaring, shake *Damascus* turrets downe.
The rogue of *Volga* holds *Zenocrate,*
The Souldans daughter for his Concubine,
And with a troope of theeves and vagabondes,

Hath spread his collours to our high disgrace:
While you faint-hearted base Egyptians,
Lie slumbering on the flowrie bankes of *Nile*,
As Crocodiles that unaffrighted rest,   10
While thundring Cannons rattle on their Skins.
Messenger.   Nay (mightie Souldan) did your greatnes see
The frowning lookes of fiery *Tamburlaine*,
That with his terrour and imperious eies,
Commandes the hearts of his associates,
It might amaze your royall majesty.
Souldan.   Villain, I tell thee, were that *Tamburlaine*
As monstrous as *Gorgon*, prince of Hell,
The Souldane would not start a foot from him.
But speake, what power hath he?
Messenger.   Mightie Lord,   20
Three hundred thousand men in armour clad,
Upon their pransing Steeds, disdainfully
With wanton paces trampling on the ground.
Five hundred thousand footmen threatning shot,
Shaking their swords, their speares and yron bils,
Environing their Standard round, that stood
As bristle-pointed as a thorny wood.
Their warlike Engins and munition
Exceed the forces of their martial men.
Souldan.   Nay could their numbers countervail the stars,   30
Or ever drisling drops of Aprill showers,
Or withered leaves that Autume shaketh downe:
Yet would the Souldane by his conquering power,
So scatter and consume them in his rage,
That not a man should live to rue their fall.
Capolin.   So might your highnesse, had you time to sort
Your fighting men, and raise your royall hoste.
But *Tamburlaine*, by expedition
Advantage takes of your unreadinesse.
Souldan.   Let him take all th'advantages he can,   40
Were all the world conspird to fight for him,
Nay, were he Devill, as he is no man,

Yet in revenge of faire *Zenocrate*,
Whom he detaineth in despight of us,
This arme should send him downe to *Erebus*,
To shroud his shame in darknes of the night.
Messenger.   Pleaseth your mightinesse to understand,
His resolution far exceedeth all:
The first day when he pitcheth downe his tentes,
White is their hew, and on his silver crest   50
A snowy Feather spangled white he beares,
To signify the mildnesse of his minde:
That satiate with spoile refuseth blood.
But when *Aurora* mounts the second time,
As red as scarlet is his furniture,
Then must his kindled wrath bee quencht with blood,
Not sparing any that can manage armes.
But if these threats moove not submission,
Black are his collours, blacke Pavilion,
His speare, his shield, his horse, his armour, plumes,   60
And Jetty Feathers menace death and hell.
Without respect of Sex, degree or age,
He raceth all his foes with fire and sword.
Souldan.   Mercilesse villaine, Pesant ignorant,
Of lawfull armes, or martiall discipline:
Pillage and murder are his usuall trades.
The slave usurps the glorious name of war.
See *Capolin*, the faire Arabian king
That hath bene disapointed by this slave,
Of my faire daughter, and his princely Love: 70
May have fresh warning to go war with us,
And be reveng'd for her disparadgement.
                                                    [*Exeunt.*]

[*Enter*] Tamburlain, Techelles, Theridamas, Usumcasane, Zeno- IV.ii
crate, Anippe, *two Moores drawing* Bajazeth *in his cage, and his wife*
following him.

Tamburlaine.   Bring out my foot-stoole.
                                    They take him out of the cage.
Bajazeth.   Ye holy Priests of heavenly *Mahomet,*
  That sacrificing slice and cut your flesh,
  Staining his Altars with your purple blood:
  Make heaven to frowne and every fixed starre
  To sucke up poison from the moorish Fens,
  And poure it in this glorious Tyrants throat.
Tamburlaine.   The chiefest God, first moover of that Spheare
  Enchac'd with thousands ever shining lamps,
  Will sooner burne the glorious frame of Heaven,   10
  Then it should so conspire my overthrow.
  But Villaine, thou that wishest this to me,
  Fall prostrate on the lowe disdainefull earth.
  And be the foot-stoole of great *Tamburlain,*
  That I may rise into my royall throne.
Bajazeth.   First shalt thou rip my bowels with thy sword,
  And sacrifice my heart to death and hell,
  Before I yeeld to such a slavery.
Tamburlaine.   Base villain, vassall, slave to *Tamburlaine:*
  Unworthy to imbrace or touch the ground,   20
  That beares the honor of my royall waight.
  Stoop villaine, stoope, stoope for so he bids,
  That may command thee peecemeale to be torne,
  Or scattered like the lofty Cedar trees,
  Strooke with the voice of thundring *Jupiter.*
Bajazeth.   Then as I look downe to the damned Feends,
  Feends looke on me, and thou dread God of hell,
  With Eban Scepter strike this hatefull earth,
  And make it swallow both of us at once.
                              He gets up upon him to his chaire.
Tamburlaine.   Now cleare the triple region of the aire,   30
  And let the majestie of heaven beholde

Their Scourge and Terrour treade on Emperours.
Smile Stars that raign'd at my nativity,
And dim the brightnesse of their neighbor Lamps:
Disdaine to borrow light of *Cynthia*,
For I the chiefest Lamp of all the earth,
First rising in the East with milde aspect,
But fixed now in the Meridian line,
Will send up fire to your turning Spheares,
And cause the Sun to borrowe light of you.   40
My sword stroke fire from his coat of steele,
Even in *Bythinia*, when I took this Turke:
As when a fiery exhalation
Wrapt in the bowels of a freezing cloude,
Fighting for passage, makes the Welkin cracke,
And casts a flash of lightning to the earth.
But ere I martch to wealthy *Persea*,
Or leave *Damascus* and th'Egyptian fields,
As was the fame of *Clymens* brain-sicke sonne,
That almost brent the Axeltree of heaven,   50
So shall our swords, our lances and our shot,
Fill all the aire with fiery meteors.
Then when the Sky shal waxe as red as blood,
It shall be said, I made it red my selfe,
To make me think of nought but blood and war.
Zabina.   Unworthy king, that by thy crueltie,
Unlawfully usurpest the Persean seat:
Dar'st thou that never saw an Emperour,
Before thou met my husband in the field,
Being thy Captive, thus abuse his state,   60
Keeping his kingly body in a Cage,
That rooffes of golde, and sun-bright Pallaces,
Should have prepar'd to entertaine his Grace?
And treading him beneath thy loathsome feet,
Whose feet the kings of *Affrica* have kist.
Techelles.   You must devise some torment worsse, my Lord,
To make these captives reine their lavish tongues.

45 makes] Oxberry; make O 1–4   49 *Clymens*] O 2 (*Clymenes*); *Clymeus* O 1, 3–4

Tamburlaine.   *Zenocrate*, looke better to your slave.

Zenocrate.   She is my Handmaids slave, and she shal looke
That these abuses flow not from her tongue: 70
Chide her *Anippe*.

Anippe.   Let these be warnings for you then my slave,
How you abuse the person of the king:
Or els I sweare to have you whipt stark nak'd.

Bajazeth.   Great *Tamburlaine*, great in my overthrow,
Ambitious pride shall make thee fall as low,
For treading on the back of *Bajazeth*,
That should be horsed on fower mightie kings.

Tamburlaine.   Thy names and tytles, and thy dignities,
Are fled from *Bajazeth*, and remaine with me,   80
That will maintaine it against a world of Kings.
Put him in againe.   [*They put him into the cage.*]

Bajazeth.   Is this a place for mighty *Bajazeth*?
Confusion light on him that helps thee thus.

Tamburlaine.   There whiles he lives, shal *Bajazeth* be kept,
And where I goe be thus in triumph drawne:
And thou his wife shalt feed him with the scraps
My servitures shall bring the from my boord.
For he that gives him other food than this:
Shall sit by him and starve to death himselfe.   90
This is my minde, and I will have it so.
Not all the Kings and Emperours of the Earth:
If they would lay their crownes before my feet,
Shall ransome him, or take him from his cage.
The ages that shall talk of *Tamburlain*,
Even from this day to *Platoes* wondrous yeare,
Shall talke how I have handled *Bajazeth*.
These Mores that drew him from *Bythinia*,
To faire *Damascus*, where we now remaine,
Shall lead him with us wheresoere we goe.   100
Techelles, and my loving followers,
Now may we see *Damascus* lofty towers,
Like to the shadowes of *Pyramides*,

88 the] *i.e.*, thee

That with their beauties grac'd the Memphion fields:
The golden stature of their feathered bird
That spreads her wings upon the citie wals,
Shall not defend it from our battering shot.
The townes-men maske in silke and cloath of gold,
And every house is as a treasurie.
The men, the treasure, and the towne is ours.   110
Theridamas.   Your tentes of white now pitch'd before the gates
And gentle flags of amitie displaid.
I doubt not but the Governour will yeeld,
Offering *Damascus* to your Majesty.
Tamburlaine.   So shall he have his life, and all the rest.
But if he stay until the bloody flag
Be once advanc'd on my vermilion Tent,
He dies, and those that kept us out so long.
And when they see me march in black aray,
With mournfull streamers hanging down their heads,   120
Were in that citie all the world contain'd,
Not one should scape: but perish by our swords.
Zenocrate.   Yet would you have some pitie for my sake,
Because it is my countries, and my Fathers.
Tamburlaine.   Not for the world *Zenocrate*, if I have sworn:
Come bring in the Turke.

                                        Exeunt.

[*Enter*] Souldane, Arabia, Capoline, *with streaming collors and*   IV.iii
                            Souldiers.

Souldan.   Me thinks we martch as *Meliager* did,
Environed with brave Argolian knightes,
To chace the savage Calidonian Boare:
Or *Cephalus* with lustie Thebane youths,
Against the Woolfe that angrie *Themis* sent,
To waste and spoile the sweet Aonian fieldes.
A monster of five hundred thousand heades,
Compact of Rapine, Pyracie, and spoile,

0.1 *streaming*] O3; *steaming* O1-2

The Scum of men, the hate and Scourge of God,
Raves in *Egyptia*, and annoyeth us.   10
My Lord it is the bloody *Tamburlaine*,
A sturdy Felon and a base-bred Thiefe,
By murder raised to the Persean Crowne,
That dares controll us in our Territories.
To tame the pride of this presumptuous Beast,
Joine your Arabians with the Souldans power:
Let us unite our royall bandes in one,
And hasten to remoove *Damascus* siege.
It is a blemish to the Majestie
And high estate of mightie Emperours,   20
That such a base usurping vagabond
Should brave a king, or weare a princely crowne.
Arabia.   Renowmed Souldane, have ye lately heard
  The overthrow of mightie *Bajazeth*,
  About the confines of *Bythinia*?
  The slaverie wherewith he persecutes
  The noble Turke and his great Emperesse?
Souldan.   I have, and sorrow for his bad successe:
  But noble Lord of great *Arabia*,
  Be so perswaded, that the Souldan is   30
  No more dismaide with tidings of his fall,
  Than in the haven when the Pilot stands
  And viewes a strangers ship rent in the winds,
  And shivered against a craggie rocke.
  Yet in compassion of his wretched state,
  A sacred vow to heaven and him I make,
  Confirming it with *Ibis* holy name,
  That *Tamburlaine* shall rue the day, the hower,
  Wherein he wrought such ignominious wrong,
  Unto the hallowed person of a prince,   40
  Or kept the faire *Zenocrate* so long,
  As Concubine I ferae, to feed his lust.
Arabia.   Let griefe and furie hasten on revenge,
  Let *Tamburlaine* for his offences feele
  Such plagues as heaven and we can poure on him.

127

I long to breake my speare upon his crest,
And proove the waight of his victorious arme:
For Fame I feare hath bene too prodigall,
In sounding through the world his partiall praise.

Souldan.   *Capolin*, hast thou survaid our powers?   50

Capolin.   Great Emperours of *Egypt* and *Arabia*,
The number of your hostes united is,
A hundred and fifty thousand horse,
Two hundred thousand foot, brave men at armes,
Couragious and full of hardinesse:
As frolike as the hunters in the chace
Of savage beastes amid the desart woods.

Arabia.   My mind presageth fortunate successe,
And *Tamburlaine*, my spirit doth foresee
The utter ruine of thy men and thee.   60

Souldan.   Then reare your standardes, let your sounding Drummes
Direct our Souldiers to *Damascus* walles.
Now *Tamburlaine*, the mightie Souldane comes,
And leads with him the great Arabian King,
To dim thy basenesse and obscurity,
Famous for nothing but for theft and spoile,
To race and scatter thy inglorious crue,
Of Scythians and slavish Persians.

Exeunt.

The Banquet, and to it commeth Tamburlain *al in scarlet,*   IV.iv
Theridamas, Techelles, Usumcasane, *the* Turke, *with others.*

Tamburlaine.   Now hang our bloody collours by *Damascus*,
Reflexing hewes of blood upon their heads,
While they walke quivering on their citie walles,
Halfe dead for feare before they feele my wrath:
Then let us freely banquet and carouse
Full bowles of wine unto the God of war,
That meanes to fill your helmets full of golde:
And make *Damascus* spoiles as rich to you,
As was to *Jason Colchos* golden fleece.

And now *Bajaʒeth*, hast thou any stomacke?   10

Bajaʒeth.   I, such a stomacke (cruel *Tamburlane*) as I could
willingly feed upon thy blood-raw hart.

Tamburlaine.   Nay, thine owne is easier to come by, plucke out
that, and twil serve thee and thy wife: Wel *Zenocrate*,
Techelles, and the rest, fall to your victuals.

Bajaʒeth.   Fall to, and never may your meat digest.
Ye Furies that can maske invisible,
Dive to the bottome of *Avernus* poole,
And in your hands bring hellish poison up,
And squease it in the cup of *Tamburlain*.   20
Or winged snakes of *Lerna* cast your stings,
And leave your venoms in this Tyrants dish.

Zabina.   And may this banquet proove as omenous,
As *Prognes* to th'adulterous Thracian King,
That fed upon the substance of his child.

Zenocrate.   My Lord, how can you suffer these outragious curses
by these slaves of yours?

Tamburlaine.   To let them see (divine *Zenocrate*)
I glorie in the curses of my foes,
Having the power from the Emperiall heaven,   30
To turne them al upon their proper heades.

Techelles.   I pray you give them leave Madam, this speech is a
goodly refreshing to them.

Theridamas.   But if his highnesse would let them be fed, it would
doe them more good.

Tamburlaine.   Sirra, why fall you not too, are you so daintily
brought up, you cannot eat your owne flesh?

Bajaʒeth.   First legions of devils shall teare thee in peeces.

Usumcasane.   Villain, knowest thou to whom thou speakest?

Tamburlaine.   O let him alone: here, eat sir, take it from my 40
swords point, or Ile thrust it to thy heart.

He takes it and stamps upon it.

Theridamas.   He stamps it under his feet my Lord.

Tamburlaine.   Take it up Villaine, and eat it, or I will make thee
slice the brawnes of thy armes into carbonadoes, and eat them.

Usumcasane.   Nay, twere better he kild his wife, and then she

shall be sure not to be starv'd, and he be provided for a moneths victuall before hand.

Tamburlaine. Here is my dagger, dispatch her while she is fat,
for if she live but a while longer, shee will fall into a consumption with freatting, and then she will not bee woorth the 50
eating.

Theridamas. Doost thou think that *Mahomet* wil suffer this?

Techelles. Tis like he wil, when he cannot let it.

Tamburlaine. Go to, fal to your meat: what, not a bit? belike he
hath not bene watered to day, give him some drinke.

> *They give him water to drinke, and he flings it on the ground.*

Faste and welcome sir, while hunger make you eat.
How now *Zenocrate*, dooth not the Turke and his wife make a
goodly showe at a banquet?

Zenocrate. Yes, my Lord.

Theridamas. Me thinks, tis a great deale better than a consort of 60
musicke.

Tamburlaine. Yet musicke woulde doe well to cheare up *Zenocrate*:
pray thee tel, why art thou so sad? If thou wilt have a song, the
Turke shall straine his voice: but why is it?

Zenocrate. My lord, to see my fathers towne besieg'd,
The countrie wasted where my selfe was borne,
How can it but afflict my verie soule?
If any love remaine in you my Lord,
Or if my love unto your majesty
May merit favour at your highnesse handes,   70
Then raise your siege from faire *Damascus* walles,
And with my father take a frindly truce.

Tamburlaine. *Zenocrate*, were *Egypt Joves* owne land,
Yet would I with my sword make *Jove* to stoope.
I will confute those blind Geographers
That make a triple region in the world,
Excluding Regions which I meane to trace,
And with this pen reduce them to a Map,
Calling the Provinces, Citties and townes
After my name and thine *Zenocrate*:   80
Here at *Damascus* will I make the Point

That shall begin the Perpendicular.
And wouldst thou have me buy thy Fathers love
With such a losse? Tell me *Zenocrate?*
Zenocrate.   Honor still waight on happy *Tamburlaine*:
Yet give me leave to plead for him my Lord.
Tamburlaine.   Content thy selfe, his person shall be safe,
And all the friendes of faire *Zenocrate,*
If with their lives they will be pleasde to yeeld,
Or may be forc'd, to make me Emperour.   90
For *Egypt* and *Arabia* must be mine.
Feede you slave, thou maist thinke thy selfe happie to be fed from
my trencher.
Bajazeth.   My empty stomacke ful of idle heat,
Drawes bloody humours from my feeble partes,
Preserving life, by hasting cruell death.
My vaines are pale, my sinowes hard and drie,
My jointes benumb'd, unlesse I eat, I die.
Zabina.   Eat *Bajazeth.* Let us live in spite of them, looking some
happie power will pitie and inlarge us.   100
Tamburlaine.   Here Turk, wilt thou have a cleane trencher?
Bajazeth.   I Tyrant, and more meat.
Tamburlaine.   Soft sir, you must be dieted, too much eating will
make you surfeit.
Theridamas.   So it would my lord, specially having so smal a
walke, and so litle exercise.

Enter a second course of Crownes.

Tamburlaine.   *Theridamas, Techelles* and *Casane,* here are the
cates you desire to finger, are they not?
Theridamas.   I (my Lord) but none save kinges must feede with
these.   110
Techelles.   Tis enough for us to see them, and for *Tamburlaine*
onely to enjoy them.
Tamburlaine.   Wel, here is now to the Souldane of *Egypt*, the
King of *Arabia*, and the Governour of *Damascus.* Now take
these three crownes, and pledge me, my contributorie Kings.
I crowne you here (*Theridamas*) King of *Argier: Techelles* King

of *Fesse*, and *Usumcasane* King of *Morocus*. How say you to
this (Turke) these are not your contributorie kings.

Bajazeth.   Nor shall they long be thine, I warrant them.

Tamburlaine.   Kings of *Argier*, *Morocus*, and of *Fesse*,   120
  You that have martcht with happy *Tamburlaine*,
  As far as from the frozen plage of heaven,
  Unto the watry mornings ruddy bower,
  And thence by land unto the Torrid Zone,
  Deserve these tytles I endow you with,
  By valure and by magnanimity.
  Your byrthes shall be no blemish to your fame,
  For vertue is the fount whence honor springs.
  And they are worthy she investeth kings.

Theridamas.   And since your highnesse hath so well vouchsaft,   130
  If we deserve them not with higher meeds
  Then erst our states and actions have retain'd,
  Take them away againe and make us slaves.

Tamburlaine.   Wel said *Theridamas*, when holy Fates
  Shall stablish me in strong *Egyptia*,
  We meane to traveile to th'Antartique Pole,
  Conquering the people underneath our feet.
  And be renowm'd, as never Emperours were.
  Zenocrate, I will not crowne thee yet,
  Until with greater honors I be grac'd.   140

[*Enter*] *The* Governour *of* Damasco, *with three or foure Citizens,* V.i
   and foure Virgins, *with branches of Laurell in their hands.*

Governour.   Stil dooth this man or rather God of war,
  Batter our walles, and beat our Turrets downe.
  And to resist with longer stubbornesse,
  Or hope of rescue from the Souldans power,
  Were but to bring our wilfull overthrow,
  And make us desperate of our threatned lives:
  We see his tents have now bene altered,

With terrours to the last and cruelst hew:
His cole-blacke collours every where advaunst,
Threaten our citie with a generall spoile: 10
And if we should with common rites of Armes,
Offer our safeties to his clemencie,
I feare the custome proper to his sword,
Which he observes as parcell of his fame,
Intending so to terrifie the world:
By any innovation or remorse,
Will never be dispenc'd with til our deaths.
Therfore, for these our harmlesse virgines sakes,
Whose honors and whose lives relie on him:
Let us have hope that their unspotted praiers, 20
Their blubbered cheekes and hartie humble mones
Will melt his furie into some remorse:
And use us like a loving Conquerour.
1. Virgin.   If humble suites or imprecations,
(Uttered with teares of wretchednesse and blood,
Shead from the heads and hearts of all our Sex,
Some made your wives, and some your children)
Might have intreated your obdurate breasts,
To entertaine some care of our securities,
Whiles only danger beat upon our walles, 30
These more than dangerous warrants of our death,
Had never bene erected as they bee,
Nor you depend on such weake helps as we.
Governour.   Wel, lovely Virgins, think our countries care,
Our love of honor loth to be enthral'd
To forraine powers, and rough imperious yokes:
Would not with too much cowardize or feare,
Before all hope of rescue were denied,
Submit your selves and us to servitude.
Therefore in that your safeties and our owne, 40
Your honors, liberties and lives were weigh'd
In equall care and ballance with our owne,
Endure as we the malice of our stars,
The wrath of *Tamburlain*, and power of warres.

Or be the means the overweighing heavens
Have kept to quallifie these hot extreames,
And bring us pardon in your chearfull lookes.

2. Virgin. Then here before the majesty of heaven,
And holy *Patrones* of *Egyptia*,
With knees and hearts submissive we intreate   50
Grace to our words and pitie to our lookes,
That this devise may proove propitious,
And through the eies and eares of *Tamburlaine*,
Convey events of mercie to his heart:
Graunt that these signes of victorie we yeeld
May bind the temples of his conquering head,
To hide the folded furrowes of his browes,
And shadow his displeased countenance,
With happy looks of ruthe and lenity.
Leave us my Lord, and loving countrimen,   60
What simple Virgins may perswade, we will.

Governour. Farewell (sweet Virgins) on whose safe return
Depends our citie, libertie, and lives.

Exeunt. [*Manent* Virgins.]

[*Enter*] Tamburlaine, Techelles, Theridamas, Usumcasane, *with
others*: Tamburlaine *all in blacke, and verie melancholy.*

Tamburlaine. What, are the Turtles fraide out of their neastes?
Alas poore fooles, must you be first shal feele
The sworne destruction of *Damascus.*
They know my custome: could they not as well
Have sent ye out, when first my milkwhite flags
Through which sweet mercie threw her gentle beams,
Reflexing them on your disdainfull eies: 70
As now when furie and incensed hate
Flings slaughtering terrour from my coleblack tents.
And tels for trueth, submissions comes too late.

1. Virgin. Most happy King and Emperour of the earth,
Image of Honor and Nobilitie.

*49 *Patrones*] stet O 1–4

134

For whome the Powers divine have made the world,
And on whose throne the holy Graces sit.
In whose sweete person is compriz'd the Sum
Of natures Skill and heavenly majestie.
Pittie our plightes, O pitie poore *Damascus*:   80
Pitie olde age, within whose silver haires
Honor and reverence evermore have raign'd,
Pitie the mariage bed, where many a Lord
In prime and glorie of his loving joy,
Embraceth now with teares of ruth and blood,
The jealous bodie of his fearfull wife,
Whose cheekes and hearts so punisht with conceit,
To thinke thy puisant never staied arme
Will part their bodies, and prevent their soules
From heavens of comfort, yet their age might beare,   90
Now waxe all pale and withered to the death,
As well for griefe our ruthlesse Governour
Have thus refusde the mercie of thy hand,
(Whose scepter Angels kisse, and Furies dread)
As for their liberties, their loves or lives.
O then for these, and such as we our selves,
For us, for infants, and for all our bloods,
That never nourisht thought against thy rule,
Pitie, O pitie, (sacred Emperour)
The prostrate service of this wretched towne.   100
And take in signe thereof this gilded wreath,
Whereto ech man of rule hath given his hand,
And wisht as worthy subjects happy meanes,
To be investers of thy royall browes,
Even with the true Egyptian Diadem.
Tamburlaine.   Virgins, in vaine ye labour to prevent
   That which mine honor sweares shal be perform'd:
   Behold my sword, what see you at the point?
1. Virgin.   Nothing but feare and fatall steele my Lord.
Tamburlaine.   Your fearfull minds are thicke and mistie then,   110
   For there sits Death, there sits imperious Death,
   Keeping his circuit by the slicing edge.

135

But I am pleasde you shall not see him there:
He now is seated on my horsmens speares,
And on their points his fleshlesse bodie feedes.
Techelles, straight goe charge a few of them
To chardge these Dames, and shew my servant death,
Sitting in scarlet on their armed speares.
Omnes.   O pitie us.
Tamburlaine.   Away with them I say and shew them death.   120
                    They [Techelles *and soldiers*] *take them away.*
I will not spare these proud Egyptians,
Nor change my Martiall observations,
For all the wealth of *Gehons* golden waves.
Or for the love of *Venus*, would she leave
The angrie God of Armes, and lie with me.
They have refusde the offer of their lives,
And know my customes are as peremptory
As wrathfull Planets, death, or destinie.
                                        Enter Techelles.
What, have your horsmen shewen the virgins Death?
Techelles.   They have my Lord, and on *Damascus* wals   130
Have hoisted up their slaughtered carcases.
Tamburlaine.   A sight as banefull to their soules I think
As are Thessalian drugs or Mithradate.
But goe my Lords, put the rest to the sword.
                            Exeunt. [*Manet* Tamburlaine.]
Ah faire *Zenocrate*, divine *Zenocrate*,
Faire is too foule an Epithite for thee,
That in thy passion for thy countries love,
And feare to see thy kingly Fathers harme,
With haire discheweld wip'st thy watery cheeks:
And like to *Flora* in her mornings pride,   140
Shaking her silver tresses in the aire,
Rain'st on the earth resolved pearle in showers,
And sprinklest Saphyrs on thy shining face,
Wher Beauty, mother to the Muses sits,
And comments vollumes with her Yvory pen:
Taking instructions from thy flowing eies,

Eies when that *Ebena* steps to heaven,
In silence of thy solemn Evenings walk,
Making the mantle of the richest night,
The Moone, the Planets, and the Meteors light.   150
There Angels in their christal armours fight
A doubtfull battell with my tempted thoughtes,
For *Egypts* freedom and the Souldans life:
His life that so consumes *Zenocrate*,
Whose sorrowes lay more siege unto my soule,
Than all my Army to *Damascus* walles.
And neither Perseans Soveraign, nor the Turk
Troubled my sences with conceit of foile,
So much by much, as dooth *Zenocrate*.
What is beauty, saith my sufferings then?   160
If all the pens that ever poets held,
Had fed the feeling of their maisters thoughts,
And every sweetnes that inspir'd their harts,
Their minds, and muses on admyred theames:
If all the heavenly Quintessence they still
From their immortall flowers of Poesy,
Wherein as in a myrrour we perceive
The highest reaches of a humaine wit:
If these had made one Poems period
And all combin'd in Beauties worthinesse,   170
Yet should ther hover in their restlesse heads,
One thought, one grace, one woonder at the least,
Which into words no vertue can digest:
But how unseemly is it for my Sex,
My discipline of armes and Chivalrie,
My nature and the terrour of my name,
To harbour thoughts effeminate and faint?
Save onely that in Beauties just applause,
With whose instinct the soule of man is toucht,
And every warriour that is rapt with love   180
Of fame, of valour, and of victory,
Must needs have beauty beat on his conceites.

*147 *Ebena*] *stet* O 1–4   *177–87 To harbour…weeds,] *stet* O 1–4

I thus conceiving and subduing both:
That which hath stoopt the tempest of the Gods,
Even from the fiery spangled vaile of heaven,
To feele the lovely warmth of shepheards flames,
And martch in cottages of strowed weeds:
Shal give the world to note, for all my byrth,
That Vertue solely is the sum of glorie,
And fashions men with true nobility. 190
Who's within there?

Enter two or three.

Hath *Bajazeth* bene fed to day?
Attendant. I, my Lord.
Tamburlaine. Bring him forth, and let us know if the towne be
ransackt. [*Exeunt attendants.*]

Enter Techelles, Theridamas, Usumcasane, *and others.*

Techelles. The town is ours my Lord, and fresh supply
Of conquest, and of spoile is offered us.
Tamburlaine. Thats wel *Techelles*, what's the newes?
Techelles. The Souldan and the Arabian king together
Martch on us with such eager violence, 200
As if there were no way but one with us.
Tamburlaine. No more there is not I warrant thee *Techelles*.

They bring in the Turke [*in his cage, and Zabina*].

Theridamas. We know the victorie is ours my Lord,
But let us save the reverend Souldans life,
For faire *Zenocrate*, that so laments his state.
Tamburlaine. That will we chiefly see unto, *Theridamas*,
For sweet *Zenocrate*, whose worthinesse
Deserves a conquest over every hart:
And now my footstoole, if I loose the field,
You hope of libertie and restitution: 210
Here let him stay my maysters from the tents,
Till we have made us ready for the field.
Pray for us *Bajazeth*, we are going.

Exeunt. [*Manent* Bajazeth *and* Zabina.]

*184 stoopt] Coll MS Dyce²; stopt *187 martch] *stet* O 1–4
   O 1–4   193 *Attendant.*] Robinson; *An.* O 1–4

Baja۬eth.   Go, never to returne with victorie:
  Millions of men encompasse thee about,
  And gore thy body with as many wounds.
  Sharpe forked arrowes light upon thy horse:
  Furies from the blacke *Cocitus* lake,
  Breake up the earth, and with their firebrands,
  Enforce thee run upon the banefull pikes.   220
  Volleyes of shot pierce through thy charmed Skin,
  And every bullet dipt in poisoned drugs,
  Or roaring Cannons sever all thy joints,
  Making thee mount as high as Eagles soare.
Zabina.   Let all the swords and Lances in the field,
  Stick in his breast, as in their proper roomes.
  At every pore let blood comme dropping foorth,
  That lingring paines may massacre his heart.
  And madnesse send his damned soule to hell.
Baja۬eth.   Ah faire *Zabina*, we may curse his power,   230
  The heavens may frowne, the earth for anger quake,
  But such a Star hath influence in his sword,
  As rules the Skies, and countermands the Gods:
  More than Cymerian *Stix* or Distinie.
  And then shall we in this detested guyse,
  With shame, with hungar, and with horror aie
  Griping our bowels with retorqued thoughtes,
  And have no hope to end our extasies.
Zabina.   Then is there left no *Mahomet*, no God,
  No Feend, no Fortune, nor no hope of end   240
  To our infamous monstrous slaveries?
  Gape earth, and let the Feends infernall view
  A hell, as hoplesse and as full of feare,
  As are the blasted banks of *Erebus*:
  Where shaking ghosts with ever howling grones,
  Hover about the ugly Ferriman,
  To get a passage to *Elisian*.
  Why should we live, O wretches, beggars, slaves,
  Why live we *Baja۬eth*, and build up neasts,

243 A] Oxberry; As O 1–4

So high within the region of the aire, 250
By living long in this oppression,
That all the world will see and laugh to scorne,
The former triumphes of our mightines,
In this obscure infernall servitude?
Bajazeth. O life more loathsome to my vexed thoughts,
Than noisome parbreak of the Stygian Snakes,
Which fils the nookes of Hell with standing aire,
Infecting all the Ghosts with curelesse griefs:
O dreary Engines of my loathed sight,
That sees my crowne, my honor and my name, 260
Thrust under yoke and thraldom of a thiefe.
Why feed ye still on daies accursed beams,
And sink not quite into my tortur'd soule.
You see my wife, my Queene and Emperesse,
Brought up and propped by the hand of fame,
Queen of fifteene contributory Queens,
Now throwen to roomes of blacke abjection,
Smear'd with blots of basest drudgery:
And Villanesse to shame, disdaine, and misery:
Accursed *Bajazeth*, whose words of ruth, 270
That would with pity chear *Zabinas* heart,
And make our soules resolve in ceasles teares:
Sharp hunger bites upon and gripes the root,
From whence the issues of my thoughts doe breake:
O poore *Zabina*, O my Queen, my Queen,
Fetch me some water for my burning breast,
To coole and comfort me with longer date,
That in the shortned sequel of my life,
I may poure foorth my soule into thine armes,
With words of love: whose moaning entercourse 280
Hath hetherto bin staid, with wrath and hate
Of our expreslesse band inflictions.
Zabina. Sweet *Bajazeth*, I will prolong thy life,
As long as any blood or sparke of breath
Can quench or coole the torments of my griefe. *She goes out.*

282 band] *i.e.,* bann'd

Bajazeth.   Now *Bajazeth*, abridge thy banefull daies,
And beat thy braines out of thy conquer'd head:
Since other meanes are all forbidden me,
That may be ministers of my decay.
O highest Lamp of everliving *Jove*,   290
Accursed day infected with my griefs,
Hide now thy stained face in endles night,
And shut the windowes of the lightsome heavens.
Let ugly darknesse with her rusty coach
Engyrt with tempests wrapt in pitchy clouds,
Smother the earth with never fading mistes:
And let her horses from their nostrels breathe
Rebellious winds and dreadfull thunderclaps:
That in this terrour *Tamburlaine* may live.
And my pin'd soule resolv'd in liquid ayre,   300
May styl excruciat his tormented thoughts.
Then let the stony dart of sencelesse colde,
Pierce through the center of my withered heart,
And make a passage for my loathed life.

> *He brains himself against the cage.*

> *Enter* Zabina.

Zabina.   What do mine eies behold, my husband dead?
His Skul al rivin in twain, his braines dasht out?
The braines of *Bajazeth*, my Lord and Soveraigne?
O *Bajazeth*, my husband and my Lord,
O *Bajazeth*, O Turk, O Emperor.
Give him his liquor? Not I, bring milk and fire, and my blood I   310
bring him againe, teare me in peeces, give me the sworde with a
ball of wildefire upon it. Downe with him, downe with him. Goe
to, my child, away, away, away. Ah, save that Infant, save him,
save him. I, even I speake to her. The Sun was downe. Streamers
white, Red, Blacke. Here, here, here. Fling the meat in his face.
Tamburlaine, Tamburlaine. Let the souldiers be buried. Hel, death,
Tamburlain, Hell. Make ready my Coch, my chaire, my jewels, I
come, I come, I come.

> *She runs against the Cage and braines her selfe.*

300 ayre] O3; ay O1–2   *315 Fling…face.] stet O1–4

Enter Zenocrate *wyth* Anippe.

Zenocrate.   Wretched *Zenocrate*, that livest to see,
  Damascus walles di'd with Egyptian blood: 320
  Thy Frathers subjects and thy countrimen.
  Thy streetes strowed with dissevered jointes of men,
  And wounded bodies gasping yet for life.
  But most accurst, to see the Sun-bright troope
  Of heavenly vyrgins and unspotted maides,
  Whose lookes might make the angry God of armes,
  To breake his sword, and mildly treat of love,
  On horsmens Lances to be hoisted up,
  And guiltlesly endure a cruell death.
  For every fell and stout Tartarian Stead   330
  That stampt on others with their thundring hooves,
  When al their riders chardg'd their quivering speares
  Began to checke the ground, and rain themselves:
  Gazing upon the beautie of their lookes:
  Ah *Tamburlaine*, wert thou the cause of this
  That tearm'st *Zenocrate* thy dearest love?
  Whose lives were dearer to *Zenocrate*
  Than her owne life, or ought save thine owne love.
  But see another bloody spectacle.
  Ah wretched eies, the enemies of my hart,   340
  How are ye glutted with these grievous objects,
  And tell my soule mor tales of bleeding ruth?
  See, se *Anippe* if they breathe or no.
Anippe.   No breath nor sence, nor motion in them both.
  Ah Madam, this their slavery hath Enforc'd,
  And ruthlesse cruelty of *Tamburlaine*.
Zenocrate.   Earth cast up fountaines from thy entralles,
  And wet thy cheeks for their untimely deathes:
  Shake with their waight in signe of feare and griefe:
  Blush heaven, that gave them honor at their birth,   350
  And let them die a death so barbarous.
  Those that are proud of fickle Empery,
  And place their chiefest good in earthly pompe:

Behold the Turke and his great Emperesse.
Ah *Tamburlaine*, my love, sweet *Tamburlaine*,
That fights for Scepters and for slippery crownes,
Behold the Turk and his great Emperesse.
Thou that in conduct of thy happy stars,
Sleep'st every night with conquest on thy browes,
And yet wouldst shun the wavering turnes of war,   360
In feare and feeling of the like distresse,
Behold the Turke and his great Emperesse.
Ah myghty *Jove* and holy *Mahomet*,
Pardon my Love, oh pardon his contempt,
Of earthly fortune, and respect of pitie,
And let not conquest ruthlesly pursewde
Be equally against his life incenst,
In this great Turk and haplesse Emperesse.
And pardon me that was not moov'd with ruthe,
To see them live so long in misery: 370
Ah what may chance to thee *Zenocrate*?
Anippe.   Madam content your self and be resolv'd,
  Your Love hath fortune so at his command,
  That she shall stay and turne her wheele no more,
  As long as life maintaines his mighty arme,
  That fights for honor to adorne your head.

            Enter [Philemus,] *a Messenger*.

Zenocrate.   What other heavie news now brings *Philemus*?
Philemus.   Madam, your father and th'Arabian king,
  The first affecter of your excellence,
  Comes now as *Turnus* gainst *Eneas* did,   380
  Armed with lance into the Egyptian fields,
  Ready for battaile gainst my Lord the King.
Zenocrate.   Now shame and duty, love and feare presents
  A thousand sorrowes to my martyred soule:
  Whom should I wish the fatall victory,
  When my poore pleasures are devided thus,
  And rackt by dutie from my cursed heart:
  My father and my first betrothed love,

                143

Must fight against my life and present love:
Wherin the change I use condemns my faith, 390
And makes my deeds infamous through the world.
But as the Gods to end the Troyans toile,
Prevented *Turnus* of *Lavinia*,
And fatally enricht *Eneas* love.
So for a finall Issue to my griefes,
To pacifie my countrie and my love,
Must *Tamburlaine* by their resistlesse powers,
With vertue of a gentle victorie,
Conclude a league of honor to my hope.
Then as the powers devine have preordainde, 400
With happy safty of my fathers life,
Send like defence of faire *Arabia*.

They sound to the battaile. And Tamburlaine *enjoyes the
victory, after* Arabia *enters wounded.*

Arabia. What cursed power guides the murthering hands,
Of this infamous Tyrants souldiers,
That no escape may save their enemies:
Nor fortune keep them selves from victory.
Lye down *Arabia*, wounded to the death,
And let *Zenocrates* faire eies beholde
That as for her thou bearst these wretched armes,
Even so for her thou diest in these armes: 410
Leaving thy blood for witnesse of thy love.
Zenocrate. Too deare a witnesse for such love my Lord.
Behold *Zenocrate*, the cursed object
Whose Fortunes never mastered her griefs:
Behold her wounded in conceit for thee,
As much as thy faire body is for me.
Arabia. Then shal I die with full contented heart,
Having beheld devine *Zenocrate*,
Whose sight with joy would take away my life,
As now it bringeth sweetnesse to my wound, 420
If I had not bin wounded as I am.
Ah that the deadly panges I suffer now,

Would lend an howers license to my tongue:
To make discourse of some sweet accidents
Have chanc'd thy merits in this worthles bondage.
And that I might be privy to the state,
Of thy deserv'd contentment and thy love:
But making now a vertue of thy sight,
To drive all sorrow from my fainting soule:
Since Death denies me further cause of joy,   430
Depriv'd of care, my heart with comfort dies,
Since thy desired hand shall close mine eies.   [*Dies.*]

> *Enter* Tamburlain *leading the* Souldane, Techelles,
> Theridamas, Usumcasane, *with others.*

Tamburlaine.   Come happy Father of *Zenocrate*,
  A title higher than thy Souldans name:
  Though my right hand have thus enthralled thee,
  Thy princely daughter here shall set thee free.
  She that hath calmde the furie of my sword,
  Which had ere this bin bathde in streames of blood,
  As vast and deep as *Euphrates* or *Nile*.
Zenocrate.   O sight thrice welcome to my joiful soule,   440
  To see the king my Father issue safe,
  From dangerous battel of my conquering Love.
Souldan.   Wel met my only deare *Zenocrate*,
  Though with the losse of *Egypt* and my Crown.
Tamburlaine.   Twas I my lord that gat the victory,
  And therfore grieve not at your overthrow,
  Since I shall render all into your hands.
  And ad more strength to your dominions
  Than ever yet confirm'd th'Egyptian Crown.
  The God of war resignes his roume to me,   450
  Meaning to make me Generall of the world,
  Jove viewing me in armes, lookes pale and wan,
  Fearing my power should pull him from his throne.
  Where ere I come the fatall sisters sweat,
  And griesly death, by running to and fro,
  To doo their ceassles homag to my sword:

And here in *Affrick* where it seldom raines,
Since I arriv'd with my triumphant hoste,
Have swelling cloudes drawen from wide gasping woundes,
Bene oft resolv'd in bloody purple showers,   460
A meteor that might terrify the earth,
And make it quake at every drop it drinks:
Millions of soules sit on the bankes of *Styx*,
Waiting the back returne of *Charons* boat,
Hell and *Elisian* swarme with ghosts of men,
That I have sent from sundry foughten fields,
To spread my fame through hell and up to heaven:
And see my Lord, a sight of strange import,
Emperours and kings lie breathlesse at my feet.
The Turk and his great Emperesse as it seems,   470
Left to themselves while we were at the fight,
Have desperatly dispatcht their slavish lives:
With them *Arabia* too hath left his life,
Al sights of power to grace my victory:
And such are objects fit for *Tamburlaine*.
Wherein as in a mirrour may be seene,
His honor, that consists in sheading blood,
When men presume to manage armes with him.
Souldan.   Mighty hath God and *Mahomet* made thy hand
(Renowmed *Tamburlain*) to whom all kings   480
Of force must yeeld their crownes and Emperies:
And I am pleasde with this my overthrow,
If as beseemes a person of thy state,
Thou hast with honor usde *Zenocrate*.
Tamburlaine.   Her state and person wants no pomp you see,
And for all blot of foule inchastity,
I record heaven, her heavenly selfe is cleare:
Then let me find no further time to grace
Her princely Temples with the Persean crowne:
But here these kings that on my fortunes wait,   490
And have bene crown'd for prooved worthynesse:
Even by this hand that shall establish them,
Shal now, adjoining al their hands with mine,

Invest her here my Queene of *Persea*.
What saith the noble Souldane and *Zenocrate?*
Souldan.   I yeeld with thanks and protestations
Of endlesse honor to thee for her love.
Tamburlaine.   Then doubt I not but faire *Zenocrate*
Will soone consent to satisfy us both.
Zenocrate.   Els should I much forget my self, my Lord.   500
Theridamas.   Then let us set the crowne upon her head,
That long hath lingred for so high a seat.
Techelles.   My hand is ready to performe the deed,
For now her mariage time shall worke us rest.
Usumcasane.   And here's the crown my Lord, help set it on.
Tamburlaine.   Then sit thou downe divine *Zenocrate*,
And here we crowne thee Queene of *Persea*,
And all the kingdomes and dominions
That late the power of *Tamburlaine* subdewed:
As *Juno*, when the Giants were supprest,   510
That darted mountaines at her brother *Jove*:
So lookes my Love, shadowing in her browes
Triumphes and Trophees for my victories:
Or as *Latonas* daughter bent to armes,
Adding more courage to my conquering mind.
To gratify the sweet *Zenocrate*,
Egyptians, Moores and men of *Asia*,
From *Barbary* unto the Westerne *Inde*,
Shall pay a yearly tribute to thy Syre.
And from the boundes of *Affrick* to the banks   520
Of *Ganges*, shall his mighty arme extend.
And now my Lords and loving followers,
That purchac'd kingdomes by your martiall deeds,
Cast off your armor, put on scarlet roabes.
Mount up your royall places of estate,
Environed with troopes of noble men,
And there make lawes to rule your provinces:
Hang up your weapons on *Alcides* poste,
For *Tamburlaine* takes truce with al the world.

*516 the] *stet* O1–4

Thy first betrothed Love, *Arabia*,   530
Shall we with honor (as beseemes) entombe,
With this great Turke and his faire Emperesse:
Then after all these solemne Exequies,
We wil our celebrated rites of mariage solemnize.

[*Exeunt.*]

TAMBURLAINE

PART II

[DRAMATIS PERSONÆ

TAMBURLAINE, king of Persia

CALYPHAS
AMYRAS } his sons
CELEBINUS

THERIDAMAS, king of Argier
TECHELLES, king of Fez
USUMCASANE, king of Morocco
ORCANES, king of Natolia
KING OF TREBIZON
KING OF SORIA
KING OF JERUSALEM
KING OF AMASIA
GAZELLUS, viceroy of Byron
URIBASSA
SIGISMUND, king of Hungary
FREDERICK } Lords of Buda
BALDWIN } and Bohemia

CALLAPINE, son to Bajazeth and prisoner to Tamburlaine
ALMEDA, his keeper
GOVERNOR OF BABYLON
CAPTAIN OF BALSERA
HIS SON
MAXIMUS, PERDICAS, *Physicians, Lords, Citizens, Messengers, Soldiers, and Attendants*

ZENOCRATE, *wife to Tamburlaine*
OLYMPIA, *wife to the Captain of Balsera*
Turkish Concubines.]

The Prologue.

The generall welcomes Tamburlain *receiv'd,*
When he arrived last upon our stage,
Hath made our Poet pen his second part,
Wher death cuts off the progres of his pomp,
And murdrous Fates throwes al his triumphs down.
But what became of faire Zenocrate,
And with how manie cities sacrifice
He celebrated her sad funerall,
Himselfe in presence shal unfold at large.

8 *sad*] Oxberry; *said* O 1–4

The Second Part of The Bloody Conquests
of mighty Tamburlaine.

With his impassionate fury, for the death of
his Lady and love, faire Zenocrate: his fourme
of exhortation and discipline to his three
sons, and the maner of his own death.

[*Enter*] Orcanes, *king of* Natolia, Gazellus, *vice-roy of* Byron,   I.i
Uribassa, *and their traine, with drums and trumpets.*

Orcanes.   Egregious Viceroyes of these Eastern parts
Plac'd by the issue of great *Bajazeth,*
And sacred Lord, the mighty *Calapine:*
Who lives in *Egypt,* prisoner to that slave,
Which kept his father in an yron cage:
Now have we martcht from faire *Natolia*
Two hundred leagues, and on *Danubius* banks,
Our warlike hoste in compleat armour rest,
Where *Sigismond* the king of *Hungary*
Should meet our person to conclude a truce.   10
What? Shall we parle with the Christian,
Or crosse the streame, and meet him in the field?
Gazellus.   King of *Natolia,* let us treat of peace,
We all are glutted with the Christians blood,
And have a greater foe to fight against,
Proud *Tamburlaine,* that now in *Asia,*
Neere *Guyrons* head doth set his conquering feet,
And means to fire *Turky* as he goes:
Gainst him my Lord must you addresse your power.
Uribassa.   Besides, king *Sigismond* hath brought from Christen-
dome,   20
More then his Camp of stout Hungarians,

0.2 Uribassa] Oxberry: Upibassa O 1–4

Sclavonians, Almans, Rutters, Muffes, and Danes,
That with the Holbard, Lance, and murthering Axe,
Will hazard that we might with surety hold.
Orcanes.   Though from the shortest Northren Paralell,
Vast *Gruntland* compast with the frozen sea,
Inhabited with tall and sturdy men,
Gyants as big as hugie *Polypheme*:
Millions of Souldiers cut the Artick line,
Bringing the strength of *Europe* to these Armes: 30
Our Turky blades shal glide through al their throats,
And make this champion mead a bloody Fen.
Danubius stream that runs to *Trebizon*,
Shall carie wrapt within his scarlet waves,
As martiall presents to our friends at home,
The slaughtered bodies of these Christians.
The Terrene main wherin *Danubius* fals,
Shall by this battell be the bloody Sea.
The wandring Sailers of proud *Italy*,
Shall meet those Christians fleeting with the tyde,   40
Beating in heaps against their Argoses,
And make faire *Europe* mounted on her bull,
Trapt with the wealth and riches of the world,
Alight and weare a woful mourning weed.
Gazellus.   Yet stout *Orcanes*, Prorex of the world,
Since *Tamburlaine* hath mustred all his men,
Marching from *Cairon* northward with his camp,
To *Alexandria*, and the frontier townes,
Meaning to make a conquest of our land:
Tis requisit to parle for a peace   50
With *Sigismond* the king of *Hungary*:
And save our forces for the hot assaults
Proud *Tamburlaine* intends *Natolia*.
Orcanes.   Viceroy of *Byron*, wisely hast thou said:
My realme, the Center of our Empery
Once lost, All *Turkie* would be overthrowne:
And for that cause the Christians shall have peace

25 *Orcanes.*] Oxberry; *omit* O 1–4

Slavonians, Almains, Rutters, Muffes, and Danes
Feare not *Orcanes*, but great *Tamburlaine*:
Nor he but Fortune that hath made him great.   60
We have revolted Grecians, Albanees,
Cicilians, Jewes, Arabians, Turks, and Moors,
Natolians, Sorians, blacke Egyptians,
Illirians, Thracians, and Bythinians,
Enough to swallow forcelesse *Sigismond*,
Yet scarse enough t'encounter *Tamburlaine*.
He brings a world of people to the field,
From *Scythia* to the Orientall Plage
Of *India*, wher raging *Lantchidol*
Beates on the regions with his boysterous blowes,   70
That never sea-man yet discovered:
All *Asia* is in Armes with *Tamburlaine*.
Even from the midst of fiery *Cancers* Tropick,
To *Amazonia* under *Capricorne*,
And thence as far as *Archipellago*:
All *Affrike* is in Armes with *Tamburlaine*.
Therefore Viceroies the Christians must have peace.

[*Enter*] Sigismond, Fredericke, Baldwine, and *their traine with
drums and trumpets.*

Sigismond.   *Orcanes* (as our Legates promist thee)
    Wee with our Peeres have crost *Danubius* stream
    To treat of friendly peace or deadly war: 80
    Take which thou wilt, for as the Romans usde
    I here present thee with a naked sword.
    Wilt thou have war, then shake this blade at me,
    If peace, restore it to my hands againe:
    And I wil sheath it to confirme the same.
Orcanes.   Stay *Sigismond*, forgetst thou I am he
    That with the Cannon shooke *Vienna* walles,
    And made it dance upon the Continent:
    As when the massy substance of the earth,
    Quiver about the Axeltree of heaven.   90

64 Illirians] O3; Illicians O1–2

Forgetst thou that I sent a shower of dartes
Mingled with powdered shot and fethered steele
So thick upon the blink-ei'd Burghers heads,
That thou thy self, then County-Pallatine,
The king of *Boheme*, and the *Austrich* Duke,
Sent Herralds out, which basely on their knees
In all your names desirde a truce of me?
Forgetst thou, that to have me raise my siege,
Wagons of gold were set before my tent:
Stampt with the princely Foule that in her wings   100
Caries the fearfull thunderbolts of *Jove*.
How canst thou think of this and offer war?
Sigismond.   *Vienna* was besieg'd, and I was there,
Then County-Pallatine, but now a king:
And what we did, was in extremity:
But now *Orcanes*, view my royall hoste,
That hides these plaines, and seems as vast and wide,
As dooth the Desart of *Arabia*
To those that stand on *Badgeths* lofty Tower,
Or as the Ocean to the Traveiler   110
That restes upon the snowy Appenines:
And tell me whether I should stoope so low,
Or treat of peace with the Natolian king?
Gazellus.   Kings of *Natolia* and of *Hungarie*,
We came from *Turky* to confirme a league,
And not to dare ech other to the field:
A friendly parle might become ye both.
Fredericke.   And we from *Europe* to the same intent,
Which if your General refuse or scorne,
Our Tents are pitcht, our men stand in array,   120
Ready to charge you ere you stir your feet.
Orcanes.   So prest are we, but yet if *Sigismond*
Speake as a friend, and stand not upon tearmes,
Here is his sword, let peace be ratified
On these conditions specified before,
Drawen with advise of our Ambassadors.
Sigismond.   Then here I sheath it, and give thee my hand,

Never to draw it out, or manage armes
Against thy selfe or thy confederates:
But whilst I live will be at truce with thee. 130
Orcanes. But (*Sigismond*) confirme it with an oath,
And sweare in sight of heaven and by thy Christ.
Sigismond. By him that made the world and sav'd my soule,
The sonne of God and issue of a Mayd,
Sweet Jesus Christ, I sollemnly protest,
And vow to keepe this peace inviolable.
Orcanes. By sacred *Mahomet*, the friend of God,
Whose holy Alcaron remaines with us,
Whose glorious body when he left the world,
Closde in a coffyn mounted up the aire, 140
And hung on stately *Mecas* Temple roofe,
I sweare to keepe this truce inviolable:
Of whose conditions, and our solemne othes
Sign'd with our handes, each shal retaine a scrowle:
As memorable witnesse of our league.
Now *Sigismond*, if any Christian King
Encroche upon the confines of thy realme,
Send woord, *Orcanes* of *Natolia*
Confirm'd this league beyond *Danubius* streame,
And they will (trembling) sound a quicke retreat, 150
So am I fear'd among all Nations.
Sigismond. If any heathen potentate or king
Invade *Natolia*, *Sigismond* will send
A hundred thousand horse train'd to the war,
And backt by stout Lanceres of *Germany*,
The strength and sinewes of the imperiall seat.
Orcanes. I thank thee *Sigismond*, but when I war
All *Asia Minor*, *Affrica*, and *Greece*
Follow my Standard and my thundring Drums:
Come let us goe and banquet in our tents: 160
I will dispatch chiefe of my army hence
To faire *Natolia*, and to *Trebizon*,
To stay my comming gainst proud *Tamburlaine*.
Freend *Sigismond*, and peeres of *Hungary*,

Come banquet and carouse with us a while,
And then depart we to our territories.

Exeunt.

[*Enter*] Callapine *with* Almeda, *his keeper.*   I.ii

Callapine.   Sweet *Almeda*, pity the ruthfull plight
Of *Callapine*, the sonne of *Bajazeth*,
Born to be Monarch of the Western world:
Yet here detain'd by cruell *Tamburlaine.*
Almeda.   My Lord I pitie it, and with my heart
Wish your release, but he whose wrath is death,
My soveraigne Lord, renowmed *Tamburlain*,
Forbids you further liberty than this.
Callapine.   Ah were I now but halfe so eloquent
To paint in woords, what Ile perfourme in deeds,   10
I know thou wouldst depart from hence with me.
Almeda.   Not for all *Affrike*, therefore moove me not.
Callapine.   Yet heare me speake my gentle *Almeda.*
Almeda.   No speach to that end, by your favour sir.
Callapine.   By *Cairo* runs——
Almeda.   No talke of running, I tell you sir.
Callapine.   A litle further, gentle *Almeda.*
Almeda.   Wel sir, what of this?
Callapine.   By *Cairo* runs to *Alexandria* Bay,
Darotes streames, wherin at anchor lies   20
A Turkish Gally of my royall fleet,
Waiting my comming to the river side,
Hoping by some means I shall be releast,
Which when I come aboord will hoist up saile,
And soon put foorth into the Terrene sea:
Where twixt the Isles of *Cyprus* and of *Creete*,
We quickly may in Turkish seas arrive.
Then shalt thou see a hundred kings and more
Upon their knees, all bid me welcome home.
Amongst so many crownes of burnisht gold,   30

15, 19 *Cairo*] Oxberry; *Cario* O 1–4

Choose which thou wilt, all are at thy command.
A thousand Gallies mann'd with Christian slaves
I freely give thee, which shall cut the straights,
And bring Armados from the coasts of *Spaine*,
Fraughted with golde of rich *America*:
The Grecian virgins shall attend on thee,
Skilful in musicke and in amorous laies:
As faire as was *Pigmalions* Ivory gyrle,
Or lovely *Io* metamorphosed.
With naked Negros shall thy coach be drawen,   40
And as thou rid'st in triumph through the streets,
The pavement underneath thy chariot wheels
With Turky Carpets shall be covered:
And cloath of Arras hung about the walles,
Fit objects for thy princely eie to pierce.
A hundred Bassoes cloath'd in crimson silk
Shall ride before the on Barbarian Steeds:
And when thou goest, a golden Canapie
Enchac'd with pretious stones, which shine as bright
As that faire vail that covers all the world: 50
When *Phœbus* leaping from his Hemi-Spheare,
Discendeth downward to th'Antipodes.
And more than this, for all I cannot tell.
Almeda.   How far hence lies the Galley, say you?
Callapine.   Sweet *Almeda*, scarse halfe a league from hence.
Almeda.   But need we not be spied going aboord?
Callapine.   Betwixt the hollow hanging of a hill
  And crooked bending of a craggy rock,
  The sailes wrapt up, the mast and tacklings downe,
  She lies so close that none can find her out.   60
Almeda.   I like that well: but tel me my Lord, if I should let you
  goe, would you bee as good as your word? Shall I be made a king
  for my labour?
Callapine.   As I am *Callapine* the Emperour,
  And by the hand of *Mahomet* I sweare,
  Thou shalt be crown'd a king and be my mate.
Almeda.   Then here I sweare, as I am *Almeda*,

158

Your Keeper under *Tamburlaine* the great,
(For that's the style and tytle I have yet)
Although he sent a thousand armed men
To intercept this haughty enterprize,   70
Yet would I venture to conduct your Grace,
And die before I brought you backe again.
Callapine.   Thanks gentle *Almeda*, then let us haste,
Least time be past, and lingring let us both.
Almeda.   When you will my Lord, I am ready.
Callapine.   Even straight: and farewell cursed *Tamburlaine.*
Now goe I to revenge my fathers death.

             Exeunt.

[*Enter*] Tamburlaine *with* Zenocrate, *and his three sonnes*, Calyphas,   I.iii
 Amyras, *and* Celebinus, *with drummes and trumpets.*

Tamburlaine.   Now, bright *Zenocrate*, the worlds faire eie,
Whose beames illuminate the lamps of heaven,
Whose chearful looks do cleare the clowdy aire
And cloath it in a christall liverie,
Now rest thee here on faire *Larissa* Plaines,
Where *Egypt* and the Turkish Empire parts,
Betweene thy sons that shall be Emperours,
And every one Commander of a world.
Zenocrate.   Sweet *Tamburlain*, when wilt thou leave these armes
And save thy sacred person free from scathe: 10
And dangerous chances of the wrathfull war?
Tamburlaine.   When heaven shal cease to moove on both the poles
And when the ground wheron my souldiers march
Shal rise aloft and touch the horned Moon,
And not before, my sweet *Zenocrate*:
Sit up and rest thee like a lovely Queene.
So, now she sits in pompe and majestie:
When these my sonnes, more precious in mine eies
Than all the wealthy kingdomes I subdewed:
Plac'd by her side, looke on their mothers face.   20
But yet me thks irinthe looks are amorous,

        159

Not martiall as the sons of *Tamburlaine.*
Water and ayre being simbolisde in one,
Argue their want of courage and of wit:
Their haire as white as milke and soft as Downe,
Which should be like the quilles of Porcupines,
As blacke as Jeat, and hard as Iron or steel,
Bewraies they are too dainty for the wars.
Their fingers made to quaver on a Lute,
Their armes to hang about a Ladies necke: 30
Their legs to dance and caper in the aire:
Would make me thinke them Bastards, not my sons,
But that I know they issued from thy wombe,
That never look'd on man but *Tamburlaine.*
Zenocrate.   My gratious Lord, they have their mothers looks,
But when they list, their conquering fathers hart:
This lovely boy the yongest of the three,
Not long agoe bestrid a Scythian Steed:
Trotting the ring, and tilting at a glove:
Which when he tainted with his slender rod,   40
He raign'd him straight and made him so curvet,
As I cried out for feare he should have falne.
Tamburlaine.   Wel done my boy, thou shalt have shield and lance,
Armour of proofe, horse, helme, and Curtle-axe,
And I will teach thee how to charge thy foe,
And harmelesse run among the deadly pikes.
If thou wilt love the warres and follow me,
Thou shalt be made a King and raigne with me,
Keeping in yron cages Emperours.
If thou exceed thy elder Brothers worth,   50
And shine in compleat vertue more than they,
Thou shalt be king before them, and thy seed
Shall issue crowned from their mothers wombe.
Celebinus.   Yes father, you shal see me if I live,
Have under me as many kings as you,
And martch with such a multitude of men,
As all the world shall tremble at their view.
Tamburlaine.   These words assure me boy, thou art my sonne,

When I am old and cannot mannage armes,
Be thou the scourge and terrour of the world.   60
Amyras.   Why may not I my Lord, as wel as he,
Be tearm'd the scourge and terrour of the world?
Tamburlaine.   Be al a scourge and terror to the world,
Or els you are not sons of *Tamburlaine.*
Calyphas.   But while my brothers follow armes my lord,
Let me accompany my gratious mother,
They are enough to conquer all the world
And you have won enough for me to keep.
Tamburlaine.   Bastardly boy, sprong from some cowards loins,
And not the issue of great *Tamburlaine*:   70
Of all the provinces I have subdued
Thou shalt not have a foot, unlesse thou beare
A mind corragious and invincible:
For he shall weare the crowne of *Persea,*
Whose head hath deepest scarres, whose breast most woundes,
Which being wroth, sends lightning from his eies,
And in the furrowes of his frowning browes,
Harbors revenge, war, death and cruelty:
For in a field whose superficies
Is covered with a liquid purple veile,   80
And sprinkled with the braines of slaughtered men,
My royal chaire of state shall be advanc'd:
And he that meanes to place himselfe therein
Must armed wade up to the chin in blood.
Zenocrate.   My Lord, such speeches to our princely sonnes,
Dismaies their mindes before they come to proove
The wounding troubles angry war affoords.
Celebinus.   No Madam, these are speeches fit for us,
For if his chaire were in a sea of blood,
I would prepare a ship and saile to it,   90
Ere I would loose the tytle of a king.
Amyras.   And I would strive to swim through pooles of blood,
Or make a bridge of murthered Carcases,
Whose arches should be fram'd with bones of Turks,

*79 superficies] Oxberry; superfluities O 1–4

Ere I would loose the tytle of a king.
Tamburlaine. Wel lovely boies, you shal be Emperours both,
Stretching your conquering armes from east to west:
And sirha, if you meane to weare a crowne,
When we shall meet the Turkish Deputie
And all his Viceroies, snatch it from his head,   100
And cleave his Pericranion with thy sword.
Calyphas.   If any man will hold him, I will strike,
And cleave him to the channell with my sword.
Tamburlaine.   Hold him, and cleave him too, or Ile cleave thee,
For we will martch against them presently.
Theridamas, Techelles, and *Casane*
Promist to meet me on *Larissa* plaines
With hostes apeece against this Turkish crue,
For I have sworne by sacred *Mahomet*,
To make it parcel of my Empery.   110
The trumpets sound, *Zenocrate*, they come.

Enter Theridamas, *and his traine with Drums*
and Trumpets.

Tamburlaine.   Welcome *Theridamas*, king of *Argier.*
Theridamas.   My Lord the great and mighty *Tamburlain*,
Arch-Monarke of the world, I offer here,
My crowne, my selfe, and all the power I have,
In all affection at thy kingly feet.
Tamburlaine.   Thanks good *Theridamas.*
Theridamas.   Under my collors march ten thousand Greeks,
And of *Argier* and *Affriks* frontier townes
Twise twenty thousand valiant men at armes,   120
All which have sworne to sacke *Natolia:*
Five hundred Briggandines are under saile,
Meet for your service on the sea, my Lord,
That lanching from *Argier* to *Tripoly*,
Will quickly ride before *Natolia:*
And batter downe the castles on the shore.
Tamburlaine.   Wel said *Argier*, receive thy crowne againe.

Enter Techelles *and* Usumcasane *together*.

Tamburlaine.   Kings of *Morocus* and of *Fesse*, welcome.
Usumcasane.   Magnificent and peerlesse *Tamburlaine*,
  I and my neighbor King of *Fesse* have brought   130
  To aide thee in this Turkish expedition,
  A hundred thousand expert souldiers:
  From *Aʒamor* to *Tunys* neare the sea,
  Is *Barbary* unpeopled for thy sake,
  And all the men in armour under me,
  Which with my crowne I gladly offer thee.
Tamburlaine.   Thanks king of *Morocus*, take your crown again.
Techelles.   And mighty *Tamburlaine*, our earthly God,
  Whose lookes make this inferiour world to quake,
  I here present thee with the crowne of *Fesse*,   140
  And with an hoste of Moores trainde to the war,
  Whose coleblacke faces make their foes retire,
  And quake for feare, as if infernall *Jove*
  Meaning to aid thee in this Turkish armes,
  Should pierce the blacke circumference of hell,
  With ugly Furies bearing fiery flags,
  And millions of his strong tormenting spirits:
  From strong *Tesella* unto *Biledull*,
  All *Barbary* is unpeopled for thy sake.
Tamburlaine.   Thanks king of *Fesse*, take here thy crowne again. 150
  Your presence (loving friends and fellow kings)
  Makes me to surfet in conceiving joy.
  If all the christall gates of *Joves* high court
  Were opened wide, and I might enter in
  To see the state and majesty of heaven,
  It could not more delight me than your sight.
  Now will we banquet on these plaines a while,
  And after martch to *Turky* with our Campe,
  In number more than are the drops that fall
  When *Boreas* rents a thousand swelling cloudes,   160
  And proud *Orcanes* of *Natolia*,

144 thee] Oxberry; them O 1–4

With all his viceroies shall be so affraide,
That though the stones, as at *Deucalions* flood,
Were turnde to men, he should be overcome:
Such lavish will I make of Turkish blood,
That *Jove* shall send his winged Messenger
To bid me sheath my sword, and leave the field:
The Sun unable to sustaine the sight,
Shall hide his head in *Thetis* watery lap,
And leave his steeds to faire *Boetes* charge: 170
For halfe the world shall perish in this fight:
But now my friends, let me examine ye,
How have ye spent your absent time from me?
Usumcasane.   My Lord, our men of *Barbary* have martcht
Foure hundred miles with armour on their backes,
And laine in leagre fifteene moneths and more,
For since we left you at the Souldans court,
We have subdude the Southerne *Guallatia*,
And all the land unto the coast of *Spaine*.
We kept the narrow straight of *Gibralter*,   180
And made *Canarea* cal us kings and Lords,
Yet never did they recreate themselves,
Or cease one day from war and hot alarms,
And therefore let them rest a while my Lord.
Tamburlaine.   They shal *Casane*, and tis time yfaith.
Techelles.   And I have march'd along the river *Nile*,
To *Machda*, where the mighty Christian Priest
Cal'd *John* the great, sits in a milk-white robe,
Whose triple Myter I did take by force,
And made him sweare obedience to my crowne.   190
From thence unto *Caʒates* did I march,
Wher Amazonians met me in the field:
With whom (being women) I vouchsaft a league,
And with my power did march to *Zansibar*,
The Westerne part of *Affrike*, where I view'd
The Ethiopian sea, rivers and lakes:
But neither man nor child in al the land:
Therfore I tooke my course to *Manico*:

Where unresisted I remoov'd my campe.
And by the coast of *Byather* at last,   200
I came to *Cubar*, where the Negros dwell,
And conquering that, made haste to *Nubia*,
There having sackt *Borno* the Kingly seat,
I took the king, and lead him bound in chaines
Unto *Damasco*, where I staid before.
Tamburlaine.   Well done *Techelles*: what saith *Theridamas?*
Theridamas.   I left the confines and the bounds of *Affrike*
And made a voyage into *Europe*,
Where by the river *Tyros* I subdew'd
Stoka, *Padalia*, and *Codemia*.   210
Then crost the sea and came to *Oblia*,
And *Nigra Silva*, where the Devils dance,
Which in despight of them I set on fire:
From thence I crost the Gulfe, call'd by the name
Mare magiore, of th'inhabitantes:
Yet shall my souldiers make no period
Untill *Natolia* kneele before your feet.
Tamburlaine.   Then wil we triumph, banquet and carouse,
Cookes shall have pensions to provide us cates,
And glut us with the dainties of the world,   220
Lachrima Christi and Calabrian wines
Shall common Souldiers drink in quaffing boules,
I, liquid golde when we have conquer'd him,
Mingled with corrall and with orient pearle:
Come let us banquet and carrouse the whiles.

                                                Exeunt.

  [*Enter*] Sigismond, Fredericke, Baldwine, *with their traine.*   II.i

Sigismond.   Now say my Lords of *Buda* and *Bohemia*,
  What motion is it that inflames your thoughts,
  And stirs your valures to such soddaine armes?
Fredericke.   Your Majesty remembers I am sure
  What cruell slaughter of our Christian bloods,
  These heathnish Turks and Pagans lately made,

224 orient] Oxberry; orientall O 1–4

Betwixt the citie *Zula* and *Danubius*,
How through the midst of *Verna* and *Bulgaria*
And almost to the very walles of *Rome*,
They have not long since massacred our Camp. 10
It resteth now then that your Majesty
Take all advantages of time and power,
And worke revenge upon these Infidels:
Your Highnesse knowes for *Tamburlaines* repaire,
That strikes a terrour to all Turkish hearts,
Natolia hath dismist the greatest part
Of all his armie, pitcht against our power
Betwixt *Cutheia* and *Orminius* mount:
And sent them marching up to *Belgasar*,
Acantha, *Antioch*, and *Cæsaria*, 20
To aid the kings of *Soria* and *Jerusalem*.
Now then my Lord, advantage take hereof,
And issue sodainly upon the rest:
That in the fortune of their overthrow,
We may discourage all the pagan troope,
That dare attempt to war with Christians.
Sigismond.   But cals not then your Grace to memorie
The league we lately made with king *Orcanes*,
Confirm'd by oth and Articles of peace,
And calling Christ for record of our trueths? 30
This should be treacherie and violence,
Against the grace of our profession.
Baldwine.   No whit my Lord: for with such Infidels,
In whom no faith nor true religion rests,
We are not bound to those accomplishments,
The holy lawes of Christendome injoine:
But as the faith which they prophanely plight
Is not by necessary pollycy,
To be esteem'd assurance for our selves,
So what we vow to them should not infringe 40
Our liberty of armes and victory.
Sigismond.   Though I confesse the othes they undertake,
Breed litle strength to our securitie,

Yet those infirmities that thus defame
Their faiths, their honors, and their religion,
Should not give us presumption to the like.
Our faiths are sound, and must be consumate,
Religious, righteous, and inviolate.

Fredericke.   Assure your Grace tis superstition
To stand so strictly on dispensive faith: 50
And should we lose the opportunity
That God hath given to venge our Christians death
And scourge their foule blasphemous Paganisme?
As fell to *Saule*, to *Balaam* and the rest,
That would not kill and curse at Gods command,
So surely will the vengeance of the highest
And jealous anger of his fearefull arme
Be pour'd with rigour on our sinfull heads,
If we neglect this offered victory.

Sigismond.   Then arme my Lords, and issue sodainly,   60
Giving commandement to our generall hoste,
With expedition to assaile the Pagan,
And take the victorie our God hath given.

Exeunt.

[*Enter*] Orcanes, Gazellus, Uribassa *with their traine.*   II.ii

Orcanes. Gaʒellus, Uribassa, and the rest,
Now will we march from proud *Orminius* mount
To faire *Natolia,* where our neighbour kings
Expect our power and our royall presence,
T'incounter with the cruell *Tamburlain,*
That nigh *Larissa* swaies a mighty hoste,
And with the thunder of his martial tooles
Makes Earthquakes in the hearts of men and heaven.

Gaʒellus.   And now come we to make his sinowes shake,
With greater power than erst his pride hath felt,   10
An hundred kings by scores wil bid him armes,
And hundred thousands subjects to each score:

*47 consumate] Dyce²; consinuate O 1–4

Which if a shower of wounding thunderbolts
Should breake out off the bowels of the clowdes
And fall as thick as haile upon our heads,
In partiall aid of that proud Scythian,
Yet should our courages and steeled crestes,
And numbers more than infinit of men,
Be able to withstand and conquer him.
Uribassa.   Me thinks I see how glad the christian King   20
Is made, for joy of your admitted truce:
That could not but before be terrified:
With unacquainted power of our hoste.

Enter a Messenger.

Messenger.   Arme dread Soveraign and my noble Lords.
The treacherous army of the Christians,
Taking advantage of your slender power,
Comes marching on us, and determines straight,
To bid us battaile for our dearest lives.
Orcanes.   Traitors, villaines, damned Christians.
Have I not here the articles of peace,   30
And solemne covenants we have both confirm'd,
He by his Christ, and I by *Mahomet*?
Gazellus.   Hel and confusion light upon their heads,
That with such treason seek our overthrow,
And cares so litle for their prophet Christ.
Orcanes.   Can there be such deceit in Christians,
Or treason in the fleshly heart of man,
Whose shape is figure of the highest God?
Then if there be a Christ, as Christians say,
But in their deeds deny him for their Christ: 40
If he be son to everliving *Jove*,
And hath the power of his outstretched arme,
If he be jealous of his name and honor,
As is our holy prophet *Mahomet*,
Take here these papers as our sacrifice
And witnesse of thy servants perjury.

14 off] *i.e.,* of *as in* O 3–4

Open thou shining vaile of *Cynthia*
And make a passage from the imperiall heaven
That he that sits on high and never sleeps,
Nor in one place is circumscriptible,   50
But every where fils every Continent,
With strange infusion of his sacred vigor,
May in his endlesse power and puritie
Behold and venge this Traitors perjury.
Thou Christ that art esteem'd omnipotent,
If thou wilt proove thy selfe a perfect God,
Worthy the worship of all faithfull hearts,
Be now reveng'd upon this Traitors soule,
And make the power I have left behind
(Too litle to defend our guiltlesse lives)   60
Sufficient to discomfort and confound
The trustlesse force of those false Christians.
To armes my Lords, on Christ still let us crie,
If there be Christ, we shall have victorie.

                                                    [*Exeunt.*]

        Sound to the battell, and Sigismond *comes out wounded.*   [II.iii]

Sigismond.   Discomfited is all the Christian hoste,
And God hath thundered vengeance from on high,
For my accurst and hatefull perjurie.
O just and dreadfull punisher of sinne,
Let the dishonor of the paines I feele,
In this my mortall well deserved wound,
End all my penance in my sodaine death,
And let this death wherein to sinne I die,
Conceive a second life in endlesse mercie.   [*Dies.*]

        Enter Orcanes, Gazellus, Uribassa, *with others.*

Orcanes.   Now lie the Christians bathing in their bloods,   10
And Christ or *Mahomet* hath bene my friend.
Gazellus.   See here the perjur'd traitor *Hungary*,
Bloody and breathlesse for his villany.

Orcanes.   Now shall his barbarous body be a pray
  To beasts and foules, and al the winds shall breath
  Through shady leaves of every sencelesse tree,
  Murmures and hisses for his hainous sin.
  Now scaldes his soule in the Tartarian streames,
  And feeds upon the banefull tree of hell,
  That *Zoacum*, that fruit of bytternesse,   20
  That in the midst of fire is ingraft,
  Yet flourisheth as *Flora* in her pride,
  With apples like the heads of damned Feends.
  The Dyvils there in chaines of quencelesse flame,
  Shall lead his soule through *Orcus* burning gulfe:
  From paine to paine, whose change shal never end:
  What saiest thou yet *Gazellus* to his foile:
  Which we referd to justice of his Christ,
  And to his power, which here appeares as full
  As raies of *Cynthia* to the clearest sight?   30
Gazellus.   Tis but the fortune of the wars my Lord,
  Whose power is often proov'd a myracle.
Orcanes.   Yet in my thoughts shall Christ be honoured,
  Not dooing *Mahomet* an injurie,
  Whose power had share in this our victory:
  And since this miscreant hath disgrac'd his faith,
  And died a traitor both to heaven and earth,
  We wil both watch and ward shall keepe his trunke
  Amidst these plaines, for Foules to pray upon.
  Go *Uribassa*, give it straight in charge.   40
Uribassa.   I will my Lord.

                    Exit Uribassa [*and soldiers with body*].
Orcanes.   And now *Gazellus*, let us haste and meete
  Our Army and our brother of *Jerusalem*,
  Of *Soria*, *Trebizon* and *Amasia*,
  And happily with full Natolian bowles
  Of Greekish wine now let us celebrate
  Our happy conquest, and his angry fate.

                                    Exeunt.

The Arras is drawn and Zenocrate *lies in her bed of state,* Tambur- II.iv
laine *sitting by her: three* Phisitians *about her bed, tempering potions.*
Theridamas, Techelles, Usumcasane, *and the three sonnes.*

Tamburlaine. Blacke is the beauty of the brightest day,
The golden balle of heavens eternal fire,
That danc'd with glorie on the silver waves,
Now wants the fewell that enflamde his beames:
And all with faintnesse and for foule disgrace,
He bindes his temples with a frowning cloude,
Ready to darken earth with endlesse night:
Zenocrate that gave him light and life,
Whose eies shot fire from their Ivory bowers,
And tempered every soule with lively heat, 10
Now by the malice of the angry Skies,
Whose jealousie admits no second Mate,
Drawes in the comfort of her latest breath
All dasled with the hellish mists of death.
Now walk the angels on the walles of heaven,
As Centinels to warne th'immortall soules,
To entertaine devine *Zenocrate.*
Apollo, Cynthia, and the ceaslesse lamps
That gently look'd upon this loathsome earth,
Shine downwards now no more, but deck the heavens 20
To entertaine divine *Zenocrate.*
The christall springs whose taste illuminates
Refined eies with an eternall sight,
Like tried silver runs through Paradice
To entertaine divine *Zenocrate.*
The Cherubins and holy Seraphins
That sing and play before the king of kings,
Use all their voices and their instruments
To entertaine divine *Zenocrate.*
And in this sweet and currious harmony, 30
The God that tunes this musicke to our soules,
Holds out his hand in highest majesty
To entertaine divine *Zenocrate.*

Then let some holy trance convay my thoughts,
Up to the pallace of th'imperiall heaven:
That this my life may be as short to me
As are the daies of sweet *Zenocrate*:
Phisitions, wil no phisicke do her good?
1. Phisitian. My Lord, your Majesty shall soone perceive:
And if she passe this fit, the worst is past.   40
Tamburlaine. Tell me, how fares my faire *Zenocrate?*
Zenocrate. I fare my Lord, as other Emperesses,
  That when this fraile and transitory flesh
  Hath suckt the measure of that vitall aire
  That feeds the body with his dated health,
  Wanes with enforst and necessary change.
Tamburlaine. May never such a change transfourme my love
  In whose sweet being I repose my life,
  Whose heavenly presence beautified with health,
  Gives light to *Phœbus* and the fixed stars,   50
  Whose absence make the sun and Moone as darke
  As when opposde in one Diamiter,
  Their Spheares are mounted on the serpents head,
  Or els discended to his winding traine:
  Live still my Love and so conserve my life,
  Or dieng, be the author of my death.
Zenocrate. Live still my Lord, O let my soveraigne live,
  And sooner let the fiery Element
  Dissolve, and make your kingdome in the Sky,
  Than this base earth should shroud your majesty: 60
  For should I but suspect your death by mine,
  The comfort of my future happinesse
  And hope to meet your highnesse in the heavens,
  Turn'd to dispaire, would break my wretched breast,
  And furie would confound my present rest.
  But let me die my Love, yet let me die,
  With love and patience let your true love die,
  Your griefe and furie hurtes my second life:
  Yet let me kisse my Lord before I die,

56 author] O4; anchor O1–3

172

And let me die with kissing of my Lord.   [*He kisses her.*] 70
But since my life is lengthened yet a while,
Let me take leave of these my loving sonnes,
And of my Lords whose true nobilitie
Have merited my latest memorie:
Sweet sons farewell, in death resemble me,
And in your lives your fathers excellency.
Some musicke, and my fit wil cease my Lord.

They call musicke.

Tamburlaine.   Proud furie and intollorable fit,
That dares torment the body of my Love,
And scourge the Scourge of the immortall God: 80
Now are those Spheares where *Cupid* usde to sit,
Wounding the world with woonder and with love,
Sadly supplied with pale and ghastly death,
Whose darts do pierce the Center of my soule:
Her sacred beauty hath enchaunted heaven,
And had she liv'd before the siege of *Troy*,
Hellen, whose beauty sommond *Greece* to armes,
And drew a thousand ships to *Tenedos*,
Had not bene nam'd in *Homers* Iliads:
Her name had bene in every line he wrote: 90
Or had those wanton Poets, for whose byrth
Olde *Rome* was proud, but gasde a while on her,
Nor *Lesbia*, nor *Corrinna* had bene nam'd,
Zenocrate had bene the argument
Of every Epigram or Eligie.

The musicke sounds, and she dies.

What, is she dead? *Techelles*, draw thy sword,
And wound the earth, that it may cleave in twaine,
And we discend into th'infernall vaults,
To haile the fatall Sisters by the haire,
And throw them in the triple mote of Hell,   100
For taking hence my faire *Zenocrate*.
Casane and *Theridamas* to armes:
Raise Cavalieros higher than the cloudes,
And with the cannon breake the frame of heaven,

Batter the shining pallace of the Sun,
And shiver all the starry firmament:
For amorous *Jove* hath snatcht my love from hence,
Meaning to make her stately Queene of heaven,
What God so ever holds thee in his armes,
Giving thee Nectar and Ambrosia,   110
Behold me here divine *Zenocrate*,
Raving, impatient, desperate and mad,
Breaking my steeled lance, with which I burst
The rusty beames of *Janus* Temple doores,
Letting out death and tyrannising war,
To martch with me under this bloody flag:
And if thou pitiest *Tamburlain* the great,
Come downe from heaven and live with me againe.
Theridamas.   Ah good my Lord be patient, she is dead,
And all this raging cannot make her live,   120
If woords might serve, our voice hath rent the aire,
If teares, our eies have watered all the earth:
If griefe, our murthered harts have straind forth blood.
Nothing prevailes, for she is dead my Lord.
Tamburlaine.   For she is dead? thy words doo pierce my
      soule.
Ah sweet *Theridamas*, say so no more,
Though she be dead, yet let me think she lives,
And feed my mind that dies for want of her:
Where ere her soule be, thou shalt stay with me
Embalm'd with Cassia, Amber Greece and Myrre,   130
Not lapt in lead but in a sheet of gold,
And till I die thou shalt not be interr'd.
Then in as rich a tombe as *Mausolus*,
We both will rest and have one Epitaph
Writ in as many severall languages,
As I have conquered kingdomes with my sword.
This cursed towne will I consume with fire,
Because this place bereft me of my Love:
The houses burnt, wil looke as if they mourn'd,
And here will I set up her stature   140

And martch about it with my mourning campe,
Drooping and pining for *Zenocrate.*

> *The Arras is drawen.*

Enter the kings of Trebisond *and* Soria, *one bringing a sword, and* III.i
another a scepter: Next Natolia *and* Jerusalem *with the Emperiall
crowne: After* Calapine, *and after him other Lordes* [*and* Almeda]:
Orcanes *and* Jerusalem *crowne him, and the other give him the scepter.*

Orcanes. Calepinus Cyricelibes, otherwise *Cybelius,* son and
successive heire to the late mighty Emperour *Bajazeth,* by
the aid of God and his friend *Mahomet,* Emperour of *Natolia,
Jerusalem, Trebizon, Soria, Amasia, Thracia, Illyria, Carmonia*
and al the hundred and thirty Kingdomes late contributory to his
mighty father. Long live *Callepinus,* Emperour of *Turky.*
Callapine.   Thrice worthy kings of *Natolia,* and the rest,
I will requite your royall gratitudes
With all the benefits my Empire yeelds:
And were the sinowes of th'imperiall seat   10
So knit and strengthned, as when *Bajazeth*
My royall Lord and father fild the throne,
Whose cursed fate hath so dismembred it,
Then should you see this Thiefe of *Scythia,*
This proud usurping king of *Persea,*
Do us such honor and supremacie,
Bearing the vengeance of our fathers wrongs,
As all the world should blot our dignities
Out of the booke of base borne infamies.
And now I doubt not but your royall cares   20
Hath so provided for this cursed foe,
That since the heire of mighty *Bajazeth*
(An Emperour so honoured for his vertues)
Revives the spirits of true Turkish heartes,
In grievous memorie of his fathers shame,
We shall not need to nourish any doubt,
But that proud Fortune, who hath followed long
The martiall sword of mighty *Tamburlaine,*

Will now retaine her olde inconstancie,
And raise our honors to as high a pitch   30
In this our strong and fortunate encounter.
For so hath heaven provided my escape,
From al the crueltie my soule sustaind,
By this my friendly keepers happy meanes,
That *Jove* surchardg'd with pity of our wrongs,
Will poure it downe in showers on our heads:
Scourging the pride of cursed *Tamburlain*.
Orcanes.   I have a hundred thousand men in armes,
Some, that in conquest of the perjur'd Christian,
Being a handfull to a mighty hoste,   40
Thinke them in number yet sufficient,
To drinke the river *Nile* or *Euphrates*,
And for their power, ynow to win the world.
Jerusalem.   And I as many from *Jerusalem*,
Judæa, *Gaza*, and *Scalonians* bounds,
That on mount *Sinay* with their ensignes spread,
Looke like the parti-coloured cloudes of heaven,
That shew faire weather to the neighbor morne.
Trebizon.   And I as many bring from *Trebizon*,
Chio, *Famastro*, and *Amasia*,   50
All bordring on the *Mare-major* sea:
Riso, *Sancina*, and the bordering townes,
That touch the end of famous *Euphrates*.
Whose courages are kindled with the flames,
The cursed Scythian sets on all their townes,
And vow to burne the villaines cruell heart.
Soria.   From *Soria* with seventy thousand strong,
Tane from *Aleppo*, *Soldino*, *Tripoly*,
And so unto my citie of *Damasco*,
I march to meet and aide my neigbor kings,   60
All which will joine against this *Tamburlain*,
And bring him captive to your highnesse feet.
Orcanes.   Our battaile then in martiall maner pitcht,
According to our ancient use, shall beare
The figure of the semi-circled Moone:

Whose hornes shall sprinkle through the tainted aire,
The poisoned braines of this proud Scythian.
Callapine.   Wel then my noble Lords, for this my friend,
That freed me from the bondage of my foe:
I thinke it requisite and honorable,   70
To keep my promise, and to make him king,
That is a Gentleman (I know) at least.
Almeda.   That's no matter sir, for being a king, for *Tamburlain*
came up of nothing.
Jerusalem.   Your Majesty may choose some pointed time,
Perfourming all your promise to the full:
Tis nought for your majesty to give a kingdome.
Callapine.   Then wil I shortly keep my promise *Almeda.*
Almeda.   Why, I thank your Majesty.

                                             Exeunt.

[*Enter*] Tamburlaine *with* Usumcasane, *and his three sons,* [Calyphas, III.ii
   Amyras, *and* Celibinus,] *foure bearing the hearse of* Zenocrate, *and
   the drums sounding a dolefull martch, the Towne burning.*

Tamburlaine.   So, burne the turrets of this cursed towne,
Flame to the highest region of the aire:
And kindle heaps of exhalations,
That being fiery meteors, may presage,
Death and destruction to th'inhabitants.
Over my Zenith hang a blazing star,
That may endure till heaven be dissolv'd,
Fed with the fresh supply of earthly dregs,
Threatning a death and famine to this land,
Flieng Dragons, lightning, fearfull thunderclaps,   10
Sindge these fair plaines, and make them seeme as black
As is the Island where the Furies maske,
Compast with *Lethe, Styx,* and *Phlegeton,*
Because my deare *Zenocrate* is dead.
Calyphas.   This Piller plac'd in memorie of her,
Where in Arabian, Hebrew, Greek, is writ
This towne being burnt by Tamburlaine *the great,*

Forbids the world to build it up againe.
Amyras.   And here this mournful streamer shal be plac'd
Wrought with the Persean and Egyptian armes,   20
To signifie she was a princesse borne,
And wife unto the Monarke of the East.
Celibinus.   And here this table as a Register
Of all her vertues and perfections.
Tamburlaine.   And here the picture of *Zenocrate*,
To shew her beautie, which the world admyr'd,
Sweet picture of divine *Zenocrate*,
That hanging here, wil draw the Gods from heaven:
And cause the stars fixt in the Southern arke,
Whose lovely faces never any viewed,   30
That have not past the Centers latitude,
As Pilgrimes traveile to our Hemi-spheare,
Onely to gaze upon *Zenocrate.*
Thou shalt not beautifie *Larissa* plaines,
But keep within the circle of mine armes.
At every towne and castle I besiege,
Thou shalt be set upon my royall tent.
And when I meet an armie in the field,
Those looks will shed such influence in my campe,
As if *Bellona*, Goddesse of the war   40
Threw naked swords and sulphur bals of fire,
Upon the heads of all our enemies.
And now my Lords, advance your speares againe,
Sorrow no more my sweet *Casane* now:
Boyes leave to mourne, this towne shall ever mourne,
Being burnt to cynders for your mothers death.
Calyphas.   If I had wept a sea of teares for her,
It would not ease the sorrow I sustaine.
Amyras.   As is that towne, so is my heart consum'd,
With griefe and sorrow for my mothers death.   50
Celibinus.   My mothers death hath mortified my mind,
And sorrow stops the passage of my speech.
Tamburlaine.   But now my boies, leave off, and list to me,

39 Those] Dyce; Whose O1–4

That meane to teach you rudiments of war:
Ile have you learne to sleepe upon the ground,
March in your armour thorowe watery Fens,
Sustaine the scortching heat and freezing cold,
Hunger and thirst, right adjuncts of the war.
And after this, to scale a castle wal,
Besiege a fort, to undermine a towne,　　　　　　　　60
And make whole cyties caper in the aire.
Then next, the way to fortifie your men,
In champion grounds, what figure serves you best,
For which the *quinque*-angle fourme is meet:
Because the corners there may fall more flat,
Whereas the Fort may fittest be assailde,
And sharpest where th'assault is desperate.
The ditches must be deepe, the Counterscarps
Narrow and steepe, the wals made high and broad,
The Bulwarks and the rampiers large and strong,　　　70
With Cavalieros and thicke counterforts,
And roome within to lodge six thousand men.
It must have privy ditches, countermines,
And secret issuings to defend the ditch.
It must have high Argins and covered waies
To keep the bulwark fronts from battery,
And Parapets to hide the Muscatters:
Casemates to place the great Artillery,
And store of ordinance that from every flanke
May scoure the outward curtaines of the Fort,　　　80
Dismount the Cannon of the adverse part,
Murther the Foe and save the walles from breach.
When this is learn'd for service on the land,
By plaine and easie demonstration,
Ile teach you how to make the water mount,
That you may dryfoot martch through lakes and pooles,
Deep rivers, havens, creekes, and litle seas,
And make a Fortresse in the raging waves,

Fenc'd with the concave of a monstrous rocke,
Invincible by nature of the place.   90
When this is done, then are ye souldiers,
And worthy sonnes of *Tamburlain* the great.
Calyphas.   My Lord, but this is dangerous to be done,
We may be slaine or wounded ere we learne.
Tamburlaine.   Villain, art thou the sonne of *Tamburlaine*,
And fear'st to die, or with a Curtle-axe
To hew thy flesh and make a gaping wound?
Hast thou beheld a peale of ordinance strike
A ring of pikes, mingled with shot and horse,
Whose shattered lims, being tost as high as heaven,   100
Hang in the aire as thicke as sunny motes,
And canst thou Coward stand in feare of death?
Hast thou not seene my horsmen charge the foe,
Shot through the armes, cut overthwart the hands,
Dieng their lances with their streaming blood,
And yet at night carrouse within my tent,
Filling their empty vaines with aiery wine,
That being concocted, turnes to crimson blood,
And wilt thou shun the field for feare of woundes?
View me thy father that hath conquered kings,   110
And with his hoste martcht round about the earth,
Quite voide of skars, and cleare from any wound,
That by the warres lost not a dram of blood,
And see him lance his flesh to teach you all.   *He cuts his arme.*
A wound is nothing be it nere so deepe,
Blood is the God of Wars rich livery.
Now look I like a souldier, and this wound
As great a grace and majesty to me,
As if a chaire of gold enamiled,
Enchac'd with Diamondes, Saphyres, Rubies   120
And fairest pearle of welthie *India*
Were mounted here under a Canapie:
And I sat downe, cloth'd with the massie robe,
That late adorn'd the Affrike Potentate,

111 martcht] O3; march O1–2

Whom I brought bound unto *Damascus* walles.
Come boyes and with your fingers search my wound,
And in my blood wash all your hands at once,
While I sit smiling to behold the sight.
Now my boyes, what think you of a wound?
Calyphas.   I know not what I should think of it. Me thinks tis a   130
   pitifull sight.
Celibinus.   Tis nothing: give me a wound father.
Amyras.   And me another my Lord.
Tamburlaine.   Come sirra, give me your arme.
Celebinus.   Here father, cut it bravely as you did your own.
Tamburlaine.   It shall suffice thou darst abide a wound.
My boy, Thou shalt not loose a drop of blood,
Before we meet the armie of the Turke.
But then run desperate through the thickest throngs,
Dreadlesse of blowes, of bloody wounds and death: 140
And let the burning of *Larissa* wals,
My speech of war, and this my wound you see,
Teach you my boyes to beare couragious minds,
Fit for the followers of great *Tamburlaine.*
Usumcasane now come let us martch
Towards *Techelles* and *Theridamas,*
That we have sent before to fire the townes,
The towers and cities of these hatefull Turks,
And hunt that Coward, faintheart runaway,
With that accursed traitor *Almeda,*   150
Til fire and sword have found them at a bay.
Usumcasane.   I long to pierce his bowels with my sword,
That hath betraied my gracious Soveraigne,
That curst and damned Traitor *Almeda.*
Tamburlaine.   Then let us see if coward *Calapine*
Dare levie armes against our puissance,
That we may tread upon his captive necke,
And treble all his fathers slaveries.

                                                    Exeunt.

[*Enter*] Techelles, Theridamas *and their traine.* III.iii

Theridamas. Thus have wee martcht Northwarde from *Tambur-
laine,*
  Unto the frontier point of *Soria*:
  And this is *Balsera* their chiefest hold,
  Wherein is all the treasure of the land.
Techelles. Then let us bring our light Artilery,
  Minions, Fauknets, and Sakars to the trench,
  Filling the ditches with the walles wide breach,
  And enter in, to seaze upon the gold:
  How say ye Souldiers, Shal we not?
Souldiers. Yes, my Lord, yes, come lets about it. 10
Theridamas. But stay a while, summon a parle, Drum,
  It may be they will yeeld it quietly,
  Knowing two kings, the friends to *Tamburlain,*
  Stand at the walles, with such a mighty power.

                                    Summon the battell.

[*Enter above*] Captaine *with his wife* [Olympia] *and sonne.*

Captaine. What requier you my maisters?
Theridamas. Captaine, that thou yeeld up thy hold to us.
Captaine. To you? Why, do you thinke me weary of it?
Techelles. Nay Captain, thou art weary of thy life,
  If thou withstand the friends of *Tamburlain.*
Theridamas. These Pioners of *Argier* in *Affrica,* 20
  Even in the cannons face shall raise a hill
  Of earth and fagots higher than thy Fort,
  And over thy Argins and covered waies
  Shal play upon the bulwarks of thy hold
  Volleies of ordinance til the breach be made,
  That with his ruine fils up all the trench.
  And when we enter in, not heaven it selfe
  Shall ransome thee, thy wife and family.
Techelles. Captaine, these Moores shall cut the leaden pipes,
  That bring fresh water to thy men and thee: 30

13 friends] O3; friend O1–2

182

And lie in trench before thy castle walles,
That no supply of victuall shall come in,
Nor any issue foorth, but they shall die:
And therefore Captaine, yeeld it quietly.
Captaine.   Were you that are the friends of *Tamburlain*,
Brothers to holy *Mahomet* himselfe,
I would not yeeld it: therefore doo your worst.
Raise mounts, batter, intrench, and undermine,
Cut off the water, all convoies that can,
Yet I am resolute, and so farewell.   [*Exeunt.*] 40
Theridamas.   Pioners away, and where I stuck the stake,
Intrench with those dimensions I prescribed:
Cast up the earth towards the castle wall,
Which til it may defend you, labour low:
And few or none shall perish by their shot.
Pioners.   We will my Lord.   *Exeunt.*
Techelles.   A hundred horse shall scout about the plaines
To spie what force comes to relieve the holde.
Both we (*Theridamas*) wil intrench our men,
And with the Jacobs staffe measure the height   50
And distance of the castle from the trench,
That we may know if our artillery
Will carie full point blancke unto their wals.
Theridamas.   Then see the bringing of our ordinance
Along the trench into the battery,
Where we will have Gabions of sixe foot broad,
To save our Cannoniers from musket shot,
Betwixt which, shall our ordinance thunder foorth,
And with the breaches fall, smoake, fire, and dust,
The cracke, the Ecchoe and the souldiers crie   60
Make deafe the aire, and dim the Christall Sky.
Techelles.   Trumpets and drums, alarum presently,
And souldiers play the men, the hold is yours.

[*Exeunt.*]

33 any] Oxberry] *omit* O 1–4   63 hold] O 3; holds O 1–2
56 Gabions] Broughton (*qy*), Cun-
ningham; Galions O 1–4

Enter [below] the Captaine *with* [Olympia] *his wife
and sonne.*

Olympia. Come good my Lord, and let us haste from hence
Along the cave that leads beyond the foe,
No hope is left to save this conquered hold.
Captaine. A deadly bullet gliding through my side,
Lies heavy on my heart, I cannot live.
I feele my liver pierc'd and all my vaines,
That there begin and nourish every part,
Mangled and torne, and all my entrals bath'd
In blood that straineth from their orifex.
Farewell sweet wife, sweet son farewell, I die.　　　*[Dies.]* 10
Olympia. Death, whether art thou gone that both we live?
Come back again (sweet death) and strike us both:
One minute end our daies, and one sepulcher
Containe our bodies: death, why comm'st thou not?
Wel, this must be the messenger for thee.　　　*[Dagger.]*
Now ugly death stretch out thy Sable wings,
And carie both our soules, where his remaines.
Tell me sweet boie, art thou content to die?
These barbarous Scythians full of cruelty,
And Moores, in whom was never pitie found,　　　20
Will hew us peecemeale, put us to the wheele,
Or els invent some torture worse than that.
Therefore die by thy loving mothers hand,
Who gently now wil lance thy Ivory throat,
And quickly rid thee both of paine and life.
Sonne. Mother dispatch me, or Ile kil my selfe,
For think ye I can live, and see him dead?
Give me your knife (good mother) or strike home:
The Scythians shall not tyrannise on me.
Sweet mother strike, that I may meet my father.　　*She stabs him.* 30
Olympia. Ah sacred *Mahomet*, if this be sin,
Intreat a pardon of the God of heaven,
And purge my soule before it come to thee.　*[Burns the bodies.]*

Enter Theridamas, Techelles *and all their traine.*

Theridamas.   How now Madam, what are you doing?
Olympia.   Killing my selfe, as I have done my sonne,
Whose body with his fathers I have burnt,
Least cruell Scythians should dismember him.
Techelles.   Twas bravely done, and like a souldiers wife.
Thou shalt with us to *Tamburlaine* the great,
Who when he heares how resolute thou wert,   40
Wil match thee with a viceroy or a king.
Olympia.   My Lord deceast, was dearer unto me,
Than any Viceroy, King or Emperour.
And for his sake here will I end my daies.
Theridamas.   But Lady goe with us to *Tamburlaine,*
And thou shalt see a man greater than *Mahomet,*
In whose high lookes is much more majesty
Than from the Concave superficies,
Of *Joves* vast pallace the imperiall Orbe,
Unto the shining bower where *Cynthia* sits,   50
Like lovely *Thetis* in a Christall robe:
That treadeth Fortune underneath his feete,
And makes the mighty God of armes his slave:
On whom death and the fatall sisters waite,
With naked swords and scarlet liveries:
Before whom (mounted on a Lions backe)
Rhamnusia beares a helmet ful of blood,
And strowes the way with braines of slaughtered men:
By whose proud side the ugly furies run,
Harkening when he shall bid them plague the world.   60
Over whose Zenith cloth'd in windy aire,
And Eagles wings join'd to her feathered breast,
Fame hovereth, sounding of her golden Trumpe:
That to the adverse poles of that straight line,
Which measureth the glorious frame of heaven,
The name of mightie *Tamburlain* is spread:
And him faire Lady shall thy eies behold.
Come.

Olympia. Take pitie of a Ladies ruthfull teares,
That humbly craves upon her knees to stay, 70
And cast her bodie in the burning flame,
That feeds upon her sonnes and husbands flesh.
Techelles. Madam, sooner shall fire consume us both,
Then scortch a face so beautiful as this,
In frame of which, Nature hath shewed more skill,
Than when she gave eternall *Chaos* forme,
Drawing from it the shining Lamps of heaven.
Theridamas. Madam, I am so far in love with you,
That you must goe with us, no remedy.
Olympia. Then carie me I care not where you will, 80
And let the end of this my fatall journey,
Be likewise end to my accursed life.
Techelles. No Madam, but the beginning of your joy,
Come willinglie, therfore.
Theridamas. Souldiers now let us meet the Generall,
Who by this time is at *Natolia*,
Ready to charge the army of the Turke.
The gold, the silver, and the pearle ye got,
Rifling this Fort, devide in equall shares:
This Lady shall have twice so much againe, 90
Out of the coffers of our treasurie.

Exeunt.

[*Enter*] Callepine, Orcanes, Jerusalem, Trebizon, Soria, Almeda, III.v
with their traine. [*To them the* Messenger.]

Messenger. Renowmed Emperour, mighty *Callepine*,
Gods great lieftenant over all the world:
Here at *Alepo* with an hoste of men
Lies *Tamburlaine*, this king of *Persea*:
In number more than are the quyvering leaves
Of *Idas* forrest, where your highnesse hounds,
With open crie pursues the wounded Stag:
Who meanes to gyrt *Natolias* walles with siege,
Fire the towne and overrun the land.

Callapine.   My royal army is as great as his,   10
  That from the bounds of *Phrigia* to the sea
  Which washeth *Cyprus* with his brinish waves,
  Covers the hils, the valleies and the plaines.
  Viceroies and Peeres of *Turky* play the men,
  Whet all your swords to mangle *Tamburlain*,
  His sonnes, his Captaines and his followers,
  By *Mahomet* not one of them shal live.
  The field wherin this battaile shall be fought,
  For ever terme, the Perseans sepulchre,
  In memorie of this our victory.   20
Orcanes.   Now, he that cals himself the scourge of *Jove*,
  The Emperour of the world, and earthly God,
  Shal end the warlike progresse he intends,
  And traveile hedlong to the lake of hell:
  Where legions of devils (knowing he must die
  Here in *Natolia*, by your highnesse hands)
  All brandishing their brands of quenchlesse fire,
  Streching their monstrous pawes, grin with their teeth,
  And guard the gates to entertaine his soule.
Callapine.   Tell me Viceroies the number of your men,   30
  And what our Army royall is esteem'd.
Jerusalem.   From *Palestina* and *Jerusalem*,
  Of Hebrewes, three score thousand fighting men
  Are come since last we shewed your majesty.
Orcanes.   So from *Arabia* desart, and the bounds
  Of that sweet land, whose brave Metropolis
  Reedified the faire *Semyramis*,
  Came forty thousand warlike foot and horse,
  Since last we numbred to your Majesty.
Trebizon.   From *Trebizon* in *Asia* the lesse,   40
  Naturalized Turks and stout Bythinians
  Came to my bands full fifty thousand more,
  That fighting, knowes not what retreat doth meane,
  Nor ere returne but with the victory,
  Since last we numbred to your majesty.
Soria.   Of Sorians from *Halla* is repair'd

187

And neighbor cities of your highnesse land,
Ten thousand horse, and thirty thousand foot,
Since last we numbred to your majestie:
So that the Army royall is esteem'd   50
Six hundred thousand valiant fighting men.
Callapine.   Then welcome *Tamburlaine* unto thy death.
Come puissant Viceroies, let us to the field,
(The Perseans Sepulchre) and sacrifice
Mountaines of breathlesse men to *Mahomet,*
Who now with *Jove* opens the firmament,
To see the slaughter of our enemies.

   [*Enter*] Tamburlaine *with his three sonnes,* Usumcasane
                     with other.

Tamburlaine.   How now *Casane?* See a knot of kings,
Sitting as if they were a telling ridles.
Usumcasane.   My Lord, your presence makes them pale and wan. 60
Poore soules they looke as if their deaths were neere.
Tamburlaine.   Why, so he is *Casane,* I am here,
But yet Ile save their lives and make them slaves.
Ye petty kings of *Turkye* I am come,
As *Hector* did into the Grecian campe,
To overdare the pride of *Græcia,*
And set his warlike person to the view
Of fierce *Achilles,* rivall of his fame.
I doe you honor in the *simile,*
For if I should as *Hector* did *Achilles,*   70
(The worthiest knight that ever brandisht sword)
Challenge in combat any of you all,
I see how fearfully ye would refuse,
And fly my glove as from a Scorpion.
Orcanes.   Now thou art fearfull of thy armies strength,
Thou wouldst with overmatch of person fight,
But Shepheards issue, base borne *Tamburlaine,*
Thinke of thy end, this sword shall lance thy throat.
Tamburlaine.   Villain, the shepheards issue, at whose byrth
Heaven did affoord a gratious aspect,   80

And join'd those stars that shall be opposite,
Even till the dissolution of the world,
And never meant to make a Conquerour,
So famous as is mighty *Tamburlain*:
Shall so torment thee and that *Callapine*,
That like a roguish runnaway, suborn'd
That villaine there, that slave, that Turkish dog,
To false his service to his Soveraigne,
As ye shal curse the byrth of *Tamburlaine*.

Callapine.   Raile not proud Scythian, I shall now revenge   90
My fathers vile abuses and mine owne.

Jerusalem.   By *Mahomet* he shal be tied in chaines,
Rowing with Christians in a Brigandine,
About the Grecian Isles to rob and spoile:
And turne him to his ancient trade againe.
Me thinks the slave should make a lusty theefe.

Callapine.   Nay, when the battaile ends, al we wil meet,
And sit in councell to invent some paine,
That most may vex his body and his soule.

Tamburlaine.   Sirha, *Callapine*, Ile hang a clogge about your necke 100
for running away againe, you shall not trouble me thus to come
and fetch you.
But as for you (Viceroy) you shal have bits,
And harnest like my horses, draw my coch,
And when ye stay, be lasht with whips of wier:
Ile have you learne to feed on provander,
And in a stable lie upon the planks.

Orcanes.   But *Tamburlaine*, first thou shalt kneele to us
And humbly crave a pardon for thy life.

Trebizon.   The common souldiers of our mighty hoste   110
Shal bring thee bound unto the Generals tent.

Soria.   And all have jointly sworne thy cruell death,
Or bind thee in eternall torments wrath.

Tamburlaine.   Wel sirs, diet your selves, you knowe I shall have
occasion shortly to journey you.

Celebinus.   See father, how *Almeda* the Jaylor lookes upon us.

Tamburlaine.   Villaine, traitor, damned fugitive,

Ile make thee wish the earth had swallowed thee:
Seest thou not death within my wrathfull lookes?
Goe villaine, cast thee headlong from a rock,   120
Or rip thy bowels, and rend out thy heart,
T'appease my wrath, or els Ile torture thee,
Searing thy hatefull flesh with burning yrons,
And drops of scalding lead, while all thy joints
Be rackt and beat asunder with the wheele,
For if thou livest, not any Element
Shal shrowde thee from the wrath of *Tamburlaine*.
Callapine.   Wel, in despight of thee he shall be king:
Come *Almeda*, receive this crowne of me,
I here invest thee king of *Ariadan*,   130
Bordering on *Mare Roso* neere to *Meca*.
Orcanes.   What, take it man.
Almeda.   Good my Lord, let me take it.
Callapine.   Doost thou aske him leave? Here, take it.
Tamburlaine.   Go too sirha, take your crown, and make up the
halfe dozen.
So sirha, now you are a king you must give armes.
Orcanes.   So he shal, and weare thy head in his Scutchion.
Tamburlaine.   No, let him hang a bunch of keies on his standerd,
to put him in remembrance he was a Jailor, that when I take him, 140
I may knocke out his braines with them, and lock you in the stable,
when you shall come sweating from my chariot.
Trebizon.   Away, let us to the field, that the villaine may be
slaine.
Tamburlaine.   Sirha, prepare whips, and bring my chariot to my
Tent: For as soone as the battaile is done, Ile ride in triumph
through the Camp.

Enter Theridamas, Techelles, *and their traine.*

How now ye pety kings, loe, here are Bugges
Wil make the haire stand upright on your heads,
And cast your crownes in slavery at their feet.
Welcome *Theridamas* and *Techelles* both,   150
See ye this rout, and know ye this same king?

Tamburlaine.   Wel, now you see hee is a king, looke to him
Theridamas.   I, my Lord, he was *Calapines* keeper.
  Theridamas, when we are fighting, least hee hide his crowne as
  the foolish king of *Persea* did.
Soria.   No *Tamburlaine*, hee shall not be put to that exigent, I
  warrant thee.
Tamburlaine.   You knowe not sir:
  But now my followers and my loving friends,
  Fight as you ever did, like Conquerours,   160
  The glorie of this happy day is yours:
  My sterne aspect shall make faire Victory,
  Hovering betwixt our armies, light on me,
  Loden with Lawrell wreathes to crowne us all.
Techelles.   I smile to think, how when this field is fought,
  And rich *Natolia* ours, our men shall sweat
  With carrieng pearle and treasure on their backes.
Tamburlaine.   You shall be princes all immediatly:
  Come fight ye Turks, or yeeld us victory.
Orcanes.   No, we wil meet thee slavish *Tamburlain*.   170

                              Exeunt.

          Alarme: Amyras *and* Celebinus, *issues from the tent*   IV.i
                  where Caliphas *sits a sleepe.*

Amyras.   Now in their glories shine the golden crownes
  Of these proud Turks, much like so many suns
  That halfe dismay the majesty of heaven:
  Now brother, follow we our fathers sword,
  That flies with fury swifter than our thoughts,
  And cuts down armies with his conquering wings.
Celebinus.   Call foorth our laisie brother from the tent,
  For if my father misse him in the field,
  Wrath kindled in the furnace of his breast,
  Wil send a deadly lightening to his heart.   10
Amyras.   Brother, ho, what, given so much to sleep
  You cannot leave it, when our enemies drums

6 conquering] O2; conquerings O1

191

And ratling cannons thunder in our eares.
Our proper ruine, and our fathers foile?
Calyphas.   Away ye fools, my father needs not me,
Nor you in faith, but that you wil be thought
More childish valourous than manly wise:
If halfe our campe should sit and sleepe with me,
My father were enough to scar the foe:
You doo dishonor to his majesty,   20
To think our helps will doe him any good.
Amyras.   What, dar'st thou then be absent from the fight,
Knowing my father hates thy cowardise,
And oft hath warn'd thee to be stil in field,
When he himselfe amidst the thickest troopes
Beats downe our foes to flesh our taintlesse swords?
Calyphas.   I know sir, what it is to kil a man,
It works remorse of conscience in me,
I take no pleasure to be murtherous,
Nor care for blood when wine wil quench my thirst.   30
Celebinus.   O cowardly boy, fie for shame, come foorth.
Thou doost dishonor manhood, and thy house.
Calyphas.   Goe, goe tall stripling, fight you for us both,
And take my other toward brother here,
For person like to proove a second *Mars.*
Twill please my mind as wel to heare both you
Have won a heape of honor in the field,
And left your slender carkasses behind,
As if I lay with you for company.
Amyras.   You wil not goe then?   40
Calyphas.   You say true.
Amyras.   Were all the lofty mounts of *Zona mundi,*
That fill the midst of farthest *Tartary,*
Turn'd into pearle and proffered for my stay,
I would not bide the furie of my father:
When made a victor in these hautie arms,
He comes and findes his sonnes have had no shares
In all the honors he proposde for us.
Calyphas.   Take you the honor, I will take my ease,

My wisedome shall excuse my cowardise: 50
I goe into the field before I need?

                             Alarme, and Amyras *and* Celebinus *run in.*

The bullets fly at random where they list.
And should I goe and kill a thousand men,
I were as soone rewarded with a shot,
And sooner far than he that never fights.
And should I goe and do nor harme nor good,
I might have harme, which all the good I have
Join'd with my fathers crowne would never cure.
Ile to cardes: *Perdicas.*

                [*Enter* Perdicas.]

Perdicas.   Here my Lord.   60
Calyphas.   Come, thou and I wil goe to cardes to drive away the
time.
Perdicas.   Content my Lord, but what shal we play for?
Calyphas.   Who shal kisse the fairest of the Turkes Concubines
first, when my father hath conquered them.
Perdicas.   Agreed yfaith.   *They play.*
Calyphas.   They say I am a coward, (*Perdicas*) and I feare as litle
their *tara, tantaras,* their swordes or their cannons, as I doe a
naked Lady in a net of golde, and for feare I should be affraid,
would put it off and come to bed with me.   70
Perdicas.   Such a feare (my Lord) would never make yee retire.
Calyphas.   I would my father would let me be put in the front of
such a battaile once, to trie my valour.   *Alarme.*
What a coyle they keepe, I beleeve there will be some hurt done
anon amongst them.   [*They go in the tent.*]

Enter [*with Souldiers*] Tamburlain, Theridamas, Techelles,
   Usumcasane, Amyras, Celebinus, *leading the Turkish kings.*

Tamburlaine.   See now ye slaves, my children stoops your pride
And leads your glories sheep-like to the sword.
Bring them my boyes, and tel me if the warres
Be not a life that may illustrate Gods,
And tickle not your Spirits with desire   80

Stil to be train'd in armes and chivalry?
Amyras. Shal we let goe these kings again my Lord
To gather greater numbers gainst our power,
That they may say, it is not chance doth this,
But matchlesse strength and magnanimity?
Tamburlaine. No, no *Amyras*, tempt not Fortune so,
Cherish thy valour stil with fresh supplies:
And glut it not with stale and daunted foes.
But wher's this coward, villaine, not my sonne,
But traitor to my name and majesty.   90

                    He goes in and brings him out.

Image of sloth, and picture of a slave,
The obloquie and skorne of my renowne,
How may my hart, thus fired with mine eies,
Wounded with shame, and kill'd with discontent,
Shrowd any thought may holde my striving hands
From martiall justice on thy wretched soule.
Theridamas. Yet pardon him I pray your Majesty.
Techelles and Usumcasane. Let al of us intreat your highnesse pardon.
Tamburlaine. Stand up, ye base unworthy souldiers,
Know ye not yet the argument of Armes?   100
Amyras. Good my Lord, let him be forgiven for once,
And we wil force him to the field hereafter.
Tamburlaine. Stand up my boyes, and I wil teach ye arms,
And what the jealousie of warres must doe.
O *Samarcanda*, where I breathed first,
And joy'd the fire of this martiall flesh,
Blush, blush faire citie, at thine honors foile,
And shame of nature which *Jaertis* streame,
Embracing thee with deepest of his love,
Can never wash from thy distained browes.   110
Here *Jove*, receive his fainting soule againe,
A Forme not meet to give that subject essence,
Whose matter is the flesh of *Tamburlain*,
Wherein an incorporeall spirit mooves,

---

*89 coward, villaine,] *stet* O 1–4   *108 *Jaertis*] *stet* O 1–4
108 which] Oxberry; with O 1–4

Made of the mould whereof thy selfe consists,
Which makes me valiant, proud, ambitious,
Ready to levie power against thy throne,
That I might moove the turning Spheares of heaven,
For earth and al this aery region
Cannot containe the state of *Tamburlaine.*   [*Stabs* Calyphas.] 120
By *Mahomet*, thy mighty friend I sweare,
In sending to my issue such a soule,
Created of the massy dregges of earth,
The scum and tartar of the Elements,
Wherein was neither corrage, strength or wit,
But follie, sloth, and damned idlenesse:
Thou hast procur'd a greater enemie,
Than he that darted mountaines at thy head,
Shaking the burthen mighty *Atlas* beares:
Whereat thou trembling hid'st thee in the aire,   130
Cloth'd with a pitchy cloud for being seene.
And now ye cankred curres of *Asia*,
That will not see the strength of *Tamburlaine*,
Although it shine as brightly as the Sun.
Now you shal feele the strength of *Tamburlain*,
And by the state of his supremacie,
Approove the difference twixt himself and you.
Orcanes.   Thou shewest the difference twixt our selves and thee
In this thy barbarous damned tyranny.
Jerusalem.   Thy victories are growne so violent,   140
That shortly heaven, fild with the meteors
Of blood and fire thy tyrannies have made,
Will poure down blood and fire on thy head:
Whose scalding drops wil pierce thy seething braines,
And with our bloods, revenge our bloods on thee.
Tamburlaine.   Villaines, these terrours and these tyrannies
(If tyrannies wars justice ye repute)
I execute, enjoin'd me from above,
To scourge the pride of such as heaven abhors:
Nor am I made Arch-monark of the world,   150
Crown'd and invested by the hand of *Jove*,

For deeds of bounty or nobility:
But since I exercise a greater name,
The Scourge of God and terrour of the world,
I must apply my selfe to fit those tearmes,
In war, in blood, in death, in crueltie,
And plague such Pesants as resist in me
The power of heavens eternall majesty.
Theridamas, Techelles, and *Casane,*
Ransacke the tents and the pavilions   160
Of these proud Turks, and take their Concubines,
Making them burie this effeminate brat,
For not a common Souldier shall defile
His manly fingers with so faint a boy.
Then bring those Turkish harlots to my tent,
And Ile dispose them as it likes me best,
Meane while take him in.
Souldiers.   We will my Lord.
                    [*Exeunt with the body of* Calyphas.]
Jerusalem.   O damned monster, nay a Feend of Hell,
    Whose cruelties are not so harsh as thine,
    Nor yet imposd, with such a bitter hate.   170
Orcanes.   Revenge it *Radamanth* and *Eacus,*
    And let your hates extended in his paines,
    Expell the hate wherewith he paines our soules.
Trebizon.   May never day give vertue to his eies,
    Whose sight composde of furie and of fire
    Doth send such sterne affections to his heart.
Soria.   May never spirit, vaine or Artier feed
    The cursed substance of that cruel heart,
    But (wanting moisture and remorsefull blood)
    Drie up with anger, and consume with heat.   180
Tamburlaine.   Wel, bark ye dogs. Ile bridle al your tongues
    And bind them close with bits of burnisht steele,
    Downe to the channels of your hatefull throats,
    And with the paines my rigour shall inflict,
    Ile make ye roare, that earth may eccho foorth

157 resist in] Broughton (*qy*), Dyce; resisting O 1–4

The far resounding torments ye sustaine,
As when an heard of lusty Cymbrian Buls,
Run mourning round about the Femals misse,
And stung with furie of their following,
Fill all the aire with troublous bellowing: 190
I will with Engines, never exercisde,
Conquer, sacke, and utterly consume
Your cities and your golden pallaces,
And with the flames that beat against the clowdes
Incense the heavens, and make the starres to melt,
As if they were the teares of *Mahomet*
For hot consumption of his countries pride:
And til by vision, or by speach I heare
Immortall *Jove* say, Cease my *Tamburlaine,*
I will persist a terrour to the world,   200
Making the Meteors, that like armed men
Are seene to march upon the towers of heaven,
Run tilting round about the firmament,
And breake their burning Lances in the aire,
For honor of my woondrous victories.
Come bring them in to our Pavilion.

Exeunt.

[*Enter*] Olympia *alone.*   IV.ii

Olympia.   Distrest *Olympia,* whose weeping eies
Since thy arrivall here beheld no Sun,
But closde within the compasse of a tent,
Hath stain'd thy cheekes, and made thee look like death,
Devise some meanes to rid thee of thy life,
Rather than yeeld to his detested suit,
Whose drift is onely to dishonor thee.
And since this earth, dew'd with thy brinish teares,
Affoords no hearbs, whose taste may poison thee,
Nor yet this aier, beat often with thy sighes,   10
Contagious smels, and vapors to infect thee,
Nor thy close Cave a sword to murther thee,
Let this invention be the instrument.

Enter Theridamas.

Theridamas.   Wel met *Olympia*, I sought thee in my tent,
  But when I saw the place obscure and darke,
  Which with thy beauty thou wast woont to light,
  Enrag'd I ran about the fields for thee,
  Supposing amorous *Jove* had sent his sonne,
  The winged *Hermes*, to convay thee hence:
  But now I finde thee, and that feare is past.   20
  Tell me *Olympia*, wilt thou graunt my suit?
Olympia.   My Lord and husbandes death, with my sweete sons,
  With whom I buried al affections,
  Save griefe and sorrow which torment my heart,
  Forbids my mind to entertaine a thought
  That tends to love, but meditate on death,
  A fitter subject for a pensive soule.
Theridamas.   *Olympia*, pitie him, in whom thy looks
  Have greater operation and more force
  Than *Cynthias* in the watery wildernes,   30
  For with thy view my joyes are at the full,
  And eb againe, as thou departst from me.
Olympia.   Ah, pity me my Lord, and draw your sword,
  Making a passage for my troubled soule,
  Which beates against this prison to get out,
  And meet my husband and my loving sonne.
Theridamas.   Nothing, but stil thy husband and thy sonne?
  Leave this my Love, and listen more to me.
  Thou shalt be stately Queene of faire *Argier*,
  And cloth'd in costly cloath of massy gold,   40
  Upon the marble turrets of my Court
  Sit like to *Venus* in her chaire of state,
  Commanding all thy princely eie desires,
  And I will cast off armes and sit with thee,
  Spending my life in sweet discourse of love.
Olympia.   No such discourse is pleasant in mine eares,
  But that where every period ends with death,
  And every line begins with death againe:

I cannot love to be an Emperesse.

Theridamas.   Nay Lady, then if nothing wil prevaile,   50
Ile use some other means to make you yeeld,
Such is the sodaine fury of my love,
I must and wil be pleasde, and you shall yeeld:
Come to the tent againe.

Olympia.   Stay good my Lord, and wil you save my honor,
Ile give your Grace a present of such price,
As all the world cannot affoord the like.

Theridamas.   What is it?

Olympia.   An ointment which a cunning Alcumist
Distilled from the purest Balsamum,   60
And simplest extracts of all Minerals,
In which the essentiall fourme of Marble stone,
Tempered by science metaphisicall,
And Spels of magicke from the mouthes of spirits,
With which if you but noint your tender Skin,
Nor Pistol, Sword, nor Lance can pierce your flesh.

Theridamas.   Why Madam, thinke ye to mocke me thus palpably?

Olympia.   To proove it, I wil noint my naked throat,
Which when you stab, looke on your weapons point,
And you shall se't rebated with the blow.   70

Theridamas.   Why gave you not your husband some of it,
If you loved him, and it so precious?

Olympia.   My purpose was (my Lord) to spend it so,
But was prevented by his sodaine end.
And for a present easie proofe hereof,
That I dissemble not, trie it on me.

Theridamas.   I wil *Olympia*, and will keep it for
The richest present of this Easterne world.

She noints her throat.

Olympia.   Now stab my Lord, and mark your weapons point
That wil be blunted if the blow be great.   80

Theridamas.   Here then *Olympia.*   [*Stabs her.*]
What, have I slaine her? Villaine, stab thy selfe:
Cut off this arme that murthered my Love:
In whom the learned Rabies of this age,

Might find as many woondrous myracles,
As in the Theoria of the world.
Now Hell is fairer than *Elisian*,
A greater Lamp than that bright eie of heaven,
From whence the starres doo borrow all their light,
Wanders about the black circumference, 90
And now the damned soules are free from paine,
For every Fury gazeth on her lookes:
Infernall *Dis* is courting of my Love,
Inventing maskes and stately showes for her,
Opening the doores of his rich treasurie,
To entertaine this Queene of chastitie,
Whose body shall be tomb'd with all the pompe
The treasure of my kingdome may affoord.

Exit, taking her away.

[*Enter*] Tamburlaine *drawn in his chariot by* Trebizon *and* Soria   IV.iii
with bittes in their mouthes, reines in his left hand, in his right hand a
whip, with which he scourgeth them, Techelles, Theridamas, Usumcasane, Amyras, Celebinus: [Orcanes *king of*] Natolia, *and*
Jerusalem *led by with five or six common souldiers.*

Tamburlaine.   Holla, ye pampered Jades of *Asia*:
What, can ye draw but twenty miles a day,
And have so proud a chariot at your heeles,
And such a Coachman as great *Tamburlaine?*
But from *Asphaltis*, where I conquer'd you,
To *Byron* here where thus I honor you?
The horse that guide the golden eie of heaven,
And blow the morning from their nosterils,
Making their fiery gate above the cloudes,
Are not so honoured in their Governour, 10
As you (ye slaves) in mighty *Tamburlain*.
The headstrong Jades of *Thrace, Alcides* tam'd,
That King *Egeus* fed with humaine flesh,
And made so wanton that they knew their strengths,
Were not subdew'd with valour more divine,

Than you by this unconquered arme of mine.
To make you fierce, and fit my appetite,
You shal be fed with flesh as raw as blood,
And drinke in pailes the strongest Muscadell:
If you can live with it, then live, and draw   20
My chariot swifter than the racking cloudes:
If not, then dy like beasts, and fit for nought
But perches for the black and fatall Ravens.
Thus am I right the Scourge of highest *Jove*,
And see the figure of my dignitie,
By which I hold my name and majesty.

Amyras.   Let me have coach my Lord, that I may ride,
And thus be drawen with these two idle kings.

Tamburlaine.   Thy youth forbids such ease my kingly boy,
They shall to morrow draw my chariot,   30
While these their fellow kings may be refresht.

Orcanes.   O thou that swaiest the region under earth,
And art a king as absolute as *Jove*,
Come as thou didst in fruitfull *Scicilie*,
Survaieng all the glories of the land:
And as thou took'st the faire *Proserpina*,
Joying the fruit of *Ceres* garden plot,
For love, for honor, and to make her Queene,
So for just hate, for shame, and to subdew
This proud contemner of thy dreadfull power,   40
Come once in furie and survay his pride,
Haling him headlong to the lowest hell.

Theridamas.   Your Majesty must get some byts for these,
To bridle their contemptuous cursing tongues,
That like unruly never broken Jades,
Breake through the hedges of their hateful mouthes,
And passe their fixed boundes exceedingly.

Techelles.   Nay, we wil break the hedges of their mouths
And pul their kicking colts out of their pastures.

Usumcasane.   Your Majesty already hath devisde   50
A meane, as fit as may be to restraine
These coltish coach-horse tongues from blasphemy.

Celebinus.   How like you that sir king? why speak you not?
Jerusalem.   Ah cruel Brat, sprung from a tyrants loines,
  How like his cursed father he begins,
  To practize tauntes and bitter tyrannies?
Tamburlaine.   I Turke, I tel thee, this same Boy is he,
  That must (advaunst in higher pompe than this)
  Rifle the kingdomes I shall leave unsackt,
  If *Jove* esteeming me too good for earth,   60
  Raise me to match the faire *Aldeboran*,
  Above the threefold Astracisme of heaven,
  Before I conquere all the triple world.
  Now fetch me out the Turkish Concubines,
  I will prefer them for the funerall
  They have bestowed on my abortive sonne.

                        The Concubines are brought in.

  Where are my common souldiers now that fought
  So Lion-like upon *Asphaltis* plaines?
Souldiers.   Here my Lord.
Tamburlaine.   Hold ye tal souldiers, take ye Queens apeece   70
  (I meane such Queens as were kings Concubines)
  Take them, devide them and their jewels too,
  And let them equally serve all your turnes.
Souldiers.   We thank your majesty.
Tamburlaine.   Brawle not (I warne you) for your lechery,
  For every man that so offends shall die.
Orcanes.   Injurious tyrant, wilt thou so defame
  The hatefull fortunes of thy victory,
  To exercise upon such guiltlesse Dames,
  The violence of thy common Souldiours lust?   80
Tamburlaine.   Live continent then (ye slaves) and meet not me
  With troopes of harlots at your sloothful heeles.
Ladies.   O pity us my Lord, and save our honours.
Tamburlaine.   Are ye not gone ye villaines with your spoiles?

                        They run away with the Ladies.

Jerusalem.   O mercilesse infernall cruelty.
Tamburlaine.   Save your honours? twere but time indeed,

81 continent] Oxberry; content O 1–4

Lost long before you knew what honour meant.
Theridamas.　It seemes they meant to conquer us my Lord,
And make us jeasting Pageants for their Trulles.
Tamburlaine.　And now themselves shal make our Pageant,　　90
And common souldiers jest with all their Truls.
Let them take pleasure soundly in their spoiles,
Till we prepare our martch to *Babylon*,
Whether we next make expedition.
Techelles.　Let us not be idle then my Lord,
But presently be prest to conquer it.
Tamburlaine.　We wil *Techelles*, forward then ye Jades:
Now crowch ye kings of greatest *Asia*,
And tremble when ye heare this Scourge wil come,
That whips downe cities, and controwleth crownes,　　100
Adding their wealth and treasure to my store.
The Euxine sea North to *Natolia*,
The Terrene west, the Caspian north north-east,
And on the south *Senus Arabicus*,
Shal al be loden with the martiall spoiles
We will convay with us to *Persea*.
Then shal my native city *Samarcanda*
And christall waves of fresh *Jaertis* streame,
The pride and beautie of her princely seat,
Be famous through the furthest continents,　　110
For there my Pallace royal shal be plac'd:
Whose shyning Turrets shal dismay the heavens,
And cast the fame of *Ilions* Tower to hell.
Thorow the streets with troops of conquered kings,
Ile ride in golden armour like the Sun,
And in my helme a triple plume shal spring,
Spangled with Diamonds dancing in the aire,
To note me Emperour of the three fold world:
Like to an almond tree ymounted high,
Upon the lofty and celestiall mount,　　120
Of ever greene *Selinus* queintly dect
With bloomes more white than *Hericinas* browes,

121 ever] Robinson; every O 1–4

Whose tender blossoms tremble every one,
At every little breath that thorow heaven is blowen:
Then in my coach like *Saturnes* royal son,
Mounted his shining chariot, gilt with fire,
And drawen with princely Eagles through the path,
Pav'd with bright Christall, and enchac'd with starres,
When all the Gods stand gazing at his pomp:
So will I ride through *Samarcanda* streets,   130
Until my soule dissevered from this flesh,
Shall mount the milk-white way and meet him there.
To *Babylon* my Lords, to *Babylon*.

Exeunt.

Enter the Governour *of* Babylon *upon the walles with*   V.i
[Maximus *and*] *others*.

Governour.   What saith *Maximus*?
Maximus.   My Lord, the breach the enimie hath made
  Gives such assurance of our overthrow,
  That litle hope is left to save our lives,
  Or hold our citie from the Conquerours hands.
  Then hang out flagges (my Lord) of humble truce,
  And satisfie the peoples generall praiers,
  That *Tamburlains* intollorable wrath
  May be suppresst by our submission.
Governour.   Villaine, respects thou more thy slavish life,   10
  Than honor of thy countrie or thy name?
  Is not my life and state as deere to me,
  The citie and my native countries weale,
  As any thing of price with thy conceit?
  Have we not hope, for all our battered walles,
  To live secure, and keep his forces out,
  When this our famous lake of *Limnasphaltis*
  Makes walles a fresh with every thing that falles
  Into the liquid substance of his streame,
  More strong than are the gates of death or hel?   20

126 chariot] Dyce; chariots O1–4

What faintnesse should dismay our courages,
When we are thus defenc'd against our Foe,
And have no terrour but his threatning lookes?

    Enter another [1. Citizen], *kneeling to the* Governour.

1. Citizen.　My Lord, if ever you did deed of ruth,
And now will work a refuge to our lives,
Offer submission, hang up flags of truce,
That *Tamburlaine* may pitie our distresse,
And use us like a loving Conquerour.
Though this be held his last daies dreadfull siege,
Wherein he spareth neither man nor child,　　　　　　30
Yet are there Christians of *Georgia* here,
Whose state he ever pitied and reliev'd,
Wil get his pardon if your grace would send.
Governour.　How is my soule environed,
And this eternisde citie *Babylon*,
Fill'd with a packe of faintheart Fugitives,
That thus intreat their shame and servitude?

    [*Enter* 2. Citizen.]

2. Citizen.　My Lord, if ever you wil win our hearts,
Yeeld up the towne, save our wives and children:
For I wil cast my selfe from off these walles,　　　　　　40
Or die some death of quickest violence,
Before I bide the wrath of *Tamburlaine*.
Governour.　Villaines, cowards, Traitors to our state,
Fall to the earth, and pierce the pit of Hel,
That legions of tormenting spirits may vex
Your slavish bosomes with continuall paines,
I care not, nor the towne will never yeeld
As long as any life is in my breast.

    Enter Theridamas *and* Techelles, *with other souldiers.*

Theridamas.　Thou desperate Governour of *Babylon*,
To save thy life, and us a litle labour,　　　　　　50
Yeeld speedily the citie to our hands,

Or els be sure thou shalt be forc'd with paines,
More exquisite than ever Traitor felt.

Governour. Tyrant, I turne the traitor in thy throat,
And wil defend it in despight of thee.
Call up the souldiers to defend these wals.

Techelles. Yeeld foolish Governour, we offer more
Than ever yet we did to such proud slaves,
As durst resist us till our third daies siege:
Thou seest us prest to give the last assault,   60
And that shal bide no more regard of parlie.

Governour. Assault and spare not, we wil never yeeld.

> *Alarme, and they scale the walles.*

Enter Tamburlaine, [*drawn in his chariot by the kings of* Trebizon
and Soria,] *with* Usumcasane, Amyras, *and* Celebinus, *with others,*
the two spare kings [Orcanes, *King of* Natolia, *and King of* Jerusalem,
led by souldiers].

Tamburlaine. The stately buildings of faire *Babylon*,
Whose lofty Pillers, higher than the cloudes,
Were woont to guide the seaman in the deepe,
Being caried thither by the cannons force,
Now fil the mouth of *Limnasphaltes* lake,
And make a bridge unto the battered walles.
Where *Belus*, *Ninus* and great *Alexander*
Have rode in triumph, triumphs *Tamburlaine*,   70
Whose chariot wheeles have burst th'Assirians bones,
Drawen with these kings on heaps of carkasses.
Now in the place where faire *Semiramis*,
Courted by kings and peeres of *Asia*,
Hath trode the Meisures, do my souldiers martch,
And in the streets, where brave Assirian Dames
Have rid in pompe like rich *Saturnia*,
With furious words and frowning visages,
My horsmen brandish their unruly blades.

Enter [below] Theridamas *and* Techelles *bringing the* Governor *of*
Babylon.

Who have ye there my Lordes?   80
Theridamas.   The sturdy Governour of *Babylon*,
  That made us all the labour for the towne,
  And usde such slender reckning of your majesty.
Tamburlaine.   Go bind the villaine, he shall hang in chaines,
  Upon the ruines of this conquered towne.
  Sirha, the view of our vermillion tents,
  Which threatned more than if the region
  Next underneath the Element of fire,
  Were full of Commets and of blazing stars,
  Whose flaming traines should reach down to the earth   90
  Could not affright you, no, nor I my selfe,
  The wrathfull messenger of mighty *Jove*,
  That with his sword hath quail'd all earthly kings,
  Could not perswade you to submission,
  But stil the ports were shut: villaine I say,
  Should I but touch the rusty gates of hell,
  The triple headed *Cerberus* would howle,
  And wake blacke *Jove* to crouch and kneele to me,
  But I have sent volleies of shot to you,
  Yet could not enter till the breach was made.   100
Governour.   Nor if my body could have stopt the breach,
  Shouldst thou have entred, cruel *Tamburlaine*:
  Tis not thy bloody tents can make me yeeld,
  Nor yet thy selfe, the anger of the highest,
  For though thy cannon shooke the citie walles,
  My heart did never quake, or corrage faint.
Tamburlaine.   Wel, now Ile make it quake, go draw him up,
  Hang him up in chaines upon the citie walles,
  And let my souldiers shoot the slave to death.
Governour.   Vile monster, borne of some infernal hag,   110
  And sent from hell to tyrannise on earth,
  Do all thy wurst, nor death, nor *Tamburlaine*,

83 your] O2; you O1

207

Torture or paine can daunt my dreadlesse minde.
Tamburlaine. Up with him then, his body shalbe scard.
Governour. But *Tamburlain*, in *Lymnasphaltis* lake,
There lies more gold than *Babylon* is worth,
Which when the citie was besieg'd I hid,
Save but my life and I wil give it thee.
Tamburlaine. Then for all your valour, you would save your life.
Where about lies it? 120
Governour. Under a hollow bank, right opposite
Against the Westerne gate of *Babylon*.
Tamburlaine. Go thither some of you and take his gold,
The rest forward with execution,
Away with him hence, let him speake no more:
I think I make your courage something quaile.
 [*Exeunt souldiers several ways, some with* Governour.]
When this is done, we'll martch from *Babylon*,
And make our greatest haste to *Persea*:
These Jades are broken winded, and halfe tyr'd,
Unharnesse them, and let me have fresh horse: 130
So, now their best is done to honour me,
Take them, and hang them both up presently.
Trebizon. Vild Tyrant, barbarous bloody *Tamburlain*.
Tamburlaine. Take them away *Theridamas*, see them dispatcht.
Theridamas. I will my Lord.
 [*Exit with the Kings of* Trebizon *and* Soria.]
Tamburlaine. Come Asian Viceroies, to your taskes a while
And take such fortune as your fellowes felt.
Orcanes. First let thy Scythyan horse teare both our limmes
Rather then we should draw thy chariot,
And like base slaves abject our princely mindes 140
To vile and ignominious servitude.
Jerusalem. Rather lend me thy weapon *Tamburlain*,
That I may sheath it in this breast of mine,
A thousand deathes could not torment our hearts
More than the thought of this dooth vexe our soules.
Amyras. They will talk still my Lord, if you doe not bridle
them.

Tamburlaine.   Bridle them, and let me to my coach.

                           They bridle them.

[*Souldiers hang the* Governour *of* Babylon *in chaines on the walles.*
              Enter Theridamas *below.*]

Amyras.   See now my Lord how brave the Captaine hangs.
Tamburlaine.   Tis brave indeed my boy, wel done,
  Shoot first my Lord, and then the rest shall follow.   150
Theridamas.   Then have at him to begin withall.

                     Theridamas *shootes.*

Governour.   Yet save my life, and let this wound appease
  The mortall furie of great *Tamburlain.*
Tamburlaine.   No, though *Asphaltis* lake were liquid gold,
  And offer'd me as ransome for thy life,
  Yet shouldst thou die, shoot at him all at once.   *They shoote.*
  So now he hangs like *Bagdets* Governour,
  Having as many bullets in his flesh,
  As there be breaches in her battered wall.
  Goe now and bind the Burghers hand and foot,   160
  And cast them headlong in the cities lake:
  Tartars and Perseans shall inhabit there,
  And to command the citie, I will build
  A Cytadell, that all *Assiria*
  Which hath bene subject to the Persean king,
  Shall pay me tribute for, in *Babylon.*
Techelles,   What shal be done with their wives and children my
  Lord.
Tamburlaine.   *Techelles,* Drowne them all, man, woman, and child,
  Leave not a Babylonian in the towne.   170
Techelles.   I will about it straight, come Souldiers.   *Exit.*
Tamburlaine.   Now *Casane,* wher's the Turkish *Alcaron,*
  And all the heapes of supersticious bookes,
  Found in the Temples of that *Mahomet,*
  Whom I have thought a God? they shal be burnt.
Usumcasane.   Here they are my Lord.
Tamburlaine.   Wel said, let there be a fire presently.
  In vaine I see men worship *Mahomet,*

My sword hath sent millions of Turks to hell,
Slew all his Priests, his kinsmen, and his friends, 180
And yet I live untoucht by *Mahomet*:
There is a God full of revenging wrath,
From whom the thunder and the lightning breaks,
Whose Scourge I am, and him will I obey.
So *Casane*, fling them in the fire.
Now *Mahomet*, if thou have any power,
Come downe thy selfe and worke a myracle,
Thou art not woorthy to be worshipped,
That suffers flames of fire to burne the writ
Wherein the sum of thy religion rests. 190
Why send'st thou not a furious whyrlwind downe,
To blow thy *Alcaron* up to thy throne,
Where men report, thou sitt'st by God himselfe,
Or vengeance on the head of *Tamburlain*,
That shakes his sword against thy majesty,
And spurns the Abstracts of thy foolish lawes.
Wel souldiers, *Mahomet* remaines in hell,
He cannot heare the voice of *Tamburlain*,
Seeke out another Godhead to adore,
The God that sits in heaven, if any God, 200
For he is God alone, and none but he.

[*Enter* Techelles.]

Techelles.   I have fulfil'd your highnes wil, my Lord,
Thousands of men drown'd in *Asphaltis* Lake,
Have made the water swell above the bankes,
And fishes fed by humaine carkasses,
Amasde, swim up and downe upon the waves,
As when they swallow *Assafitida*,
Which makes them fleet aloft and gaspe for aire.
Tamburlaine.   Wel then my friendly Lordes, what now remaines
But that we leave sufficient garrison 210
And presently depart to *Persea*,
To triumph after all our victories.

205 fed] Oxberry; feed O 1–4

Theridamas.   I, good my Lord, let us in hast to *Persea*,
And let this Captaine be remoov'd the walles,
To some high hill about the citie here.
Tamburlaine.   Let it be so, about it souldiers:
But stay, I feele my selfe distempered sudainly.
Techelles.   What is it dares distemper *Tamburlain?*
Tamburlaine.   Something *Techelles*, but I know not what,
But foorth ye vassals, what so ere it be,   220
Sicknes or death can never conquer me.

                                      Exeunt.

     Enter Callapine, Amasia, [Captaine, *Souldiers*,] *with drums*   V.ii
                  and trumpets.

Callapine.   King of *Amasia*, now our mighty hoste,
Marcheth in *Asia major*, where the streames,
Of *Euphrates* and *Tigris* swiftly runs,
And here may we behold great *Babylon*,
Circled about with *Limnasphaltis* Lake,
Where *Tamburlaine* with all his armie lies,
Which being faint and weary with the siege,
Wee may lie ready to encounter him,
Before his hoste be full from *Babylon*,
And so revenge our latest grievous losse,   10
If God or *Mahomet* send any aide.
Amasia.   Doubt not my lord, but we shal conquer him.
The Monster that hath drunke a sea of blood,
And yet gapes stil for more to quench his thirst,
Our Turkish swords shal headlong send to hell,
And that vile Carkasse drawne by warlike kings,
The Foules shall eate, for never sepulchre
Shall grace that base-borne Tyrant *Tamburlaine*.
Callapine.   When I record my Parents slavish life,
Their cruel death, mine owne captivity,   20
My Viceroies bondage under *Tamburlaine*,
Me thinks I could sustaine a thousand deaths,

*215 about] *stet* O 1–4

To be reveng'd of all his Villanie.
Ah sacred *Mahomet*, thou that hast seene
Millions of Turkes perish by *Tamburlaine*,
Kingdomes made waste, brave cities sackt and burnt,
And but one hoste is left to honor thee:
Aid thy obedient servant *Callapine*,
And make him after all these overthrowes,
To triumph over cursed *Tamburlaine*. 30
Amasia. Feare not my Lord, I see great *Mahomet*
Clothed in purple clowdes, and on his head
A Chaplet brighter than *Apollos* crowne,
Marching about the ayer with armed men,
To joine with you against this *Tamburlaine*.
Renowmed Generall mighty *Callapine*,
Though God himselfe and holy *Mahomet*,
Should come in person to resist your power,
Yet might your mighty hoste incounter all,
And pull proud *Tamburlaine* upon his knees, 40
To sue for mercie at your highnesse feete.
Callapine. Captaine, the force of *Tamburlaine* is great,
His fortune greater, and the victories
Wherewith he hath so sore dismaide the world,
Are greatest to discourage all our drifts,
Yet when the pride of *Cynthia* is at full,
She waines againe, and so shall his I hope,
For we have here the chiefe selected men
Of twenty severall kingdomes at the least:
Nor plowman, Priest, nor Merchant staies at home, 50
All *Turkie* is in armes with *Callapine*.
And never wil we sunder camps and armes,
Before himselfe or his be conquered.
This is the time that must eternize me,
For conquering the Tyrant of the world.
Come Souldiers, let us lie in wait for him
And if we find him absent from his campe,
Or that it be rejoin'd again at full,
Assaile it and be sure of victorie.
　　　　　　　　　　　　　　　　　Exeunt.

[*Enter*] Theridamas, Techelles, Usumcasane.   V.iii

Theridamas.   Weepe heavens, and vanish into liquid teares,
  Fal starres that governe his nativity,
  And sommon al the shining lamps of heaven
  To cast their bootlesse fires to the earth,
  And shed their feble influence in the aire.
  Muffle your beauties with eternall clowdes,
  For hell and darknesse pitch their pitchy tentes,
  And Death with armies of Cymerian spirits
  Gives battile gainst the heart of *Tamburlaine.*
  Now in defiance of that woonted love,   10
  Your sacred vertues pour'd upon his throne,
  And made his state an honor to the heavens,
  These cowards invisiblie assaile hys soule,
  And threaten conquest on our Soveraigne:
  But if he die, your glories are disgrac'd,
  Earth droopes and saies, that hell in heaven is plac'd.
Techelles.   O then ye Powers that sway eternal seates,
  And guide this massy substance of the earthe,
  If you retaine desert of holinesse,
  As your supreame estates instruct our thoughtes,   20
  Be not inconstant, carelesse of your fame,
  Beare not the burthen of your enemies joyes,
  Triumphing in his fall whom you advaunst,
  But as his birth, life, health and majesty
  Were strangely blest and governed by heaven,
  So honour heaven til heaven dissolved be,
  His byrth, his life, his health and majesty.
Usumcasane.   Blush heaven to loose the honor of thy name,
  To see thy foot-stoole set upon thy head,
  And let no basenesse in thy haughty breast,   30
  Sustaine a shame of such inexcellence:
  To see the devils mount in Angels throanes,
  And Angels dive into the pooles of hell.
  And though they think their painfull date is out,
  And that their power is puissant as *Joves,*

Which makes them manage armes against thy state,
Yet make them feele the strength of *Tamburlain*,
Thy instrument and note of Majesty,
Is greater far, than they can thus subdue.
For if he die, thy glorie is disgrac'd, 40
Earth droopes and saies that hel in heaven is plac'd.

[*Enter* Tamburlaine, *drawn by the captive kings;* Amyras,
Celebinus, Physitians.]

Tamburlaine. What daring God torments my body thus,
And seeks to conquer mighty *Tamburlaine*,
Shall sicknesse proove me now to be a man,
That have bene tearm'd the terrour of the world?
Techelles and the rest, come take your swords,
And threaten him whose hand afflicts my soul,
Come let us march against the powers of heaven,
And set blacke streamers in the firmament,
To signifie the slaughter of the Gods. 50
Ah friends, what shal I doe, I cannot stand,
Come carie me to war against the Gods,
That thus invie the health of *Tamburlaine*.
Theridamas. Ah good my Lord, leave these impatient words,
Which ad much danger to your malladie.
Tamburlaine. Why, shal I sit and languish in this paine?
No, strike the drums, and in revenge of this,
Come let us chardge our speares and pierce his breast,
Whose shoulders beare the Axis of the world,
That if I perish, heaven and earth may fade. 60
Theridamas, haste to the court of *Jove*,
Will him to send *Apollo* hether straight,
To cure me, or Ile fetch him downe my selfe.
Techelles. Sit stil my gratious Lord, this griefe wil cease,
And cannot last, it is so violent.
Tamburlaine. Not last *Techelles*, no, for I shall die.
See where my slave, the uglie monster death
Shaking and quivering, pale and wan for feare,
Stands aiming at me with his murthering dart,

Who flies away at every glance I give,　　　　　　　　　70
And when I look away, comes stealing on:
Villaine away, and hie thee to the field,
I and myne armie come to lode thy barke
With soules of thousand mangled carkasses.
Looke where he goes, but see, he comes againe
Because I stay: *Techelles* let us march,
And weary Death with bearing soules to hell.
Phisitian.　Pleaseth your Majesty to drink this potion,
　Which wil abate the furie of your fit,
And cause some milder spirits governe you.　　　　　80
Tamburlaine.　Tel me, what think you of my sicknes now?
Phisitian.　I view'd your urine, and the Hipostasis
　Thick and obscure doth make your danger great,
　Your vaines are full of accidentall heat,
　Whereby the moisture of your blood is dried,
　The *Humidum* and *Calor*, which some holde
　Is not a parcell of the Elements,
　But of a substance more divine and pure,
　Is almost cleane extinguished and spent,
　Which being the cause of life, imports your death.　　90
　Besides my Lord, this day is Criticall,
　Dangerous to those, whose Chrisis is as yours:
　Your Artiers which alongst the vaines convey
　The lively spirits which the heart ingenders
　Are partcht and void of spirit, that the soule
　Wanting those Organnons by which it mooves,
　Can not indure by argument of art.
　Yet if your majesty may escape this day,
　No doubt, but you shal soone recover all.
Tamburlaine.　Then will I comfort all my vital parts,　　100
　And live in spight of death above a day.
　　　　　　　　　　　　　　　　Alarme within.

82 Hipostasis] Robinson; Hipostates O 1–4

[*Enter a* Messenger.]

Messenger. My Lord, yong *Callapine* that lately fled from your
majesty, hath nowe gathered a fresh Armie, and hearing your
absence in the field, offers to set upon us presently.
Tamburlaine. See my Phisitions now, how *Jove* hath sent
A present medicine to recure my paine:
My looks shall make them flie, and might I follow,
There should not one of all the villaines power
Live to give offer of another fight.
Usumcasane. I joy my Lord, your highnesse is so strong, 110
That can endure so well your royall presence,
Which onely will dismay the enemy.
Tamburlaine. I know it wil *Casane*: draw you slaves,
In spight of death I will goe show my face.

Alarme, Tamburlaine *goes in, and comes out againe with al the rest.*

Thus are the villaines, cowards fled for feare,
Like Summers vapours, vanisht by the Sun.
And could I but a while pursue the field,
That *Callapine* should be my slave againe.
But I perceive my martial strength is spent,
In vaine I strive and raile against those powers, 120
That meane t'invest me in a higher throane,
As much too high for this disdainfull earth.
Give me a Map, then let me see how much
Is left for me to conquer all the world,
That these my boies may finish all my wantes.

One brings a Map.

Here I began to martch towards *Persea,*
Along *Armenia* and the Caspian sea,
And thence unto *Bythinia,* where I tooke
The Turke and his great Empresse prisoners,
Then martcht I into *Egypt* and *Arabia,* 130
And here not far from *Alexandria,*
Whereas the Terren and the red sea meet,
Being distant lesse than ful a hundred leagues,

I meant to cut a channell to them both,
That men might quickly saile to *India*.
From thence to *Nubia* neere *Borno* Lake,
And so along the Ethiopian sea,
Cutting the Tropicke line of *Capricorne*,
I conquered all as far as *Zansibar*.
Then by the Northerne part of *Affrica*,   140
I came at last to *Græcia*, and from thence
To *Asia*, where I stay against my will,
Which is from *Scythia*, where I first began,
Backeward and forwards nere five thousand leagues.
Looke here my boies, see what a world of ground,
Lies westward from the midst of *Cancers* line,
Unto the rising of this earthly globe,
Whereas the Sun declining from our sight,
Begins the day with our Antypodes:
And shall I die, and this unconquered?   150
Loe here my sonnes, are all the golden Mines,
Inestimable drugs and precious stones,
More worth than *Asia*, and the world beside,
And from th'Antartique Pole, Eastward behold
As much more land, which never was descried,
Wherein are rockes of Pearle, that shine as bright
As all the Lamps that beautifie the Sky,
And shal I die, and this unconquered?
Here lovely boies, what death forbids my life,
That let your lives commaund in spight of death.   160
Amyras.   Alas my Lord, how should our bleeding harts
Wounded and broken with your Highnesse griefe,
Retaine a thought of joy, or sparke of life?
Your soul gives essence to our wretched subjects,
Whose matter is incorporat in your flesh.
Celebinus.   Your paines do pierce our soules, no hope survives,
For by your life we entertaine our lives.
Tamburlaine.   But sons, this subject not of force enough,
To hold the fiery spirit it containes,
Must part, imparting his impressions,   170

By equall portions into both your breasts:
My flesh devided in your precious shapes,
Shal still retaine my spirit, though I die,
And live in all your seedes immortally:
Then now remoove me, that I may resigne
My place and proper tytle to my sonne:
First take my Scourge and my imperiall Crowne,   [*To* Amyras.]
And mount my royall chariot of estate,
That I may see thee crown'd before I die.
Help me (my Lords) to make my last remoove.   180
Theridamas.   A woful change my Lord, that daunts our thoughts,
More than the ruine of our proper soules.
Tamburlaine.   Sit up my sonne, let me see how well
Thou wilt become thy fathers majestie.

                                        They crowne him.

Amyras.   With what a flinty bosome should I joy,
The breath of life, and burthen of my soule,
If not resolv'd into resolved paines,
My bodies mortified lineaments
Should exercise the motions of my heart,
Pierc'd with the joy of any dignity?   190
O father, if the unrelenting eares
Of death and hell be shut against my praiers,
And that the spightfull influence of heaven,
Denie my soule fruition of her joy,
How should I step or stir my hatefull feete,
Against the inward powers of my heart,
Leading a life that onely strives to die,
And plead in vaine, unpleasing soveranity.
Tamburlaine.   Let not thy love exceed thyne honor sonne,
Nor bar thy mind that magnanimitie,   200
That nobly must admit necessity:
Sit up my boy, and with those silken raines,
Bridle the steeled stomackes of those Jades.
Theridamas.   My Lord, you must obey his majesty,
Since Fate commands, and proud necessity.
Amyras.   Heavens witnes me, with what a broken hart

And damned spirit I ascend this seat,
And send my soule before my father die,
His anguish and his burning agony.
Tamburlaine.　Now fetch the hearse of faire *Zenocrate*, 210
Let it be plac'd by this my fatall chaire,
And serve as parcell of my funerall.
Usumcasane.　Then feeles your majesty no sovereraigne ease,
Nor may our hearts all drown'd in teares of blood,
Joy any hope of your recovery?
Tamburlaine.　*Casane* no, the Monarke of the earth,
And eielesse Monster that torments my soule,
Cannot behold the teares ye shed for me,
And therefore stil augments his cruelty.
Techelles.　Then let some God oppose his holy power, 220
Against the wrath and tyranny of death,
That his teare-thyrsty and unquenched hate,
May be upon himselfe reverberate.

　　　　　　　　　　　　　They bring in the hearse.

Tamburlaine.　Now eies, injoy your latest benefite,
And when my soule hath vertue of your sight,
Pierce through the coffin and the sheet of gold,
And glut your longings with a heaven of joy.
So, raigne my sonne, scourge and controlle those slaves,
Guiding thy chariot with thy Fathers hand.
As precious is the charge thou undertak'st 230
As that which *Clymens* brainsicke sonne did guide,
When wandring *Phœbes* Ivory cheeks were scortcht
And all the earth like *Ætna* breathing fire:
Be warn'd by him then, learne with awfull eie
To sway a throane as dangerous as his:
For if thy body thrive not full of thoughtes
As pure and fiery as *Phyteus* beames,
The nature of these proud rebelling Jades
Wil take occasion by the slenderest haire,
And draw thee peecemeale like *Hyppolitus*, 240
Through rocks more steepe and sharp than Caspian cliftes.

231 *Clymens*] O2(*Clymenes*); *Clymeus* O1, 3–4.

The nature of thy chariot wil not beare
A guide of baser temper than my selfe,
More then heavens coach, the pride of *Phaeton*.
Farewel my boies, my dearest friends, farewel,
My body feeles, my soule dooth weepe to see
Your sweet desires depriv'd my company,
For *Tamburlaine*, the Scourge of God must die.　　　[*Dies*.]
Amyras.　　Meet heaven and earth, and here let al things end,
For earth hath spent the pride of all her fruit,　　　　250
And heaven consum'd his choisest living fire.
Let earth and heaven his timelesse death deplore,
For both their woorths wil equall him no more.

FINIS

TEXTUAL NOTES

PART I

I.i

89 of *Affrica*]   Most editors have followed O4's filling out of the line with 'of all *Affrica*'. It is possible that 'all' has been omitted in O1 by error, even though the O1 compositor is seldom guilty of this lapse. On the other hand, if this is a nine-syllable pentameter (the first syllable omitted), the line would be regular enough although something of an unnecessary stress would then be placed on 'him'.

169 Long live]   Earlier editors found irresistible the assignment of this line to '*All.*' as in O3–4. However, for what it is worth, the colon after 'Lake' in the preceding line does not favor any hypothesis of eyeskip. The compositor must have believed that the speech ended with line 169. There is no difficulty, of course, with Ortygius ending his speech with the traditional formula.

I.ii

0.2 Magnetes]   This name is Oxberry's guess for the attendant lord on Zenocrate who has only two brief speeches, each assigned the speech-prefix '*Mag.*', at I.ii.17, 80.

161 And]   It is extremely odd that all editors have overlooked the importance of this catchword on sig. A8ᵛ in O1 and have selected instead the text's following word beginning sig. B1. Catchwords may have peculiar significance because they were set presumably with the compositor's eye directly on the copy. It would be strictly a speculation, of course, to argue that when the compositor began his setting of B1, after making up the last pages of sheet A, he read over some of the preceding text from sig. A8ᵛ in the manuscript so that he could proceed with an under-standing of the sense, in the process memorizing the first line of sig. B1 before turning to his cases. If so, he might easily have picked up 'To pull' in line 161 from memorial contamination with 'to pierce' that he had just read in line 160.

225 Are]   This is a notable crux with no entirely satisfactory resolution. Dyce[1] is the only editor to follow O1, but he changed his mind in the revision Dyce[2] and reverted to the earlier editors who, following Oxberry, boldly changed 'Are' to 'To'. This makes the smoothest sense of all emendations and has the advantage of leaving O1 'soule' in the line above with no punctuation, as is found in O1 (but see below). Tucker Brooke heeding a suggestion by Brereton placed a query after 'soule' and changed 'Are' to 'Ah', an authentic Marlovian form as we know from the manuscript fragment of *The Massacre at Paris* but a less desirable alternative since the 'h' of 'Ah' is not very likely to be mistaken in the secretary hand for 're'. This is the reading adopted by the Methuen and Regent's editors, however. The present editor has considerable confidence in the original O1 'Are', even though it requires repunctuating 'soule'. In the first place, 'soule' with a preceding round bracket is turned up above the line with very little space to its left, and under such circumstances it is not unusual for a compositor to omit following punctuation when cut off by his measure. The absence of a query (actually an exclamation) after 'soule' is not very weighty evidence, therefore, against the authority of O1 'Are'. Secondly, it has not been remarked that 'Are' is the catchword on sig. B1ᵛ and is repeated as the following word beginning the first line of text on sig. B2, indicating that in normal course the compositor would have looked at the individual word in manuscript before setting it as the catchword. Moreover, after tieing up page B1ᵛ he would have come back to the typesetting and would have scrutinized the manuscript again before continuing to set the text. (This is not a case as at I.ii.161 where the first text word of a page has been memorially contaminated by preceding words.) If normality obtained, therefore, he would have read the manuscript word twice as 'are' (capitals not being present at the start of verse lines in manuscript). This evidence may suggest that misreading is not very likely, particularly since none of the proposed emendations is close in appearance to 'are'. If, then, the original is to stand with only the minor emendation of supplied punctuation after turned-up 'soule', the syntax is indeed somewhat strained, but sufficient sense may be made out of the sentence. One could untangle the syntax to take it that the query is, *Are these noble Scythians so resolved?* But we may notice that 'these' in line 225 may well refer back to Usumcasane's boast in line 223 that kings will be forced to confess 'Theise are the men that all the world admires.' The aristocratic Theridamas, whose first contemptuous words in line 152 must not be forgotten, is now borne down by the eloquence of Tamburlaine and his followers. In direct reference back to Usumcasane's line 223, then, he questions whether he should believe his eyes or the intoxicating promises of future conquests that tempt him so strongly, and he asks of himself, in effect, are these not mere shepherds, as I have believed, but instead noble and resolved Scythian warriors whom I should join? Alternatively, 'noble Scythians' might be a parenthesis, and 'these' refer back to the conquests that are planned. But 'resolved' is not used in the sense of 'planned' or 'decided' in the play, and the suggestion is unlikely.

II.iii

55 Cutle-axe is an acceptable although uncommon form, according to *O.E.D.*, and therefore has been retained. However, it is a tossup whether the compositor here has not omitted a letter, for it is 'Curtle-axe' elsewhere in the play.

III.iii

158 our strokes to wound the sencelesse aire] Dyce's query 'air' for O1 'lure' is adopted by modern editors and is preferable to Cunningham's query 'wind'. It is unfortunate that his emendation of 'your' for O1 'our' has been taken up as well. This whole speech by Tamburlaine is addressed as much to his followers as to Bajazeth, and nowhere else in it is there a contrast between what his host can do and what 'your' or Bajazeth's supporters can do. 'Our' is the consistent point of view. Under these circumstances the neat antithesis proposed by Dyce is false. The O1 reading merely increases the hyperbole. To wound the air is not necessarily futile, or to miss one's opponent, but instead to make one's strokes more fearsome.

The bullets and points will be directed home; the strokes against Bajazeth's men will be so vehement as even to wound the air, which being senseless is not easily wounded. If the air will be wounded in this manner, Bajazeth's men, being sensible, will be killed. Emendation destroys what is indeed the climax of the threat.

IV.iv

126 valure] Dyce's emendation of O 1–4 'value' is useful to provide the necessary wordplay. 'Valure' can mean simple 'valour' (*O.E.D.*, *sb.* 5.11*b*); on the other hand, it can have the same sense as 'value', as in I.ii.96–7: 'Enchast with precious juelles of mine owne: More rich and valurous than *Zenocrates*.'

V.i

49 *Patrones*] No doubt for metrical reasons all editors have followed Oxberry in reading 'Patrons' for O 1–4 '*Patrones*'. Yet the O 1 italic setting for the word encourages Broughton's query whether the reference is not to the patroness of Egypt, Isis. The O 1 compositor evidently had some reason to believe that this was a technical word. To swear by a female goddess Isis would be appropriate for *Second Virgin*, of course.

147 *Ebena*] We are no forwarder than in Oxberry's day in knowing whether Marlowe was inventing the name of this goddess, perhaps from 'ebony', or whether what he wrote in the manuscript has been so corrupted in print as to be unrecognizable.

177–87 To harbour...weeds:] It is possible that this difficult passage is more corrupt than the single emendation in this text, adopted from Dyce at line 184, would suggest. The main intent of the passage is clear enough, however. Tamburlaine is, in a sense, forecasting the debates between love and honour so popular in Restoration heroic tragedy. Love is represented by the mysterious effect on him of Zenocrate's beauty, which is weakening his resolve to keep to his word and destroy Damascus. Speaking with Marlowe's own voice, he associates this power with the mysterious reaches of the imagination in poetry which seem to penetrate reality farther than physical deeds can manage. Even after he has abruptly pulled himself up short with an accusation of effeminacy, he still returns to the effects of beauty that he feels working within him upon his resolve. The conclusion is not very systematically presented but seems to represent an attempted apotheosis by which he joins both incentives to greatness into a new whole that resolves their apparent differences. Presumably this resolution motivates his decision to satisfy both parts, the one by devastating Damascus but the other by sparing the life of Zenocrate's father.

184 stoopt] Dyce's emendation, in the common enough sense of *make stoop* (Part II, IV.i.76), restores a word that constantly appears in this play and is certainly appropriate in linking the descent of the gods to earthly loves.

187 martch] Although Dyce's 'mask' is a most ingenious substitution, the original does not need changing. As in *Edward II*, I.ii.20, 'Thus arme in arme the king and he dooth marche', the word may mean only *walk*, *stroll*, or *move*, with no necessary

connotation of the military or of any other pace. The rest of the line may be corrupt, but proper emendation is obscure. The humble cottages which the gods enter
or stroll among are certainly like the 'strawie cabins' of ancient Rome in *Elegy*
II.ix.18. It is tempting, therefore, to adopt 'reeds' from Dyce[2]; but the composition
of the cottages (if that is the sense) is difficult to reconcile with 'strowed', and
double corruption – as of *strawie reeds* – is not convincing as a hypothesis. It
would seem that the 'strowed weeds' are the covering for the floors, even though
this sense is difficult to adjust to 'of' in 'cottages of strowed weeds'. If so, 'weeds'
is about as acceptable as 'reeds', and emendation does not seem to be positively
required.

315 Fling...face.]　It is not beyond possibility that a stage-direction here has been
incorporated with the text to go with preceding 'Here, here, here.' On the other
hand, the speech consists of a series of imperatives at this point.

516 the sweet]　The spelling 'the' for *thee* is sufficiently common in the period to
justify Dyce[2]'s emendation to 'thee', followed by the most recent editors. This
may very well be the construction, which would place the phrase in parallel with
'thy Syre' in line 519. On the other hand, earlier at II.iii.34 the O1 text reads 'to
the faire *Cosroe*' where the article and not the pronoun seems more clearly intended,
despite the alteration of O3–4 to 'thee faire'. It is also worth notice that in *Elegy*
III.viii.66 'The godly, sweete *Tibullus* doth increase' definitely means *the* and not
thee. It is more than possible, therefore, that the construction here in *Tamburlaine*
is the same as that at II.iii.34 and also in the elegy, in which case no emendation
to 'thee' to indicate the meaning would be correct.

PART II

I.iii

79 superficies]　Editors have all adopted Oxberry's emendation of 'superficies' for
O1–4 'superfluities'. They are probably right to do so, but it is worth pointing
out that Marlowe just possibly may have written 'superfluities', derived from *fluere*,
which is the root of the rare 'superfluitance' or *that which floats on the surface*. The
O.E.D. remarks, incidentally, that at least once this *superfluitance* was confused
with *superfluities*. But the appearance in III.iv.48 of 'superficies' in somewhat the
same sense encourages the adoption of Dyce's emendation.

II.i

47 consumate]　O1–4 read 'consinuate' on which *O.E.D.* is silent. Robinson's
emendation, approved by Broughton, of 'continuate' retains the letters *uate* and is
acceptable in meaning, as *continued intact, without a break*, or *lasting, long-continued*.
Yet Dyce[2]'s emendation *consummate* for his original acceptance of *continuate* has
several advantages. In secretary hand the confusion of *um* as *inu* is perhaps easier
to account for than that of *t* for *s*; and though *continuate* is acceptable metrically, the
couplet here perhaps requires regularity in both its lines as provided by *consumate*.

Finally, although 'consumate' as *complete, perfect, of highest degree or quality* is a shade more strained, its association to 'religious' and 'righteous' is perhaps less tautological than that of 'inviolate' to 'continuate'.

III.iii

13 friends]　O3 'friends' for O1–2 'friend' may just possibly be a sophistication, since the collective singular could be defended as the antonym of *enemy* (*O.E.D. sb.* A. 6). A good example would be one quoted by *O.E.D.* under *adj.* B. from *Julius Caesar*: 'whether yond tropps are friend or enemy'. But the reiteration of the plural 'friends' in lines 19 and 35 is probably decisive despite the change in preposition from 'to' to 'of'; the plural 'Brothers be' at line 36 is also helpful.

IV.i

89 coward, villaine,]　In approving of the absence of the O1–4 comma after 'coward' that he found in Robinson (inherited from Oxberry), Broughton noted what he thought to be the appearance of *coward* as an adjective in V.iii.115 'Thus are the villain cowards fled'; but particularly III.ii.149, 'And hunt that Coward faintheart runaway'. Unfortunately, however, Robinson's text deceived him. At V.iii.115 'villain‸' had been Oxberry's alteration of O1–4 'villaines,' with a comma, and at III.ii.149 O1–4 places commas after 'Coward' and 'faintheart'. Tempting as is the emendation here at line 89, then, to treat 'coward' as an adjective has no support from parallels in the text.

108 *Jaertis*]　This is the Jaxartes river. The form here does not seem to be a compositorial error, for it is repeated at IV.iii.108. If emendation were to be made, *Jacertis*, or Oxberry's *Jakertis* would be proper.

V.i

215 about]　Some merit may reside in Oxberry's alteration to 'above' in view of the possibility that the compositor picked up 'about' by memorial contamination from 'about' in line 216. But the case is insufficiently certain to justify emendation. Curiously, no editor after Robinson has felt tempted.

PRESS-VARIANTS IN Q1 (1590)

[Copies collated; Bodl. (Bodleian Library), and CSmH (Huntington Library.]

SHEET A (*outer forme*)

Corrected: CSmH
Uncorrected: Bodl.

Sig. A3
    I.i.6 *Persea,*] *Persea.*
      10 *Europe,*] *Europe*
      14 Sun] Sun,
Sig. A4ᵛ
    I.i.108 himselfe?] himselfe.

SHEET B (*outer forme*)

Corrected: CSmH
Uncorrected: Bodl.

Sig. B6ᵛ
    II.iv.42.1 *trumpets*] *trunpets*

EMENDATIONS OF ACCIDENTALS

PART I

Foreword

20 *ever more*] *possibly* evermore *as in* O2

Prologue

3 War:] O3; ~ . O1; ~ , O2
4 *Tamburlaine*,] O4; ~ : O1–3

6 sword.] O2; ~ ∧ O1

I.i

0.1 I.i] *Actus.1. Scæna.1.* O1–4
10 *Europe*∧] O1(u); ~ , O1(c)
14 Sun,] O1(u); ~ ∧ O1(c)
16 thee,] O2; ~ ∧ | O1
30 *Tamburlaine*,] O4; ~ . O1–3±
32 Passengers,] O4; ~ . O1, 3; ~ :
O2
33 plumes.] ~ , O1–4
40 outrages,] ~ . O1–4
46 *Theridamas*] O2; *Theridimas* O1
49 lord,] O4; ~ ∧ | O1–3
57 *Theridamas*,] *Theridimas*∧ | O1–4;
(O4: *Theridamas*)
66 Dame:] ~ , O1–4
74 swords,] O2; ~ ∧ | O1
77 mine,] O4; ~ . O1–3
82 *Theridamas*,] *Therid.* O1–3; ~ ∧
O4
82 times.] O3; ~ , O1–2
97 seat——] ~ . O1, 3; ~ , O2, 4

99 state,] O2; ~ . O1
106 *Exeunt*.] *Exit.* O1–4
108 threaten] O2; thraten O1
112 *Asia*.] ~ , O1–4
117 scorne:] ~ , O1–4
118 teares,] O4; ~ : O1–3
126 Emperie.] ~ , O1–4
132 Christendome?] O4; ~ . | O1–3
133 *Menaphon*,] *Menaph.* O1–4
133 sound?] O2; ~ ∧ | O1
135.1 *Crowne*,] O4; ~ ∧ | O1–3
145 Crestes:] ~ , O1–4
147 discipline,] O4; ~ . | O1–3
148 warre,] O2; ~ . O1
157 th'emperiall]] O2 (th'imperiall);
th'mperiall O1
180 neere∧] ~ , O1–4
188 O1–4 *line*: then, | God (O3–4: *All.*
God)

I.ii

0.1 I.ii] *Actus.1.Scæna.2.* O1–4
1 thoughts.] ~ ∧ | O1–4
4 *Siria*,] O2; ~ . O1
18 Cham] *Cham* O1–4
40 *Phœbus*] O4; *Phœbus* O1–3
49 quake,] ~ . O1–2; ~ ∧ | O3–4
53 Beastes,] ~ . O1–4

60 followers.] ~ , O1–4±
61–2 estimates, . . .spirits:]O4(spirits.);
~ : . . .~ , O1–3
91 Crowne,] O2; ~ . O1
92 birth.] O4; ~ , O1–3
103 waves,] O2; ~ . O1–3
137 first.] O4; ~ , O1–3

145 swords,] O3; ~ . O1; ~ ₍ₐ₎ O2
154-5 *One line in* O1-4
156 furniture?] O2; ~ , O1
158 earth,] O4; ~ . O1-3
160 *Avernus*] O2; *Avernas* O1
160 vaults,] O4; ~ . O1-3
162 Persean] O2; Perseau O1
165 lookes:——] ~ : ₍ₐ₎ O1-4±
166, 242 *Persea*] Persea O1-4
181 harme.] O4; ~ , O1-3±
182 showers,] O3; ~ . O1-2
185 East,] O3; ~ . O1-2
187 Emperesse.] ~ , O1-4

192 sackt.] ~ , O1-4
195 sea,] O2; ~ . O1
198 Senators.] ~ , O1-4
207 Boötes] Botëes O1-2; Bo-otes O3; Boetes O4
207 light,] O3; ~ . O1-2
216 that₍ₐ₎] O3; ~ , O1-2
218 expect,] O2; ~ . O1
224 soule?] O4; ~ ₍ₐ₎ | O1-3
232 hand,] O2; ~ . O1
244 *Scythia*] Scythia O1-4
249 *Tamburlain,*] ~ ₍ₐ₎ | O1-4
256 with] O2; wtth O1

II.i

0.1 II.i] *Actus.2. Scœna.1.* O1-4
11 burthen. Twixt] burthen, twixt O1-4
16 Spheares₍ₐ₎] ~ : O1-4
17 throne,] O2; ~ . O1
20 Thirsting] O2; Thrirsting O1
20 soveraitny,] ~ ₍ₐ₎ O1-4
23 heire,] O3; ~ . O1-2

35 made₍ₐ₎] O2; ~ : O1
36 men,] O3; ~ . O1-2
40 join'd] O3; ~ ₍ₐ₎ | O1-2
59 treasure] O2; trasure O1
59 thoughts?] ~ , O1; ~ . O2-4
64 King,] O2; ~ . O1
65 *Parthia:*] Parthia. O1-2; Parthia, O3; *Parthia,* O4

II.ii

0.1 II.ii] *Act.2 Scœna.2,* O1
4 brother.] ~ ₍ₐ₎ | O1, 3; ~ , O2, 4
5 abusde,] ~ . O1; ~ ? O2-4
15 hilles,] O2; ~ . O1
25 promises₍ₐ₎] O2; ~ . O1

51 say,] ~ ₍ₐ₎ | O1-4
52 venomous?] O2; ~ . O1
68 subdu'd,] O4; ~ : O1-3±
69 carkasses:] ~ , O1-4
71 *Persea.*] ~ , O1-4

II.iii

0.1 II.iii] *Actus.2. Scœna.3.* O1-2, 4; Actus.1. Scœna.2. O3
0.2 Ortygius,] O2; ~ . O1
3 attemptes?] O2; ~ . O1
13 armes,] O2; ~ . O1
14 support.] O3; ~ , O1-2
38 Armes,] O3; ~ : O1-2
39 *Asia:*] ~ , O1-4

42 alone,] O2; ~ . O1
44 Fate.] O3; ~ , O1-2
53 *Perseas*] O4; Perseas O1-3
55 -axe,] ~ ₍ₐ₎ O1, 3-4; ~ . O2
56 Armes.] ~ , O1-4
58 lightening,] O4; ~ : O1-3
58 heaven:] ~ , O1-4

II.iv

16 What,...coward,] ~ ∧ ... ~ ∧ O1–4
17 field?] ~ . O1–4

21 kneele,] O3; ~ . O1–2
42.1 and] O2; aud O1

II.v

0.2 *Ortygius, Techelles,*] O2; ~ . ~ . O1
8 *Persea*] O3; Persea O1–2
16 Majestie,] O2; ~ . O1
19 *Persea*] Persea O1–4
48 wish,] O3; ~ . O1–2

59 earth.] ~ , O1–4
67 What] O2; what O1
72 *Casane,*] *Casanes*∧ O1–4
74 attemplesse,] ~ ∧ O1–4
104 Haste thee] O2; Haste the O1

II.vi

0.1 II.vi] *Actus.2. Scæna.6.* O1–4
2 presumption,] O3; ~ . O1–2
13 rule,] O4; ~ . O1–3
26 Elements∧] ~ , O1–4

28 death.] O3; ~ , O1–2
30 ingratitude] O2; ingratude O1
31 Soveraigntie] O2; Soveraingtie O1

II.vii

8 voice,] ~ . O1–4
10 heart.] ~ , O1–4
23 course:] ~ . O1; ~ , O2–4
25 Spheares,] O2; ~ . O1
26 rest,] O2; ~ . O1
27 all,] O2; ~ . O1
28 felicitie,] O2; ~ . O1
30 *Tamburlain,*] O2; ~ ∧ | O1
34 us,] ~ ∧ O1–4
34 *Tamburlaine,*] O2; ~ . O1

37 Crowne,] O4; ~ . O1–3 (O3 *doubtful comma*)
39, 67 *Persea*] O3; Persea O1–2
43 wound,] O2; ~ . O1
44 hell:] ~ . O1; ~ , O2–4
45 depart.] ~ : O1–4
47 both,] O2; ~ . O1
49 hart,] O2; ~ . O1
58 armes,] O3; ~ ∧ | O1–2
67.1 *Finis Actus 2.* O1–4

III.i

0.1 III.i] *Actus.3. Scæna. 1.* O1–4
0.1 Fesse,] Fess. O1–4
0.1 Argier,] O2; ~ . O1
14 yeeld,] O3; ~ . O1–2
16 Generall,] O4; ~ ∧ | O1–3
17 guard,] O2; ~ . O1
23 *Asia,*] O2; ~ . O1
24 *Grecia*] Grecia O1–4

26 highest] O2; higest O1
26 world,] O2; ~ . O1
29 *Grecia,*] O3; Grecia. O1–2
38 arise∧] O3; ~ . O1–2
43 Persean,] O2; ~ . O1
52 thereon,] O3; ~ . O1; ~ : O2
60 *Carnon.*] O3; ~ , O1–2

III.ii

0.1 III.ii] *Actus.3. Scæna. 2.* O1
1 *Agidas.*] *omit* O1–4
5 pale,] O2; ~ . O1
9 agoe,] O2; ~ . O1
11 well,] O4; ~ : O1–3
14 conceits,] O2; ~ . O1
18 dissolv'd,] O2; ~ . O1
21 life‸] O3; ~ , O1–2
21 Breast,] O2; ~ . O1
25 *Zenocrate,*] O3; ~ . O1; ~ ‸ O1
28 Queene,] O2; ~ . O1
29 Concubine,] O3; ~ . O1–2
35 words:] ~ . O1; ~ , O2–4
36 deserves.] ~ : O1–4
48 armes:] ~ . O1–2; ~ , O3–4

49 *Tamburlaine.*] O4; ~ : O1–3
51 Pierides,] ~ . O1–2; ~ : O3–4
52 strive.] ~ , O1–4
54 God,] O2; ~ . O1
58 enjoy] O2 (injoy); ejoy O1
66 love,] O2; ~ . O1
67 jealousie,] O2; ~ . O1
68, 74 revenge,] O2; ~ . O1
73 hart,] O2; ~ . O1
80 thunderclaps,] O2; ~ . O1
95 die,] O2; ~ . O1
96 least.] ~ , O1–4
102 rage,] O4; ~ . O1–3
105 die,] O4; ~ . O1–3

III.iii

0.1 III.iii] *Act.3. Scæna.3,* O1–4
1 Bassoe] *Bassoe* O1–4
3 See] O2; see O1
12 hoste.] ~ , O1–4
16 Steeds,] O2; ~ . O1
17 *Tripoly:*] ~ . O1–4±;
19 *Grecia*] Grecia O1–4
25 Steeds,] O2; ~ . O1
30 yours.] ~ ‸ | O1, 4; ~ , O2–3
38, 135 *Europe*] O3; Europe O1–2
48 chaines,] O2; ~ . O1
53 side,] O3; ~ . O1–2
54 give.] O3; ~ , O1–2
56 *Affrica,*] O2; ~ . O1
60, 73, 99 *Affrica*] Affrica O1–4
64 swordes,] O2; ~ ‸ | O1
75 sepulcher,] O2; ~ . O1
80 Emperesse,] O2; ~ . O1
88 *Tamburlaine?*] O2; ~ . O1
89 *Barbary,*] O2; ~ . O1
90 indignities?] O2; ~ . O1
91 pointes,] O2; ~ . O1
98 swords,] ~ ‸ | O1–4
106 Lance,] O3; ~ . O1–2
120 heaven,] O2; ~ . O1
128 kings,] O2; ~ . O1
132 *Persea,*] O4; ~ ‸ O1–3
137 *Bythinia.*] O3; ~ , O1–2

139 Shall] O1 (*cw*); Shal O1 (*text*)
158 aire.] ~ , O1–4
159 spread,] O3; ~ . O1–2
164 Bassoes,] O2; ~ ‸ O1
169 Cal'st] O1 (*cw*); Call'st O1 (*text*)
173 selfe,] O3; ~ : O1; ~ ‸ O2
180 weedes,] O3; ~ . O1–2
182 Hearst] O2; hearst O1
189 *Persea,*] O3; Persea. O1; Persea, O2
199 shrine,] O2; ~ . O1
205, 221, 223 *Affrica*] O4; Affrica O1–3
209 conquered,] O2; ~ . O1
210 otherwise,] O2; ~ . O1
215 crownes,] O2; ~ ‸ O1
216 ifaith.] O4; ~ ‸ | O1–2; ~ , O3
218 Lord,] O2; ~ . O1
220 *Zenocrate,*] ʒen. | O1–2; ~ ‸ O3–4
222 best,] O4; ~ ‸ | O1–3
224 Turkesse,] ~ ‸ O1–4
224.1 *her,*] O2; ~ . O1
241 lost,] O2; ~ . O1
251 *Asant,*] O3; ~ . O1–2
257 one,] O2; ~ . O1
258 *Portingale:*] ~ . O1–2; ~ , O3–4
259 shore.] O4; ~ : O1; ~ , O2–3
262 gold?] O2; ~ , O1
268 armes?] O2; ~ . O1
273.2 *Finis Actus tertii.* O1–4

IV.i

0.1 IV.i] *Actus.4. Scæna. 1.* O 1–4
6 vagabonds,] ~ . O 1–2; ~ ₍ O 3–4
17 Villain,] O 4; ~ . O 1, 3; ~ ₍ O 2
17 *Tamburlaine*₍] ~ . O 1; ~ : O 2; ~ , O 3–4
30 stars,] O 3; ~ ₍ | O 1–2
32 downe:] ~ . O 1; ~ , O 2–4
33 power,] ~ : O 1–2; ~ ₍ O 3–4
45 *Erebus,*] O 2; ~ . O 1
52 minde:] O 4; ~ . O 1, 3; ~ , O 2
53 blood.] ~ : O 1–4±

56 blood:] O 4; ~ . O 1–3±
57 armes.] ~ : O 1–4
58 submission,] O 2; ~ . O 1
61 hell.] ~ , O 1–4
62 age,] O 4; ~ . O 1–3
68 *Capolin,...king,*₍] ~ ₍ ... ~ , O 1–4
69 slave,] O 3; ~ : O 1–2
72 disparadgement] O 3 (disparagement); dispardgement O 1–2

IV.ii

0.1 IV.ii] *Actus.4. Scæna. 2.* O 1–4
8 God,] O 3; ~ ₍ O 1–2
8 Spheare₍] ~ . O 1, 4; ~ , O 2–3
10 Heaven,] O 2; ~ . O 1
20 ground,] O 2; ~ . O 1
26 Feends,] O 2; ~ . O 1
27 hell,] O 2; ~ . O 1
32 Emperours.] *point uncertain and may be broken comma*

33 nativity,] ~ : O 1–4
34 Lamps:] ~ , O 1–3; ~ . O 4
50 heaven,] ~ . O 1–2; ~ : O 3–4
51 shot,] O 2; ~ . O 1
66 Lord,] ~ ₍ | O 1–4
76 low,] O 2; ~ . O 1
79 dignities,] ~ ₍ O 1–4
108 gold,] O 2; ~ . O 1
121 contain'd,] O 3; ~ . O 1; ~ : O 2

IV.iii

0.1 IV.iii] *Act.4. Scæna.3,* O 1–4
2 knightes,] ~ : O 1–3; ~ ₍ O 4
3 Calidonian] O 2; Caldonian O 1
3 Boare:] ~ , O 1–4
4 youths,] O 2; ~ . O 1
5 sent,] O 2; ~ . O 1
8 spoile,] ~ . O 1–2; ~ : O 3–4
11 *Tamburlaine,*] O 2; ~ . O 1
12 Thiefe,] ~ . O 1; ~ : O 2–4
13 Crowne,] O 2; ~ . O 1
15 presumptuous O 2; presumotuous O 1
27 Emperesse?] O 4; ~ . O 1–3
34 rocke.] ~ , O 1–3; ~ : O 4

38 hower,] *point doubtful and could be broken full stop*
39 wrong,] O 2; ~ . O 1
41 long,] O 2; ~ . O 1
42 Concubine₍ I feare,] ~ , ~ ~ ₍ O 1–3; ~ (~ ~) O 4
48 prodigall,] ~ : O 2, 4; ~ ₍ O 3
50 powers?] O 2; ~ . O 1
51 *Arabia,*] O 2; ~ . O 1
56 chace₍] O 3; ~ : O 1–2
64 Arabian] *Arabian* O 1–4
65 King,] O 2; ~ . O 1
65 obscurity,] O 2; ~ . O 1

IV.iv

0.1 IV.iv] *Actus:4. Scæna.5.* O 1–4
0.2 Theridamas,] O 2; ~ . O 1
1 *Damascus,*] O 2; *Damascns.* O 1
2 heads,] O 3; ~ . O 1–2

3 walles,] O 3; ~ . O 1–2
11–12 O 1–4 *line*: could | Willingly
13–14 O 1–4 *line*: Nay...that, | And ...*Zenocrate,* | *Techelles*...victuals

18 *Avernus*] *Avernas* O1–4
19 up,] O3; ~ . O1–2
24 King,] O2; ~ . O1
26–7 O1–2 *line*: curses | By
29 foes,] O2; ~ . O1
39 speakest?] ~ ₐ | O1; ~ . O2–4
43 Villaine,] *point uncertain*
52 this?] O2; ~ ₐ | O1
54 what,] ~ ₐ O1–4
73 *Egypt*] Egypt O1–4
74 stoope.] ~ , O1–4
77 trace,] O2; ~ . O1
78 Map,] O3; ~ . O1; ~ : O2
87 safe,] O2; ~ . O1
90 forc'd,] ~ ₐ O1–4

91 *Egypt…Arabia*] O3; Egypt…
Arabia O1–2
92 Feede] O1 *cw*; Feed O1 *text*
99 *Bajazeth.*] ~ , O1–4
99–100 O1–4 *line*: them, | Looking
113 here] O3; Here O1–2
113 *Egypt,*] O3; ~ ₐ | O1–2
114 Governour] O2; Governout O1
120 *Fesse,*] O2; ~ . O1
122 heaven,] O2; ~ . O1
123 bower,] ~ . O1–4
125 with,] O2; ~ . O1
127 fame,] O2; ~ . O1
135 *Egyptia,*] O3; ~ . O1–2
136 Antartique] O2; Antatique O1
140.1 *Finis Actus quarti.* O1–4

V.i

0.1 V.i] *Actus:5.Scæna.1.* O1(*with
turned* 5)–4
14 fame,] O3; ~ : O1–2
15 world:] O4; ~ , O1–3
17 deaths.] ~ , O1–2; ~ : O3–4
20 praiers,] O2; ~ ₐ O1
24 *1. Virgin.*] *Virgin.* O1–4
28 breasts,] O3; ~ . O1–2
29 securities,] O2; ~ . O1
31 death,] *point doubtful*
34 care,] O2; ~ ₐ | O1
40 owne,] O3; ~ ₐ O1–2
43 stars,] O2; ~ . O1
46 extreames,] O2; ~ . O1
50 intreate ₐ] O2; ~ , O1
51 lookes,] O2; ~ ₐ O1
59 lenity.] ~ , O1–4
63.1.0 *Actus.5. Scæna.2.* O1–4
63.2 Tamburlaine,] O2; ~ . O1
63.2 Techelles,] O3; ~ ₐ O1–2
63.2 Usumcasane,] O2; Usumcasan, |
O1
69 beams,] ~ ₐ | O1–4
74 earth,] O2; ~ . O1
84 joy,] ~ . O1; ~ : O2; ~ ₐ O3–4
95 lives.] O4; ~ , O1–3
110 then,] O3; ~ ₐ | O1–2
111 imperious Death,] O2; ~ ~ . O1

113 I am] *probably a space mark, not a
point, between the two*
113 there:] ~ , O1–4
114 speares,] O3; ~ : O1–2
117 death,] O2; ~ . O1
121 Egyptians,] O2; ~ . O1
123 *Gehons*] Gehons O1–4
141 tresses] O2; treshes O1
141 aire,] O2; ~ . O1
147 heaven,] O3; ~ . (*uncertain*) O1;
~ : O2
148 walk,] O2; ~ . O1
149 night,] O3; ~ . O1–2
150 light.] O4; ~ , O1–3
153 *Egypts*] Egypts O1–4
160 beauty,] *point slightly doubtful*
168 wit:] ~ . O1–2; ~ , O3–4
174 Sex,] O2; ~ ₐ O1
176 name,] O2; ~ . O1
179 toucht,] ~ . O1; ~ : O2; ~ ₐ O3–4
180 love ₐ] ~ , O1–4
181 victory,] O4; ~ ₐ O1–3
182 conceites.] ~ , O1–4
186 flames,] O3; ~ . O1–4
187 weeds:] O3; ~ , O1–2
188 note,] ~ ₐ O1–4
195.1 Usumcasane,] O2; Usumcasan ₐ |
O1

206 *Theridamas,*] O2; ~ . O1
215 about,] O2; ~ . O1
216 wounds.] ~ , O1–4
221 Skin,] O4; ~ . O1–3
223 joints,] O2; ~ . O1
226 roomes.] ~ , O1–4
227 foorth,] O4; ~ . O1–3
233 Gods:] ~ . O1; ~ , O2, 4; ~ ₐ O3
234 Distinie.] ~ : O1–4
240 end_ₐ] O3; ~ ? O1–2
241 slaveries?] O3; ~ : O1–2
242 view_ₐ] ~ , O1–4
243 feare,] ~ ₐ O1–4
246–7 *One line in* O1–4
247 *Elisian.*] ~ ₐ | O1–4
248 Why] O2; why O1
248 beggars,] O2; ~ ₐ O1
248 slaves,] ~ ₐ O1–4
252 scorne,] O2; ~ . O1
271 heart,] ~ : O1–4
272 teares:] ~ , O1–4
273 root,] ~ : O1–4
274 breake:] ~ , O1–4
282 inflictions] O2 (*doubtful*); inflictious O1
293 heavens.] O4; ~ , O1–3
304.2 *Enter*] O1 (*text*); *Zab.* O1 (*cw*)
309 O *Bajazeth*] O1–4 *start prose here, joined to* l. 310
310 Give] give O1–4
310 liquor?] ~ ₐ | O1–2; ~ , O3–4
313 to,] ~ ₐ O1–4
314 her. The] her, the O1–2; ~ : ~ O3–4
315 white,] O3; ~ . O1–2
315 Blacke. Here] Blacke, here O1–4
316 *Tamburlaine.*] O2; ~ , O1
317 Hell.] ~ , O1–2; ~ ₐ O3–4
318.2 *Enter*] O4; *omit* O1–3
320 blood:] ~ . O1–3; ~ , O4
321 countrimen.] ~ : O1–4

330 Stead_ₐ] ~ , O1–4
331 hooves,] O2; ~ ₐ O1
344 both.] ~ ₐ | O1–4
347 entralles,] O2; ~ . O1
357 Emperesse.] O2; ~ , O1
360 war,] O3; ~ . O1–2
378 Arabian] O3; *Arabian* O1–2
380 did,] O3; ~ . O1; ~ : O2
393 *Lavinia,*] O4; ~ . O1–2; ~ : O3
399 hope.] O4; ~ , O1–2; ~ : O3
404 souldiers,] O3; ~ ; O1–2
409 armes,] O2; ~ . O1
412 Lord.] ~ : O1, 4; ~ , O2–3
430 joy,] O3; ~ . O1–2
431 dies,] O2; ~ . O1
435 thee,] O4; ~ ₐ O1–3
437 sword,] O3; ~ . O1–2
440 soule,] O2; ~ . O1
444 *Egypt*] O3; Egypt O1–2
446 overthrow,] ~ . O1; ~ : O2–4
455 death,] ~ ₐ O1–4
457 *Affrick*] O3; Affrick O1–2
458 triumphant] O2; triumphat O1
459 woundes,] ~ . O1–3; ~ ₐ O4
466 fields,] O4; ~ . O1–3
469 feet.] ~ , O1–4
471 fight,] O2; ~ . O1
481 Emperies:] ~ , O1–4
482 overthrow,] O3; ~ : O1–2
490 wait,] O3; ~ : O1–2
491 worthynesse:] ~ , O1–4
494 *Persea.*] O3; ~ , O1–2
505 here's] O3; her's O1–2
515 mind.] ~ , O1–4
517 *Asia*] O3; Asia O1–2
518 *Inde*] *Indie* O1–4
523 martiall] O2; matiall O1
530 betrothed_ₐ] O3; ~ , O1–2
530 Love,] ~ ₐ O1–4
534.1 *Finis Actus quinti et ultimi huius primæ partis.* O1–3; *Finis.* O4

PART II

Prologue

4 *pomp*,] O4; ∼ . O1–2; O3 *un-certain*   5 *down*.] ∼ , O1–4

I.i

0.1 I.i] *Actus.1. Scæna. 1.* O1–4
2 *Bajazeth*,] ∼ : O1–4
3 Lord,] ∼ ₐ O1–4
11–12 Christian,...field?] O4; ∼?...
∼ . O1–3
13, 45, 114 *Gazellus*.] *Byr.* O1–4
18 *Turky*] O4 (*Turkie*); Turky O1–3
30 Armes:] ∼ . O1, 3–4; ∼ ₐ O2
32 Fen.] ∼ , O1–4
35 home,] O2; ∼ . O1
41 Argoses,] O3; ∼ . O1–2
56 *Turkie*] Turkie O1–4
59 *Tamburlaine*:] ∼ . O1–3; ∼ , O4
65 *Sigismond*,] *point doubtful*
72 *Tamburlaine*.] ∼ , O1–4

74 *Capricorne*,] O3; ∼ . O1–2
75 *Archipellago*:] O2; ∼ . O1
77.0 *Act.1. Scæna.2*, O1–4
78 *Sigismond*.] omit O1–4
80 To] O2; to O1
82 sword.] ∼ , O1–4
87 walles,] O2; ∼ . O1
101 *Jove*.] ∼ , O1–4
108 *Arabia*ₐ] O3; ∼ . O1–2
115 *Turky*] O4 (*Turkie*); Turky O1–3
120 array,] O3; ∼ . O1–2
122 *et seq. this scene Orcanes*.] *Nat.*
O1–4
133 soule,] O3; ∼ ₐ O1–2
155 *Germany*,] O3; ∼ . O1–2

I.ii

0.1 I.ii] *Act.1. Scæna. 3.* O1–4
7 *Tamburlain*,] O2; ∼ . O1
15 runs——] ∼ . O1–2; ∼ , O3–4

30 many] O2; mady O1
31 command.] ∼ , O1–4
34 *Spaine*] O3; Spaine O1–2

I.iii

0.1 I.iii] *Actus.1. Scæna.4.* O1–4
6 *Egypt*] O3; Egypt O1–2
11 war?] O2; ∼ . O1
15 before,] O3; ∼ ₐ O1–2
18 precious] O2; procions O1
20 face.] ∼ , O1–4
22 *Tamburlaine*.] ∼ ₐ O1–2; ∼ : O3–4
23 one,] O3; ∼ : O1–2
24 wit:] ∼ , O1–4
25 Downe,] O2; ∼ . O1
26 Porcupines,] O3; ∼ . O1–2
35 looks,] O2; ∼ ₐ | O1
43 lance,] O3; ∼ ₐ | O1–2
44 -axe,] O4; ∼ ₐ O1–3

48 me,] O2; ∼ . O1
65 lord,] *point uncertain; may be none*
69 loins,] O3; ∼ ; O1–2
70 *Tamburlaine*:] ∼ , O1–4
76 eies,] O4; ∼ . O1–3
90–1 it,...king.] O2; ∼ ....∼ , O1
96 both,] O3; ∼ ₐ | O1–2
101 Pericranion] O4; pecicranion O1–3
104 thee,] O2; ∼ ₐ | O1
110 Empery.] O3; ∼ , O1–2
111 sound,] O3; ∼ ₐ O1–2
111.0 *Actus:1. Scæna.5.* O1–4
118 Greeks,] O4; ∼ ₐ | O1–3
119 townesₐ] ∼ , O1–3; ∼ . O4

121 sworne] O2; sworue O1
127.0 *Actus.1. Scæna. 6.* O1-4
150 again.] O3; ~ | O1-2
152 joy.] ~ , O1-4
158 *Turky*] Turky O1-4
160 cloudes,] O3; ~ . O1-2
179 *Spaine*] O3; Spaine O1-2
186 Nile,] *point uncertain*

194 *Zansibar,*] ~ ‸ O1-4
195 view'd‸] O2; ~ . O1
198 *Manico:*] ~ . O1-3; ~ , O4
199 campe.] ~ : O1-2; ~ , O3-4
211 *Oblia,*] O3; ~ . O1-2
223 him,] O3; ~ . O1-2
225.2 *Finis Actus primi.* O1-4

II.i

0.1 II.i] *Actus.2. Scæna. 1.* O1-4

10 Camp.] ~ , O1-4

II.ii

0.1 II.ii] *Actus.2. Scæna.2.*
2 *Orminius*] O2 *Orminus* O1
23.1 Messenger] O3; messenger O1-2

24 Lords.] ~ ‸ O1-3; ~ , O4
36 Christians,] *point uncertain*

II.iii

0.1 *to*] O2; *ro* O1
20 *Zoacum*] O2; ʒoacum O1

23 Feends.] ~ , O1-4

II.iv

0.1 II.iv] *Actus.2.Scæna ultima.* O1-4
    (O3: *Actus 1.*)
3 waves,] O3; ~ : O1-2
4 beames:] ~ ‸ O1-2; ~ , O3-4
31 soules,] O3; ~ : O1-2
39 *1. Physitian.] Phys.* O1-4
52 Diamiter,] O3; ~ : O1-2
64 breast,] O3; ~ . O1-2
67 die,] ~ : O1-2; ~ . O3-4
68 life:] ~ , O1-2; ~ . O3-4
83 death,] O3; ~ : O1-2

84 soule:] ~ , O1-4
102 armes:] ~ , O1-4
103 cloudes,] O3; ~ : O1-2
115 war,] O3; ~ : O1-2
116 flag:] ~ , O1-4
123 blood.] ~ ‸ | O1-3; ~ , O4
125 soule.] ~ ‸ | O1-4
136 sword.] O4; ~ , O1-2; ~ : O3
139 mourn'd,] O3; ~ ‸ O1-2
140 stature‸] O4; ~ , O1-3

III.i

0.1 III.i] *Actus.3. Scæna.1,* O1-4
2 mighty] O2; mtghty O1
5 and] O3; And O1-2
6 *Turky*] Turky O1-4
31 encounter.] ~ , O1-4

38 thousand] O2; thousad O1
39 Christian,] O2; ~ . O1
57 strong,] O2; ~ . O1
73-4 O1-4 *line*: king, | For
75 time,] O2; ~ . O1

III.ii

0.1 III.ii] *Actus.2. Scæna.2.* O1–4
5 inhabitants.] ~ ₐ O1–2; ~ : O3–4
11 Sindge] O3 (Singe); sindge O1–2
12 maske,] O3; ~ ₐ O1–2
19 mournful] O2; mourful O1
20 armes,] *point uncertain*
31 latitude,] O4; ~ . O1–2; ~ : O3
32 -spheare,] O2; ~ . O1
34 plaines,] O2; ~ . O1
56 thorowe] O2; throwe O1

64 meet:] ~ , O1–2; ~ . O3; ~ ₐ O4
65 flat,] O3; ~ : O1–2
124 Potentate,] O3; ~ . O1–2
130–1 O1–4 *line*: it, | Me
130 it.] ~ , O1–4
136 wound.] ~ ₐ O1–3; ~ , O4
141 wals,] O4; ~ ₐ O1–3
142 see,] O4; ~ ₐ O1–3
149 faintheart ₐ] ~ , O1–4

III.iii

0.1 III.iii] *Actus.3. Scæna.1,* O1–4
20 *Affrica*] O3; Affrica O1–2

30–1 thee:…walles,] O3; ~ , …~ :
O1–2
35 *Tamburlain,*] O4; ~ ₐ | O1–3

III.iv

1 *Olympia.*] O1 *speech-prefix in this
scene is* Olym. *or* Olim.
15 thee.] ~ , O1–4
22 that.] ~ , O1–4
28 knife (good] ~ , ~ O1–2; ~ ₐ ~
O3–4
33.1 *Enter*] O2; *Entert* O1

38 wife.] ~ , O1, 3; ~ ₐ | O2, 4
46 *Mahomet,*] O2; ~ . O1
48 superficies,] O4; ~ . O1–2; ~ ₐ O3
51 robe:] ~ , O1–4
59 run,] O4; ~ . O1–3
67–8 *One line in* O1–4
74 this,] O2; ~ . O1

III.v

0.1 III.v] *Actus:3. Scæna.5.* O1–4
0.1 Callepine] O2; *first* e *turned in* O1
14 *Turky*] Turky O1–4
15 *Tamburlain,*] O3; ~ ₐ O1–2
19 ever ₐ] ~ , O1–4
28 teeth,] O4; ~ . O1–2; ~ ₐ | O3
55 *Mahomet,*] O2; ~ . O1
57.0 *Actus.2.Scæna.* 1. O1, 3; *Actus.2.
Scæna II.* O2; *Actus 4. Scena 1.*
O3–4

64 *Turkye*] Turkye O1–4
65 campe,] O2; ~ . O1
66 *Græcia,*] O3 (Grecia); Grœcia. O1
68 fame.] O3; ~ , O1–2
69 *simile,*] ~ . O1–4
104 coch,] O3; ~ : O1–2
105 wier:] ~ , O1–4
119 looks?] O2; ~ . O1
156 exigent] O3; | Exigent O1; Exigent |
O2

IV.i

0.1 IV.i] *Actus.4.Scæna. 1.* O1–4
1 *Amyras.*] omit O1–4
26 swords?] O3; ~ . O1–2

35 *Mars.*] ~ , O1–4
46 arms,] O2; ~ . O1
85 magnanimity?] O2; ~ . O1

88 foes.] O3; ∼ , O1–2
115 consists,] O4; ∼ . O1–2 (O2 doubtful); ∼ : O3
128 head,] O2; ∼ . O1
130 aire,] O2; ∼ . O1
138 thee∧] O2; ∼ . O1

148 above,] ∼ : O1–4
149 abhors:] ∼ , O1–4
161 Concubines,] O2; ∼ . O1
188 about∧] ∼ , O1–4
195 heavens,] O2; ∼ . O1

IV.ii

0.1 IV.ii] *Actus.4. Scæna.3,*] O1–4
1 *Olympia.*] *omit* O1–4
4 death,] O3; ∼ ∧ O1–2
5 life,] O2; ∼ . O1
14 tent,] O3; ∼ ∧ | O1–2

38 me.] ∼ , O1–4
58 it?] O3; ∼ . O1–2
68 wil] O2; mil O1
71–2 Why...precious?] *Prose* in O1–4

IV.iii

0.1 IV.iii] *Actus.4. Scæna.4.* O1–4
59 unsackt,] ∼ . O1–2; ∼ : O3–4
80 lust?] O4; ∼ . O1–3
91 Truls.] ∼ , O1–2, 4; ∼ : O3
101 store.] ∼ , O1–2; ∼ : O3–4

104 *Arabicus,*] O3; ∼ . O1; ∼ ∧ O2
118 world:] O2; ∼ . O1
129 pomp:] O3; ∼ . O1–2
133.2 *Finis Actus quarti.* O1–4

V.i

0.1 V.i] *Actus.5.Scæna. 1.* O1–4
6 my Lord)] ∼ ∼ ∧ O1–2; ∼ ∼ , O3–4
20 hel?] ∼ . O1–2; ∼ : O3–4
24 *1. Citizen. omit* O1–4
28 Conquerour.] ∼ , O1–4
32 reliev'd,] O3; ∼ : O1–2
38 *2. Citizen.*] *Another.* O1–4
49 *Theridamas.*] *omit* O1–4
65 deepe,] O3; ∼ . O1–2
68 walles.] ∼ , O1–4
72 carkasses.] ∼ , O1–4

85 towne.] O3; ∼ , O1–2
119 life.] ∼ , O1–4
126 quaile.] ∼ , O1–4
139 chariot,] O4; ∼ . O1–3
164 *Affrica*] O4; Affrica O1–3
174 *Mahomet,*] O3; ∼ ? O1–2
175 God?] ∼ , O1–4
177 presently.] ∼ , O1–4
179 hell,] O4; ∼ . O1–3
192 *Alcaron*] Alcaron O1–4
195 majesty,] ∼ . O1–2; ∼ : O3–4

V.ii

0.1 V.ii] *Actus.5. Scæna.4.* O1–4
4 *Babylon*] O3; Babylon O1–2
8 him,] O3; ∼ . O1–2
12 him.] ∼ ∧ | O1–3; ∼ , O4
22 sustaine] O2; sustaiue O1

24 seene∧] O3; ∼ , O1–2
27 thee:] ∼ . O1–2; ∼ , O3–4
28 *Callapine,*] O4; ∼ . O1–3
51 *Turkie*] Turkie O1–4

V.iii

0.1 V.iii] *Actus.5. Scæna.6.* O1–4
1 *Theridamas.*] *omit* O1–4
1 teares,] O2; ∼ ∧ O1
4 earth,] O4; ∼ . O1–3
38 Majesty,] O2; Majsty. O1

39 subdue.] *point uncertain and might be comma*
50 Gods.] O2 (*doubtful*), O4; ∼ , O1–3
51 doe,] O2; ∼ ∧ O1

56 Why,] ~ ∧ O1–4
56 paine?] O2; ~ , O1
60 fade.] O2; ~ , O1
64 cease,] O2; ~ . O1
66 die.] ~ , O1–4
74 carkasses.] O3; ~ , O1–2
76 stay:] O3; ~ , O1–2
78 potion,] O2; ~ . O1
89 spent,] O2; ~ . O1
97 art.] *point uncertain and may be comma*
106 medicine] O2; medicince O1
125 wantes.] O2; ~ , O1
139 *Zansibar.*] ~ , O1–2; ~ : O3–4
140 *Affrica,*] O2; ~ . O1

144 leagues.] ~ , O1–3; ~ ∧ O4
156 bright] O2; kright O1
159 life,] O2; ~ . O1
164 subjects,] O2; ~ . O1
165 incorporat] O2 (incorporate); incorporoat O1
170 Must] O2; must O1
179 die.] ~ , O1–4
189 Should] O2; should O1
193 heaven,] O2; ~ . O1
228 slaves,] O2; ~ ∧ | O1
234 him∧ then,] ~ , ~ ∧ O1–4
247 company,] O2; ~ . O1
249 end,] O3; ~ ∧ | O1–2

HISTORICAL COLLATION

[NOTE: The following editions are herein collated: O1 (1590), O2 (1593), O3 (1597), O4 (1605, 1606), Ox (ed. Oxberry, 1820), R (*Works*, ed. Robinson, 1826), D¹ (*Works*, ed. Dyce, 1850), D² (*Works*, rev. 1858), C (*Works*, ed. Cunningham, 1870), B (*Works*, ed. Bullen, 1884–5), W (*1 Tamburlaine*, ed. Wagner, 1885), TB (*Works*, ed. Tucker Brooke, 1910), M (Methuen, ed. Ellis-Fermor, 1930), K (*Plays*, ed. Kirschbaum, 1962); Ri (*Plays*, ed. Ribner, 1963), Rg (Regent's ed. Jump, 1967). Reference is made to Mal (MS notes by Malone in Bodleian copy of O4), Br (MS notes by Broughton in BM copy of Robinson) and Coll (MS notes by Collier in BM copy of 1850 Dyce).]

PART I

Dedication

1–23 *omit* Ox, R
2 *the two*] this O4
2 *Discourses*] discourse O4
4 *they*] it O4
6 *they have*] it hath O4
7 *were*] was O4
10 *happly*] happilye O4
12 *times*] time O2, D, C, B

13 *mixtured*] mingled O3–4
16 *them*] it O4
17 *leave*] leave it O4
17–18 *both...other,*] *omit* O4
18 *of them*] thereof O4
19 *protection*] protections O3–4
20 *accept*] doo O3–4
22 *humble*] *omit* O4

Prologue

HT The two...mighty] The First Part of ...mighty O2; The tragicall Conquests of O3–4

8 *fortunes*] fortune C, B
8 *you please*] they passe Coll MS

I.i

9 *Affrike*] Affrica O3–4
10 dares scarce] scarce dares Ox, R
11 meteors] waters Coll MS
15 their] his O1–4
15 in] on Ox, R
19 Planets] plainness Coll MS
23 you] yon O3
32 of] & Coll MS
38 Trading] Treading O1, 3–4, W, K, Ri

40 incivill] uncivill O3–4, Ox, R, C, Ri
54 How] How you O3
58 chiefest] chiefe O4
87 you] *omit* O3–4
87 task] *omit* O1–4; feat Mal MS
89 *Assiria*] Affrica O1–3 all Affrica O4, Ox, R, C, B, W, M, K, Rg
90 Babylonians] Babylonian Ox, R
96 Lament] Laments Ox, R, C, B
97 my royal] my my royal O2

 98 then.] then, *Mycetes.* W (*after* Elze)
103 What,...thee_∧] What_∧...thee?
    Ox, R, C, B
105 for] so Coll MS
117 sits and laughs] sit and laugh Ox, R,
    D, C, B
118 resolve] dissolve O 3–4
121 shippes] shippe O 2
123 intreat] incite Coll MS
130 Passe] Haste O 3–4
132 you] they O 4
134 Lord, *Ortigius* _∧] ~ _∧ ~ , O 1–4, TB
135.1 Ceneus] Conerus O 1–4
138 this] the Ox, R, C, B, K
149 the] their O 2, Ox, R, D, C, B

150 stay] stop Ox, R, C, B, K
162 of *Persea*] *Persea* O 2, Ox, R, D, B
164 *Assiria*] *Affrica* O 1–4
167 wide vast] vase wide R
168 ever] river O 4
169 Long] *All.* Long O 3–4, Ox, R, D,
    C, B
170 *Jove* may] may *Jove* Br MS
174 desires] desire Ox, R, C, B
174 of] and Coll MS
179 knew] knowe O 4
182 Lords] Lord O 1–2
183 injure] injurie O 2–3, D, C, B, W
188 God] *All.* God O 3–4, D, C, B

I.ii

 0.2 *other*] & *other* O 4
 11 Medean] my uncle's C
 12 my uncles] his C
 12 *Medea*] *Meda* O 3–4
 33 do you do] do you Ox, R
 67 they] thee O 1
 79 th'arrivall] the arrivall O 2
 88 Rhodope] Rhodolfe O 1–4
 93 hundreth] hundred Ox, R, D, C, B,
    M, K, Ri, Rg
 99 Pooles] Poles O 4
101 resolv'd] dessolv'd O 4
104 Shall all we] Shall we O 2, Ox, R;
    We all shall O 4; Shall we all D, C,
    B
108 in] *omit* O 4
113 Now] How ! Ox, R, C, B
115 triumpht] tryumph O 4
115 so] to Ox, R
116 Lordings] lordlings M, Ri
126 Hangs] Hang Ox, R, C, B
132 Orators] orator Ox, R, C, B
133 foot] top O 4, D, C, B

134 an] a Ox, R, C, B, K
137 *Techelles*] *omit* Ox, R, C
138 Males] ways Ox, R
152 this] the O 4
152 Scythian] Scythian Shepherd D (*qy*);
    Scythian, this C
153 Whom] Who Ox, R, C
161 And] To O 1–4, Ox+ ; As TB (*qy*)
167 thy] the O 3–4
175 turne] turns Ox, R
199 sometime] sometimes Ox, R, D, C,
    B, M, K, Ri
220 Where] When Ox, R, C, B
225 Are] To Ox, R, D², C, W; Ah TB
    (*after* Brereton), M, Ri, Rg; These
    are resolved B
228 thy looks] looks O 3
244 statutes] statues O 3–4, R+
246 kings] King O 4
248 leave] leane O 3
248 till] to Ox, R
249 thee...them] they...theirs Ox, R
254 will] *omit* O 3–4

II.i

  2 the] that O 3–4
 11 his] this R
 11 pitch] brows Ox, R
 20 with love] and love O 3–4, Ox, R, C,
    B
 27 and fingers...sinowy] and fingers

...snowy O 1–3; long, his fingers
snowy-white O 4; and fingers, long
and snowy-white Ox, R
 30 subdued] subdue O 4
 44 is] in O 4

II.ii

4 of] on R, C, B, K
7 worst] worse O2, Ox, R, D, C, B, W, M, Ri
15 pitcht] pitch O1
24 the] that O4
27 his King] the King O3-4
28 are] be O2, R, D, C, B, K
34 Beside] Besides O4
39 An] A Ox, R, C, B, K

40 champion] camp ion O3
42 make reports] make report O2, Ox, R, C, B, M; makes reporte O4
45 after greedy] greedy after D1 (qy),D
46 than] them O4
48 teeth of] omit O3-4
51 there] their W
72 the] omit O3-4
75 ye] you O4

II.iii

7 of] omit O1-4, K
12 To some] To scorne O2; Nor scorne Br MS
13 will] shall O3-4
15 host] hosts M, Ri
16 To drinke] T'have drank R; To have dranke C, B
25 see] hear C
26 top] stop O1-4, Ox (top [qy]), R, C, B, K

31 thrust] thrist O4; thirst D, C, B
33 and] not O1-3
34 the] thee O3-4
35 Which...crown.] omit Ox, R
40 meeds] deeds O4, Ox, R
55 Cutle-axe] Curtle-axe O3
58 or the breath] o'er the breadth Coll MS
59 sure] surely Ox, R
64 enough] enow O2, D, C, B, W, K

II.iv

3 were] wh'ere Ox, R
4 Stand] Stand those O4
13 not I] I not Ox, R, C, B, K
16 coward] coward's Ox, R

19 give] give me O4, D2, C
25 to speak but] but to speak Ox, R; speak but C, B, K
29 ye] you Ox, R, D, C, B

II.v

6 man] men O4
11 chiefest] chiefe O2
15 happy] happiest O3-4, C
16 your] you O3
32 aim'd] and O1-2
33 it] is O2
34 our lives] lives O2
41 we] I O3-4, Ox, R, C
48 *Menaphon.*] *Meander.* Ox, R, D C, B

67 saies] say Ox, R, D, C, B
68 I,] omit Ox, R
86 apace] apeece O3-4, Ox, R, D, B, TB, M
96 gaine] game B, K, Ri
97 the] this O2, Ox, R, D, C, B, K
100 him back] his back O1-4, Ox, TB, Ri
103 and] with O4, Ox, R

II.vi

11 of] from Ox, R
13 dares] dare O3–4, C, B, K
18 state] fate D, K

20 Thiefe] chief Ox, R, C, B
25 one] on O2, W
37 my] his Coll MS

II.vii

0.1 *Exeunt*] *Enter* O1–4, K, Ri, Rg
1 Barbarous] O barbarous Ox, D (*qy*)
10 Sackes] Sucks Coll MS
11 Bloody] O bloody Ox
18 fram'd] form'd Ox, R
26 Wils] Will Ox, R, D, C
26 weare] weary Coll MS
26 our] orr O3

27 fruit] fruites O2
31 massie] massive Ox
32 deeds] deed Ox
42 chill] child O3
48 Is] Are Ox, R, D, C
50 Harpyr] Harpye O2, Ox, R, C, B,
　　W, M, K, Ri, Rg; Harper O4
53 the furies] thy furies O2

III.i

5 thinks] think R, C, B
9 renied] renegades Ox
25 Ocean,] ~ ‸ Ox, R, C
28 Not] Nor O4
28 in] on O4, R, C, B
29 collours] colours forth C; colours
　　once B

29 in] over W (*qy*)
36 heaven] the heaven O3–4
49 tremble] trembles Ox, R, D, C, B
50 host] hosts Ox, R
56 greatnes] highness Ox, R
65 mouth'd] mouths Ox, R
67.1 *Exeunt*.] *omit* O3

III.ii

14 ceaselesse] carelesse O4
15 dies] dye R, D, C
19 *Phœbes*] *Phœbus* O4, Ox, R, D, C, B
21 his] the O4
23 you] me O3–4
35 *Agidas*,] *omit* O1–4, Ox, R, K, Ri,
　　Rg; Leave, Agydas C
42–3 Who . . . slew] *lines transposed in* R
50 much] more O4, C
65 love] loving R

68 of] and O2, Ox, R
73 furie] furies O2, Ox, R, C, B, K
74 shine] shone D¹ (*qy*), D²
75 casts] cast Ox, R, D, C, K
86 sent] send D²
87 makes] make D, C, B
89 *Exit*.] *omit* O3–4, Ox, R, C, B, K,
　　Ri
106 [*Dies*]] *Stabs himselfe.* O4, Ox, R, C,
　　B, K, Ri

III.iii

4 menace] meane O4
5 fetch] fetcht O4
25 seate] set O2, D, B, K, Ri
42 gives] give O2, Ox, R, D, C, B

51 breath and rest] rest or breath O2,
　　Ox, R, D, C, B, K
53 they] *omit* O4
60 set] sets Br MS

60.1 *contributorie*] *his contributorie* O 3–4

65 t'] to O 2

70 tytles] title O 3–4, Ox, R

84 Ile] I wil O 3–4

87 the] this O 4

90 ye] you O 4

94 hugie] huge Ox

97 all] of O 2, R, D, C, B

99 raigne] rule O 2, Ox, R, D, C, B, K

103 braver] brave O 4

105 pash] part Ox, R

109 ysprong] ere sprung Ox, R

127 Me] We Ox, R

142 they should] they they should O 3

144 thee] them D²

145 foolish hardy] foolish-hardy Br MS, M

149 use] us'd Ox, R

151 on] o'er Ox, R

151 the] *omit* D (*qy*)

158 our] your D, C, B, W, K, Rg

158 aire] lure O 1, 3–4, M; lute O 2; light Ox, R, D (*but qy* air), C, B, W; wind C (*qy*)

175 Advocates] Advocate O 3–4, Ox, R, D, C, B

178 *et seq. Ebea*] Ebra Ox

179 she thinks perhaps] perhaps she thinks Ox, R, C, B

180 other] her other Ox

180 weedes] weed O 3

181–2 And make...talk,] *repeated in* O 4, *but transposed, between sigs.* F 1–F 1ʳ

183 mistresse] mistreth O 2

188.1 *to*] *omit* O 1–2, TB, K, Ri

191 Turkish] fearful Ox, R

198 him] *Bajazeth* W

201 lie] lies O 4

202 And] as O 4 (*prose*)

203 Trumpets] trumpet Ox, R, B

204 As] and O 4 (*prose*)

208–11 If...Conqueror.] *omit* Ox, R

211.2 *short*] *is short* O 3; *shout* K

213 foile] soile O 1–4, Ox, R, D¹

220 Turkish] *omit* Ox, R, C, B, K

233–4 *Bajazeth. Ah...Emperour*] O 4 *transposes ll.* 233–4

234 And...Emperour] *omit* Ox

246 furthest] farthest O 4

250 Christians] Christian Ox, R, C

251 *Asant*] à Zante Coll MS

259 British] brightest O 2

262 thinkst] thinksts O 2; thinks O 4

268 ye] you O 2, D, B, W, K, Ri

270 makest] makes O 4, Ox, R, C, B

273 martiall] materiall O 4

IV.i

18 *Gorgon*] the Gorgon Ox, R

31 ever] *omit* O 2

35 should] shal O 2

42 Devill] the devill O 4

50 White] While O 4

59 blacke] black h's R; black's Br MS

59 Pavilion] pavilions Ox, R

61 Jetty] petty Ox, R

IV.ii

4 his] your Ox, R

6 moorish] Moorish Ox, R

7 it] *omit* O 2, W

8 Spheare] speare O 4

9 thousands] thousand Ox, R

11 it should] should it O 2, O 4

12 this] it O 4

15 into] unto O 2, Ox, R

17 heart] soule O 2, Ox, R, D¹, C, B, K

22 stoope, stoope] stoop, stoop, stoop Ox, D (*qy*)

26 Then] When Ox, R, C

34 their] your D¹ (*qy*), D², C, B, W

45 makes] make O 1–4, K

46 to] or O 4

49 *Clymens*] *Clymeus* O 1, 3–4; *Clymenes* O 2

50 brent] burnt O 3–4

65 kings] King O 4

70 from] in O2
72 for you then] then for you O3–4, D
79 dignities] dignitis O3; dignitie O4
85 whiles] while O4, Ox, R, C
87 shalt] shal O2
104 grac'd] grace Br MS, D, C, B, W
105 stature] statue O3–4, Ox, R, C, K

106 citie] city's Ox, R, C, B
110 is] are R, D, C
119 me] us Ox, R, C, B
120 their] our Ox, R
123 would] should Br MS
124 countries] country Ox, R, D, C, B
125 if I have] I've Ox, R, C, B

IV.iii

0.1 streaming] steaming O1–2
3 Calidonian] Caldonian O1; Calce-
donian O3–4
4 lustie] omit O4
10 Raves] Roves Br MS
12 and] omit O2, Ox, R
14 dares] dare O2–4, D, B
17 bandes] handes O4
23 ye] you D, B, K

35 of] to B
37 Ibis] Isis' Ox, R
45 heaven and we] we and Heaven Ox,
R, C, B, K
47 And] An O1 (cw)
55 and] omit O4
65 thy basenesse and] the basenesse of
O4

IV.iv

17 maske] walke O3–4, Ox, R
26 My Lord] My lord, my lord B
26 suffer] tamely suffer D (qy), W, K
33 goodly] good O3–4
33 to] for O2, D
36 you not] ye not O3–4
40 here] there O3–4
44 slice] flice O3; fleece O4
45 she] he Ox, R, C, B
49 will] will not O4
57 dooth] do R, C, B
60 a great deale] omit Ox, R
63 art thou] thou art Ox, R, C, B, K
83 thy] my O4

89 will] may Ox, R, C, B K,
96 hasting] hastening O3–4, Ox, R, D,
C
98 benumb'd] be numb'd O3–4
99 Let] and let Ox, R, C, B
105 specially] especially O3–4, Ox, R, C
110 these] them Ox, R
122 plage] place O1–4, Ox, R, D¹, W,
TB, M, K, Ri, Rg
123 bower] hower O1–2
126 valure] value O1–4
127 byrthes] birth Ox, R
128 whence] where O4
133 againe] omit O3–4

V.i

18 sakes] sake O3–4
29 care] cares O2
30 Whiles] While Ox, R, C
33 helps] help O4
37 or] for O4
41 weigh'd] weigh O2
44 power] powers O4
49 Patrones] Patrons Ox, R, D, C, B,
M, K, Ri, Rg

54 events] intents Coll MS
66 Damascus] Damascus walls B
67 know] knew O2, Ox, R, D, C, B
70 Reflexing] Reflexed Ox, R, D, C, B
70 your] their D¹ (qy), D², W
71 As] and O4
72 tents] tent O3–4, R
73 submissions] submission Ox, R, D,
C, W, K

73 comes] come O3
85 of ruth and] and ruth of O4
93 Have] Hath O3–4, D, C, B, K; Has Ox, R
97 for] our C, B
98 nourisht] nourish O3–4
103 wisht] wish O3–4
106 ye] you O2, Ox, R, D, C, B, K
111 imperious] imprecious O4
123 *Gehons*] Gelion's Ox
140 mornings] morning Ox, R, C, B, K
147 when that] that when B (*after* Mermaid); which when that W
149 Making] Make in B (*after* Mermaid)
151 There] these Ox, R, C, B
151 fight] fights O3–4
157 Perseans] Persia's Ox, R, C, B, M
172 least] last Br MS
180 rapt] wrapt O2, Ox, R, B
184 stoopt] stopt O1–4, Ox, R, D¹, M, K, Ri, Rg
184 tempest] temper Coll MS; chiefest D², C, B
185 fiery spangled] spangled firie O3–4; fire-yspangled Coll MS, D (*qy*)
185 vaile] vault Coll MS
186 lovely] lowly Coll MS, C, B, K
187 martch] mask D, C, B, W
187 cottages] cottges O3; coatches O4; cottagers' off-strowed Br MS
187 weeds] reeds D², C, B, K
191.1 *two or three*] Anippe Ox
193 *Attendant.*] *An.* O1–4, Ox
195.1 *and*] with O3–4
200 March…with] Martcht on with us with O2
202 not] *omit* Ox
218 Furies] May Furies Br MS
227 pore] dore Ox
232 in] on Ox, R
236 With] Live aye Ox
236 aie] *omit* Ox; live R; stay D, C, B
237 retorqued] retortued O4
240 Feend] friend Ox
240 nor no] no, nor Ox
243 A] As O1–4
255 thoughts] thought O3–4
257 fils] fill Ox, R
260 sees] see Ox, R, C, B

262 ye] you O4
263 soule] scull Br MS
267 abjection] objection O2, 4
270 ruth] truth O4, C
282 band] hard Ox, R
287 thy braines] the braines O3–4, Ox, R, D
290 everliving] everlasting O4
300 ayre] ay O1–2
310–11 I bring him] Ay, bring him Br MS
311 peeces, give] peeces & give O2, Ox, R
316–17 Let…*Tamburlaine*] *omit* O3–4
316 buried] cursed Ox, R; burn'd C
317–18 I come…come.] I come, I come. O3–4
318.2 *Enter*] *omit* O1–3
320 Egyptian] Egyptians' D, C, B, W
322 Thy] The D, C, B, W, K
336 tearm'st] tearmest O2
340 Ah] Oh C
347 thy] thine O3–4, C
356 fights] fightst O3–4, Ox, R, D, C, B, K
356 slippery] fickle Ox, R
359 conquest] conquests Ox, R, C, K
360 war] warres O3–4
365 respect of] respective Br MS
380 Comes] Come Ox, R, D
383 presents] present Ox, R, D, C, B
395 finall] small O2
411 thy blood] my blood O2
432.2 Usumcasane] *omit* O2
435 have] hath O3–4; has Ox, R, C
453 should] shall O3–4
454 sweat] sweare O3–4
457 raines] raignes O2
459 gasping] gaping Ox, R, Br MS (gasping), D
463 Millions] Million O4
473, 502 hath] has Ox, R
485 wants] want Ox, R, D, C, B, K
494 my] the O2, Ox, R, D, B, K
495 saith] say Ox, R
498 I not] not I O3–4
500 Els] Then O2
505 on] *omit* O2
514 daughter] daughters Ox, R, C, B

516 the] thee D², M, Ri, Rg
521 arme] hand Ox, R
523 your] you O3
528 poste] posts D, C

531 beseemes] best beseemes O2
531 entombe] entomb'd Ox, R
534 celebrated] *omit* D, C, B, K, Ri

PART II

Prologue

2 *our*] *the* O4, Ox, R, D, C, B, K
3 *Hath*] Have D
5 *Fates*] fate Ox, R
5 *throwes*] throw D, C, B

5 *triumphs*] tryumph O4, Ox, R
8 *sad*] said O1–4, K
9 *at large*] *at at large* O3

I.i

HT With . . . *death*.] *omit* O4
0.2 Uribassa] Upibassa O1–4
14 all are] are all M, K
19 must you] you must O2, R, D, C, B, K
20 *Uribassa*.] *Upibas.* O1–4
22, 58 Almans, Rutters] Almain Rutters Coll MS, B
22, 58 Muffes] Russ Coll MS, K
24 surety] safety Ox, R
25 *Orcanes*.] *omit* O1–4
26 *Gruntland*] *Grantland* O3–4, Ox, R, D, C, B
28 hugie] huge Ox
29 cut the] out the O3; out of O4
32 champion] champaign'd R
56 Once] Being Ox, R
62 Cicilians] Cilicians TB (*qy*)
63 Sorians] Syrians O2, Ox, R, C, B
63 blacke] and black O3–4
63–4 Egyptians, | Illirians] *Egyptians,* | *Fred.* And we from *Europe* to the

same intent | Illirians O3–4 (*transposed* from 118) Ox, R (*Gazellus,*)
64 Illirians] Illicians O1–2
64 Bythinians] Bithymans O3–4
66 t'] to O2
68 Plage] Place O3–4
72 in] *omit* O3
77 Viceroies] Viceroie O2, Ox, R, D, C, B
87 *Vienna*] Vienna's Ox, R
90 Quiver] Quivers Ox, R, D, C, B
99 tent] tents Ox, R, C, B, K
113 Or] As Ox, R, C
117 ye] you O2, Ox, R, D, C, B
118 *Fredericke.* And . . . intent,] *omit* O3–4 (*see ll.* 63–4)
120 stand] are O3–4
128 or] and O3–4
143 conditions] condition O2, Ox, R
149 Confirm'd] Confirme O2
155 by] with O3–4

I.ii

5 with] with all Ox, R, C, B, K
6 your] you B, K
15, 19 *Cairo*] *Cario* O1–4, TB
20 streames] stream D²
20 at] an O2
22 river] river's Ox, R
26 Where] Whence Ox, R

28 a] an O3–4
34 from] to O2, Ox, R
51 his] the Ox, R, C, B
52 th'] the O2
58 bending] landing Ox, R
59 tacklings] tackling Ox, R

I.iii

6 parts] part D, C, B
9 wilt] wile O 3
18 When] While Ox, R
25 and] as O 3–4
31 Their...aire:] *omit* Ox, R, C, B
50 Brothers] brother's Ox, R
57 shall] should O 4
58 words] word O 3
62 of] to O 4
63 to] of O 4
68 won] now Ox, R
79 superficies] superfluities O 1–4
86 Dismaies] Dismay Ox, R, D, C, B
92 through] thorow O 2
93 Carcases] Carkasse O 4
96 you] ye O 2, 4; Ox, R, D, C, B, K
99 we] yon O 4
107 *Larissa*] *Larissa's* Ox, R

119 *Argier*] *Argier's* Ox, R, C, B
141 war] warres O 3–4
143 infernall] the infernall O 4
144 thee] them O 1–4
144 this] these O 3–4, Ox, R, D, C, B, M, K, Ri, Rg
167 my] the Ox, R
170 *Boetes*] Bootes O 3–4, Ox
179 coast] coasts Ox, R, C
180 straight] straits Ox, R
195 Westerne] eastern Br MS, C, B
198 *Manico*] Mexico Ox, R
199 Where] Whence Ox, R
208 made] thence I made C, B
208 *Europe*] Europa W (*qy after* Elze)
211 Then] Thence Ox, R, C, B, K
224 orient] oriental O 1–4, K
225 whiles] while Ox, R, C

II.i

18 *Cutheia*] Cuthea O 3–4; Bretheia Ox
20 *Acantha*] *Acanthia* O 3
21 *et seq. Soria*] Syria Ox, R, C
22 hereof] thereof O 2, Ox, R, D, C, B
24 the] th' O 2
40 what we] that we O 2, D, C, B; we that R
41 and] or Ox, R, C, B, K

45 faiths] fame O 4
45 and their] their R; and Ox, D, C, B
47 consumate] consinuate O 1–4; continuate Ox, R, D¹
50 dispensive] defensive Ox
52 venge] avenge C
59 this] the O 4

II.ii

7 martial] materiall O 2
8 heaven] heavens Ox, R
12 And] An Ox, R, C
12 thousands] thousand Ox, R, C, W

21 your] our O 3–4, D
23 With] Which O 2
35 cares] care Ox, R, C, B
63 Lords] Lord O 4

II.iii

1 Christian] Christians O 3–4
5 of] and Coll MS
22 flourisheth] flourishes R, C, B
32 is] has Ox, R

34 an] any O 4
38 shall] and O 2
40 give] and give O 4
43 brother] brothers Ox, R, D, C, B, M

247

II.iv

9 their] *omit* O2
9 bowers] brows D
19 this] the O3–4
22 springs] spring D
38 no] not O2
40 And] An D, B
43 and] a O2
46 Wanes] Wane Ox, R, D, C, Ri; Wade B
47 May] Nay O2
51 make] makes O3–4, Ox
56 author] anchor O1–3, K
65 And] An O3
66 yet] yes Ox, R, D

68 hurtes] hurt Ox, R
73 Lords] lord Ox, R
74 Have] Hath Coll MS
76 excellency] excellence O3–4, D, C, B
77.1 call] *call for* O3–4, Ox, R, C, B, Ri
96 What] *Tam.* What O2
132 shalt] shall O4
134 one] on O2; our O4, Ox, R, C, B
140 stature] statue O3–4, Ox, R, K, Ri; statua Br MS, D (*qy*), C, B; statuè Coll MS

III.i

13 fate] Fates O4
14 Thiefe] chief Ox, R, C, B
18 our] his D, B
21 Hath] Have R, D, C, B, K
24 true] all true O2, Ox, R, D, C, B
30 honors] honor O3–4
37 cursed] *omit* Ox, R

39 conquest] the conquest O2
43 ynow] know Ox, R
45 *Judæa*] *Juda* O4
45 *Scalonians*] *Sclavonians* O4; Sclavonia's R, D, C, B
59 unto] on to C, B, K
74 of] from Ox, R

III.ii

9 death] dearth D, C, B, Ri
10 thunderclaps] thunderbolts, Ox, R
14 deare] dear'st Ox, R, C, B
20 Egyptian] the Egyptian O2, Ox, R, D, C, B
34 *Larissa*] Larissa's R
39 Those] Whose O1–4, Ox, R
39 campe] camps C
48 sorrow] sorrowes O2, Ox, R, D, C, B, Ri
58 thirst] cold O1–3, K
64 which] with O1–4, Ox
68 the Counterscarps] and Counterscarps O3–4
78 great] greatst O4
80 curtaines] curtain Ox, R
82 the walles] their walles O1–4
90 Invincible] Invisible R
90 by] by the O4
91 ye] you O3–4

96 a] the O2, R, B, K
99 mingled...horse] of mingled foot and horse C (*qy*)
99 shot] foot D (*qy*)
101 Hang...motes,] *omit* R
111 his] this O3–4
111 hoste] horse B
111 martcht] martch O1–2, TB, K
113 dram] drop O2, Ox, R, D, C, B
119 chaire] chain Ox, R, D, C, B
123 the] a O2–4, Ox, R, D, C, B, K
129 you] ye O2, D, C, B
130 tis] it is Ox, R, C, B
132 Tis] This O2; This? Ox, R, C, B
139 throngs] dregs Ox, R, C
141 *Larissa*] Larissa's Ox, R
147 the] *omit* O3
150 accursed] cursed O2
152 his] the O2

III.iii

1 *Theridamas*.] *Tamb*. C
1 Northwarde] southward C (*ay*)
2 point] port O 3–4, Ox, R
2 *et seq. Soria*] Syria Ox, R, C, B
8 gold] hold D, W
9 ye] you O 2, 4; Ox, R, D, C, B, K
9 we] we or B
12 quietly] quickely O 4
13 friends] friend O 1–2
17 do you] do thou O 2
20 These] The R, C
21 in] to O 4
22 thy] the Ox, R, C, B, K
33 any] *omit* O 1–4, K
34 quietly] quickely O 4

35 you] all you O 3–4
35 the] *omit* O 4
36 to] of O 2, Ox, R, D, C, B, K
39 that can] that come Ox, R; you can C
40 I am] am I O 4
43 wall] walls Ox, R
45 their] the Ox, R
53 unto their wals] into their castle Ox, R
55 into] unto O 4
56 Gabions] Galions O 1–4, Ox, R, D
56 foot] feet B, K
63 hold] holds O 1–2, K

III.iv

0.1 *the*] *omit* O 3–4
5 on] at Ox, R
9 straineth] staineth O 2
22 Or] And Ox, R
27 ye] you Ox, R, C, B, K
28 home] have O 4
30 meet] see Ox, R, C
40 wert] art O 4, Ox, R, C, B
41 thee with] with thee O 4
46 man] *omit* TB (*qy*)
62 join'd] injoin'd O 2

63 Fame] Fume O 3–4
63 of] in O 4, C
67 thy] thine Ox, R
69 Take] Tame O 2
83 the] *omit* C, B
86 time] times O 3
88 the silver] and silver O 2, Ox, R, D, C, B, K
88 ye] we B
90 so] as C, B

III.v

1 mighty] and mighty O 4
2 all] half Ox, R
3 an] a R, C, B
5 In] With Ox, R
5 number] numbers Ox, R, C, B
5 the] this O 2
7 pursues] pursue Ox, R, D, C, B
11 of] from Ox, R
15 your] our O 4
19 terme] term'd D¹ (*qy*), D²
21 the] *omit* O 2
26 your] our O 4
27 their] in their O 2, D
28 pawes] jaws C
28 with] *omit* O 2

30 me] us Ox, R
34 your] to your O 4, R
42 bands] band Ox, R
43 knowes] know Ox, R, D, C, B, M
46 repair'd] prepar'd O 4
47 And...land,] *omit* O 4
50 Army royall] royal army Ox, R, C, K
57.1 *other*] *others* O 2
61 deaths] death C, K
62 Why] And Ox, R, C, B, K
65 into] unto R
84 is] the O 4
90 proud] vile Ox, R, C, B
101 away againe,] ~ ; ~ ₍ Ox, R, C

103 Viceroy] Viceroys Ox, R, D, C, B
104 harnest] harnesse O 3–4
106 on] with O 2
108 thou shalt] shalt thou O 4
111 the] our O 3–4, Ox, R, C, B
118 had swallowed] did swallow R, C
121 and] or O 4
121 rend] rent O 2, D, C, B

125 beat] rent Coll MS
135 too] *omit* O 4
139 No] Go O 2
140 in] *omit* R
151 know ye] know you O 3–4
153 you] ye O 2, Ox, R, D, C, B, K
162 aspect] aspects O 4
164 Loden] Laden O 3–4, Ox, R

IV.i

6 conquering] conquerings O 1; conquering's K, Rg
6 wings] swings W, TB
12 You cannot] Can you not O 4
14 ruine] ruins Ox, R, C
22 fight] field Ox, R, C, B, K
36 both you] you both O 4, C, B
46 arms] aims Coll MS
51.1 *run*] *runnes* O 2
53 should I] I should O 4
56 nor harme] no harme O 2, 4; Ox, R,
   D, C, B
59 Ile] I will Ox, R, C, B
61 goe] go away Ox, R, C
76 now] how R
76 ye] my O 4
76 stoops] stoop Ox, R, D, C
77 leads] lead Ox, R, D, C
77 glories] bodies O 2, Ox, R, D, C, B,
   K
83 gainst] against O 4
93 mine] my O 2, Ox, R
95 may] nay O 2
99 up] by R

101 once] one O 2
103 ye] you O 3–4
106 martiall] materiall O 3–4
107 thine] thy O 4
108 which] with O 1–4
108 *Jaertis*] Laertes O 4; Laertis' Ox;
   Jakertis' R
114 incorporeall] incorporall O 3–4
135 you shal] shall ye O 3–4
135 feele] see Ox, R, C
142 have] *omit* Ox, R
145 bloods on] blood on O 2, Ox, R
146 Villaines] Villaine O 4
152 or] and Ox, R
157 resist in] resisting O 1–4, Ox, R, K
157 Pesants] parsants O 4
158 The power] Resist the pow'r Ox, R
159 *Casane*] *Usumcasane* O 2, Ox, R
163 defile] befile O 2
170 imposd] so impos'd] Ox, R
171 it] *omit* O 3–4
173 Expell] Excel D, C, B
185 ye] you O 3–4

IV.ii

2 beheld] beholde O 2, 4; D, C, B, K
3 a] the O 2, Ox, R, C
4 Hath] Have R, D, C, Ri
16 wast] was O 2
18 *Jove*] love Ox, R
22 sons] Sonne O 4
25 Forbids] Forbid Ox, R, C
44 and] to O 2, Ox, R, D, C, B, K
46 in] to O 4
55 good] now O 2, Ox, R, D, C, B
55 and wil you] if you will O 4, R

64 mouthes] mother O 2
66 Pistol] pistols Ox, R, C, B
67 ye] you O 3–4, Ox, R, D, C, B, K
75 hereof] thereof O 2, Ox, R, D, C, B,
   K
77 wil] I wil O 2; I'll Ox, R, C
83 my] thy Ox, R, C, B, K
86 Theoria] Theona Ox
89 doo borrow] borrow doo O 2
98 my] thy O 2; this Ox, R

IV.iii

0.2 *his left*] *their left* O2, Ox
0.5 *with*] *omit* O4, Ox, R, D, C, B, M, Ri
10 in] as O4
27 coach] a coch O3–4
28 with] by O4, Ox, R, D, C
37 garden] garded O2
53 speak you] speake ye O2, Ox, R, C
57 same] *omit* O4
61 match] march O3–4
62 Above] about O4
72 their] *omit* O2
74 your majesty] you Ox, R, C, B
81 continent] content O1–4
87 you] ye O2, Ox, R, D, C, B, K

87 honour] honours R
90 Pageant] pageants Ox, R, C, B
104 *Senus*] *Sinus* O2
105 al] *omit* O4
108 *Jaertis*] *Laertes* O4; Laertis' Ox; Jakertis' R
114 Thorow] Through O3; & through O4
119 ymounted] mounted Ox, R
121 ever] every O1–4, Ox
122 browes] bowes O2
124 that thorow] from O4; through C, B
126 chariot] chariots O1–4, Ox, R

V.i

6 out] our O2–4, B
12 Is] Are Ox, R, C, B, K
14 of] in O4
14 with] in Ox, R, C
22 Foe] foes Ox, R, C, B
23 lookes] look Ox, R, C
25 to] for Ox, R, C, B
32 he] was O2, Ox, R, D1, C, B
33 Wil] Would Ox, R, C, B
34 How] Alas *or* Ay me how] W (*qy*)
34 environed] environed with cares Br MS, B; environed. How am I bereft Br MS (*later*); environed with grief D1 (*qy*)
35 eternisde] enternisde O2
38 you] ye O2, Ox, R, C
39 save] and save O4, Ox, R, D, C, B
47 never] ever C, B
70 triumphs] triumph Ox, R
75 do] I and Ox, R
83 of] for O4
83 your] you O1
84 villaine] traitor Ox, R
93 quail'd] qual'd O2; quell'd Ox, R
98 wake] make O4, D2, W, K, Ri
101 breach] breath O2
105 citie] *omit* O4
106 or] nor Ox, R
107 him] it O2, R
108 up] *omit* Ox, R, D2, C, B, K

113 or] nor Ox, R, C, B
114 him then,] them Ox
114 scard] scard O3–4, Ox, R, C; scared B
124 execution] th'execution R
133 Vild] Wild Ox, R
134 dispatcht] dispatche O3
146 doe not] don't Ox, R, C, B
149 done,] done, *Theridamas* Br MS
157 *Bagdets*] Babylon's Coll MS
159 her] the R
159 wall] walls Ox, R
164 Cytadell] lofty citadel B
164 *Assiria*] *Affrica* O1–4; *Arabia* Br MS
180 Slew] Slain Ox, R, C, B
182 revenging] revengeful Ox, R
184 will I] I wil O3–4
189 flames] flame Ox, R, C, B, K
191 send'st] sends O3–4
193 sitt'st] sits O3–4
194 head] blood O4
204 water] waters R, C, B, K
205 fed] feed O1–4
206 upon] *omit* O3–4
208 gaspe] gape O2, Ox, R, D, C, B, K
209 now] more Ox, R, C
213 in] *omit* O3–4
215 about] above Ox, R
220 so ere] so ever O4

V.ii

3 runs] run Ox, R, D, C, B
4 may we] we may O 4, Ox, R, C
18 that] this O 2, D, C, B, K
21 Viceroies] Viceroy's Ox, R, C;

viceroys' D, B, M, K, Ri, Rg
27 hoste] post Ox, R
28 Aid] And O 3–4
50 at home] here Ox, R

V.iii

10 Now] How Ox, R
13 invisiblie] invincible O 2, Ox; invisible R, C, B
23 whom you] you most Ox, R
31 inexcellence] inexcellencie O 2
35 that] *omit* Ox, R
36 makes] make R
53 thus invie] envy thus Ox, R
64 cease] case O 3
73 barke] backe O 3–4, Ox, R, D, C, B
82 Hipostasis] Hipostates O 1–4, Ox
85 moisture] moister O 3
87, 89 Is] Are R, C
93 alongst] along Ox, R, C
94 the] thy Ox, R
95 spirit] spirits C, B, K
96 Organnons] organisms Ox, R
104 upon] on O 2
115 villaines,] villain_Λ Ox, R, D², C, B, K
116 Summers] summer Ox, R, C
116 vanisht] banish'd Coll MS
121 t'] to O 2
128 unto] to O 4, Ox, R

130 Then] Thence Ox, R, C, B
143 began] begun O 4
147 this] the O 4, Ox, R
164 subjects] substance Coll MS
168 subject] substance Coll MS
171 into] unto O 4, Ox, R
174 your] our O 4, Ox, R
181 A] *omit* Ox, R
181 Lord] lords Ox, R, C, B
181 that] it Ox, R
183 let] and let Ox, R, D, C, B, K
186 breath] breach O 4
188 lineaments] laments O 3–4, Ox, R
190 Pierc'd] Piec'd Coll MS
202, 203 those] these O 3–4, Ox, R, D, C, Ri (*line* 202 *only*)
207 damned] dampned Coll MS
231 *Clymens*] *Clymeus* O 1,3–4; *Clymenes* O 2
232 *Phœbes*] *Phœbus* O 4, Ox, R
237 *Phyteus*] Phoebus' Ox, R
240 thee] me O 4
241 cliftes] clefts Coll MS

THE RICH JEW OF MALTA

The Jew of Malta (Greg, *Bibliography*, no. 475) was entered in the Stationers' Register on 17 May 1594 to Nicholas Ling and Thomas Millington as *the famouse tragedie of The Riche Jewe of Malta*. So far as is known, no edition was published. The next entry refers to the 1633 quarto. On 20 November 1632 the Register records the entry to Nicholas Vavasour, licensed by Sir Henry Herbert, a tragedy called *The Jew of Malta*. The quarto should have been published in late December 1632 or early 1633. Greg identifies the printer by his initials as John Beale. The quarto collates A–I⁴ K², A 1 blank and the text starting on B 1. The type is worn so that the imperfect inking leads to questions of the actual pointing that can be resolved only by the comparison of a number of copies. The substantive corruption does not seem to be excessive, but the number of literals is rather high. The only known press-correction repaired a single such literal in each of three formes.

The play had long been popular. Its first recorded performance was on 26 February 1592, its title in Henslowe's version being *the Jewe of malltuse* and the receipts 50 shillings. It was played again on 10 March, noted as *the Jewe of Malta* with receipts of 56 shillings. On both occasions the company was Lord Strange's men. The last record of a performance by this company was on 1 February 1593 when 35 shillings were taken in. On 4 February 1594 the Earl of Sussex's men acted it, with receipts of 50 shillings. On 3 April, 7 April, and 14 May Sussex's and the Queen's companies, combined, staged it for receipts of £3, 26 shillings, and 48 shillings respectively. Henslowe then records it in a list of the Admiral's company and the Chamberlain's company productions on 4 June 1594 (10s.) and a number of other performances up to 9 December 1594 (3s.). It was revived on 9 January 1596 (56s.) and acted through 21 June (13s.). For another revival, Henslowe lent £5 10s. probably for costumes on 19 May 1601. Thereafter records cease. The performances at the Cockpit and at court, presumably in 1632, for which Heywood wrote the prologues and epilogues are not recorded.

Given this history, no doubt only a small part of the actual facts, the odds favour two speculations. The first is that more likely than not it would have been the earlier promptbook which was preserved and used as the basis for the 1632 revival, the text of which seems to be represented in the quarto of 1633. Whether the actual prompt-book or a transcript was sent to the printer, or a revised, marked-up copy, perhaps intercalated with new leaves, of the old book which had been transcribed to form a new book for the revival and was thus available for printing, is not to be determined. Critics have speculated that the forms of the speech-prefixes might encourage a hypothesis that the quarto had some relation to Marlowe's original manuscript, but the evidence – if evidence it is – is very slight and perhaps such a circumstance may appear to be most improbable. That Heywood, or whoever was the actual entrepreneur for the revival, would not touch up an old play for a new audience is also most improbable. The different forms *Basso* and *Bashaw* in the first and second halves of the play have been noticed, the first being that found in *Tamburlaine*. Also possible evidence of textual disruption comes in the variant forms of the speech-prefixes of the two friars Jacomo and Bernardine. It has not been noticed that one or two typographical conventions differ between the first two and the last three acts. In Acts I and II 'Turk(e)' is invariably in italic, as are words like 'Spanish', 'Grecian' and so on. Starting with Act III, however, of all the various occurrences of 'Turke' only once, at IV.i.111, is the word italicized; the others are all in roman, completely in contrast with the usage of the first two acts.[1] Also, at V.ii.7 'Turkish' is in roman whereas it and other such adjectives are invariably in italic in the first two acts (although *Italian* in italic appears at III.iv.69). Just possibly another piece of evidence is significant. The word 'master' is spelled out in the four times it occurs in Act II, as at II.iii.173, 202, 365, 368. But starting with III.iii.18 it is sometimes abbreviated to 'M^r.' and sometimes spelled out. A few minor anomalies exist in the last three acts, such as roman 'Turkey' at V.v.115 versus italic at V.iii.16 and earlier, or italic *Curtezane* at IV.iii.2 but roman elsewhere. At IV.iv.30 'French' is in roman. It is probably a reasonable theory that the comic scenes,

[1] Cf. roman at III.ii.13, III.iii.48, IV.i.127, 198, IV.ii.39, V.i.27, 51.

more prominent in the last three acts, were among those that were touched up in preparation for the revival, but bibliographical evidence about any distinction in authorship would seem to be wanting.

Anomalies such as those noticed cannot be assigned to differences in the number of workmen. Dr Robert F. Welsh, in his 1964 dissertation *The Printing of the Early Editions of Marlowe's Plays* (University Microfilms), pp. 158–83, has made a thorough analysis of the printing of the quarto, with the following results. The running-titles show that one skeleton-forme printed both formes of sheets B–D, but the outer formes of sheets D–I and half-sheet K were printed from a newly made-up skeleton-forme so that these sheets were machined more speedily by the use of two skeleton-formes. Recurring pieces of identifiable types show that Sheets D–I were typeset by formes, as were sheets B and C. Throughout, the characteristics of only one compositor can be detected, a workman who seems to have set Beale's quartos of Forde's *Broken Heart* and *Loves Sacrifice*, both in 1633 also.

To establish the 1633 form of the text, twelve of the numerous preserved copies of the quarto were collated, with only three trifling press-variants of literals being disclosed. These copies were British Museum[1] (82.c.22[6]), BM[2] (644.e.70; imperfect, wanting D1, I4, K1.2), BM[3] (Ashley; a made-up copy), Bodleian[1] (Mal. 133[2]), Bodl[2] (Mal. 172[2]), Bodl[3] (Mal. 915[5]), CSmH (Huntington), DFo[1] (Folger, Halliwell-Phillipps), DFo[2] (H-P Warwick Castle), DFo[3] (Malone), MH (Harvard), MWiW–C (Chapin, Williams College).

In 1818 J. Chappell Jr printed an edition of this play, as he did for most of Marlowe's other plays, some readings of which represent the earliest emendations for readings adopted in the present text. This edition is not recorded in the Historical Collation, however, for it differs in so many small modernizations and sophistications of language that the listing of these variants would expand the Collation beyond normal size. Moreover, so far as can be told, the Chappell edition was not in the mainstream of the textual history and did not influence later texts. Although the present editor regrets the necessity to omit this interesting Chappell edition from consideration, no regrets may be wasted on another 1818 edition, put out by S. Penley, Comedian, and published by Richard White. The titlepage advertises 'considerable alterations and additions' and states that the play is in the form being acted at the Theatre Royal in Drury Lane. The very extensive rewriting and vulgarization prevent any attempt to record its variant readings.

TO MY WORTHY FRIEND,

M^R. THOMAS HAMMON,

OF GRAYES INNE, &c.

This Play, composed by so worthy an Authour as Master *Marlo*; and the part of the Jew presented by so unimitable an Actor as Master *Allin*, being in this later Age commended to the Stage: As I usher'd it unto the Court, and presented it to the Cock-pit, with these Prologues and Epilogues here inserted, so now being newly brought to the Presse, I was loath it should be published without the ornament of an Epistle; making choyce of you unto whom to devote it; then whom (of all those Gentlemen and acquaintance, within the compasse of my long knowledge) there is none more able to taxe Ignorance, or attribute right to merit. Sir, you have bin 10 pleased to grace some of mine owne workes with your curteous patronage; I hope this will not be the worse accepted, because commended by mee; over whom, none can clayme more power or privilege than your selfe. I had no better a New-yeares gift to present you with; receive it therefore as a continuance of that inviolable obliegement, by which, he rests still ingaged; who as he ever hath, shall always remaine,

Tuissimus:

THOMAS HEYWOOD.

The Prologue spoken at Court.

Gracious and Great, that we so boldly dare,
('Mongst other Playes that now in fashion are)
To present this; writ many yeares agone,
And in that Age, thought second unto none;
We humbly crave your pardon: we pursue
The story of a rich and famous *Jew*
Who liv'd in *Malta*: you shall find him still,
In all his projects, a sound *Machevill*;
And that's his Character: He that hath past
So many Censures, is now come at last   10
To have your princely Eares; grace you him, then
You crowne the Action, and renowne the pen.

Epilogue.

It is our feare (dread Soveraigne) we have bin
Too tedious; neither can't be lesse than sinne
To wrong your Princely patience: If we have,
(Thus low dejected) we your pardon crave:
And if ought here offend your eare or sight,
We onely Act, and Speake, what others write.

The Prologue to the Stage, at the Cocke-pit.

We know not how our Play may passe this Stage,
But by the best of* Poets in that age   * Marlo.
The *Malta Jew* had being, and was made;
And He, then by the best of* Actors play'd: * Allin.
In *Hero* and *Leander*, one did gaine
A lasting memorie: in *Tamberlaine*,
This *Jew*, with others many, th'other wan
The Attribute of peerelesse, being a man
Whom we may ranke with (doing no one wrong)
Proteus for shapes, and *Roscius* for a tongue,   10
So could he speake, so vary; nor is't hate
To merit in* him who doth personate   * Perkins
Our *Jew* this day, nor is it his ambition
To exceed, or equall, being of condition
More modest; this is all that he intends,
(And that too, at the urgence of some friends)
To prove his best, and if none here gaine-say it,
The part he hath studied, and intends to play it.

Epilogue.

In Graving, with *Pigmalion* to contend;
Or Painting, with *Apelles*; doubtlesse the end
Must be disgrace: our Actor did not so,
He onely aym'd to goe, but not out-goe.
Nor thinke that this day any prize was plaid,
Here were no betts at all, no wagers laid;
All the ambition that his mind doth swell,
Is but to heare from you, (by me) 'twas well.

[DRAMATIS PERSONÆ

MACHIAVEL, the Prologue
BARABAS, the Jew
FERNEZE, Governor of Malta
CALYMATH, Son to the Grand Signior
CALLAPINE, Bashaw to Calymath
DON LODOWICK, the Governor's son
DON MATHIAS
ITHAMORE, a Turkish Slave
DEL BOSCO, the Spanish Vice Admiral
JACOMO
BARNARDINO } Friars
PILIA BORZA

TWO MERCHANTS
Three JEWS
KNIGHTS
BASHAWS
OFFICERS
READER
ABIGAIL, Daughter to Barabas
KATHERINE, Mother to Mathias
TWO NUNS
ABBESS
BELLAMIRA, a Courtezan]

The Jew of Malta

[*Enter*] Machevil [*as Prologue*].

Albeit the world thinke *Machevill* is dead,
Yet was his soule but flowne beyond the *Alpes*,
And now the *Guize* is dead, is come from *France*
To view this Land, and frolicke with his friends.
To some perhaps my name is odious,
But such as love me, gard me from their tongues,
And let them know that I am *Machevill*,
And weigh not men, and therefore not mens words.
Admir'd I am of those that hate me most:
Though some speake openly against my bookes,   10
Yet will they reade me, and thereby attaine
To *Peters* Chayre: And when they cast me off,
Are poyson'd by my climing followers.
I count Religion but a childish Toy,
And hold there is no sinne but Ignorance.
Birds of the Aire will tell of murders past;
I am asham'd to heare such fooleries.
Many will talke of Title to a Crowne:
What right had *Cæsar* to the Empery?
Might first made Kings, and Lawes were then most sure   20
When like the *Dracos* they were writ in blood.
Hence comes it, that a strong built Citadell
Commands much more then letters can import:
Which maxime had *Phaleris* observ'd,
H'had never bellowed in a brasen Bull
Of great ones envy; o'th poore petty wites,
Let me be envy'd and not pittied!
But whither am I bound, I come not, I,
To reade a lecture here in *Britanie*,

19 Empery] Scott; Empire Q
21 *Dracos*] Dodsley² (Draco's);
    Drancus Q

26 wites] *almost certainly* wights, *not*
    wits
*29 *Britanie*] Bullen; *Britaine* Q

But to present the Tragedy of a Jew,   30
Who smiles to see how full his bags are cramb'd,
Which mony was not got without my meanes.
I crave but this, Grace him as he deserves,
And let him not be entertain'd the worse
Because he favours me.

                                              [*Exit.*]

Enter Barabas *in his Counting-house, with heapes*   [I.i]
of gold before him.

Barabas.   So that of thus much that returne was made:
And of the third part of the Persian ships,
There was the venture summ'd and satisfied.
As for those Samnites, and the men of *Uzz*,
That bought my Spanish Oyles, and Wines of *Greece*,
Here have I purst their paltry silverlings.
Fye; what a trouble tis to count this trash.
Well fare the Arabians who so richly pay
The things they traffique for with wedge of gold,
Whereof a man may easily in a day   10
Tell that which may maintaine him all his life.
The needy groome that never fingred groat,
Would make a miracle of thus much coyne:
But he whose steele-bard coffers are cramb'd full,
And all his life time hath bin tired,
Wearying his fingers ends with telling it,
Would in his age be loath to labour so,
And for a pound to sweat himselfe to death:
Give me the Merchants of the Indian Mynes,
That trade in mettall of the purest mould;   20
The wealthy Moore, that in the Easterne rockes
Without controule can picke his riches up,
And in his house heape pearle like pibble-stones,
Receive them free, and sell them by the weight;

---

4 Samnites] Chappell, Dodsley[3]   6 silverlings] Dodsley[2] (*qy*), Robin-
   Samintes Q   son; silverbings Q

Bags of fiery *Opals*, *Saphires*, *Amatists*,
Jacints, hard *Topas*, grasse-greene *Emeraulds*,
Beauteous *Rubyes*, sparkling *Diamonds*,
And seildsene costly stones of so great price,
As one of them indifferently rated,
And of a Carrect of this quantity,   30
May serve in perill of calamity
To ransome great Kings from captivity.
This is the ware wherein consists my wealth:
And thus me thinkes should men of judgement frame
Their meanes of traffique from the vulgar trade,
And as their wealth increaseth, so inclose
Infinite riches in a little roome.
But now how stands the wind?
Into what corner peeres my Halcions bill?
Ha, to the East? yes: See how stands the Vanes?   40
East and by-South: why then I hope my ships
I sent for *Egypt* and the bordering Iles
Are gotten up by *Nilus* winding bankes:
Mine Argosie from *Alexandria*,
Loaden with Spice and Silkes, now under saile,
Are smoothly gliding downe by *Candie* shoare
To *Malta*, through our Mediterranean sea.
But who comes heare? How now.

Enter a Merchant.

1. Merchant.   *Barabas*,
Thy ships are safe, riding in *Malta* Rhode: 50
And all the Merchants with other Merchandize
Are safe arriv'd, and have sent me to know
Whether your selfe will come and custome them.
Barabas.   The ships are safe thou saist, and richly fraught.
1. Merchant.   They are.
Barabas.   Why then goe bid them come ashore,
And bring with them their bils of entry:
I hope our credit in the Custome-house
Will serve as well as I were present there.

Goe send 'um threescore Camels, thirty Mules,
And twenty Waggons to bring up the ware.   60
But art thou master in a ship of mine,
And is thy credit not enough for that?
1. Merchant.   The very Custome barely comes to more
Then many Merchants of the Towne are worth,
And therefore farre exceeds my credit, Sir.
Barabas.   Goe tell 'em the Jew of *Malta* sent thee, man:
Tush, who amongst 'em knowes not *Barrabas*?
1 Merchant.   I goe.
Barabas.   So then, there's somewhat come.
Sirra, which of my ships art thou Master of?   70
1 Merchant.   Of the *Speranza*, Sir.
Barabas.   And saw'st thou not
Mine Argosie at *Alexandria*?
Thou couldst not come from *Egypt*, or by *Caire*
But at the entry there into the sea,
Where *Nilus* payes his tribute to the maine,
Thou needs must saile by *Alexandria*.
1 Merchant.   I neither saw them, nor inquir'd of them.
But this we heard some of our sea-men say,
They wondred how you durst with so much wealth
Trust such a crazed Vessell, and so farre.   80
Barabas.   Tush, they are wise; I know her and her strength:
But goe, goe thou thy wayes, discharge thy Ship,
And bid my Factor bring his loading in.   [*Exit* 1. Merchant.]
And yet I wonder at this Argosie.

Enter a second Merchant.

2. Merchant.   Thine Argosie from *Alexandria*,
Know *Barabas*, doth ride in *Malta* Rhode,
Laden with riches, and exceeding store
Of *Persian* silkes, of gold, and Orient Perle.
Barabas.   How chance you came not with those other ships
That sail'd by *Egypt*?
2 Merchant.   Sir we saw 'em not.   90

82 But] Chappell, Robinson; By Q

Barabas.   Belike they coasted round by *Candie* shoare
About their Oyles, or other businesses.
But 'twas ill done of you to come so farre
Without the ayd or conduct of their ships.
2 Merchant.   Sir, we were wafted by a Spanish Fleet
That never left us till within a league,
That had the Gallies of the Turke in chase.
Barabas.   Oh they were going up to *Sicily*:
Well, goe
And bid the Merchants and my men dispatch   100
And come ashore, and see the fraught discharg'd.
2 Merchant.   I goe.   *Exit.*
Barabas.   Thus trowles our fortune in by land and Sea,
And thus are wee on every side inrich'd:
These are the Blessings promis'd to the Jewes,
And herein was old *Abrams* happinesse:
What more may Heaven doe for earthly man
Then thus to powre out plenty in their laps,
Ripping the bowels of the earth for them,
Making the Sea their servant, and the winds   110
To drive their substance with successefull blasts?
Who hateth me but for my happinesse?
Or who is honour'd now but for his wealth?
Rather had I a Jew be hated thus,
Then pittied in a Christian poverty:
For I can see no fruits in all their faith,
But malice, falshood, and excessive pride,
Which me thinkes fits not their profession.
Happily some haplesse man hath conscience,
And for his conscience lives in beggery.   120
They say we are a scatter'd Nation:
I cannot tell, but we have scambled up
More wealth by farre then those that brag of faith.
There's *Kirriah Jairim*, the great Jew of *Greece*,
Obed in *Bairseth*, *Nones* in *Portugall*,
My selfe in *Malta*, some in *Italy*,

*110 servant] Wagner; servants Q

Many in *France*, and wealthy every one:
I, wealthier farre then any Christian.
I must confesse we come not to be Kings:
That's not our fault: Alas, our number's few,   130
And Crownes come either by succession,
Or urg'd by force; and nothing violent,
Oft have I heard tell, can be permanent.
Give us a peacefull rule, make Christians Kings,
That thirst so much for Principality.
I have no charge, nor many children,
But one sole Daughter, whom I hold as deare
As *Agamemnon* did his *Iphigen*:
And all I have is hers. But who comes here?

Enter three Jewes.

1. Jew.   Tush, tell not me 'twas done of policie.   140
2. Jew.   Come therefore let us goe to *Barrabas*;
For he can counsell best in these affaires;
And here he comes.
Barabas.   Why, how now Countrymen?
Why flocke you thus to me in multitudes?
What accident's betided to the Jewes?
1. Jew.   A Fleet of warlike Gallyes, *Barabas*,
Are come from *Turkey*, and lye in our Rhode:
And they this day sit in the Counsell-house
To entertaine them and their Embassie.
Barabas.   Why let 'em come, so they come not to warre;   150
Or let 'em warre, so we be conquerors:
Nay let 'em combat, conquer, and kill all,   *Aside.*
So they spare me, my daughter, and my wealth.
1. Jew.   Were it for confirmation of a League,
They would not come in warlike manner thus.
2. Jew.   I feare their comming will afflict us all.
Barabas.   Fond men, what dreame you of their multitudes?
What need they treat of peace that are in league?
The Turkes and those of *Malta* are in league.
Tut, tut, there is some other matter in't.   160

1. Jew.   Why, *Barabas*, they come for peace or warre.
Barabas.   Happily for neither, but to passe along
Towards *Venice* by the Adriatick Sea;
With whom they have attempted many times,
But never could effect their Stratagem.
3. Jew.   And very wisely sayd, it may be so.
2. Jew.   But there's a meeting in the Senate-house,
And all the Jewes in *Malta* must be there.
Barabas.   Umh; All the Jewes in *Malta* must be there?
I, like enough, why then let every man   170
Provide him, and be there for fashion-sake.
If any thing shall there concerne our state
Assure your selves I'le looke——*unto my selfe.*   *Aside.*
1. Jew.   I know you will; well brethren let us goe.
2. Jew.   Let's take our leaves; Farewell good *Barabas.*
Barabas.   Doe so; Farewell *Zaareth*, farewell *Temainte.*
                              [*Exeunt three* Jewes.]
And *Barabas* now search this secret out.
Summon thy sences, call thy wits together:
These silly men mistake the matter cleane.
Long to the Turke did *Malta* contribute;   180
Which Tribute all in policie, I feare,
The Turkes have let increase to such a summe,
As all the wealth of *Malta* cannot pay;
And now by that advantage thinkes, belike,
To seize upon the Towne: I, that he seekes.
How ere the world goe, I'le make sure for one,
And seeke in time to intercept the worst,
Warily garding that which I ha got.
Ego mihimet sum semper proximus.
Why let 'em enter, let 'em take the Towne.   190
                                   [*Exit.*]

Enter [Ferneze] *Governor of* Malta, Knights [*and* Officers,] *met by* [I.ii
[Callapine *and other*] Bassoes *of the* Turke; Calymath.

Governor.   Now Bassoes, what demand you at our hands?
Basso.   Know Knights of *Malta*, that we came from *Rhodes*,
From *Cyprus*, *Candy*, and those other Iles
That lye betwixt the Mediterranean seas.
Governor.   What's *Cyprus*, *Candy*, and those other Iles
To us, or *Malta*? What at our hands demand ye?
Calymath.   The ten yeares tribute that remaines unpaid.
Governor.   Alas, my Lord, the summe is overgreat,
I hope your Highnesse will consider us.
Calymath.   I wish, grave Governour, 'twere in my power   10
To favour you, but 'tis my fathers cause,
Wherein I may not, nay I dare not dally.
Governor.   Then give us leave, great *Selim-Calymath*.
Calymath.   Stand all aside, and let the Knights determine,
And send to keepe our Gallies under-saile,
For happily we shall not tarry here:
Now Governour, how are you resolv'd?
Governor.   Thus: Since your hard conditions are such
That you will needs have ten yeares tribute past,
We may have time to make collection   20
Amongst the Inhabitants of *Malta* for't.
Basso.   That's more then is in our Commission.
Calymath.   What *Callapine*, a little curtesie.
Let's know their time, perhaps it is not long;
And 'tis more Kingly to obtaine by peace
Then to enforce conditions by constraint.
What respit aske you Governour?
Governor.   But a month.
Calymath.   We grant a month, but see you keep your promise.
Now lanch our Gallies backe againe to Sea,
Where wee'll attend the respit you have tane,   30
And for the mony send our messenger.

0.1; 10, 17, 27, 32 *Governor*] Chap-   *Governors* Q (Governours 10, 17, 27)
pell, Dyce (*except* 0.1 Robinson);

Farewell great Governor, and brave Knights of *Malta*.

Exeunt [*Turkes*].

Governor.　And all good fortune wait on *Calymath*.
Goe one and call those Jewes of *Malta* hither:
Were they not summon'd to appeare to day?
Officer.　They were, my Lord, and here they come.

Enter Barabas, *and three* Jewes.

1. Knight.　Have you determin'd what to say to them?
Governor.　Yes, give me leave, and Hebrews now come neare.
From the Emperour of *Turkey* is arriv'd
Great *Selim-Calymath*, his Highnesse sonne,　　　　　　40
To levie of us ten yeares tribute past,
Now then here know that it concerneth us——
Barabas.　Then good my Lord, to keepe your quiet still,
Your Lordship shall doe well to let them have it.
Governor.　Soft *Barabas*, there's more longs too't than so.
To what this ten yeares tribute will amount
That we have cast, but cannot compasse it
By reason of the warres, that robb'd our store;
And therefore are we to request your ayd.
Barabas.　Alas, my Lord, we are no souldiers:　　　　50
And what's our aid against so great a Prince?
1. Knight.　Tut, Jew, we know thou art no souldier;
Thou art a Merchant, and a monied man,
And 'tis thy mony, *Barabas*, we seeke.
Barabas.　How, my Lord, my mony?
Governor.　　　　　　　　　　　Thine and the rest.
For to be short, amongst you 'tmust be had.
1. Jew.　Alas, my Lord, the most of us are poore!
Governor.　Then let the rich increase your portions.
Barabas.　Are strangers with your tribute to be tax'd?
2. Knight.　Have strangers leave with us to get their wealth?　　60
Then let them with us contribute.
Barabas.　How, equally?
Governor.　　　　　　　No, Jew, like infidels.
For through our sufferance of your hatefull lives,

271

Who stand accursed in the sight of heaven,
These taxes and afflictions are befal'ne,
And therefore thus we are determined;
Reade there the Articles of our decrees.

Reader. First, the tribute mony of the Turkes shall all be levyed amongst the Jewes, and each of them to pay one halfe of his estate. 70

Barabas. How, halfe his estate? *I hope you meane not mine.*

[*Aside.*]

Governor. Read on.

Reader. Secondly, hee that denies to pay, shal straight become a Christian.

Barabas. How, a Christian? *Hum, what's here to doe?* [*Aside.*]

Reader. Lastly, he that denies this, shall absolutely lose al he has.

All 3 Jewes. Oh my Lord we will give halfe.

Barabas. Oh earth-mettall'd villaines, and no Hebrews born!
And will you basely thus submit your selves
To leave your goods to their arbitrament? 80

Governor. Why *Barabas* wilt thou be christened?

Barabas. No, Governour, I will be no convertite.

Governor. Then pay thy halfe.

Barabas. Why know you what you did by this device?
Halfe of my substance is a Cities wealth.
Governour, it was not got so easily;
Nor will I part so slightly therewithall.

Governor. Sir, halfe is the penalty of our decree,
Either pay that, or we will seize on all.

Barabas. *Corpo di dio*; stay, you shall have halfe, 90
Let me be us'd but as my brethren are.

Governor. No, Jew, thou hast denied the Articles,
And now it cannot be recall'd. [*Exeunt* Officers.]

Barabas. Will you then steale my goods?
Is theft the ground of your Religion?

Governor. No, Jew, we take particularly thine
To save the ruine of a multitude:
And better one want for a common good,
Then many perish for a private man:

Yet *Barrabas* we will not banish thee,　　　100
But here in *Malta*, where thou gotst thy wealth,
Live still; and if thou canst, get more.
Barabas.　Christians; what, or how can I multiply?
Of nought is nothing made.
1. Knight.　From nought at first thou camst to little welth,
From little unto more, from more to most:
If your first curse fall heavy on thy head,
And make thee poore and scorn'd of all the world,
'Tis not our fault, but thy inherent sinne.
Barabas.　What? bring you Scripture to confirm your wrongs?　110
Preach me not out of my possessions.
Some Jewes are wicked, as all Christians are:
But say the Tribe that I descended of
Were all in generall cast away for sinne,
Shall I be tryed by their transgression?
The man that dealeth righteously shall live:
And which of you can charge me otherwise?
Governor.　Out wretched *Barabas*,
Sham'st thou not thus to justifie thy selfe,
As if we knew not thy profession?　　　120
If thou rely upon thy righteousnesse,
Be patient and thy riches will increase.
Excesse of wealth is cause of covetousnesse:
And covetousnesse, oh 'tis a monstrous sinne.
Barabas.　I, but theft is worse: tush, take not from me then,
For that is theft; and if you rob me thus,
I must be forc'd to steale and compasse more.
1. Knight.　Grave Governor, list not to his exclames:
Convert his mansion to a Nunnery,
His house will harbour many holy Nuns.　　　130

Enter Officers.

Governor.　It shall be so: now Officers have you done?
Officers.　I, my Lord, we have seiz'd upon the goods
And wares of *Barabas*, which being valued

128 Governor] Dyce; Governors Q

Amount to more then all the wealth in *Malta.*
And of the other we have seized halfe.
Governor. Then wee'll take order for the residue.
Barabas. Well then my Lord, say, are you satisfied?
You have my goods, my mony, and my wealth,
My ships, my store, and all that I enjoy'd;
And having all, you can request no more; 140
Unlesse your unrelenting flinty hearts
Suppresse all pitty in your stony breasts,
And now shall move you to bereave my life.
Governor. No, *Barabas*, to staine our hands with blood
Is farre from us and our profession.
Barabas. Why I esteeme the injury farre lesse,
To take the lives of miserable men,
Then be the causers of their misery.
You have my wealth, the labour of my life,
The comfort of mine age, my childrens hope, 150
And therefore ne're distinguish of the wrong.
Governor. Content thee, *Barabas*, thou hast nought but right.
Barabas. Your extreme right does me exceeding wrong:
But take it to you i'th devils name.
Governor. Come, let us in, and gather of these goods
The mony for this tribute of the Turke.
1. Knight. 'Tis necessary that be look'd unto:
For if we breake our day, we breake the league,
And that will prove but simple policie.

     Exeunt. [*Manent* Barabas *and the three* Jewes.]

Barabas. I, policie? that's their profession, 160
And not simplicity, as they suggest.
The plagues of *Egypt*, and the curse of heaven,
Earths barrennesse, and all mens hatred
Inflict upon them, thou great *Primus Motor*.
And here upon my knees, striking the earth,
I banne their soules to everlasting paines
And extreme tortures of the fiery deepe,

136 *Governor.*] Robinson; *omit* Q

That thus have dealt with me in my distresse.

1. Jew.   Oh yet be patient, gentle *Barabas*.

Barabas.   Oh silly brethren, borne to see this day!   170
Why stand you thus unmov'd with my laments?
Why weepe you not to thinke upon my wrongs?
Why pine not I, and dye in this distresse?

1. Jew.   Why, *Barabas*, as hardly can we brooke
The cruell handling of our selves in this:
Thou seest they have taken halfe our goods.

Barabas.   Why did you yeeld to their extortion?
You were a multitude, and I but one,
And of me onely have they taken all.

1. Jew.   Yet brother *Barabas* remember *Job*.   180

Barabas.   What tell you me of *Job*? I wot his wealth
Was written thus: he had seven thousand sheepe,
Three thousand Camels, and two hundred yoake
Of labouring Oxen, and five hundred
Shee Asses: but for every one of those,
Had they beene valued at indifferent rate,
I had at home, and in mine Argosie
And other ships that came from *Egypt* last,
As much as would have bought his beasts and him,
And yet have kept enough to live upon;   190
So that not he, but I may curse the day,
Thy fatall birth-day, forlorne *Barabas*;
And henceforth wish for an eternall night,
That clouds of darkenesse may inclose my flesh,
And hide these extreme sorrowes from mine eyes:
For onely I have toyl'd to inherit here
The months of vanity and losse of time,
And painefull nights have bin appointed me.

2. Jew.   Good *Barabas* be patient.

Barabas.   I, I,
Pray leave me in my patience. You that   200
Were ne're possest of wealth, are pleas'd with want.
But give him liberty at least to mourne,

*199 I, I,] Methuen (Ay, ay,); I, I, Q

275

That in a field amidst his enemies,
Doth see his souldiers slaine, himselfe disarm'd,
And knowes no meanes of his recoverie:
I, let me sorrow for this sudden chance,
'Tis in the trouble of my spirit I speake;
Great injuries are not so soone forgot.

1. Jew.   Come, let us leave him in his irefull mood,
Our words will but increase his extasie.   210

2. Jew.   On then: but trust me 'tis a misery
To see a man in such affliction:
Farewell *Barabas*.   *Exeunt.*

Barabas.   I, fare you well.
See the simplicitie of these base slaves,
Who for the villaines have no wit themselves,
Thinke me to be a senselesse lumpe of clay
That will with every water wash to dirt:
No, *Barabas* is borne to better chance,
And fram'd of finer mold then common men,
That measure nought but by the present time.   220
A reaching thought will search his deepest wits,
And cast with cunning for the time to come:
For evils are apt to happen every day.

Enter Abigall *the Jewes daughter.*

But whither wends my beauteous *Abigall*?
Oh what has made my lovely daughter sad?
What, woman, moane not for a little losse:
Thy father has enough in store for thee.

Abigall.   Not for my selfe, but aged *Barabas*:
Father, for thee lamenteth *Abigaile*:
But I will learne to leave these fruitlesse teares,   230
And urg'd thereto with my afflictions,
With fierce exclaimes run to the Senate-house,
And in the Senate reprehend them all,
And rent their hearts with tearing of my haire,
Till they reduce the wrongs done to my father.

Barabas.   No, *Abigail*, things past recovery

Are hardly cur'd with exclamations.
Be silent, Daughter, sufferance breeds ease,
And time may yeeld us an occasion
Which on the sudden cannot serve the turne.   240
Besides, my girle, thinke me not all so fond
As negligently to forgoe so much
Without provision for thy selfe and me.
Ten thousand Portagues besides great Perles,
Rich costly Jewels, and Stones infinite,
Fearing the worst of this before it fell,
I closely hid.
Abigall.   Where father?
Barabas.   In my house, my girle.
Abigall.   Then shall they ne're be seene of *Barrabas*:   250
For they have seiz'd upon thy house and wares.
Barabas.   But they will give me leave once more, I trow,
To goe into my house.
Abigall.   That may they not:
For there I left the Governour placing Nunnes,
Displacing me; and of thy house they meane
To make a Nunnery, where none but their owne sect
Must enter in; men generally barr'd.
Barabas.   My gold, my gold, and all my wealth is gone.
You partiall heavens, have I deserv'd this plague?
What, will you thus oppose me, lucklesse Starres,   260
To make me desperate in my poverty?
And knowing me impatient in distresse
Thinke me so mad as I will hang my selfe,
That I may vanish ore the earth in ayre,
And leave no memory that e're I was.
No, I will live; nor loath I this my life:
And since you leave me in the Ocean thus
To sinke or swim, and put me to my shifts,
I'le rouse my senses, and awake my selfe.
Daughter, I have it: thou perceiv'st the plight   270
Wherein these Christians have oppressed me:
Be rul'd by me, for in extremitie

277

We ought to make barre of no policie.
Abigall. Father, what e're it be to injure them
That have so manifestly wronged us,
What will not *Abigall* attempt?
Barabas. Why so,
Then thus; thou toldst me they have turn'd my house
Into a Nunnery, and some Nuns are there.
Abigall. I did.
Barabas. Then *Abigall*, there must my girle
Intreat the Abbasse to be entertain'd. 280
Abigall. How, as a Nunne?
Barabas. I, Daughter, for Religion
Hides many mischiefes from suspition.
Abigall. I, but father they will suspect me there.
Barabas. Let 'em suspect, but be thou so precise
As they may thinke it done of Holinesse.
Intreat 'em faire, and give them friendly speech,
And seeme to them as if thy sinnes were great,
Till thou hast gotten to be entertain'd.
Abigall. Thus father shall I much dissemble.
Barabas. Tush,
As good dissemble that thou never mean'st 290
As first meane truth, and then dissemble it,
A counterfet profession is better
Then unseene hypocrisie.
Abigall. Well father, say I be entertain'd,
What then shall follow?
Barabas. This shall follow then;
There have I hid close underneath the plancke
That runs along the upper chamber floore,
The gold and Jewels which I kept for thee.
But here they come; be cunning *Abigall*.
Abigall. Then father, goe with me. 300
Barabas. No, *Abigall*, in this
It is not necessary I be seene.
For I will seeme offended with thee for't.
Be close, my girle, for this must fetch my gold.

Enter two Fryars *and three* Nuns [, *one the* Abbasse].

1. Fryar.　Sisters,
We now are almost at the new made Nunnery.
Abbasse.　The better; for we love not to be seene:
'Tis thirtie winters long since some of us
Did stray so farre amongst the multitude.
1. Fryar.　But, Madam, this house　　　　　　　　　310
And waters of this new made Nunnery
Will much delight you.
Abbasse.　It may be so: but who comes here?
Abigall.　Grave Abbasse, and you happy Virgins guide,
Pitty the state of a distressed Maid.
Abbasse.　What art thou, daughter?
Abigall.　The hopelesse daughter of a haplesse Jew,
The Jew of *Malta*, wretched *Barabas*;
Sometimes the owner of a goodly house,
Which they have now turn'd to a Nunnery.　　　　320
Abbasse.　Well, daughter, say, what is thy suit with us?
Abigall.　Fearing the afflictions which my father feeles,
Proceed from sinne, or want of faith in us,
I'de passe away my life in penitence,
And be a Novice in your Nunnery,
To make attonement for my labouring soule.
1. Fryar.　No doubt, brother, but this proceedeth of the spirit.
2. Fryar.　I, and of a moving spirit too, brother; but come,
Let us intreat she may be entertain'd.
Abbasse.　Well, daughter, we admit you for a Nun.　　　330
Abigall.　First let me as a Novice learne to frame
My solitary life to your streight lawes,
And let me lodge where I was wont to lye.
I doe not doubt by your divine precepts
And mine owne industry, but to profit much.
Barabas.　*As much I hope as all I hid is worth.*　　　*Aside.*
Abbasse.　Come daughter, follow us.

304.1 *two*] Chappell, Dyce; *three* Q　　　307 *Abbasse.*] Dyce; *1 Nun.* Q
*304.1 *three*] *two* Q　　　　　　　　　　313 *Abbasse.*] Dyce; *Nun* Q

Barabas. Why how now *Abigall*, what mak'st thou
Amongst these hateful Christians?

1. Fryar. Hinder her not, thou man of little faith, 340
For she has mortified her selfe.

Barabas. How, mortified!

1. Fryar. And is admitted to the Sister-hood.

Barabas. Child of perdition, and thy fathers shame,
What wilt thou doe among these hatefull fiends?
I charge thee on my blessing that thou leave
These divels, and their damned heresie.

Abigall. Father, give me——

Barabas. *Nay backe,* Abigall, *Whispers to her.*
And thinke upon the Jewels and the gold,
The boord is marked thus that covers it. 350
Away accursed from thy fathers sight.

1. Fryar. *Barabas,* although thou art in mis-beleefe,
And wilt not see thine owne afflictions,
Yet let thy daughter be no longer blinde.

Barabas. Blind, Fryer, I wrecke not thy perswasions.
The boord is marked thus † that covers it, [*Aside to her.*]
For I had rather dye, then see her thus.
Wilt thou forsake mee too in my distresse,
Seduced Daughter, *Goe, forget not.* *Aside to her.*
Becomes it Jewes to be so credulous, 360
To morrow early I'le be at the doore. *Aside to her.*
No come not at me, if thou wilt be damn'd,
Forget me, see me not, and so be gone.
Farewell, Remember to morrow morning. *Aside.*
Out, out thou wretch.

[*As they are leaving*] *Enter* Mathias.

Mathias. Whose this? Faire *Abigall* the rich Jewes daughter
Become a Nun? her fathers sudden fall
Has humbled her and brought her downe to this:
Tut, she were fitter for a tale of love
Then to be tired out with Orizons: 370
And better would she farre become a bed

Embraced in a friendly lovers armes,
Then rise at midnight to a solemne masse.

Enter Lodowicke.

Lodowicke.   Why how now Don *Mathias*, in a dump?
Mathias.   Beleeve me, Noble *Lodowicke*, I have seene
  The strangest sight, in my opinion,
  That ever I beheld.
Lodowicke.   What wast I prethe?
Mathias.   A faire young maid scarce fourteene yeares of age,
  The sweetest flower in *Citherea's* field,
  Cropt from the pleasures of the fruitfull earth,   380
  And strangely metamorphis'd Nun.
Lodowicke.   But say, What was she?
Mathias.   Why, the rich Jewes daughter.
Lodowicke.   What, *Barabas*, whose goods were lately seiz'd?
  Is she so faire?
Mathias.   And matchlesse beautifull;
  As had you seene her 'twould have mov'd your heart,
  Tho countermin'd with walls of brasse, to love,
  Or at the least to pitty.
Lodowicke.   And if she be so faire as you report,
  'Twere time well spent to goe and visit her:
  How say you, shall we?   390
Mathias.   I must and will, Sir, there's no remedy.
Lodowicke.   *And so will I too, or it shall goe hard.*——   [*Aside.*]
  Farewell *Mathias.*
Mathias.   Farewell *Lodowicke.*

Exeunt.

Enter Barabas *with a light.*   II.[i]

Barabas.   Thus like the sad presaging Raven that tolls
  The sicke mans passeport in her hollow beake,
  And in the shadow of the silent night
  Doth shake contagion from her sable wings;

*386 countermin'd] *stet* Q

Vex'd and tormented runnes poore *Barabas*
With fatall curses towards these Christians.
The incertaine pleasures of swift-footed time
Have tane their flight, and left me in despaire;
And of my former riches rests no more
But bare remembrance; like a souldiers skarre,   10
That has no further comfort for his maime.
Oh thou that with a fiery piller led'st
The sonnes of *Israel* through the dismall shades,
Light *Abrahams* off-spring; and direct the hand
Of *Abigall* this night; or let the day
Turne to eternall darkenesse after this:
No sleepe can fasten on my watchfull eyes,
Nor quiet enter my distemper'd thoughts,
Till I have answer of my *Abigall*.

Enter Abigall *above.*

Abigall.   Now have I happily espy'd a time   20
To search the plancke my father did appoint;
And here behold (unseene) where I have found
The gold, the perles, and Jewels which he hid.
Barabas.   Now I remember those old womens words,
Who in my wealth wud tell me winters tales,
And speake of spirits and ghosts that glide by night
About the place where Treasure hath bin hid:
And now me thinkes that I am one of those:
For whilst I live, here lives my soules sole hope,
And when I dye, here shall my spirit walke.   30
Abigall.   Now that my fathers fortune were so good
As but to be about this happy place;
'Tis not so happy: yet when we parted last,
He said he wud attend me in the morne.
Then, gentle sleepe, where e're his bodie rests,
Give charge to *Morpheus* that he may dreame
A golden dreame, and of the sudden walke,
Come and receive the Treasure I have found.

*37 walke] stet Q

282

Barabas.   *Bien para todos mi ganado no es:*
As good goe on, as sit so sadly thus.   40
But stay, what starre shines yonder in the *East?*
The Loadstarre of my life, if *Abigall.*
Who's there?
Abigall.   Who's that?
Barabas.   Peace, *Abigal*, 'tis I.
Abigall.   Then father here receive thy happinesse.
Barabas.   Hast thou't?
Abigall.   Here,   *Throwes downe bags.*
          Hast thou't?
                              There's more, and more, and more.
Barabas.   Oh my girle,
My gold, my fortune, my felicity;
Strength to my soule, death to mine enemy;
Welcome the first beginner of my blisse: 50
Oh *Abigal, Abigal,* that I had thee here too,
Then my desires were fully satisfied,
But I will practise thy enlargement thence:
Oh girle, oh gold, oh beauty, oh my blisse!   *Hugs his bags.*
Abigall.   Father, it draweth towards midnight now,
And 'bout this time the Nuns begin to wake;
To shun suspition, therefore, let us part.
Barabas.   Farewell my joy, and by my fingers take
A kisse from him that sends it from his soule.
Now *Phœbus* ope the eye-lids of the day,   60
And for the Raven wake the morning Larke,
That I may hover with her in the Ayre,
Singing ore these, as she does ore her young.
Hermoso Placer de los Dineros.
                                                  Exeunt.

Enter Governor, Martin del Bosco, *the* Knights [*and* Officers].   [II.ii]

Governor.   Now Captaine tell us whither thou art bound?
Whence is thy ship that anchors in our Rhoad?
And why thou cam'st ashore without our leave?
Bosco.   Governor of *Malta*, hither am I bound;

My Ship, *the flying Dragon*, is of *Spaine*,
And so am I, *Delbosco* is my name;
Vizadmirall unto the Catholike King.

1. Knight.   'Tis true, my Lord, therefore intreat him well.

Bosco.   Our fraught is Grecians, Turks, and Africk Moores.
For late upon the coast of *Corsica*,   10
Because we vail'd not to the Turkish Fleet,
Their creeping Gallyes had us in the chase:
But suddenly the wind began to rise,
And then we luft, and tackt, and fought at ease:
Some have we fir'd, and many have we sunke;
But one amongst the rest became our prize:
The Captain's slaine, the rest remaine our slaves,
Of whom we would make sale in *Malta* here.

Governor.   *Martin del Bosco*, I have heard of thee;
Welcome to *Malta*, and to all of us;   20
But to admit a sale of these thy Turkes
We may not, nay we dare not give consent
By reason of a Tributary league.

1. Knight.   *Delbosco*, as thou lovest and honour'st us,
Perswade our Governor against the Turke;
This truce we have is but in hope of gold,
And with that summe he craves might we wage warre.

Bosco.   Will Knights of *Malta* be in league with Turkes,
And buy it basely too for summes of gold?
My Lord, Remember that to *Europ's* shame,   30
The Christian Ile of *Rhodes*, from whence you came,
Was lately lost, and you were stated here
To be at deadly enmity with Turkes.

Governor.   Captaine we know it, but our force is small.

Bosco.   What is the summe that *Calymath* requires?

Governor.   A hundred thousand Crownes.

Bosco.   My Lord and King hath title to this Isle,
And he meanes quickly to expell you hence;
Therefore be rul'd by me, and keepe the gold:
I'le write unto his Majesty for ayd,   40

11 Turkish] Scott; Spanish Q   14 luft and tackt] Dyce; left, and tooke Q

And not depart untill I see you free.

Governor.   On this condition shall thy Turkes be sold.
Goe Officers and set them straight in shew.   [*Exeunt* Officers.]
Bosco, thou shalt be *Malta's* Generall;
We and our warlike Knights will follow thee
Against these barbarous mis-beleeving Turkes.

Bosco.   So shall you imitate those you succeed:
For when their hideous force inviron'd *Rhodes,*
Small though the number was that kept the Towne,
They fought it out, and not a man surviv'd   50
To bring the haplesse newes to Christendome.

Governor.   So will we fight it out; come, let's away:
Proud-daring *Calymath,* instead of gold,
Wee'll send thee bullets wrapt in smoake and fire:
Claime tribute where thou wilt, we are resolv'd,
Honor is bought with bloud and not with gold.

                                                    Exeunt.

Enter Officers *with slaves.*   [II.iii]

1. Officer.   This is the Market-place, here let 'em stand:
Feare not their sale, for they'll be quickly bought.
2. Officer.   Every ones price is written on his backe,
And so much must they yeeld or not be sold.

Enter Barabas.

1. Officer.   Here comes the Jew, had not his goods bin seiz'd,
He'de give us present mony for them all.
Barabas.   In spite of these swine-eating Christians,
(Unchosen Nation, never circumciz'd;
Such as, poore villaines, were ne're thought upon
Till *Titus* and *Vespasian* conquer'd us)   10
Am I become as wealthy as I was:
They hop'd my daughter would ha bin a Nun;
But she's at home, and I have bought a house
As great and faire as is the Governors;

*54 thee] Dodsley²; the Q

And there in spite of *Malta* will I dwell:
Having *Fernezes* hand, whose heart I'le have;
I, and his sonnes too, or it shall goe hard.
I am not of the Tribe of *Levy*, I,
That can so soone forget an injury.
We Jewes can fawne like Spaniels when we please; 20
And when we grin we bite, yet are our lookes
As innocent and harmelesse as a Lambes.
I learn'd in *Florence* how to kisse my hand,
Heave up my shoulders when they call me dogge,
And ducke as low as any bare-foot Fryar,
Hoping to see them starve upon a stall,
Or else be gather'd for in our Synagogue;
That when the offering-Bason comes to me,
Even for charity I may spit intoo't.
Here comes Don *Lodowicke* the Governor's sonne, 30
One that I love for his good fathers sake.

Enter Lodowicke.

Lodowicke.   I heare the wealthy Jew walked this way;
I'le seeke him out, and so insinuate,
That I may have a sight of *Abigall*;
For Don *Mathias* tels me she is faire.
Barabas.   Now will I shew my selfe to have more of the Serpent
then the Dove; that is, more knave than foole.
Lodowicke.   Yond walks the Jew, now for faire *Abigall*.
Barabas.   I, I, no doubt but shee's at your command.
Lodowicke.   *Barabas*, thou know'st I am the Governors sonne. 40
Barabas.   I wud you were his father too, Sir, that's al the harm I
wish you: *the slave looks like a hogs cheek new sindg'd.*   [*Aside.*]
Lodowicke.   Whither walk'st thou, *Barabas?*
Barabas.   No further: 'tis a custome held with us,
That when we speake with Gentiles like to you,
We turne into the Ayre to purge our selves:
For unto us the Promise doth belong.
Lodowicke.   Well, *Barabas*, canst helpe me to a Diamond?
Barabas.   Oh, Sir, your father had my Diamonds.

Yet I have one left that will serve your turne: 50
I meane my daughter:—but e're he shall have her   *Aside.*
I'le sacrifice her on a pile of wood.
I ha the poyson of the City for him,
And the white leprosie.
Lodowicke.   What sparkle does it give without a foile?
Barabas.   The Diamond that I talke of, ne'r was foild:
But when he touches it, it will be foild: [*Aside.*]
Lord *Lodowicke*, it sparkles bright and faire.
Lodowicke.   Is it square or pointed, pray let me know.
Barabas.   Pointed it is, good Sir,——*but not for you.*   *Aside.* 60
Lodowicke.   I like it much the better.
Barabas.   So doe I too.
Lodowicke.   How showes it by night?
Barabas.   Outshines *Cinthia's* rayes:
You'le like it better farre a nights than dayes.   *Aside.*
Lodowicke.   And what's the price?
Barabas.   *Your life and if you have it.*—— [*Aside.*]
Oh my Lord we will not jarre about the price;
Come to my house and I will giv't your honour——   *Aside.*
With a vengeance.
Lodowicke.   No, *Barabas*, I will deserve it first.
Barabas.   Good Sir,
Your father has deserv'd it at my hands,   70
Who of meere charity and Christian ruth,
To bring me to religious purity,
And as it were in Catechising sort,
To make me mindfull of my mortall sinnes,
Against my will, and whether I would or no,
Seiz'd all I had, and thrust me out a doores,
And made my house a place for Nuns most chast.
Lodowicke.   No doubt your soule shall reape the fruit of it.
Barabas.   I, but my Lord, the harvest is farre off:
And yet I know the prayers of those Nuns   80
And holy Fryers, having mony for their paines,
Are wondrous; *and indeed doe no man good*:   *Aside.*
And seeing they are not idle, but still doing,

'Tis likely they in time may reape some fruit,
I meane in fulnesse of perfection.

Lodowicke.   Good *Barabas* glance not at our holy Nuns.

Barabas.   No, but I doe it through a burning zeale,
Hoping ere long to set the house a fire;   *Aside.*
For though they doe a while increase and multiply,
I'le have a saying to that Nunnery.   90
As for the Diamond, Sir, I told you of,
Come home and there's no price shall make us part,
Even for your Honourable fathers sake.
It shall goe hard but I will see your death.   *Aside.*
But now I must be gone to buy a slave.

Lodowicke.   And, *Barabas*, I'le beare thee company.

Barabas.   Come then, here's the marketplace; whats the price of
this slave, two hundred Crowns? Do the Turkes weigh so much?

1. Officer.   Sir, that's his price.

Barabas.   What, can he steale that you demand so much?   100
Belike he has some new tricke for a purse;
And if he has, he is worth three hundred plats.
So that, being bought, the Towne-seale might be got
To keepe him for his life time from the gallowes.
The Sessions day is criticall to theeves,
And few or none scape but by being purg'd.

Lodowicke.   Ratest thou this Moore but at two hundred plats?

1. Officer.   No more, my Lord.

Barabas.   Why should this Turke be dearer then that
Moore?

1. Officer.   Because he is young and has more qualities.   110

Barabas.   What, hast the Philosophers stone? and thou hast,
breake my head with it, I'le forgive thee.

Slave.   No Sir, I can cut and shave.

Barabas.   Let me see, sirra, are you not an old shaver?

Slave.   Alas, Sir, I am a very youth.

Barabas.   A youth? I'le buy you, and marry you to Lady vanity,
if you doe well.

Slave.   I will serve you, Sir.

---

98 Turkes] Dodsley²; *Turke* Q   113, 115, 118, 122 *Slave.*] Dodsley²; *Ith.* Q

Barabas.   Some wicked trick or other. It may be under colour of
shaving, thou'lt cut my throat for my goods.   120
  Tell me, hast thou thy health well?
Slave.   I, passing well.
Barabas.   So much the worse; I must have one that's sickly, and
  be but for sparing vittles: 'tis not a stone of beef a day will main-
  taine you in these chops; let me see one that's somewhat
  leaner.
1. Officer.   Here's a leaner, how like you him?
Barabas.   Where was thou borne?
Ithimore.   In *Trace*; brought up in *Arabia.*
Barabas.   So much the better, thou art for my turne.
  An hundred Crownes, I'le have him; there's the coyne.   130
1. Officer.   Then marke him, Sir, and take him hence.
Barabas.   *I, marke him, you were best, for this is he*   [*Aside.*]
    That by my helpe shall doe much villanie.
  My Lord farewell: Come Sirra you are mine.
  As for the Diamond it shall be yours;
  I pray, Sir, be no stranger at my house,
  All that I have shall be at your command.

                    Enter Mathias, Mater.

Mathias.   What makes the Jew and *Lodowicke* so private?
  I feare me 'tis about faire *Abigall.*   [*Aside.*]
Barabas.   Yonder comes Don *Mathias,* let us stay;   140
  He loves my daughter, and she holds him deare:
  But I have sworne to frustrate both their hopes,
  And be reveng'd upon the——*Governor.*   [*Aside.*]
                                                    [*Exit* Lodowicke.]
Mater.   This Moore is comeliest, is he not? speake son.
Mathias.   No, this is the better, mother, view this well.
Barabas.   Seeme not to know me here before your mother
  Lest she mistrust the match that is in hand:
  When you have brought her home, come to my house;
  Thinke of me as thy father; Sonne farewell.
Mathias.   But wherefore talk'd Don *Lodowick* with you?   150

Barabas.   Tush man, we talk'd of Diamonds, not of *Abigal.*
Mater.   Tell me, *Mathias,* is not that the Jew?
Barabas.   As for the Comment on the *Machabees*
  I have it, Sir, and 'tis at your command.
Mathias.   Yes, Madam, and my talke with him was but
  About the borrowing of a booke or two.
Mater.   Converse not with him, he is cast off from heaven.
  Thou hast thy Crownes, fellow, come let's away.

                          Exeunt [Mater *and slave*].

Mathias.   Sirra, Jew, remember the booke.
Barabas.   Marry will I, Sir.   [*Exit* Mathias.]   160
1. Officer.   Come, I have made a reasonable market,
  Lets away.   [*Exeunt* Officers *with slaves.*]
Barabas.   Now let me know thy name, and therewithall
  Thy birth, condition, and profession.
Ithimore.   Faith, Sir, my birth is but meane, my name's *Ithimor,*
  My profession what you please.
Barabas.   Hast thou no Trade? then listen to my words,
  And I will teach thee that shall sticke by thee:
  First be thou voyd of these affections,
  Compassion, love, vaine hope, and hartlesse feare,   170
  Be mov'd at nothing, see thou pitty none,
  But to thy selfe smile when the Christians moane.
Ithimore.   Oh brave, master, I worship your nose for this.
Barabas.   As for my selfe, I walke abroad a nights
  And kill sicke people groaning under walls:
  Sometimes I goe about and poyson wells;
  And now and then, to cherish Christian theeves,
  I am content to lose some of my Crownes;
  That I may, walking in my Gallery,
  See 'em goe pinion'd along by my doore.   180
  Being young I studied Physicke, and began
  To practise first upon the Italian;
  There I enrich'd the Priests with burials,
  And alwayes kept the Sexton's armes in ure
  With digging graves and ringing dead mens knels:

155 but] Dyce (*qy*), Methuen; *omit* Q   168 *thee*] Dodsley²; *omit* Q

And after that I was an Engineere,
And in the warres 'twixt *France* and *Germanie*,
Under pretence of helping *Charles* the fifth,
Slew friend and enemy with my stratagems.
Then after that was I an Usurer,   190
And with extorting, cozening, forfeiting,
And tricks belonging unto Brokery,
I fill'd the Jailes with Bankrouts in a yeare,
And with young Orphans planted Hospitals,
And every Moone made some or other mad,
And now and then one hang himselfe for griefe,
Pinning upon his breast a long great Scrowle
How I with interest tormented him.
But marke how I am blest for plaguing them,
I have as much coyne as will buy the Towne.   200
But tell me now, How hast thou spent thy time?
Ithimore.   Faith, Master,
In setting Christian villages on fire,
Chaining of Eunuches, binding gally-slaves.
One time I was an Hostler in an Inne,
And in the night time secretly would I steale
To travellers Chambers, and there cut their throats:
Once at *Jerusalem*, where the pilgrims kneel'd,
I strowed powder on the Marble stones,
And therewithall their knees would ranckle, so   210
That I have laugh'd agood to see the cripples
Goe limping home to Christendome on stilts.
Barabas.   Why this is something: make account of me
As of thy fellow; we are villaines both:
Both circumcized, we hate Christians both:
Be true and secret, thou shalt want no gold.
But stand aside, here comes Don *Lodowicke*.

                    Enter Lodowicke.

Lodowicke.   Oh *Barabas* well met;
Where is the Diamond you told me of?

Barabas. I have it for you, Sir; please you walke in with me: 220
What, ho, *Abigall*; open the doore I say.

Enter Abigall.

Abigall. In good time, father, here are letters come
From *Ormus*, and the Post stayes here within.
Barabas. Give me the letters, daughter, doe you heare?
Entertaine *Lodowicke* the Governors sonne
With all the curtesie you can affoord;
Provided, that you keepe your Maiden-head.
Use him as if he were a——*Philistine.*   *Aside.*
Dissemble, sweare, protest, vow to love him,
He is not of the seed of Abraham.   230
I am a little busie, Sir, pray pardon me.
Abigall, bid him welcome for my sake.
Abigall. For your sake and his own he's welcome hither.
Barabas. Daughter, a word more; *kisse him, speake him faire,*
[*Aside.*]
And like a cunning Jew so cast about,
That ye be both made sure e're you come out.
Abigall. O father, Don Mathias is my love.
Barabas. I know it: yet I say make love to him;
Doe, it is requisite it should be so.   240
Nay on my life it is my Factors hand,
But goe you in, I'le thinke upon the account:
[*Exeunt* Lodowicke *and* Abigall.]
The account is made, for *Lodovico* dyes.
My Factor sends me word a Merchant's fled
That owes me for a hundred Tun of Wine:
I weigh it thus much; I have wealth enough.
For now by this has he kist *Abigall*;
And she vowes love to him, and hee to her.
As sure as heaven rain'd Manna for the Jewes,
So sure shall he and Don *Mathias* dye: 250
His father was my chiefest enemie.

*242 *Lodovico*] Dyce; Lodowicke Q

Enter Mathias.

Whither goes Don *Mathias?* stay a while.

Mathias.   Whither but to my faire love *Abigall?*

Barabas.   Thou know'st, and heaven can witnesse it is true,
That I intend my daughter shall be thine.

Mathias.   I, *Barabas*, or else thou wrong'st me much.

Barabas.   Oh heaven forbid I should have such a thought.
Pardon me though I weepe; the Governors sonne
Will, whether I will or no, have *Abigall:*
He sends her letters, bracelets, jewels, rings.

Mathias.   Does she receive them?   260

Barabas.   Shee? No, *Mathias*, no, but sends them backe,
And when he comes, she lockes her selfe up fast;
Yet through the key-hole will he talke to her,
While she runs to the window looking out
When you should come and hale him from the doore.

Mathias.   Oh treacherous *Lodowicke!*

Barabas.   Even now as I came home, he slipt me in,
And I am sure he is with *Abigall.*

Mathias.   I'le rouze him thence.

Barabas.   Not for all *Malta*, therefore sheath your sword;   270
If you love me, no quarrels in my house;
But steale you in, and seeme to see him not;
I'le give him such a warning e're he goes
As he shall have small hopes of *Abigall.*
Away, for here they come.

Enter Lodowicke, Abigall.

Mathias.   What, hand in hand, I cannot suffer this.

Barabas.   *Mathias*, as thou lov'st me, not a word.

Mathias.   Well, let it passe, another time shall serve.   *Exit.*

Lodowicke.   *Barabas*, is not that the widowes sonne?

Barabas.   I, and take heed, for he hath sworne your death.   280

Lodowicke.   My death? what, is the base borne peasant mad?

Barabas.   No, no, but happily he stands in feare
Of that which you, I thinke, ne're dreame upon,

My daughter here, a paltry silly girle.
Lodowicke. Why, loves she Don *Mathias?*
Barabas. Doth she not with her smiling answer you?
Abigall. He has my heart, I smile against my will. [*Aside.*]
Lodowicke. *Barabas,* thou know'st I have lov'd thy daughter long.
Barabas. And so has she done you, even from a child.
Lodowicke. And now I can no longer hold my minde. 290
Barabas. Nor I the affection that I beare to you.
Lodowicke. This is thy Diamond, tell me, shall I have it?
Barabas. Win it, and weare it, it is yet unfoyl'd.
Oh but I know your Lordship wud disdaine
To marry with the daughter of a Jew:
And yet I'le give her many a golden crosse
With Christian posies round about the ring.
Lodowicke. 'Tis not thy wealth, but her that I esteeme,
Yet crave I thy consent.
Barabas. And mine you have, yet let me talke to her; 300
This off-spring of Cain, *this Jebusite*
That never tasted of the Passeover,
Nor e're shall see the land of Canaan,
Nor our Messias *that is yet to come,*
This gentle Magot, Lodowicke *I meane,*
Must be deluded: let him have thy hand,
But keepe thy heart till Don Mathias *comes.*
Abigall. *What, shall I be betroth'd to* Lodowicke?
Barabas. *It's no sinne to deceive a Christian;*
For they themselves hold it a principle, 310
Faith is not to be held with Heretickes;
But all are Hereticks that are not Jewes;
This followes well, and therefore daughter feare not.
I have intreated her, and she will grant.
Lodowicke. Then gentle *Abigal* plight thy faith to me.
Abigall. I cannot chuse, seeing my father bids:—— [*Aside.*]
Nothing but death shall part my love and me.
Lodowicke. Now have I that for which my soule hath long'd.
Barabas. So have not I, but yet I hope I shall. [*Aside.*]

*293 unfoyl'd] Dodsley³ (*qy*), Dyce (*qy*) unsoyl'd Q

Abigall.   Oh wretched *Abigal,* what hast thou done?   320
Lodowicke.   Why on the sudden is your colour chang'd?
Abigall.   I know not, but farewell, I must be gone.
Barabas.   Stay her,——but let her not speake one word
  more.   [*Aside.*]
Lodowicke.   Mute a the sudden; here's a sudden change.
Barabas.   Oh muse not at it, 'tis the Hebrewes guize,
  That maidens new betroth'd should weepe a while:
  Trouble her not, sweet *Lodowicke* depart:
  Shee is thy wife, and thou shalt be mine heire.
Lodowicke.   Oh, is't the custome, then I am resolv'd:
  But rather let the brightsome heavens be dim,   330
  And Natures beauty choake with stifeling clouds,
  Then my faire *Abigal* should frowne on me.
  There comes the villaine, now I'le be reveng'd.

Enter Mathias.

Barabas.   Be quiet *Lodowicke,* it is enough
  That I have made thee sure to *Abigal.*
Lodowicke.   Well, let him goe.   *Exit.*
Barabas.   Well, but for me, as you went in at dores
  You had bin stab'd, but not a word on't now;
  Here must no speeches passe, nor swords be drawne.
Mathias.   Suffer me, *Barabas,* but to follow him.   340
Barabas.   No; so shall I, if any hurt be done,
  Be made an accessary of your deeds;
  Revenge it on him when you meet him next.
Mathias.   For this I'le have his heart.
Barabas.   Doe so; loe here I give thee *Abigall.*
Mathias.   What greater gift can poore *Mathias* have?
  Shall *Lodowicke* rob me of so faire a love?
  My life is not so deare as *Abigall.*
Barabas.   My heart misgives me, that to crosse your love,
  Hee's with your mother, therefore after him.   350
Mathias.   What, is he gone unto my mother?
Barabas.   Nay, if you will, stay till she comes her selfe.

320 thou] Scott; thee Q

Mathias. I cannot stay; for if my mother come,
 Shee'll dye with griefe. *Exit.*
Abigall. I cannot take my leave of him for teares:
 Father, why have you thus incenst them both?
Barabas. What's that to thee?
Abigall. I'le make 'em friends againe.
Barabas. You'll make 'em friends?
 Are there not Jewes enow in *Malta,*
 But thou must dote upon a Christian? 360
Abigall. I will have Don *Mathias,* he is my love.
Barabas. Yes, you shall have him: Goe put her in.
Ithimore. I, I'le put her in. [*Exit* Abigall.]
Barabas. Now tell me, *Ithimore,* how lik'st thou this?
Ithimore. Faith Master, I thinke by this
 You purchase both their lives; is it not so?
Barabas. True; and it shall be cunningly perform'd.
Ithimore. Oh, master, that I might have a hand in this.
Barabas. I, so thou shalt, 'tis thou must doe the deed:
 Take this and beare it to *Mathias* streight, 370
 And tell him that it comes from *Lodowicke.*
Ithimore. 'Tis poyson'd, is it not?
Barabas. No, no, and yet it might be done that way:
 It is a challenge feign'd from *Lodowicke.*
Ithimore. Feare not, I'le so set his heart a fire,
 That he shall verily thinke it comes from him.
Barabas. I cannot choose but like thy readinesse:
 Yet be not rash, but doe it cunningly.
Ithimore. As I behave my selfe in this, imploy me hereafter. *Exit.*
Barabas. Away then. 380
 So, now will I goe in to *Lodowicke,*
 And like a cunning spirit feigne some lye,
 Till I have set 'em both at enmitie.
 Exit.

Enter a Curtezane. III.[i]

Curtezane. Since this Towne was besieg'd, my gaine growes cold:
  The time has bin, that but for one bare night
  A hundred Duckets have bin freely given:
  But now against my will I must be chast.
  And yet I know my beauty doth not faile.
  From *Venice* Merchants, and from *Padua*
  Were wont to come rare witted Gentlemen,
  Schollers I meane, learned and liberall;
  And now, save *Pilia-borza*, comes there none,
  And he is very seldome from my house; 10
  And here he comes.

Enter Pilia-borza.

Pilia-borza. Hold thee, wench, there's something for thee to spend.
Curtezene. 'Tis silver, I disdaine it.
Pilia-borza. I, but the Jew has gold,
  And I will have it or it shall goe hard.
Curtezane. Tell me, how cam'st thou by this?
Pilia-borza. Faith, walking the backe lanes through the Gardens
  I chanc'd to cast mine eye up to the Jewes counting-house where
  I saw some bags of mony, and in the night I clamber'd up with my
  hooks, and as I was taking my choyce, I heard a rumbling in the 20
  house; so I tooke onely this, and runne my way: but here's the
  Jews man.

Enter Ithimore.

Curtezane. Hide the bagge.
Pilia-borza. Looke not towards him, let's away:
  Zoon's what a looking thou keep'st, thou'lt betraye's anon.
Ithimore. O the sweetest face that ever I beheld! I know she is a
  Curtezane by her attire: now would I give a hundred of the Jewes
  Crownes that I had such a Concubine.
  Well, I have deliver'd the challenge in such sort,
  As meet they will, and fighting dye; brave sport. 30
                                                Exit.

Enter Mathias.   [III.ii]

Mathias.   This is the place, now *Abigall* shall see
Whether *Mathias* holds her deare or no.

Enter Lodowicke *reading.*

Lodowicke.   What, dares the villain write in such base terms?
Mathias.   I did it, and revenge it if thou dar'st.

Fight: Enter Barabas *above.*

Barabas.   Oh bravely fought, and yet they thrust not home.
 Now *Lodowicke*, now *Mathias*, so;   [*Kill each other.*]
 So, now they have shew'd themselves to be tall fellowes.
Within.   Part 'em, part 'em.
Barabas.   I, part 'em now they are dead: Farewell, farewell.

                                                              Exit.

Enter Governor, Mater [*attended*].

Governor.   What sight is this? my *Lodovico* slaine!   10
 These armes of mine shall be thy Sepulchre.
Mater.   Who is this? my sonne *Mathias* slaine!
Governor.   Oh *Lodowicke*! hadst thou perish'd by the Turke,
 Wretched *Ferneze* might have veng'd thy death.
Mater.   Thy sonne slew mine, and I'le revenge his death.
Governor.   Looke, *Katherin*, looke, thy sonne gave mine these
   wounds.
Mater.   Oh leave to grieve me, I am griev'd enough.
Governor.   Oh that my sighs could turne to lively breath;
 And these my teares to blood, that he might live.
Mater.   Who made them enemies?   20
Governor.   I know not, and that grieves me most of all.
Mater.   My sonne lov'd thine.
Governor.   And so did *Lodowicke* him.
Mater.   Lend me that weapon that did kill my sonne,
 And it shall murder me.

*3 *Lodowicke.*] Oxberry; *Math.* Q   10 *Lodovico*] Dyce; *Lodowicke* Q
 4 *Mathias.*] Oxberry; *Lod.* Q

Governor.   Nay Madam stay, that weapon was my son's,
And on that rather should *Fernexe* dye.
Mater.   Hold, let's inquire the causers of their deaths,
That we may venge their blood upon their heads.
Governor.   Then take them up, and let them be interr'd
Within one sacred monument of stone;   30
Upon which Altar I will offer up
My daily sacrifice of sighes and teares,
And with my prayers pierce th'impartiall heavens,
Till they reveal the causers of our smarts,
Which forc'd their hands divide united hearts:
Come, *Katherina*, our losses equall are,
Then of true griefe let us take equall share.

Exeunt [*with bodies*].

Enter Ithimore.   [III.iii]

Ithimore.   Why, was there ever seene such villany,
So neatly plotted, and so well perform'd?
Both held in hand, and flatly both beguil'd.

Enter Abigall.

Abigall.   Why, how now *Ithimore*, why laugh'st thou so?
Ithimore.   Oh, Mistresse, ha ha ha.
Abigall.   Why what ayl'st thou?
Ithimore.   Oh my master.
Abigall.   Ha.
Ithimore.   Oh Mistris! I have the bravest, gravest, secret, subtil,
bottle-nos'd knave to my Master, that ever Gentleman had.   10
Abigall.   Say, knave, why rail'st upon my father thus?
Ithimore.   Oh, my master has the bravest policy.
Abigall.   Wherein?
Ithimore.   Why, know you not?
Abigall.   Why, no.
Ithimore.   Know you not of *Mathias* and Don *Lodowickes* disaster?
Abigall.   No, what was it?

33 th'] Chappell (the); *omit* Q   34 reveal] Dyce; *omit* Q

Ithimore.   Why the devil invented a challenge, my master writ it,
and I carried it, first to *Lodowicke*, and *imprimis* to *Mathias*.
And then they met, and as the story sayes,   20
In dolefull wise they ended both their dayes.
Abigall.   And was my father furtherer of their deaths?
Ithimore.   Am I *Ithimore*?
Abigall.   Yes.
Ithimore.   So sure did your father write, and I cary the chalenge.
Abigall.   Well, *Ithimore*, let me request thee this,
Goe to the new made Nunnery, and inquire
For any of the Fryars of Saint *Jaques*,
And say, I pray them come and speake with me.
Ithimore.   I pray, mistris, wil you answer me to one question?   30
Abigall.   Well, sirra, what is't?
Ithimore.   A very feeling one; have not the Nuns fine sport with
the Fryars now and then?
Abigall.   Go to, sirra sauce, is this your question? get ye gon.
Ithimore.   I will forsooth, Mistris.   *Exit.*
Abigall.   Hard-hearted Father, unkind *Barabas*,
Was this the pursuit of thy policie?
To make me shew them favour severally,
That by my favour they should both be slaine?
Admit thou lov'dst not *Lodowicke* for his sire,   40
Yet Don *Mathias* ne're offended thee:
But thou wert set upon extreme revenge,
Because the Pryor dispossest thee once,
And couldst not venge it, but upon his sonne,
Nor on his sonne, but by *Mathias* meanes;
Nor on *Mathias*, but by murdering me.
But I perceive there is no love on earth,
Pitty in Jewes, nor piety in Turkes.
But here comes cursed *Ithimore* with the Fryar.

20 and] Chappell, Robinson; *omit* Q   40 sire] Dyce; sinne Q
28 *Jaques*] Scott; Jaynes Q   *43 Pryor] *stet* Q

Enter Ithimore, 1. Fryar.

1. Fryar. *Virgo, salve.*   50
Ithimore. When, ducke you?
Abigall. Welcome grave Fryar; *Ithamore* begon,
                                        [*Exit* Ithimore.]
 Know, holy Sir, I am bold to sollicite thee.
1. Fryar. Wherein?
Abigall. To get me be admitted for a Nun.
1. Fryar. Why *Abigal* it is not yet long since
 That I did labour thy admition,
 And then thou didst not like that holy life.
Abigall. Then were my thoughts so fraile and unconfirm'd,
 And I was chain'd to follies of the world: 60
 But now experience, purchased with griefe,
 Has made me see the difference of things.
 My sinfull soule, alas, hath pac'd too long
 The fatall Labyrinth of misbeleefe,
 Farre from the Sonne that gives eternall life.
1. Fryar. Who taught thee this?
Abigall.   The Abbasse of the house
 Whose zealous admonition I embrace:
 Oh therefore, *Jacomo*, let me be one,
 Although unworthy of that Sister-hood.
1. Fryar. *Abigal* I will, but see thou change no more,   70
 For that will be most heavy to thy soule.
Abigall. That was my father's fault.
1. Fryar.   Thy father's, how?
Abigall. Nay, you shall pardon me: oh *Barabas*,   [*Aside.*]
 Though thou deservest hardly at my hands,
 Yet never shall these lips bewray thy life.
1. Fryar. Come, shall we goe?
Abigall.   My duty waits on you.
                                        Exeunt.

Enter Barabas *reading a letter.*

Barabas.   What, *Abigall* become a Nunne againe?
  False, and unkinde; what, hast thou lost thy father?
  And all unknowne, and unconstrain'd of me,
  Art thou againe got to the Nunnery?
  Now here she writes, and wils me to repent.
  Repentance? *Spurca*: what pretendeth this?
  I feare she knowes ('tis so) of my device
  In Don *Mathias* and *Lodovicoes* deaths:
  If so, 'tis time that it be seene into:
  For she that varies from me in beleefe   10
  Gives great presumption that she loves me not;
  Or loving, doth dislike of something done.

[*Enter* Ithimore.]

  But who comes here? Oh *Ithimore* come neere;
  Come neere, my love, come neere, thy masters life,
  My trusty servant, nay, my second selfe;
  For I have now no hope but even in thee;
  And on that hope my happinesse is built:
  When saw'st thou *Abigall*?
Ithimore.   To day.
Barabas.   With whom?   20
Ithimore.   A Fryar.
Barabas.   A Fryar? false villaine, he hath done the deed.
Ithimore.   How, Sir?
Barabas.   Why, made mine *Abigall* a Nunne.
Ithimore.   That's no lye, for she sent me for him.
Barabas.   Oh unhappy day,
  False, credulous, inconstant *Abigall*!
  But let 'em goe: And *Ithimore*, from hence
  Ne're shall she grieve me more with her disgrace;
  Ne're shall she live to inherit ought of mine,   30
  Be blest of me, nor come within my gates,
  But perish underneath my bitter curse

15 selfe] Penley, Dyce²; life Q

302

Like *Cain* by *Adam*, for his brother's death.

Ithimore. Oh master.

Barabas. *Ithimore*, intreat not for her, I am mov'd,
And she is hatefull to my soule and me:
And least thou yeeld to this that I intreat,
I cannot thinke but that thou hat'st my life.

Ithimore. Who I, master? Why I'le run to some rocke and throw
my selfe headlong into the sea; why I'le doe any thing for your 40
sweet sake.

Barabas. Oh trusty *Ithimore*; no servant, but my friend;
I here adopt thee for mine onely heire,
All that I have is thine when I am dead,
And whilst I live use halfe; spend as my selfe;
Here take my keyes, I'le give 'em thee anon:
Goe buy thee garments: but thou shalt not want:
Onely know this, that thus thou art to doe:
But first goe fetch me in the pot of Rice
That for our supper stands upon the fire.   50

Ithimore. I hold my head my master's hungry: I goe Sir. *Exit.*

Barabas. Thus every villaine ambles after wealth
Although he ne're be richer then in hope:
But hush't.

     Enter Ithimore *with the pot.*

Ithimore. Here 'tis, Master.

Barabas. Well said, *Ithimore*;
What, hast thou brought the Ladle with thee too?

Ithimore. Yes, Sir, the proverb saies, he that eats with the devil
had need of a long spoone. I have brought you a Ladle.

Barabas. Very well, *Ithimore*, then now be secret; 60
And for thy sake, whom I so dearely love,
Now shalt thou see the death of *Abigall*,
That thou mayst freely live to be my heire.

Ithimore. Why, master, wil you poison her with a messe of rice
porredge? that wil preserve life, make her round and plump, and
batten more then you are aware.

Barabas. I but *Ithimore* seest thou this?
It is a precious powder that I bought
Of an Italian in *Ancona* once,
Whose operation is to binde, infect,   70
And poyson deeply: yet not appeare
In forty houres after it is tane.
Ithimore. How master?
Barabas. Thus *Ithimore*:
This Even they use in *Malta* here ('tis call'd
Saint *Jaques* Even) and then I say they use
To send their Almes unto the Nunneries:
Among the rest beare this, and set it there;
There's a darke entry where they take it in,
Where they must neither see the messenger,   80
Nor make enquiry who hath sent it them.
Ithimore. How so?
Barabas. Belike there is some Ceremony in't.
There *Ithimore* must thou goe place this pot:
Stay, let me spice it first.
Ithimore. Pray doe, and let me help you, master. Pray let me
taste first.
Barabas. Prethe doe: what saist thou now?
Ithimore. Troth master, I'm loth such a pot of pottage should be
spoyld.   90
Barabas. Peace, *Ithimore*, 'tis better so then spar'd.
Assure thy selfe thou shalt have broth by the eye.
My purse, my Coffer, and my selfe is thine.
Ithimore. Well, master, I goe.
Barabas. Stay, first let me stirre it *Ithimore*.
As fatall be it to her as the draught
Of which great *Alexander* drunke, and dyed:
And with her let it worke like *Borgias* wine,
Whereof his sire, the Pope, was poysoned.
In few, the blood of *Hydra*, *Lerna's* bane;   100
The jouyce of Hebon, and *Cocitus* breath,
And all the poysons of the Stygian poole

84 pot] Dodsley²; plot Q

Breake from the fiery kingdome; and in this
Vomit your venome, and invenome her
That like a fiend hath left her father thus.

Ithimore.   What a blessing has he given't? was ever pot of
rice porredge so sauc't? what shall I doe with it?

Barabas.   Oh my sweet *Ithimore* go set it downe
And come againe so soone as thou hast done,
For I have other businesse for thee.   110

Ithimore.   Here's a drench to poyson a whole stable of Flanders
mares: I'le carry't to the Nuns with a powder.

Barabas.   And the horse pestilence to boot; away.

Ithimore.   I am gone.
Pay me my wages for my worke is done.   *Exit.*

Barabas.   Ile pay thee with a vengeance *Ithamore.*

                                                                    Exit.

Enter Governor, Bosco, Knights, [Callapine, the] Bashaw.   [III.v]

Governor.   Welcome, great Bashaw, how fares *Callymath*,
What wind drives you thus into *Malta* rhode?

Basso.   The wind that bloweth all the world besides,
Desire of gold.

Governor.   Desire of gold, great Sir?
That's to be gotten in the Westerne *Inde*:
In *Malta* are no golden Minerals.

Basso.   To you of *Malta* thus saith *Calymath*:
The time you tooke for respite, is at hand,
For the performance of your promise past;
And for the Tribute-mony I am sent.   10

Governor.   Bashaw, in briefe, shalt have no tribute here,
Nor shall the Heathens live upon our spoyle:
First will we race the City wals our selves,
Lay waste the Iland, hew the Temples downe,
And shipping of our goods to *Sicily*,
Open an entrance for the wastfull sea,
Whose billowes beating the resistlesse bankes,

1 Bashaw] Dodsley²; *Bashaws* Q   15 of] *i.e.,* off

Shall overflow it with their refluence.
Basso.   Well, Governor, since thou hast broke the league
By flat denyall of the promis'd Tribute,   20
Talke not of racing downe your City wals,
You shall not need trouble your selves so farre,
For *Selim-Calymath* shall come himselfe,
And with brasse-bullets batter downe your Towers,
And turne proud *Malta* to a wildernesse
For these intolerable wrongs of yours;
And so farewell.   [*Exit.*]
Governor.   Farewell:
And now you men of *Malta* looke about,
And let's provide to welcome *Calymath*:   30
Close your Port-cullise, charge your Basiliskes,
And as you profitably take up Armes,
So now couragiously encounter them;
For by this Answer, broken is the league,
And nought is to be look'd for now but warres,
And nought to us more welcome is then wars.

Exeunt.

Enter [*the*] *two* Fryars.   [III.vi]

1. Fryar.   Oh brother, brother, all the Nuns are sicke,
And Physicke will not helpe them; they must dye.
2. Fryar.   The Abbasse sent for me to be confest:
Oh what a sad confession will there be?
1. Fryar.   And so did faire *Maria* send for me:
I'le to her lodging; hereabouts she lyes.   *Exit.*

Enter Abigall.

2. Fryar.   What, all dead save onely *Abigall*?
Abigall.   And I shall dye too, for I feele death comming.
Where is the Fryar that converst with me?
2. Fryar.   Oh he is gone to see the other Nuns.   10
Abigall.   I sent for him, but seeing you are come

0.1 Fryars] Dodsley²; *Fryars and Abigall* Q

Be you my ghostly father; and first know,
That in this house I liv'd religiously,
Chast, and devout, much sorrowing for my sinnes,
But e're I came——

2. Fryar.   What then?

Abigall.   I did offend high heaven so grievously,
As I am almost desperate for my sinnes:
And one offence torments me more then all.
You knew *Mathias* and Don *Lodowicke?*   20

2. Fryar.   Yes, what of them?

Abigall.   My father did contract me to 'em both:
First to Don *Lodowicke*, him I never lov'd;
Mathias was the man that I held deare,
And for his sake did I become a Nunne.

2. Fryar.   So, say how was their end?

Abigall.   Both jealous of my love, envied each other:
And by my father's practice, which is there
Set downe at large, the Gallants were both slaine.   [*Gives paper.*]

2. Fryar.   Oh monstrous villany.   30

Abigall.   To worke my peace, this I confesse to thee;
Reveale it not, for then my father dyes.

2. Fryar.   Know that Confession must not be reveal'd,
The Canon Law forbids it, and the Priest
That makes it knowne, being degraded first,
Shall be condemn'd, and then sent to the fire.

Abigall.   So I have heard; pray therefore keepe it close.
Death seizeth on my heart: ah gentle Fryar,
Convert my father that he may be sav'd,
And witnesse that I dye a Christian.   [*Dies.*] 40

2. Fryar.   I, and a Virgin too, that grieves me most:
But I must to the Jew and exclaime on him,
And make him stand in feare of me.

Enter 1. Fryar.

1. Fryar.   Oh brother, all the Nuns are dead, let's bury them.

2. Fryar.   First helpe to bury this, then goe with me
And helpe me to exclaime against the Jew.

1. Fryar.   Why? what has he done?

2. Fryar.   A thing that makes me tremble to unfold.

1. Fryar.   What, has he crucified a child?

2. Fryar.   No, but a worse thing: 'twas told me in shrift,   50
Thou know'st 'tis death and if it be reveal'd.
Come let's away.

Exeunt.

Enter Barabas, Ithamore. *Bells within.*   IV.[i]

Barabas.   There is no musicke to a Christians knell:
How sweet the Bels ring now the Nuns are dead
That sound at other times like Tinkers pans?
I was afraid the poyson had not wrought;
Or though it wrought, it would have done no good,
For every yeare they swell, and yet they live;
Now all are dead, not one remaines alive.

Ithimore.   That's brave, master, but think you it wil not be known?

Barabas.   How can it if we two be secret.

Ithimore.   For my part feare you not.   10

Barabas.   I'de cut thy throat if I did.

Ithimore.   And reason too;
But here's a royall Monastry hard by,
Good master let me poyson all the Monks.

Barabas.   Thou shalt not need, for now the Nuns are dead,
They'll dye with griefe.

Ithimore.   Doe you not sorrow for your daughters death?

Barabas.   No, but I grieve because she liv'd so long.
An Hebrew borne, and would become a Christian?
Cazzo, diabolo.   20

Enter the two Fryars.

Ithimore.   Look, look, master, here come two religious Caterpillers.

Barabas.   I smelt 'em e're they came.

Ithimore.   God-a-mercy nose; come let's begone.

2. Fryar.   Stay wicked Jew, repent, I say, and stay.

1. Fryar.   Thou hast offended, therefore must be damn'd.

Barabas.   I feare they know we sent the poyson'd broth.
Ithimore.   And so doe I, master, therefore speake 'em faire.
2. Fryar.   *Barabas,* thou hast——
1. Fryar.   I, that thou hast——
Barabas.   True, I have mony, what though I have?   30
2. Fryar.   Thou art a——
1. Fryar.   I, that thou art a——
Barabas.   What needs all this? I know I am a Jew.
2. Fryar.   Thy daughter——
1. Fryar.   I, thy daughter——
Barabas.   Oh speake not of her, then I dye with griefe.
2. Fryar.   Remember that——
1. Fryar.   I, remember that——
Barabas.   I must needs say that I have beene a great usurer.
2. Fryar.   Thou hast committed——   40
Barabas.   Fornication? but that was in another Country:
And besides, the Wench is dead.
2. Fryar.   I, but *Barabas,* remember *Mathias* and Don *Lodowick.*
Barabas.   Why, what of them?
2. Fryar.   I will not say that by a forged challenge they met.
Barabas.   She has confest, and we are both undone,
My bosome inmate, *but I must dissemble.*   *Aside.*
Oh holy Fryars, the burthen of my sinnes
Lye heavy on my soule; then pray you tell me,
Is't not too late now to turne Christian?   50
I have beene zealous in the Jewish faith,
Hard harted to the poore, a covetous wretch,
That would for Lucars sake have sold my soule.
A hundred for a hundred I have tane;
And now for store of wealth may I compare
With all the Jewes in *Malta*; but what is wealth?
I am a Jew, and therefore am I lost.
Would pennance serve for this my sinne,
I could afford to whip my selfe to death.
Ithimore.   And so could I; but pennance will not serve.   60
Barabas.   To fast, to pray, and weare a shirt of haire,

*46–7 undone,...inmate] Chappell, Dyce; ~ ; ...inmates Q

And on my knees creepe to *Jerusalem.*
Cellers of Wine, and Sollers full of Wheat,
Ware-houses stuft with spices and with drugs,
Whole Chests of Gold, in Bullion, and in Coyne,
Besides I know not how much weight in Pearle
Orient and round, have I within my house;
At *Alexandria*, Merchandize unsold:
But yesterday two ships went from this Towne,
Their voyage will be worth ten thousand Crownes.   70
In *Florence*, *Venice*, *Antwerpe*, *London*, *Civill*,
Frankeford, *Lubecke*, *Mosco*, and where not,
Have I debts owing; and in most of these,
Great summes of mony lying in the bancho;
All this I'le give to some religious house
So I may be baptiz'd and live therein.
1. Fryar.   Oh good *Barabas* come to our house.
2. Fryar.   Oh no, good *Barabas* come to our house.
And *Barabas*, you know———
Barabas.   I know that I have highly sinn'd,   80
You shall convert me, you shall have all my wealth.
                                        [*Aside to* 2. Fryar.]
1. Fryar.   Oh *Barabas*, their Lawes are strict.
Barabas.   I know they are, *and I will be with you.*
                                        [*Aside to* 2. Fryar.]
1. Fryar.   They weare no shirts, and they goe bare-foot too.
Barabas.   *Then 'tis not for me; and I am resolv'd*
You shall confesse me, and have all my goods.   [*Aside to* 1. Fryar.]
2. Fryar.   Good *Barabas*, come to me.
Barabas.   *You see I answer him, and yet he stayes;*
Rid him away, and goe you home with me.   [*Aside to* 1. Fryar.]
2. Fryar.   I'le be with you to night.   90
Barabas.   *Come to my house at one a clocke this night.*
                                        [*Aside to* 2. Fryar.]
1. Fryar.   You heare your answer, and you may be gone.
2. Fryar.   Why goe, get you away.
1. Fryar.   I will not goe for thee.

*87 2. Fryar.] 1. Q

310

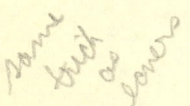

2. *Fryar.*　Not? then I'le make thee, rogue.

1. *Fryar.*　How, dost call me rogue?　　　　　　　　*Fight.*

Ithimore.　Part 'em, master, part 'em.

Barabas.　This is meere frailty, brethren, be content.
　Fryar *Barnardine* goe you with *Ithimore.*
　You know my mind, let me alone with him.　　[*Aside to* 2. Fryar.] 100

1. *Fryar.*　Why does he goe to thy house? let him begone.
　　　　　　　　　　　　　　　　Exit [Ithimore *and* 2. Fryar].

Barabas.　I'le give him something and so stop his mouth.
　I never heard of any man but he
　Malign'd the order of the *Jacobines*:
　But doe you thinke that I beleeve his words?
　Why, Brother, you converted *Abigall*;
　And I am bound in charitie to requite it,
　And so I will, oh *Jacomo*, faile not but come.

1. *Fryar.*　But *Barabas*, who shall be your godfathers,
　For presently you shall be shriv'd.　　　　　　　　110

Barabas.　Marry the Turke shall be one of my godfathers,
　But not a word to any of your Covent.

1. *Fryar.*　I warrant thee, *Barabas*.　　　　　　*Exit.*

Barabas.　So, now the feare is past, and I am safe:
　For he that shriv'd her is within my house.
　What if I murder'd him e're *Jacomo* comes?
　Now I have such a plot for both their lives,
　As never Jew nor Christian knew the like:
　One turn'd my daughter, therefore he shall dye;
　The other knowes enough to have my life,　　　　120
　Therefore 'tis not requisite he should live.
　But are not both these wise men to suppose
　That I will leave my house, my goods, and all,
　To fast and be well whipt; I'le none of that.
　Now Fryar *Bernardine* I come to you,
　I'le feast you, lodge you, give you faire words,
　And after that, I and my trusty Turke——

95　rogue] Coll MS, TB; goe Q　　　101　1. *Fryar.*] Dyce; *omit* Q
100　*You*] Dyce; *Ith. You* Q

No more but so: it must and shall be done.
Ithimore, tell me, is the Fryar asleepe?

Enter Ithimore.

Ithimore. Yes; and I know not what the reason is: 130
Doe what I can he will not strip himselfe,
Nor goe to bed, but sleepes in his owne clothes;
I feare me he mistrusts what we intend.
Barabas. No, 'tis an order which the Fryars use:
Yet if he knew our meanings, could he scape?
Ithimore. No, none can heare him, cry he ne're so loud.
Barabas. Why true, therefore did I place him there:
The other Chambers open towards the street.
Ithimore. You loyter, master, wherefore stay we thus?
Oh how I long to see him shake his heeles.   140
Barabas. Come on, sirra,
Off with your girdle, make a hansom noose;
Fryar, awake.
2. Fryar. What, doe you meane to strangle me?
Ithimore. Yes, 'cause you use to confesse.
Barabas. Blame not us but the proverb, Confes and be hang'd.
Pull hard.
2. Fryar. What, will you have my life?
Barabas. Pull hard, I say, you would have had my goods.
Ithimore. I, and our lives too, therefore pull amaine.   [*Dies.*] 150
'Tis neatly done, Sir, here's no print at all.
Barabas. Then is it as it should be, take him up.
Ithimore. Nay, master, be rul'd by me a little; so, let him leane
upon his staffe; excellent, he stands as if he were begging of
Bacon.
Barabas. Who would not thinke but that this Fryar liv'd?
What time a night is't now, sweet *Ithimore?*
Ithimore. Towards one.
Barabas. Then will not *Jacomo* be long from hence.
[*They go aside.*]

148 have] Chappell, Oxberry; save Q

312

Enter [1. Fryar] Jacomo.

1. Fryar.　　This is the houre　　　　　　　　　　　　　160
Wherein I shall proceed; Oh happy houre,
Wherein I shall convert an Infidell,
And bring his gold into our treasury.
But soft, is not this *Bernardine*? it is;
And understanding I should come this way,
Stands here a purpose, meaning me some wrong,
And intercept my going to the Jew;
Bernardine——
Wilt thou not speake? thou think'st I see thee not;
Away, I'de wish thee, and let me goe by:　　　　　170
No, wilt thou not? nay then I'le force my way;
And see, a staffe stands ready for the purpose:
As thou lik'st that, stop me another time.

Strike him, he fals. Enter [*come forward*] Barabas [*and* Ithimore].

Barabas.　　Why, how now *Jacomo*, what hast thou done?
1. Fryar.　　Why, stricken him that would have stroke at me.
Barabas.　　Who is it? *Bernardine*? now out alas,
He is slaine.
Ithimore.　　I, master, he's slain; look how his brains drop out on's
nose.
1. Fryar.　　Good sirs I have don't, but no body knowes it but you　180
two, I may escape.
Barabas.　　So might my man and I hang with you for company.
Ithimore.　　No, let us beare him to the Magistrates.
1. Fryar.　　Good *Barabas* let me goe.
Barabas.　　No, pardon me, the Law must have his course.
I must be forc'd to give in evidence,
That being importun'd by this *Bernardine*
To be a Christian, I shut him out,
And there he sate: now I to keepe my word,
And give my goods and substance to your house,　　190
Was up thus early; with intent to goe
Unto your Friery, because you staid.

Ithimore. Fie upon 'em, master, will you turne Christian, when
holy Friars turne devils and murder one another.
Barabas. No, for this example I'le remaine a Jew:
Heaven blesse me; what, a Fryar a murderer?
When shall you see a Jew commit the like?
Ithimore. Why, a Turke could ha done no more.
Barabas. To morrow is the Sessions; you shall to it.
Come *Ithimore*, let's helpe to take him hence. 200
1. Fryar. Villaines, I am a sacred person, touch me not.
Barabas. The Law shall touch you, we'll but lead you, we:
'Las I could weepe at your calamity.
Take in the staffe too, for that must be showne:
Law wils that each particular be knowne.

                                  Exeunt.

         Enter Curtezane, *and* Pilia-borza.   [IV.ii]

Curtezane. *Pilia-borza*, didst thou meet with *Ithimore?*
Pilia-borza. I did.
Curtezane. And didst thou deliver my letter?
Pilia-borza. I did.
Curtezane. And what think'st thou, will he come?
Pilia-borza. I think so, and yet I cannot tell, for at the reading
of the letter, he look'd like a man of another world.
Curtezane. Why so?
Pilia-borza. That such a base slave as he should be saluted by
such a tall man as I am, from such a beautifull dame as you. 10
Curtezane. And what said he?
Pilia-borza. Not a wise word, only gave me a nod, as who shold
say, Is it even so; and so I left him, being driven to a *non-plus* at
the critical aspect of my terrible countenance.
Curtezane. And where didst meet him?
Pilia-borza. Upon mine owne free-hold within fortie foot of the
gallowes, conning his neck-verse I take it, looking of a Fryars
Execution, whom I saluted with an old hempen proverb, *Hodie
tibi, cras mihi,* and so I left him to the mercy of the Hangman:
but the Exercise being done, see where he comes. 20

                        314

Enter Ithimore.

Ithimore. I never knew a man take his death so patiently as this
Fryar: he was ready to leape off e're the halter was about his
necke; and when the Hangman had put on his hempen Tippet,
he made such haste to his prayers, as if hee had had another
Cure to serve; well, goe whither he will, I'le be none of his
followers in haste:

And now I thinke on't, going to the execution, a fellow met me
with a muschatoes like a Ravens wing, and a Dagger with a
hilt like a warming-pan, and he gave me a letter from one
Madam *Bellamira*, saluting me in such sort as if he had meant to 30
make cleane my Boots with his lips; the effect was, that I should
come to her house. I wonder what the reason is. It may be she
sees more in me than I can find in my selfe: for she writes further,
that she loves me ever since she saw me, and who would not
requite such love? here's her house, and here she comes, and now
would I were gone, I am not worthy to looke upon her.

Pilia-borza. This is the Gentleman you writ to.

Ithimore. Gentleman, he flouts me, what gentry can be in a
poore Turke of ten pence? I'le be gone.   [*Aside.*]

Curtezane. Is't not a sweet fac'd youth, *Pilia?*   40

Ithimore. Agen, sweet youth; did not you, Sir, bring the sweet
youth a letter?

Pilia-borza. I did Sir, and from this Gentlewoman, who as my
selfe, and the rest of the family, stand or fall at your service.

Curtezane. Though womans modesty should hale me backe,
I can with-hold no longer; welcome sweet love.   [*Kisse him.*]

Ithimore. Now am I cleane, or rather fouly out of the way. [*Aside.*]

Curtezane. Whither so soone?

Ithimore. I'le goe steale some mony from my Master to make
me hansome: [*Aside.*] 50
Pray pardon me, I must goe see a ship discharg'd.

Curtezane. Canst thou be so unkind to leave me thus?

Pilia-borza. And ye did but know how she loves you, Sir.

Ithimore. Nay, I care not how much she loves me;
Sweet *Bellamira*, would I had my Masters wealth for thy sake.

Pilia-borȝa. And you can have it, Sir, and if you please.

Ithimore. If 'twere above ground I could, and would have it; but hee hides and buries it up as Partridges doe their egges, under the earth.

Pilia-borȝa. And is't not possible to find it out? 60

Ithimore. By no meanes possible.

Curteȝane. *What shall we doe with this base villaine then?*

[*Aside to* Pilia-borza.]

Pilia-borȝa. *Let me alone, doe but you speake him faire:*
But you know some secrets of the Jew,
Which if they were reveal'd, would doe him harme.

Ithimore. I, and such as——Goe to, no more,
I'le make him send me half he has, and glad he scapes so too.
Pen and Inke:
I'le write unto him, we'le have mony strait.

Pilia-borȝa. Send for a hundred Crownes at least. 70

Ithimore. Ten hundred thousand crownes,——Master *Barabas.*

He writes.

Pilia-borȝa. Write not so submissively, but threatning him.

Ithimore. Sirra *Barabas*, send me a hundred crownes.

Pilia-borȝa. Put in two hundred at least.

Ithimore. I charge thee send me three hundred by this bearer, and this shall be your warrant; if you doe not, no more but so.

Pilia-borȝa. Tell him you will confesse.

Ithimore. Otherwise I'le confesse all:——
Vanish and returne in a twinckle.

Pilia-borȝa. Let me alone, I'le use him in his kinde. [*Exit.*] 80

Ithimore. Hang him, Jew.

Curteȝane. Now, gentle *Ithimore*, lye in my lap.
Where are my Maids? provide a running Banquet;
Send to the Merchant, bid him bring me silkes,
Shall *Ithimore* my love goe in such rags?

Ithimore. And bid the Jeweller come hither too.

Curteȝane. I have no husband, sweet, I'le marry thee.

Ithimore. Content, but we will leave this paltry land,
And saile from hence to *Greece*, to lovely *Greece*,
I'le be thy *Jason*, thou my golden Fleece; 90

Where painted Carpets o're the meads are hurl'd,
And *Bacchus* vineyards over-spread the world:
Where Woods and Forrests goe in goodly greene,
I'le be *Adonis*, thou shalt be Loves Queene.
The Meads, the Orchards, and the Primrose lanes,
Instead of Sedge and Reed, beare Sugar Canes:
Thou in those Groves, by *Dis* above,
Shalt live with me and be my love.

CurteƷane.   Whither will I not goe with gentle *Ithimore?*

Enter Pilea-borza.

Ithimore.   How now? hast thou the gold?   100
Pilia-borƷa.   Yes.   [*Gives him bag.*]
Ithimore.   But came it freely, did the Cow give down her milk
freely?
Pilia-borƷa.   At reading of the letter, he star'd and stamp'd, and
turnd aside. I tooke him by the beard, and look'd upon him thus;
told him he were best to send it; then he hug'd and imbrac'd me.
Ithimore.   Rather for feare then love.
Pilia-borƷa.   Then like a Jew he laugh'd and jeer'd, and told me
he lov'd me for your sake, and said what a faithfull servant you
had bin.   110
Ithimore.   The more villaine he to keep me thus:
Here's goodly 'parrell, is there not?
Pilia-borƷa.   To conclude, he gave me ten crownes.
Ithimore.   But ten? I'le not leave him worth a gray groat. Give me
a Reame of paper, we'll have a kingdome of gold for't.
Pilia-borƷa.   Write for five hundred Crownes.
Ithimore.   Sirra Jew, as you love your life send me five hundred
crowns, and give the Bearer one hundred. Tell him I must hav't.
Pilia-borƷa.   I warrant your worship shall hav't.
Ithimore.   And if he aske why I demand so much, tell him, I   120
scorne to write a line under a hundred crownes.
Pilia-borƷa.   You'd make a rich Poet, Sir. I am gone.   *Exit.*
Ithimore.   Take thou the mony, spend it for my sake.
CurteƷane.   'Tis not thy mony, but thy selfe I weigh:

92 over-spread] Dodsley²; ore-spread Q   105 beard] Dodsley²; sterd Q

Thus *Bellamira* esteemes of gold;   [*Throw it aside.*]
But thus of thee.———   *Kisse him.*
Ithimore.   That kisse againe; she runs division of my lips. What
an eye she casts on me? It twinckles like a Starre.
Curtezane.   Come my deare love, let's in and sleepe together.
Ithimore.   Oh that ten thousand nights were put in one,   130
That wee might sleepe seven yeeres together afore we wake.
Curtezane.   Come Amorous wag, first banquet and then sleep.
                                                          [*Exeunt.*]

                Enter Barabas, *reading a letter.*   [IV.iii]

Barabas.   *Barabas* send me three hundred Crownes.
Plaine *Barabas*: oh that wicked Curtezane!
He was not wont to call me *Barabas*.
Or else I will confesse: I, there it goes:
But if I get him, *Coupe de Gorge* for that.
He sent a shaggy totter'd staring slave,
That when he speakes, drawes out his grisly beard,
And winds it twice or thrice about his eare;
Whose face has bin a grind-stone for mens swords,
His hands are hackt, some fingers cut quite off;   10
Who when he speakes, grunts like a hog, and looks
Like one that is imploy'd in Catzerie
And crosbiting, such a Rogue
As is the husband to a hundred whores:
And I by him must send three hundred crownes.
Well, my hope is, he will not stay there still;
And when he comes: Oh that he were but here!

                    Enter Pilia-borza.

Pilia-borza.   Jew, I must ha more gold.
Barabas.   Why, wantst thou any of thy tale?
Pilia-borza.   No; but three hundred will not serve his turne.   20
Barabas.   Not serve his turne, Sir?
Pilia-borza.   No Sir; and therefore I must have five hundred more.
Barabas.   I'le rather———

Pilia-borza.   Oh good words, Sir, and send it you, weere best se;
there's his letter.

Barabas.   Might he not as well come as send; pray bid him come
and fetch it: what hee writes for you, ye shall have streight.

Pilia-borza.   I, and the rest too, or else——

Barabas.   *I must make this villaine away*: please you dine with me,
Sir, *and you shal be most hartily poyson'd.*   *Aside.* 30

Pilia-borza.   No god-a-mercy, shall I have these crownes?

Barabas.   I cannot doe it, I have lost my keyes.

Pilia-borza.   Oh, if that be all, I can picke ope your locks.

Barabas.   Or climbe up to my Counting-house window: you know
my meaning.

Pilia-borza.   I know enough, and therfore talke not to me of your
Counting-house: the gold, or know Jew it is in my power to
hang thee.

Barabas.   I am betraid.——   [*Aside.*]
'Tis not five hundred Crownes that I esteeme,   40
I am not mov'd at that: this angers me,
That he who knowes I love him as my selfe
Should write in this imperious vaine! why Sir,
You know I have no childe, and unto whom
Should I leave all but unto *Ithimore*?

Pilia-borza.   Here's many words but no crownes; the crownes.

Barabas.   Commend me to him, Sir, most humbly,
And unto your good mistris as unknowne.

Pilia-borza.   Speake, shall I have 'um, Sir?

Barabas.   Sir, here they are.   50
Oh that I should part with so much gold!   [*Aside.*]
Here take 'em, fellow, with as good a will——
As I wud see thee hang'd; oh, love stops my breath:
Never lov'd man servant as I doe *Ithimore*.

Pilia-borza.   I know it, Sir.

Barabas.   Pray when, Sir, shall I see you at my house?

Pilia-borza.   Soone enough to your cost, Sir:
Fare you well.   *Exit.*

Barabas.   Nay to thine owne cost, villaine, if thou com'st.
Was ever Jew tormented as I am?   60

To have a shag-rag knave to come demand
Three hundred Crownes, and then five hundred Crownes?
Well, I must seeke a meanes to rid 'em all,
And presently: for in his villany
He will tell all he knowes and I shall dye for't.
I have it.
I will in some disguize goe see the slave,
And how the villaine revels with my gold.

Exit.

Enter Curtezane, Ithimore, Pilia-borza.   [IV.iv]

Curtezane.   I'le pledge thee, love, and therefore drinke it off.
Ithimore.   Saist thou me so? have at it; and doe you heare?
                                                [*Whispers her.*]
Curtezane.   Goe to, it shall be so.
Ithimore.   Of that condition I wil drink it up; here's to thee.
Curtezane.   Nay, I'le have all or none.
Ithimore.   There, if thou lov'st me doe not leave a drop.
Curtezane.   Love thee, fill me three glasses.
Ithimore.   Three and fifty dozen, I'le pledge thee.
Pilia-borza.   Knavely spoke, and like a Knight at Armes.
Ithimore.   Hey *Rivo Castiliano*, a man's a man.   10
Curtezane.   Now to the Jew.
Ithimore.   Ha, to the Jew, and send me mony you were best.
Pilia-borza.   What wudst thou doe if he should send thee none?
Ithimore.   Doe? nothing; but I know what I know.
He's a murderer.
Curtezane.   I had not thought he had been so brave a man.
Ithimore.   You knew *Mathias* and the Governors son; he and I
  kild 'em both, and yet never touch'd 'em.
Pilia-borza.   Oh bravely done.
Ithimore.   I carried the broth that poyson'd the Nuns, and he 20
  and I, snicle hand too fast, strangled a Fryar.
Curtezane.   You two alone?

61 demand] *omit* Q   *21 snicle hand too fast] *stet* Q
 5 *Curtezane.*] Chappell, Dyce; *Pil.* Q

Ithimore.   We two, and 'twas never knowne, nor never shall be
for me.

Pilia-borza.   This shall with me unto the Governor.

[Aside to Bellamira.]

Curtezane.   And fit it should: but first let's ha more gold.

[Aside to Pilia-borza.]

Come gentle *Ithimore*, lye in my lap.

Ithimore.   Love me little, love me long, let musicke rumble,
Whilst I in thy *incony* lap doe tumble.

Enter Barabas with a Lute, disguis'd.

Curtezane.   A French Musician, come let's heare your skill?   30

Barabas.   Must tuna my Lute for sound, twang twang first.

Ithimore.   Wilt drinke French-man, here's to thee with a—pox on
this drunken hick-up.

Barabas.   Gramercy Mounsier.

Curtezane.   Prethe, *Pilia-borza*, bid the Fidler give me the posey
in his hat there.

Pilia-borza.   Sirra, you must give my mistris your posey.

Barabas.   *A voustre commandemente Madam.*

Curtezane.   How sweet, my *Ithimore*, the flowers smell.

Ithimore.   Like thy breath, sweet-hart, no violet like 'em.   40

Pilia-borza.   Foh, me thinkes they stinke like a Holly-Hoke.

Barabas.   So, now I am reveng'd upon 'em all.   [*Aside.*]
The scent thereof was death, I poyson'd it.

Ithimore.   Play, Fidler, or I'le cut your cats guts into chitterlins.

Barabas.   Pardona moy, be no in tune yet; so, now, now all be in.

Ithimore.   Give him a crowne, and fill me out more wine.

Pilia-borza.   There's two crownes for thee, play.

Barabas.   How liberally the villian gives me mine own gold.

Aside.

Pilia-borza.   Me thinkes he fingers very well.

Barabas.   So did you when you stole my gold.   *Aside.* 50

Pilia-borza.   How swift he runnes.

Barabas.   You run swifter when you threw my gold out of my
Window.   *Aside.*

Curtezane.   Musician, hast beene in *Malta* long?

Barabas. Two, three, foure month Madam.

Ithimore. Dost not know a Jew, one *Barabas*?

Barabas. Very mush, Mounsier, you no be his man?

Pilia-borza. His man?

Ithimore. I scorne the Peasant, tell him so.

Barabas. He knowes it already. [*Aside.*] 60

Ithimore. 'Tis a strange thing of that Jew, he lives upon pickled Grashoppers, and sauc'd Mushrumbs.

Barabas. What a slave's this? The Governour feeds not as I doe.

Aside.

Ithimore. He never put on cleane shirt since he was circumcis'd.

Barabas. Oh raskall! I change my selfe twice a day. *Aside.*

Ithimore. The Hat he weares, *Judas* left under the Elder when he hang'd himselfe.

Barabas. 'Twas sent me for a present from the great *Cham.*

Aside.

Pilia-borza. A masty slave he is.

Whether now, Fidler?

Barabas. Pardona moy, Mounsier, me be no well. *Exit.* 70

Pilia-borza. Farewell Fidler: One letter more to the Jew.

Curteʒane. Prethe sweet love, one more, and write it sharp.

Ithimore. No, I'le send by word of mouth now;

Bid him deliver thee a thousand Crownes, by the same token, that the Nuns lov'd Rice, that Fryar *Bernardine* slept in his owne clothes.

Any of 'em will doe it.

Pilia-borza. Let me alone to urge it now I know the meaning.

Ithimore. The meaning has a meaning; come let's in:

To undoe a Jew is charity, and not sinne. 80

Exeunt.

Enter Governor, Knights, Martin Del-Bosco. V.[i]

Governor. Now, Gentlemen, betake you to your Armes,

And see that *Malta* be well fortifi'd;

And it behoves you to be resolute;

For *Calymath* having hover'd here so long,

*69 masty] stet Q   70 me] Dodsley²; we Q

Will winne the Towne, or dye before the wals.
1. Knight.   And dye he shall, for we will never yeeld.

Enter Curtezane, Pilia-borza.

Curtezane.   Oh bring us to the Governor.
Governor.   Away with her, she is a Curtezane.
Curtezane.   What e're I am, yet Governor heare me speake;
I bring thee newes by whom thy sonne was slaine: 10
Mathias did it not, it was the Jew.
Pilia-borza.   Who, besides the slaughter of these Gentlemen,
poyson'd his owne daughter and the Nuns, strangled a Fryar,
and I know not what mischiefe beside.
Governor.   Had we but proofe of this——
Curtezane.   Strong proofe, my Lord, his man's now at my lodging
That was his Agent, he'll confesse it all.
Governor.   Goe fetch him straight.   [*Exit* Officers.]
                                        I always fear'd that Jew.

Enter Jew, Ithimore [*with* Officers].

Barabas.   I'le goe alone, dogs, do not hale me thus.
Ithimore.   Nor me neither, I cannot out-run you Constable, oh 20
my belly.
Barabas.   One dram of powder more had made all sure. [*Aside.*]
What a damn'd slave was I?
Governor.   Make fires, heat irons, let the racke be fetch'd.
1. Knight.   Nay stay, my Lord, 'tmay be he will confesse.
Barabas.   Confesse; what meane you, Lords, who should confesse?
Governor.   Thou and thy Turk; 'twas you that slew my son.
Ithimore.   Gilty, my Lord, I confesse; your sonne and *Mathias*
were both contracted unto *Abigall*; he forg'd a counterfeit
challenge.   30
Barabas.   Who carried that challenge?
Ithimore.   I carried it, I confesse, but who writ it?
Marry, even he that strangled *Bernardine*, poyson'd the Nuns, and
his owne daughter.

29 he] Dodsley²; *omit* Q

Governor. Away with him, his sight is death to me.

Barabas. For what? you men of *Malta*, heare me speake;
Shee is a Curtezane and he a theefe,
And he my bondman, let me have law,
For none of this can prejudice my life.

Governor. Once more away with him; you shall have law. 40

Barabas. Devils doe your worst, I'le live in spite of you.
As these have spoke so be it to their soules:——
I hope the poyson'd flowers will worke anon.

    Exit [Barabas, Curtezane, Pilia-borza, *with* Officers].

     Enter Mater.

Mater. Was my *Mathias* murder'd by the Jew?
Ferneze, 'twas thy sonne that murder'd him.

Governor. Be patient, gentle Madam, it was he,
He forged the daring challenge made them fight.

Mater. Where is the Jew, where is that murderer?

Governor. In prison till the Law has past on him.

     Enter 1. Officer.

1. Officer. My Lord, the Curtezane and her man are dead; 50
So is the Turke, and *Barabas* the Jew.

Governor. Dead?

1. Officer. Dead, my Lord, and here they bring his body.

    [*Enter* Officers *carrying* Barabas, *as dead.*]

Bosco. This sudden death of his is very strange.

Governor. Wonder not at it, Sir, the heavens are just:
Their deaths were like their lives, then think not of 'em;
Since they are dead, let them be buried.
For the Jewes body, throw that o're the wals,
To be a prey for Vultures and wild beasts.

    [*They take body aside.*]

So, now away and fortifie the Towne. 60

    Exeunt. [*Manet* Barabas.]

Barabas. What, all alone? well fare sleepy drinke.
I'le be reveng'd on this accursed Towne;

41 I'le] Dyce; I Q

For by my meanes *Calymath* shall enter in.
I'le helpe to slay their children and their wives,
To fire the Churches, pull their houses downe,
Take my goods too, and seize upon my lands:
I hope to see the Governour a slave,
And, rowing in a Gally, whipt to death.

　　　　　Enter Calymath, Bashawes, Turkes.

Calymath.　Whom have we there, a spy?
Barabas.　Yes, my good Lord, one that can spy a place　　70
Where you may enter, and surprize the Towne:
My name is *Barabas*; I am a Jew.
Calymath.　Art thou that Jew whose goods we heard were sold
For Tribute-mony?
Barabas.　　　　　The very same, my Lord:
And since that time they have hir'd a slave my man
To accuse me of a thousand villanies:
I was imprison'd, but escap'd their hands.
Calymath.　Didst breake prison?
Barabas.　No, no:
I dranke of Poppy and cold mandrake juyce;　　80
And being asleepe, belike they thought me dead,
And threw me o're the wals: so, or how else,
The Jew is here, and rests at your command.
Calymath.　'Twas bravely done: but tell me, *Barabas*,
Canst thou, as thou reportest, make *Malta* ours?
Barabas.　Feare not, my Lord, for here, against the sluice,
The rocke is hollow, and of purpose digg'd,
To make a passage for the running streames
And common channels of the City.
Now whilst you give assault unto the wals,　　90
I'le lead five hundred souldiers through the Vault,
And rise with them i'th middle of the Towne,
Open the gates for you to enter in,
And by this meanes the City is your owne.
Calymath.　If this be true, I'le make thee Governor.

*86 sluice] Chappell, Dodsley³ (*qy*), Cunningham; Truce Q

Barabas. And if it be not true, then let me dye.
Calymath. Thou'st doom'd thy selfe, assault it presently.

Exeunt.

Alarmes. *Enter* Turkes, Barabas, Governour, *and* [V.ii]
Knights *prisoners.*

Calymath. Now vaile your pride you captive Christians,
And kneele for mercy to your conquering foe:
Now where's the hope you had of haughty *Spaine?*
Ferneʒe, speake, had it not beene much better
To keep thy promise then be thus surpriz'd?
Governor. What should I say? we are captives and must yeeld.
Calymath. I, villains, you must yeeld, and under Turkish yokes
Shall groning beare the burthen of our ire;
And *Barabas,* as erst we promis'd thee,
For thy desert we make thee Governor,   10
Use them at thy discretion.
Barabas.   Thankes, my Lord.
Governor. Oh fatall day, to fall into the hands
Of such a Traitor and unhallowed Jew!
What greater misery could heaven inflict?
Calymath. 'Tis our command: and *Barabas* we give
To guard thy person, these our Janizaries:
Intreat them well, as we have used thee.
And now, brave Bashawes, come, wee'll walke about
The ruin'd Towne, and see the wracke we made:
Farewell brave Jew, farewell great *Barabas.*   *Exeunt.* 20
Barabas. May all good fortune follow *Calymath.*
And now, as entrance to our safety,
To prison with the Governour and these
Captaines, his consorts and confederates.
Governor. Oh villaine, Heaven will be reveng'd on thee.

Exeunt. [*Manet* Barabas.]
Barabas. Away, no more, let him not trouble me.
Thus hast thou gotten, by thy policie,

5 keep] kept Q

No simple place, no small authority,
I now am Governour of *Malta*; true,
But *Malta* hates me, and in hating me   30
My life's in danger, and what boots it thee
Poore *Barabas*, to be the Governour,
When as thy life shall be at their command?
No, *Barabas*, this must be look'd into;
And since by wrong thou got'st Authority,
Maintaine it bravely by firme policy,
At least unprofitably lose it not:
For he that liveth in Authority,
And neither gets him friends, nor fils his bags,
Lives like the Asse that *Æsope* speaketh of,   40
That labours with a load of bread and wine,
And leaves it off to snap on Thistle tops:
But *Barabas* will be more circumspect.
Begin betimes, Occasion's bald behind,
Slip not thine opportunity, for feare too late
Thou seek'st for much, but canst not compasse it.
Within here.

              Enter Governor *with a guard.*

Governor.   My Lord?
Barabas.   I, Lord, thus slaves will learne.
Now Governor——stand by there, wait within.——   50

                                    [*Exeunt guard.*]

This is the reason that I sent for thee;
Thou seest thy life, and *Malta's* happinesse,
Are at my Arbitrament; and *Barabas*
At his discretion may dispose of both:
Now tell me, Governor, and plainely too,
What thinkst thou shall become of it and thee?
Governor.   This, *Barabas*; since things are in thy power,
I see no reason but of *Malta's* wracke,
Nor hope of thee but extreme cruelty,
Nor feare I death, nor will I flatter thee.   60
Barabas.   Governor, good words, be not so furious;

'Tis not thy life which can availe me ought,
Yet you doe live, and live for me you shall:
And as for *Malta's* ruine, thinke you not
'Twere slender policy for *Barabas*
To dispossesse himselfe of such a place?
For sith, as once you said, within this Ile
In *Malta* here, that I have got my goods,
And in this City still have had successe,
And now at length am growne your Governor,   70
Your selves shall see it shall not be forgot:
For as a friend not knowne, but in distresse,
I'le reare up *Malta* now remedilesse.
Governor.   Will *Barabas* recover *Malta's* losse?
Will *Barabas* be good to Christians?
Barabas.   What wilt thou give me, Governor, to procure
A dissolution of the slavish Bands
Wherein the Turke hath yoak'd your land and you?
What will you give me if I render you
The life of *Calymath*, surprize his men,   80
And in an out-house of the City shut
His souldiers, till I have consum'd 'em all with fire?
What will you give him that procureth this?
Governor.   Doe but bring this to passe which thou pretendest,
Deale truly with us as thou intimatest,
And I will send amongst the Citizens
And by my letters privately procure
Great summes of mony for thy recompence:
Nay more, doe this, and live thou Governor still.
Barabas.   Nay, doe thou this, *Ferneze*, and be free;   90
Governor, I enlarge thee, live with me,
Goe walke about the City, see thy friends:
Tush, send not letters to 'em, goe thy selfe,
And let me see what mony thou canst make;
Here is my hand that I'le set *Malta* free:
And thus we cast it: To a solemne feast
I will invite young *Selim-Calymath*,
Where be thou present onely to performe

One stratagem that I'le impart to thee,
Wherein no danger shall betide thy life,   100
And I will warrant *Malta* free for ever.
Governor.   Here is my hand, beleeve me, *Barabas*,
I will be there, and doe as thou desirest;
When is the time?
Barabas.   Governor, presently.
For *Callymath*, when he hath view'd the Towne,
Will take his leave and saile toward *Ottoman*.
Governor.   Then will I, *Barabas*, about this coyne,
And bring it with me to thee in the evening.
Barabas.   Doe so, but faile not; now farewell *Ferneze*:
                              [*Exit* Governor.]

And thus farre roundly goes the businesse: 110
Thus loving neither, will I live with both,
Making a profit of my policie;
And he from whom my most advantage comes,
Shall be my friend.
This is the life we Jewes are us'd to lead;
And reason too, for Christians doe the like:
Well, now about effecting this device:
First to surprize great *Selims* souldiers,
And then to make provision for the feast,
That at one instant all things may be done,   120
My policie detests prevention:
To what event my secret purpose drives,
I know; and they shall witnesse with their lives.

                                        Exit.

            Enter Calymath, Bashawes.   [V.iii]

Calymath.   Thus have we view'd the City, seene the sacke,
And caus'd the ruines to be new repair'd,
Which with our Bombards shot and Basiliske,
We rent in sunder at our entry:
And now I see the Scituation,
And how secure this conquer'd Iland stands

Inviron'd with the mediterranean Sea,
Strong contermin'd with other petty Iles;
And toward *Calabria*, back'd by *Sicily*,
Where *Siracusian Dionisius* reign'd,   10
Two lofty Turrets that command the Towne.
I wonder how it could be conquer'd thus?

Enter a Messenger.

Messenger.   From *Barabas*, *Malta's* Governor, I bring
A message unto mighty *Calymath*;
Hearing his Soveraigne was bound for Sea,
To saile to *Turkey*, to great *Ottoman*,
He humbly would intreat your Majesty
To come and see his homely Citadell,
And banquet with him e're thou leav'st the Ile.
Calymath.   To banquet with him in his Citadell?   20
I feare me, Messenger, to feast my traine
Within a Towne of warre so lately pillag'd,
Will be too costly and too troublesome:
Yet would I gladly visit *Barabas*,
For well has *Barabas* deserv'd of us.
Messenger.   *Selim*, for that, thus saith the Governor,
That he hath in store a Pearle so big,
So precious, and withall so orient,
As be it valued but indifferently,
The price thereof will serve to entertaine   30
Selim and all his souldiers for a month;
Therefore he humbly would intreat your Highnesse
Not to depart till he has feasted you.
Calymath.   I cannot feast my men in *Malta* wals,
Except he place his Tables in the streets.
Messenger.   Know, *Selim*, that there is a monastery
Which standeth as an out-house to the Towne;
There will he banquet them, but thee at home,
With all thy Bashawes and brave followers.

10–11 Where…Towne.] Robinson;   10 Where] Robinson; When Q
        Q *transposes lines*

Calymath.   Well, tell the Governor we grant his suit,   40
  Wee'll in this Summer Evening feast with him.
Messenger.   I shall, my Lord.   *Exit*.
Calymath.   And now, bold Bashawes, let us to our Tents,
  And meditate how we may grace us best
  To solemnize our Governors great feast.

                          Exeunt.

      Enter Governor, Knights, Del-bosco.   [V.iv]

Governor.   In this, my Countrimen, be rul'd by me,
  Have speciall care that no man sally forth
  Till you shall heare a Culverin discharg'd
  By him that beares the Linstocke, kindled thus;
  Then issue out and come to rescue me,
  For happily I shall be in distresse,
  Or you released of this servitude.
1. Knight.   Rather then thus to live as Turkish thrals,
  What will we not adventure?
Governor.   On then, begone.
1. Knight.   Farewell grave Governor.   10

                    [*Exeunt severally*.]

     Enter [Barabas] *with a Hammar above, very busie*.   [V.v]
         [*His men work with him*.]

Barabas.   How stand the cords? How hang these hinges, fast?
  Are all the Cranes and Pulleyes sure?
Servant.   All fast.
Barabas.   Leave nothing loose, all leveld to my mind.
  Why now I see that you have Art indeed.
  There, Carpenters, divide that gold amongst you:
  Goe swill in bowles of Sacke and Muscadine:
  Downe to the Celler, taste of all my wines.
Carpenter.   We shall, my Lord, and thanke you.   *Exeunt*.
Barabas.   And if you like them, drinke your fill and dye:
  For so I live, perish may all the world.   10

              331

Now *Selim-Calymath*, returne me word
That thou wilt come, and I am satisfied.
Now sirra, what, will he come?

Enter Messenger.

Messenger. He will; and has commanded all his men
To come ashore, and march through *Malta* streets,
That thou maist feast them in thy Citadell.
Barabas. Then now are all things as my wish wud have 'em,
There wanteth nothing but the Governors pelfe,
And see he brings it: Now, Governor, the summe?

Enter Governour.

Governor. With free consent a hundred thousand pounds.   20
Barabas. Pounds saist thou, Governor, wel since it is no more
I'le satisfie my selfe with that; nay, keepe it still,
For if I keepe not promise, trust not me.
And Governour, now partake my policy:
First, for his Army, they are sent before,
Enter'd the Monastery, and underneath
In severall places are field-pieces pitch'd,
Bombards, whole Barrels full of Gunpowder,
That on the sudden shall dissever it,
And batter all the stones about their eares,   30
Whence none can possibly escape alive:
Now as for *Calymath* and his consorts,
Here have I made a dainty Gallery,
The floore whereof, this Cable being cut,
Doth fall asunder; so that it doth sinke
Into a deepe pit past recovery.
Here, hold that knife, and when thou seest he comes,
And with his Bashawes shall be blithely set,
A warning-peece shall be shot off from the Tower,
To give thee knowledge when to cut the cord,   40
And fire the house; say, will not this be brave?
Governor. Oh excellent! here, hold thee, *Barabas*,
I trust thy word, take what I promis'd thee.

Barabas.   No, Governor, I'le satisfie thee first,
Thou shalt not live in doubt of any thing.
Stand close, for here they come: [Governor *stands aloof.*]

Why, is not this
A kingly kinde of trade to purchase Townes
By treachery, and sell 'em by deceit?
Now tell me, worldlings, underneath the sunne,
If greater falshood ever has bin done.   50

Enter Calymath *and* Bashawes.

Calymath.   Come, my Companion-Bashawes, see I pray
How busie *Barrabas* is there above
To entertaine us in his Gallery;
Let us salute him. Save thee, *Barabas.*
Barabas.   Welcome great *Calymath.*
Governor.   How the slave jeeres at him?
Barabas.   Will't please thee, mighty *Selim-Calymath,*
To ascend our homely stayres?
Calymath.   I, *Barabas,* come Bashawes, attend.
Governor.   Stay, *Calymath;*   [*Comes forward.*] 60
For I will shew thee greater curtesie
Then *Barabas* would have affoorded thee.
1. Knight.   Sound a charge there.   [*Within.*]

A charge, the cable cut, a Caldron discovered.
[Barabas *falls into it. Enter* del Bosco *and* Knights.]

Calymath.   How now, what means this?
Barabas.   Helpe, helpe me, Christians, helpe.
Governor.   See *Calymath,* this was devis'd for thee.
Calymath.   Treason, treason! Bashawes, flye.
Governor.   No, *Selim,* doe not flye;
See his end first, and flye then if thou canst.
Barabas.   Oh helpe me, *Selim,* helpe me, Christians.   70
Governour, why stand you all so pittilesse?
Governor.   Should I in pitty of thy plaints or thee,

49 sunne] Dodsley²; summe Q

Accursed *Barabas*, base Jew, relent?
No, thus I'le see thy treachery repaid,
But wish thou hadst behav'd thee otherwise.
Barabas. You will not helpe me then?
Governor.   No, villaine, no.
Barabas. And villaines, know you cannot helpe me now.
Then *Barabas* breath forth thy latest fate,
And in the fury of thy torments, strive
To end thy life with resolution: 80
Know, Governor, 'twas I that slew thy sonne;
I fram'd the challenge that did make them meet:
Know, *Calymath*, I aym'd thy overthrow,
And had I but escap'd this stratagem,
I would have brought confusion on you all,
Damn'd Christians, dogges, and Turkish Infidels;
But now begins the extremity of heat
To pinch me with intolerable pangs:
Dye life, flye soule, tongue curse thy fill and dye.   [*Dyes.*]
Calymath. Tell me, you Christians, what doth this portend?   90
Governor. This traine he laid to have intrap'd thy life;
Now *Selim* note the unhallowed deeds of Jewes:
Thus he determin'd to have handled thee,
But I have rather chose to save thy life.
Calymath. Was this the banquet he prepar'd for us?
Let's hence, lest further mischiefe be pretended.
Governor. Nay, *Selim*, stay, for since we have thee here,
We will not let thee part so suddenly:
Besides, if we should let thee goe, all's one,
For with thy Gallyes couldst thou not get hence,   100
Without fresh men to rigge and furnish them.
Calymath. Tush, Governor, take thou no care for that,
My men are all aboord,
And doe attend my comming there by this.
Governor. Why, hardst thou not the trumpet sound a charge?
Calymath. Yes, what of that?
Governor.   Why, then the house was fir'd,
Blowne up, and all thy souldiers massacred.

Calymath.　　Oh monstrous treason!
Governor.　　　　　　　　　　　　A Jewes curtesie:
　For he that did by treason worke our fall,
　By treason hath delivered thee to us:　　　　　　　　　　110
　Know therefore, till thy father hath made good
　The ruines done to *Malta* and to us,
　Thou canst not part: for *Malta* shall be freed,
　Or *Selim* ne're returne to *Ottoman.*
Calymath.　　Nay rather, Christians, let me goe to *Turkey,*
　In person there to mediate your peace;
　To keepe me here will nought advantage you.
Governor.　　Content thee, *Calymath,* here thou must stay,
　And live in *Malta* prisoner; for come all the world
　To rescue thee, so will we guard us now,　　　　　　　　120
　As sooner shall they drinke the Ocean dry,
　Then conquer *Malta,* or endanger us.
　So march away, and let due praise be given
　Neither to Fate nor Fortune, but to Heaven.

FINIS

116 mediate] Chappell, Dodsley³ (*qy*),　　119 all] Dodsley²; call Q
　　Robinson; meditate Q

TEXTUAL NOTES

Machiavel Prologue

29 *Britanie*] A four-stress line with a feminine ending may seem a little unusual here, as would occur with Q '*Britaine*'. Bullen suggested the emendation '*Britanie*' from its appearance in *Edward II*, II.ii.42. The emendation has not been adopted elsewhere but seems a more than plausible one, mending the metre and readily explaining Q as a compositorial slip.

I.i

110 servant] Why Wagner's emendation of Q 'servants' has not been taken up by editors is hard to explain. That the sea would be servants, in the plural, instead of 'servant' strains the sense, especially since in the midst of all the plurals in these lines the compositor could readily have become confused and have set 'servants'.

I.ii

199 I, I,] This sense of 'Ay, ay,' seems now established in the editorial tradition; its correctness over Q 'I, I$_\wedge$', usually modernized to *Ay, I*, is perhaps somewhat emphasized if for metrical reasons it is given a separate line.

304.1 *three*] The Q stage-direction provided an entrance for three friars and two nuns, an assignment that is certainly wrong for the friars so that it is only the number of nuns that is in question. The speech-prefixes for the nuns are respectively '*1. Nun.*', '*Nun.*', and '*Abbasse.*' Whether a '*1.*' or a '*2.*' is missing before the second is uncertain, the more particularly because it is customary, and properly so, to assign all the speeches to the abbess. It may be thought a more natural error for the numbers to have been transposed so that three nuns, the abbess and two mute attendants, stand for the transfer of the convent to their new quarters. Three is certainly a better number than two for such a circumstance, and two attendants for the abbess are better than one.

386 countermin'd] That this Q reading is not a misreading of correct 'countermur'd' is suggested by the reappearance of the word in V.iii.8. *O.E.D.* quotes from the *Jew of Malta* and gives another example in 1630 of this confusion between the two words. In a sense editors of modernized texts may properly emend to *countermur'd* (with double walls of fortifications), but there is little doubt that 'countermin'd' stood in the printer's copy and should represent what Marlowe wrote.

II.i

37 walke] Robinson's emendation of Q 'walke' to 'wake' was popular with earlier editors but seems unnecessary. *O.E.D.*, vb.10 gives *to walk* as a rare use of *to walk in one's sleep* as in *Macbeth*, V.i.3, and that would seem to be the meaning here. The

context suggests nothing about a golden dream that would awaken Barabas, whereas it is wholly appropriate to beg Morpheus to send a dream that will bring him to the place to receive his jewels without interrupting his slumbers. Indeed, to request 'gentle sleepe' with the help of Morpheus to awaken Barabas is rather anomalous. The real problem is whether a full stop should follow 'walke', so that 'Come and receive the Treasure' is addressed as if to Barabas in the form of a plea, or whether, as suggested by the Q comma, we have a series of three verbs — walk, come, and receive. Although the first possibility is tempting, no real need exists to emend Q's comma after 'walke'.

II.ii

54 thee]　Q 'the' is an acceptable early spelling for *thee* although perhaps uncommon as late as 1633. Ordinarily an old-spelling text would retain 'the', but in this case the possible ambiguity dictates the convenience of an emendation.

II.iii

242 *Lodovico*]　Here and at III.ii.10 Dyce's suggested emendation of Q '*Lodowicke*' by the metrical '*Lodovico*' may well be right, on the analogy of the Italian form in III.iv.8, since otherwise these lines would be tetrameters. It is suspicious that Q uses '*Lodovico*' for the metre once and limps several times with the English form. Dyce also emended III.ii.6 but the metre does not require '*Lodovico*' if one stresses the first 'Now', taking it to be an iamb with its initial unstressed syllable dropped.

293 unfoyl'd]　Q 'unsoyl'd' by applying only to Abigail would break the diamond image which is clearly being continued by 'it is yet'. The reference is directly back to II.iii.55, 'The Diamond that I talke of, ne'r was foild', and to the double entendre that results. If 'soyl'd' were to be correct here in line 293, then 'foild' in II.iii.56 would need to be emended to 'soild', not a good proposition.

III.ii

3 *Lodowicke*.]　The question of who says what in these lines is a vexed one, and the solution is not aided by Q's assignment of both speeches at lines 1 and 3 to Mathias and of line 4 to Lodowick, or by Q's account of the writing and delivery of the challenge(s). The original plan, as detailed in II.iii.370–6, was for Ithimore to deliver to Mathias a challenge that Barabas had written as from Lodowick and to convince him that Lodowick was the author. Then, in lines 381–3 Barabas announces his plan to go in to Lodowick, and to tell him some lie that will set him and Mathias at enmity. Here there is only one challenge written and delivered, that ostensibly from Lodowick to Mathias. At III.i.29–30 Ithimore refers to his delivery of the challenge, still in the singular, although he adds that he has done so 'in such sort, | As meet they will, and fighting dye'. The scene of the duel follows immediately. Mathias's opening words, 'This is the place, now *Abigall* shall see | Whether *Mathias* holds her deare or no' appear to refer to the place for a meeting appointed in the challenge. The stage-direction '*Enter Lodow. reading*' must refer to his reading a response to the challenge. Under these circumstances, the Q assignment

of speeches cannot be right, for the next speech, given in Q to Mathias, 'What, dares the villain write in such base terms?' would naturally refer to Lodowick's reaction to what he is reading. Moreover, since Lodowick has in fact sent no challenge, the response in Q given to him, 'I did it, and revenge it if thou dar'st' makes no sense. The last evidence we have in Ithimore's statement in III.iii.18–19 to Abigail, 'Why the devil invented a challenge, my master writ it, and I carried it, first to *Lodowicke*, and *imprimis* to *Mathias*.' This can scarcely be taken literally, for only an unsigned and unaddressed challenge could serve for both young men and Barabas has given no instructions for this double use. Putting all the evidence together we can arrive quite simply at an explanation of the events that will serve as a guide to emendation. Barabas wrote a challenge in Lodowick's name, which Ithimore delivered to Mathias. Mathias then wrote a response to Lodowick which agreed upon the place and time and apparently indulged in abusive language. This he gave Ithimore to deliver to Lodowick, which Ithimore did. It is this delivery to Lodowick that Ithimore refers to in III.i.29–30 as definitely confirming their meeting. Lodowick, having no knowledge of the original challenge, receives the letter from Mathias as in effect challenging him, and it is this that he is reading as he enters and it is this that calls from him the remark, wrongly assigned to Mathias in Q, 'What, dares the villain write in such base terms?' Since what Lodowick is reading is Mathias's actual letter, of which Mathias knows the contents, it is only natural that in response Mathias (not *Lodowick* as in Q) should acknowledge the authorship and invite Lodowick to the combat. Thus the early Oxberry emendation, followed only by Robinson and through him picked up by Cunningham, turns out to be the right one. The customary treatment, which merely confirms the Q assignment of line 3 to *Mathias* by dropping the redundant speech-prefix, begs the question of Lodowick speaking line 4 when in fact he has written nothing whereas Mathias should be the responder, since it was he who had penned the abusive letter that brought Lodowick to the assigned place.

III.iii

43 Pryor]   According to *O.E.D.* sb.1a, the commander of the priory of the Knights of St John of Jerusalem, or of Malta, was given the title of Grand Prior. In Marlowe's view, therefore, it would seem an appropriate title for the Governor. Emendation is not required.

IV.i

46–7 undone,...inmate]   The Q semicolon after 'undone' seems wrong under any circumstance and the reading 'inmates' difficult to defend as meaning that the friars are now acquainted with his most intimate secrets. Tucker Brooke's suggested 'intimates' has been adopted by all recent editors and is certainly possible. On the other hand, Dyce's simpler 'inmate' is perhaps preferable. From the italics in the Q for '*I must dissemble*' it is clear that these words are an aside; hence, the preceding part of the speech can be addressed only to Ithimore. After the extravagances of III.iv.42–5 it is appropriate enough for Barabas to call him the inmate of his bosom as he exclaims in alarm that they have both been betrayed.

87 *2. Fryar*.] The compositor seems to have confused the speech-prefixes here by assigning this speech to '*1. Fryar*.', a mistake easy enough to make when the copy probably read simply '1.' and '2.' All editors have followed Q, but the context suggests that an error has been made. Q does not have the italics of the present edition to indicate the asides but there would seem to be little difficulty in their identification. The sequence goes thus. Both friars clamor for Barabas's attention and at line 80 he answers the second neutrally but in line 81 secretly gives him a promise. The first friar does not need to hear line 81 to make his argument in line 82. When in line 83 Barabas agrees, he is still answering publicly in a neutral manner, but his following aside must be addressed to the second friar else the first would not persist in the same argument. With lines 85–6 Barabas pretends to make his decision in the first's favor. Barabas's next aside in lines 88–9 must again be addressed to the first friar since the second friar's line 90 could not be in answer to such an invitation. Moreover, the aside in lines 88–9 could not be addressed to the first friar if he had spoken line 87 but only if the second friar had spoken. Yet line 92 shows clearly to whom lines 88–9 were addressed, as well as to whom line 91. If this be so, then the speaker of line 87 can only be the second friar. This assignment gives a symmetrical pattern: after the first alternation in lines 77–8, each friar has two speeches in sequence until the alternation is resumed with line 91. Barabas's aside replies are contrapuntal. To the sequence of the two speeches in order for each friar he responds in the order of two, one, one, two. It is very neat.

IV.iv

21 snicle hand too fast] *O.E.D.* referring to this passage remarks that 'the reading is uncertain and the meaning obscure'. No subsequent scholar has untangled it. *Snickle* is a noose; as a verb it means *to catch with a snickle or noose, to snare*.

69 masty] Although most editors have opted for the easy emendation 'nasty', Marlowe's 'masty' appears to be correct, as approved by Tucker Brooke and the Methuen and Regents editors. In the seventeenth century the use of *masty* for *mastiff* came in to denote hugeness and burliness. But the earlier usage associated the word with *mast* as food for swine, and with its adjective *masted*, or fat like swine from eating mast or coarse food. In this sense it fits the context perfectly and must be retained as a late occurrence of philological interest.

V.i

86 sluice] Q 'against the Truce' has been defended, most succintly, perhaps, by the Regents editor, as referring to the month's time between the demand for tribute and the promise to pay, as at II.ii.26, the phrase then taken to mean, 'either (1) contrary to the treaty or (2) in anticipation of the cessation of hostilities.' A difficulty appears in the meaning of 'against', but *O.E.D.* VI.17 *near the beginning of* might take care of that although with some strain in the idiom. However, the context does not support any speculation that the hollowed rock had something to do with the defences of the city. What Barabas is saying is that at this specific point the rock is very thin since, inside, it had been hollowed out for a sewer channel.

No suggestion is made that in some way this sewer was a special measure taken in the month's respite for the city's defence, and indeed it would be difficult to imagine the circumstances. The inference is that under cover of the bombardment Barabas and his men can break through the thin rock wall, gain entrance to the city, and admit Calymath. It would seem, then, that 'against the Truce' is corrupt, and that 'against' is used in its familiar sense of *near to, right beside*. The error then centers on 'Truce', and here Collier's query, in his Dd[2] (1825) edition, of 'sluice' finds support from *O.E.D.*, which under sb.4 gives *sluice* as a rare word for drawbridge. This drawbridge would presumably be before the portcullis mentioned in III.v.31. It is an irony that the formal defences of drawbridge and portcullis that guarded the entrance should prove useless because of the hidden weakness in the rock below them.

PRESS-VARIANTS IN Q (1633)

[Copies collated: BM¹, BM², BM³, Bodl¹, Bodl², Bodl³, CSmH, DFo¹, DFo², DFo³, MH, MWiW–C.]

SHEET A (*inner forme*)

Corrected: BM¹⁻³, Bodl¹⁻³, CSmH, DFo¹⁻², MWiW–C
Uncorrected: MH, DFo³

Sig. A4
  Prologue at Court, 5 *pardon*] *parpon*

SHEET E (*outer forme*)

Corrected: BM¹⁻³, Bodl¹ ³, CSmH, DFo¹⁻³, MH, MWiW–C
Uncorrected: Bodl²

Sig. E2ᵛ
  II.iii.203 villages] villagss

SHEET H (*outer forme*)

Corrected: BM²⁻³, Bodl¹⁻³, DFo²⁻³, CSmH, MH, MWiW–C
Uncorrected: BM¹, DFo¹

Sig. H1
  IV.ii.18 *Hodie*] *Hidie*

EMENDATIONS OF ACCIDENTALS

Dedication

1 composed by] composedby　　　　　1, 3 Master] Mr.

Prologue at Court

11 Eares;...him,] ~ ,...~ ;

Prologue to the Stage

7 many,] ~ :　　　　　　　　　12 merit$_\wedge$] ~ :

Machiavel Prologue

8–9 words. ...most:] ~ :...~ .　　　17–18 fooleries. ...Crowne: ~ :...
12 off,] ~ ;　　　　　　　　　　　　~ .
　　　　　　　　　　　　　　　　　31 cramb'd,] ~ $_\wedge$

I.i

1 *Barabas.*] *Throughout this scene the*
　speech-prefix is Jew *until at line* 273 *it*
　changes to Barabas
2 Persian] *Persian*
5 Spanish] *Spanish*
8 Arabians] *Arabians*
8 pay$_\wedge$] ~ ,
19 Indian] *Indian*
21 Moore...Easterne] *Moore...*
　Easterne
23–4 -stones,...weight;] ~ ;...~ ,
39–41 Halcions...South] *Halcions...*
　East...East...South
49 *1. Merchant.*] *Throughout this scene*
　the speech-prefix is Merchant
49–53 Q *lines: Barabas...*safe, |
　Riding...Merchants | With...
　arriv'd, | And...selfe, | Will...
　them. (*The relining* from Mal MS)

67 amongst] amougst
70 of] off
71–2 *One line in* Q
73 *Caire*] Caire
75 maine,] ~ . (*point slightly un-*
　certain)
81 Tush,...wise;] ~ ;...~ .
86 *Barabas,*...Rhode,] ~ $_\wedge$...~ .
97, 159, 180, 182 Turke] *Turke*
98–9 *One line in* Q
104 every] enery
140 *1. Jew.*] *Throughout this scene the*
　speech-prefixes are 1., 2., 3.
152–3, 173 *Roman in* Q
163 Adriatick] *Adriatick*
173 looke——] ~ $_\wedge$
178 together] togethre
189 *proximus*] *proximas*

I.ii

2 *Malta*] Malta
2 *Rhodes*,] ~ ₍
10, 17 Governour,] ~ ₍
23 *Callapine*,] ~ ₍
35 day?] ~ .
38 Hebrews] *Hebwres*
42 us——] ~ :
68–70 *Prose in* Q, *but* | Levy'd... |
　Halfe
68–9, 78, 156 Turkes...Jewes] *Turkes
　...Jewes (...Hebrews, line 78*)
71 *I...mine.*] *Roman in* Q
73–4 *Prose in* Q, *but* | A
75 How,] ~ ₍
75 *Hum...doe?*] *Roman in* Q
81 christened] christned
90 *dio*] deo
118–21 Q *lines*: Out...thus | To...
　not | Thy...righteousnesse,
130.1 Q *places s.d. to right of line* 129
149 wealth,] ~ ₍
164 *Primus*] *Primas*
223 day.] ~ ₍

223.1 Q *places s.d. below line* 222
226 What,] Q *cw*; ~ ? Q *text*
230 teares,] ~ .
244 Portagues] *Portagues*
249 house,] ~ ₍
260 What,] ~ ₍
276–7, 289–90, 305–6 *One line in* Q
276–7 so,...thus;] ~ ;...~ ,
300 father,] ~ ₍
308 thirtie] 30
316 thou,] ~ ₍
333 lye.] ~ ,
336, 348–50, 392 *Roman in* Q
348 *Whisper to her.*] Q *places, braced, to
　right of lines 349–50*
359 *Goe*,] ~ ₍
359 *not*] net
361 *I'le*] *Il'e*
367 Nun?] ~ ,
378 fourteene] 14
382 Why,] ~ ₍
383 What,] ~ ₍

II.i

o II. i] *Actus Secundus.*
39 *Bien...es*] *Birn para todos, my ga
　nada no er*
45 Q *places s.d. to right of* Hast thou't
　alone

51 Oh *Abigal*] Oh *Aigal*
62 Ayre,] ~ ; (*point slightly uncertain*)
64 *Hermoso...Dineros*] *Hermoso
　Piarer, de les Denireh*

II.ii

0.1 Knights] *knights*
9 Grecians...Moores] *Grecians,
　Turks,* and *Africk Moores*

21, 25, 28, 33, 42, 46 Turkes] *Turkes*
56.1 *Exeunt*] *Extant*

II.iii

4.1 Q *places s.d. to right of line* 4 *and
　then repeats at* 6.1 *before Barabas's
　speech*
9 as,...villaines,] ~ ₍...~ ₍
10 us₍)] ~ .)
22 and] aud
36–7 Q *lines*: Serpent | Then
42, 51–3, 57, 60, 63, 64, 67 *Roman in* Q

43 *Barabas*] *Barobas*
45 Gentiles] *Gentiles*
53–4 *One line in* Q
64–7 Q *lines*: Your...Lord | We...
　house | And...vengeance.
69–70 *One line in* Q
88 *Aside.*] Q *places to right of line* 89
102 three hundred] 300

107, 109 Moore] *Moore*
109 Turke] *Turke*
111–12 *Prose in* Q, *but* | Breake
99, 110, 161 *1. Officer.] Off.*
116–17 Q *lines:* vanity | If
119–20 Q *lines:* colour | Of
123–5 *Prose in* Q, *but* | And... |
  Will... | That's
129 turne.] ~ ,
132–3 *Roman in* Q
137.1 Mathias,] ~ .
143 *Governor]* Governor
161–2 *One line in* Q
165 *Ithimor]* Ithimer
182 Italian] *Italian*
183 enrich'd] enric'd
187 France...Germanie] *France...
Germanie*

202–3, 218–19 *One line in* Q
228 a——] ~ ∧
234–9 *Roman in* Q
248 Manna...Jewes] *Manna...Jewes*
250.1 Q *places s.d. as line* 251.1
275.1 Lodowicke,] ~ .
276 What,] ~ ∧
281 what,] ~ ∧
285 Why,] ~ ∧
296 yet] yer
301–13 *Roman in* Q
316 bids:——] ~ : ∧
323 her,——] ~ , ∧
325 Hebrewes] *Hebrewes*
358–9 *Prose in* Q, *but* | Enow
359 Malta,] ~ .
375–6 Q *lines:* Feare...he | Shall...
him.

III.i

0 III.i] *Actus Tertius.*
1 *Curtezane.]* omit Q
6 *Padua∧]* ~ ,
17–22 Q *lines:* Faith...Gardens | I...
  -house | Where...I | Clamber'd...
  taking | My...tooke | Onely...

man.
25 Q *lines:* keep'st | Thou'lt
26–8 Q *lines:* O...is | A...hundred |
  Of...Concubine.
28 such] snch

III.ii

7 So,] ~ ∧
9.1 Governor,] ~ .

17 grieve me] grive me
25 Madam] Madem

III.iii

1–3 *Prose in* Q, *but* | Plotted... |
  Flatly
9–10 *Prose in* Q, *but* | Bottle-
15 Why,] ~ ∧
16 *Mathias]* Mathia
16 *Lodowickes]* Lodowick
18–19 *Prose in* Q, *but* | And I... |
  And then... | In
18 master] M^r.

32–3 *Prose in* Q, *but* | With
49 comes] Comes
49.1 Ithimore,] ~ .
49.1 *1. Fryar]* Fryar
50 *1. Fryar.]* Q *throughout this scene has
speech-prefix* Fry.
51 When,] ~ ∧
68 *Jacomo]* Jacome

III.iv

2 what,] ~ ∧
12 done.] *Point doubtful; may be italic colon*
14 neere,...neere,] ~ ∧...~ ∧
24 Why,] ~ ∧
39–41 *Prose in* Q, *but* | Throw... | Thing
45 halfe] helfe
56–7 Q *lines*: Well...brought | The ...too?
65–6 *Prose in* Q, *but* | Porredge... |

And batten
69 Italian] *Italian*
76 *Jaques*] *Jagues*
86 master.] M^r.
89 master,] M^r.
99 poysoned] poyson'd
100 *Lerna's*] Lerna's
101 Hebon] *Hebon*
106–7 Q *lines*: of | Rice
106 given't] give'nt
111–12 Q *lines*: of | Flanders

III.v

0.1 Governor, Bosco, Knights,] ~ . ~ . ~ .
1, 11 Bashaw] *Bashaw*

3 *Basso.*] Q *throughout this scene has speech-prefix* Bashaw.
26–7 *One line in* Q

III.vi

37 close.] ~ ,
38 heart:] ~ ,

38 Fryar,] ~ ∧
49 What,] ~ ∧

IV.i

0 IV.i] *Actus Quartus.*
0.1 Barabas,] ~ .
8 master,] M^r.
8 known?] ~ ∧|
12–14 *Prose in* Q, *but* | By
18–20 *Prose in* Q, *but* | Borne
18 long.] ~ ∧
19 Christian?] ~ .
19 Hebrew] *Hebrew*
20 *Cazzo, diabolo*] *Catho diobola*
21 master,] Mr.
28 2. *Fryar.*] Q *starting here has for the rest of the scene speech-prefixes* 1. *and* 2. *except lines* 109, 113, 144, 148 *where speech-prefix is* Fry. *and* 160 *et seq. where speech-prefix is* Ioco.
35 daughter∧——] ~ ,——
62 *Jerusalem.*] ~ ,
65 Bullion] *Bulloine*
81, 83, 85–6, 88–9, 91, 100 *Roman in* Q
93 goe,] ~ ∧

95 Not?] ~ ,
101.1 *Exit.*] Q *places as line* 102.1
111 Turke] *Turke*
114 So,] ~ ∧
115 house.] ~ ,
116 *Jacomo*] *Jocoma*
130 is:] *point uncertain; may be a turned full stop*
141–2 *One line in* Q
143 Fryar,] ~ ∧
144 What,] ~ ∧
146 hang'd.] ~ ∧|
153–5 *Prose in* Q, *but* | Upon
159.1 Q *places s.d. as line* 158.1
159.1, 174 Jacomo] *Jocoma*
160 1. *Fryar.*] Q *starting here has for the rest of the scene the speech-prefix* Ioco. (*i.e.,* Iacomo)
160–3 Q *lines*: Oh...convert | An... treasury.

345

168–9 *One line in Q*
168 *Bernadine*——] ~ ;
174, 175 Why,] ~ ∧
176–7 *One line in Q*

176 it?] ~ ∧
178, 193 master,] Mr.
180–1 *Prose in Q, but* | You
193–4 *Prose in Q, but* | Holy

IV.ii

0.1 Curtezane] *Curtezant*
6–7 *Prose in Q, but* | *The letter*
9–10 *Prose in Q, but* | A tall
12–14 *Prose in Q, but* | Non-plus
16–20 *Prose in Q, but* | Gallowes...|
  Of the... | He
16 fortie] 40
21–6 *Prose in Q, but* | This... |
  About... | Hempen.. | Hee had
  ... | He will
27–36 Q *lines*: And...fellow | Met...
  and | A Dagger...he | Gave...
  Bellamira, | Saluting...make |
  Cleane...that | I...is; | It...in |
  My...me | Ever...such | Love?
  ...now | Would...her.
32 house.] ~ ,
32 is.] ~ ;
38–9 *Prose in Q, but* | Poore
41–2 *Prose in Q, but* | Youth
43–4 *Prose in Q, but* | Selfe
49–50 Q *lines*: to | Make
55 *Bellamira*] *Allamira*

57–9 Q *lines*: If...it; | But...doe |
  Their...earth.
62–3 *Roman in Q*
64–5 *Prose in Q, but* | Reveal'd
71 Master] Mr.
75–6 *Prose in Q, but* | Shall
75 three hundred] 300
78 all:——] ~ , ∧
81 him,] ~ ∧
92 over-] ore-
99 Whither] Whiiher
104–6 *Prose in Q, but* | Aside... | Told
105 aside.] ~ ,
106 it;] ~ ,
114–15 *Prose in Q, but* | Me
114 groat. Give] ~ , give
116, 117 five hundred] 500
117–18 *Prose in Q, but* | And
118 one hundred] 100
126 *him*∧] ~ .——
127–8 Q *lines*: That...lips. | What...
  me? | It...Starre.
131 Q *lines*: afore | We

IV.iii

1, 20, 62 three hundred] 300
2 Curtezane] *Curtezane*
5 him,...*Gorge*∧] ~ ∧...~ ,
5 that.] ~ ∧
12–13 Catzerie∧...crosbiting,] ~ ,
  ...~ ∧
19 Why,] ~ ∧
22, 62 five hundred] 500
24–5 *Prose in Q, but* | There's
26–7 *Prose in Q, but* | Come

27 it:] ~ ,
29–30 *Prose in Q, but* | With
29–30, 51 *Roman in Q*
34–5 *Prose in Q, but* | You
37 -house:] ~ ,
39 betraid.——] ~ . ∧
43 vaine!] ~ ?
52–3 ∧*As*] ——*As*
65–6 *One line in Q*

IV.iv

0.1 Curtezane, Ithimore,] ~ . ~ .
12 Ha,] ~ ∧
14 Doe?...know.] ~ ∧...~ ,
17 son;] ~ ,

20–1 *Prose in Q, but* | And I
21 I,] ~ ∧
22 alone?] ~ .
23–4 *Prose in Q, but* | Be

29 *incony*] *incoomy*
32–3 *Prose in Q, but* | Pox
35–6 Q *lines*: Prethe...me | The...
there.
45 so,] ∼ ∧
52–3 *Prose in Q, but* | My
52 *you*] *yon*
57 man?] ∼ .
61–2 Q *lines*: 'Tis . . . . . . upon | Pickled

...Mushrumbs.
63 Q *lines*: What...this? | The...
doe.
66–7 Q *lines*: The...Elder | When...
himselfe.
69 is.] ∼ ;
75–7 *Prose in Q, but* | Token... |
Slept
77 clothes.] ∼ ,

V.i

0 V.i] *Actus Quintus.*
0.1 Governor, Knights,] ∼ . ∼ .
6, 25 *1. Knight.*] *Kni.*
12–14 Q *lines*: Who...Gentlemen, |
Poyson'd...Nuns, | Strangled...
what | Mischiefe beside.
15 this——] ∼ .
16–17 *Prose in Q, but* | Lodging
18 straight.] ∼ ,
19 dogs,] ∼ ∧
22 sure.] ∼ ,
25 *1. Knight.*] *Kni.*

28–30 Q *lines*: Gilty...*Mathias* |
Were...*Abigall*; | Forg'd... chal-
lenge.
29 *Abigall*;] ∼ ,
36 what?] ∼ ,
42 soules:——] ∼ : ∧
49.1, 50, 53 *1. Officer.*] Officer
56 'em;] *point uncertain*
77 escap'd] scap'd
86 here,] ∼ ∧
91 five hundred] 500

V.ii

0.1 *Alarmes*] Alarmes
6 say?] ∼ ,
10 thee] the
12 day,] ∼ ∧
46 it.] ∼ ∧

50 Governor——] ∼ ∧
50 within.——] ∼ ,
57 This, *Barabas*;] ∼ ; ∼ ,
106 toward∧] ∼ ,

V.iii

9 *Calabria*,] ∼ ∧
10 reign'd,] ∼ ;
12.1 Messenger] *messenger*
16 Ottoman] *Ottamon*

20 Citadell?] ∼ ,
24 *Barabas,*] ∼ .
39, 43 Bashawes] *Bashawes*

V.iv

10 *1. Knight.*] *Kni.*

V.v

11 -*Calymath,*] ∼ ∧
19 summe?] ∼ .
25 First,...Army,] ∼ ∧...∼ ∧
46 Why] why
54 him.] ∼ ,
63 *1. Knight.*] *Kni.*
63.1 a] | *A*
64 this?] ∼ ∧

67 treason !] ∼ ∧
73 *Barabas*,...Jew, relent?] ∼ ;...
∼ ∧ ∼ :
106 Why,] ∼ ∧
114 Ottoman] *Ottamen*
115 *Turkey*] Turkey
124 Fortune] Fottune

[NOTE: The following editions are herein collated: Q (1633), Dd² (Dodsley's *Select Old Plays*, 2nd ed., ed. Reed, 1780, vol. VIII), S (*Ancient British Drama*, ed. Sir Walter Scott[?], 1810, vol. I), Ox (ed. Oxberry, 1818), Dd³ (Dodsley's *Select Collection of Old Plays*, 3rd ed., ed. Collier, 1825, vol. VIII), R (*Works*, ed. Robinson, 1826, vol. I), D¹ (*Works*, ed. Dyce, 1850, vol. I), D² (*Works*, ed. Dyce, rev. 1858), C (*Works*, ed. Cunningham, 1870), B (*Works*, ed. Bullen, 1885, vol. II), TB (*Works*, ed. Tucker Brooke, 1910), M (Methuen, ed. Bennett, 1931), K (*Plays*, ed. Kirschbaum, 1962), Ri (*Plays*, ed. Ribner, 1963), Rg (Regents, ed. Van Fossen, 1964). Reference is made to Mal (MS notes by Malone in the Bodleian copy), Br (MS notes by Broughton in the BM copy of Robinson), and Coll (Collier's MS notes in the BM copy of Dyce¹).]

Dedication

1–19 *omit* Ox
2 unimitable] inimitable Dd², S, Ri

3 later] latter Dd², S, Dd³

Prologue at Court

11 him, then₍ₐ₎] ~ ᴧ ~ , Dd², S, Ox, R ±

Prologue to the Stage

6 *Tamberlaine*] Tamerlane Dd², S, Ox

Machiavel Prologue

1 thinke] thinks R, C, B, K
11 will they] they will R, C, B, K
19 Empery] Empire Q, R, C, K, Rg
21 *Dracos*] *Drancus* Q

24 had] had but S, Ox, D (*qy*), C, B, M
29 here] to you here D² (*qy*)
29 *Britanie*] *Britaine* Q, Dd² + (−B)

I.i

4 Samnites] Saminites Q, Dd², S, Ox, TB; Sabans B; Saenites K; Scenites Rg (*after* Seaton)
5 bought] brought M
6 silverlings] silverbings Q, Dd², S, Ox, Dd³ (*all qy* silverings *or* silverlings)
15 And] And he who B

16 Wearying] Wearing S, Ox
23 pearle] pearls B, K
30 quantity] quality Br MS
31 of] or Coll MS
40 stands] stand Dd²–C
73 *Caire*] Cairo Dd², S, Ox
80 crazed] crazy Dd², S, Ox, Dd³
82 But] By Q; Bye Dd², S, Ox, Dd³

101 fraught] freight Dd², S, Ox, Dd³, R
107 man] men Ox
110 Sea] seas D, C, B, M, K
110 servant] servants Q, Dd²+
122 scambled] scrambled R, C

173 *unto my selfe*] unto't Dd³ (*qy*)
176 Doe so] *omit* D² (*qy*), D³, C, B
182 Turkes have] Turk has R, D, C
183 of] in C
186 for one] of one Dd², S, Ox

I.ii

0.1, 10, 17, 27, 32 *Governor*] Gover-
　nors Q, Dd², S, Ox, Dd³, R
　(*except* 0.1), C (*except* 0.1, 10), K
　(0.1 *only*), Rg (0.1 *only*)
2 came] come C
17 how] say how B
22 *Basso.*] *Calymath.* C
23 *Calymath.*] *Basso.* C
46 this] these Dd², S, Ox, Dd³
57 *1. Jew.*] *Barabas.* Dd²–C (−D)
65 are] have C
90 halfe] the half B
98 a] the B
128 Governor] Governors Q, Dd²–R,
　K
128 list] listen C, B
136 *Governor.*] *omit* Q, Dd², S, Ox, Dd³
148 causers] causes C
164 great] *omit* Dd², S, Ox, Dd³
185 those] these S, Ox
199 I, I,] Ay, I Dd²–TB
200–1 that Were] *omit* B (*qy*)

228 Not] Nor D², B (*qy*)
235 reduce] redress D² (*qy*)
290 mean'st] meant'st C
293 unseene] unforeseen C
294 say] say that B
304.1 *two*] *three* Q, Dd²–R, TB, K, Rg
304.1 *three*] *two* Q, Dd²+
307 *Abbasse.*] *1 Nun.* Q, Dd²–R, C, TB
311 waters] cloisters B (*qy*); quarters TB
313 *Abbasse.*] *Nun.* Dd²·³, R, C, TB;
　1. Nun. S, Ox
314 Virgins,] ~ , Ox; Virgin's Dd³, Ri;
　Virgins' D+ (−Ri)
319 Sometimes] Sometime Ox, R, C
348 give] forgive D, M
350 *marked thus*] thus marked Ox
359 *Goe, forget not*] forget it not D²
　(*qy*); forget not, go B
365 Out...wretch.] *omit* R, C
381 Nun] to a nun D, B, M; a nun C
386 countermin'd] countermur'd Coll
　MS, B, M, Ri, Rg

II.i

7 incertaine] uncertain S, Ox, R, C,
　B, Ri
25 wealth] youth B (*qy*)

25 winters] winter's S+ (−Dd³); win-
　ters' Dd³
37 walke] wake R, D, C, B

II.ii

9 fraught] freight Dd², S, Ox, Dd³, D
11 Turkish] *Spanish* Q, Dd², Dd³ (*but
　qy* Turkish), R

14 luft, and tackt] left, and tooke Q,
　Dd²–R
38 you] them S, Ox, K

II.iii

6 give] given C, B
9 as, poore villaines,] poor villains as
　Dd², S, Ox, Dd³; poor villains such
　as D, C

46 into] unto D¹
57 *it*] he C, B
71 ruth] truth R, C, B
91 the] that Dd², S, Ox, Dd³

349

97 whats...of] What price is on C
98 Turkes] *Turke* Q, Rg
113, 115, 118, 122 *Slave*,] *Ith.* Q
123 and] and't *or* an't Dd², S, Ox, Dd³,
    D, B, M
127 was] wast Dd²–B (−D¹), K
138 makes] make D²
155 but] *omit* Q, Dd²–R, D (*but qy*
    but), C, K
159 booke] books Dd², S, Ox, Dd³
168 thee] *omit* Q
184 ure] use R, C

190 was I] I was Ox
206 I] *omit* Dd³, Coll MS, C
229 *to love*] love to D (*qy*), B
242 *Lodovico*] *Lodowicke* Q, Dd²–R,
    TB+; Lodowick he C, B
253 it] this R, C, B
280–1 I...mad?] *omit* Dd², S, Ox, Dd³
293 unfoyl'd] unsoyl'd Q, Dd²+ (*but*
    Dd², D *qy* unfoil'd)
309 *It's*] It is Dd², S, Ox, Dd³
320 thou] thee Q, Dd², TB, Rg
381 in to] unto D¹, C

III.ii

3 *Lodowicke.*] *Math.* Q, Dd², S, Dd³,
    B, TB; *omit* D, B, M, K, Ri, Rg
3 write] to write R
4 *Mathias.*] *Lod.* Q, Dd², S, Dd³, D,
    B, TB, M, K, Ri, Rg
4 I did...dar'st.] R *places in quotes*
    before line 3 *with speech-prefix*
    Lodowick, *making it Lodowick's*

    first line
6 *Lodowicke*] Lodovico D
6 now] and now C
10 *Lodovico*] *Lodowicke* Q, Dd²+
    (−D)
33 th'] *omit* Q, Dd²+
34 reveal] *omit* Q, Dd²–R; disclose
    Dd³ (*qy*)

III.iii

20 and] *omit* Q, Dd², S, Ox, Dd³
28 *Jaques*] *Jaynes* Q, Dd²
30 to] *omit* Dd², S, Ox, Dd³, Ri; *but*
    R, C, B
34 ye] you Dd², S, Ox, Dd³, D¹
37 pursuit] purpose Coll MS
40 lov'dst] lovest S, Ox

40 sire] sinne Q, Dd²–R
43 Pryor] Governor C, M; Sire TB, K,
    Ri
48 nor] or R, C, B
65 Sonne] son Dd²–D¹, K, Ri, Rg;
    sun D², C, B, M

III.iv

6 pretendeth] portendeth Dd², S, Ox,
    Dd³
8 *Lodovicoes*] Lodowick's Dd², S, Ox,
    Dd³, C
15 selfe] life Q, Dd²–D¹
37 less] least Q, Dd², S, Ox, Dd³ (*qy*
    less), R

39 rocke] huge rock C
65 porredge?] ∼ ∧ Q; ∼ , *or* ∼ ∧ Dd²,
    Dd³, R, D, C
78 Among] Amongst M
81 hath] had Ox
84 pot] plot Q
109 so] as M, Ri

III.v

1 Bashaw] *Bashaws* Q, K
2 drives you thus] thus drives you C, B

29 you] ye B

III.vi

0.1 Fryars] Fryars *and* Abigall Q

IV.i

1 to] like R
21 come] comes M
25 therefore] and therefore Ox
47 inmate] inmates Q, Dd²–R; inti-
    mates TB, K, Ri, Rg
49 Lye] Lies R
58 pennance] any penance C
58 serve] serve to atone D
68 unsold] untold D
87 *2. Fryar.*] *1 Friar.* Q, Dd² +
89 *Rid*] Bid Dd², S, Ox, Dd³
95 rogue] goe Q, Dd²–R, D (*but qy*
    rogue), C, B, K, Ri

100 *You*] *Ith. you* Q, Dd²–R
101 *1. Fryar.*] *omit* Q, Dd²–R
128 done.] done. *Exit.* | IV.ii *Enter*
    Barabas. R, C, M
139 we] me Q
148 have] save Q, Dd², S, Dd³ (*qy* have)
152 is it] it is R, C
154 of] for Ox
166 a] on Ox
167 And] To Ox
174 hast] has M
185 his] its Ox, R, C, B, K
197 commit] commit it R

IV.ii

6 and] but B
16 mine] my Ox
16 foot] feet B
28 muschatoes] mustachios Dd²–R, C
30 had] *omit* Dd², S, Ox, Dd³
38 poore] *omit* Dd², S, Ox, Dd³
51 see] and see C, B, K
53 ye] you D
63 *you*] *omit* S, Ox
64 But you know] But you know sir D

(*qy*); But, sir, you know C, B
68 Pen and Inke] *Omit text and made*
    s.d. C, B
72 threatning] threaten Dd², S, Ox, Dd³
83 running] cunning D², C
92 over-spread] ore-spread Q, TB, K,
    Rg
105 beard] sterd Q
118 one hundred] a hundred M, Ri
125 Thus] See thus C

IV.iii

5 *de*] *le* R
13 Rogue] sort of rogue C
51 *should*] e'er should D (*qy*)
59 to] *omit* Q, Dd², S, Ox, Dd³

61 demand] *omit* Q, Dd²–R, C, B, TB,
    K, Ri, Rg; and force from me D¹;
    force from me D²; convey M

IV.iv

5 *Curtezane.*] *Pil.* Q, Dd²–R
12 you] he D², C, B, M
21 snicle...fast] snickle hand to fist
    Dd², ³ (*qy*); snicle hard and fast C
    (*qy*)
23 be] | But Ox
30 heare] have R

52 run] ran S, Ox
64 cleane] a cleane Ox
69 masty] nasty Dd²–C, K, Ri; musty
    B
71 me] we Q
71 letter more] more letter Ox

V.i

10 thee] the S ,Ox
18 him] 'em D (qy)
25 *1. Knight.*] *Kni.* Q; *Knights.* Dd²–R,
   C, B
27 you] thou S, Ox
29 he] *omit* Q
41 I'le] I Q, Dd²+ (–D)
45 'twas] it was Dd², S, Ox, Dd³

47 made] and made Ox
65 the] their Ox
69 there] here B, K
75 have] *omit* Dd³
86 sluice] Truce Q, Dd², S, Ox, R, Dd³
   (qy sluice), R, Rg; trench D (qy
   sluice)
96 be] is Ox

V.ii

5 To] To've C, M, K, Rg; T'have B;
  To have TN
5 keep] kept Q, Dd²+

12 hands] hand B
67 within] 'tis in C, B

V.iii

3 Basiliske] basiliskes D, C, B, M
8 countermin'd] countermur'd M
  (*after* Deighton), K, Ri, Rg
10–11 Where...Towne.] *lines trans-*

posed Q, Dd², S, Ox, Dd³
10 Where] When Q, Dd², S, Ox, Dd³
27 in] his D², B, M

V.v

24 partake] take C, B
33 a] *omit* R
39 off] *omit* D (qy)
49 sunne] summe Q
59 attend] ascend D, C, K
63 *1. Knight.*] *Kni.* Q; *Knight.* R, C, B,

M, K, Ri; *Knights.* Dd², S, Ox, Dd³
78 fate] hate C, B
86 Christians,] Christian‸ D, C
116 mediate] meditate Q, Dd², S, Ox,
   Dd³ (qy mediate), TB, K, Ri, Rg
119 all] call Q, K

THE MASSACRE AT PARIS

TEXTUAL INTRODUCTION

The Massacre at Paris (Greg, *Bibliography*, no. 133), acted by the Admiral's Men, exists in a single early edition, an undated octavo printed for Edward White by Edward Allde. The collation is 8^0, A–D^8, 32 leaves unnumbered, A 1, D 7, 8 blank. The text begins on A 3 and ends on D 6^v. No entry was made in the Stationers' Register.

The date of printing cannot be fixed with certainty. In his *Bibliography* Greg conjectured late 1594, and H. J. Oliver in the Revels edition suggests 1602. Typographical evidence discovered by Robert F. Welsh and analyzed in his dissertation (University Microfilms, 1964), pp. 33ff., establishes that the octavo could not have been printed after 1603 since Allde's intact ornament above the head-title on sig. A 3 was damaged in 1602 or 1603 (only books from 1603 show this heavy damage on the lower right side). The titlepage device seems to appear in Allde's books first in 1591, and at this date has the three breaks found in the octavo. The ornament on sig. A 3 seems to appear first in 1592 but no deterioration can be observed before the 1603 damage. The ornamental P on sig. A 3 was observed only in a book of 1604, at which time it had the breaks present in *The Massacre*.

Dr Welsh continues his examination by the analysis of eleven of the twelve plays printed by Allde between 1589 (the date of the murder of Henry III) and 1603, in respect to a curious typesetting characteristic. In four of these plays – *The Massacre*, the undated *Spanish Tragedy* (entered 1592), and the two 1594 plays *The Battle of Alcaʒar* and *The Wars of Cyrus* – a double-'f' ligature is used invariably when the following letter is 'e', 'a', 'u', and 'w' but an unligatured 'fs' when the following letter is 'i', a characteristic not found in the remaining seven Allde plays examined.[1] Dr Welsh conjectures that this is a compositorial characteristic and thus

---

[1] The distinction is invariable in *The Massacre* and *The Spanish Tragedy*. In *The Wars of Cyrus* the ligature is used in three of the twenty-one occurrences before 'i'; in *The Battle of Alcaʒar* the 'fs' before 'i' is invariable, but this 'fs' without ligature is used in two of the numerous occurrences before other letters.

proceeds to a spelling analysis in search of confirmation. The first conclusion is that only one compositor set *The Massacre*, this on the evidence of an even distribution of relatively strong predilections for certain spellings: *doe*(28)–*do*(2), *goe*(22)–*go*(1); *then*(7)–*than*(0), *heer*(*e*)(23)–*here*(0), *fre*(*e*)*nd*(14)–*friend*(0), -*es*(32)–-*esse*(3), *Ile*(16)–*ile*(1), *bloud*(16)–*blood*(1).[1] The second conclusion is that the undated *Spanish Tragedy* from Allde's press not only has the same treatment of 'ſs' before 'i' but also has substantially the same spelling characteristics: *doe*(19)–*do*(8)–*doo*(8), *goe*(38)–*go*(5), *then*(30)–*than*(1), *heer*(*e*)(81)–*here*(0), *freend*(34)–*friend*(4), -*es*(76)–-*esse*(9), *Ile*(10)–*ile*(23), *bloud*(14)–*blood*(14). Here only the proportion of *ile* and of *blood* is out of line with the characteristics of *The Massacre* spellings, and it is a reasonable hypothesis that the two compositors were the same.

A serious anomaly appears in the spelling characteristics of the two 1594 plays, *The Battle of Alcaȥar* and *The Wars of Cyrus*, which are almost consistently opposite to the spelling habits of the compositor of *The Massacre* and *The Spanish Tragedy*.[2] On the other hand, substantially the same treatment of ligatured and un-ligatured 'ſs' is found in these 1594 plays. The present editor cannot share Dr Welsh's confidence (pp. 44–8) that the spelling habits of the compositors of these four plays are sufficiently close to justify the hypothesis that all four prints are the products of the same work-man, with the variations attributable only to a difference in date. If it were not for the matter of the ligaturing practice, the compositor of *The Massacre* and of *The Spanish Tragedy* would never, on the

[1] In view of this evidence, and of the odd treatment of 'ſs', the statement by H. J. Oliver that his own analysis of recurrent spellings and identifiable types (Revels, p. lx and n. 1) leads him to conjecture that two compositors were employed must be viewed with some concern and one wishes that the evidence had been offered. Dr Welsh's study of identifiable types (pp. 53–8) appears to demonstrate setting by formes from cast-off copy, and would not seem to permit typesetting by two compositors. Irregular spacing in some pages of the octavo, like C3ᵛ–C4, supports the conclusion that setting was by formes and that copy had sometimes to be adjusted in the inner forme to pages of the outer forme already composed.

[2] The same spellings in *The Battle of Alcaȥar* are as follows: *doe*(2)–*do*(9)–*doo*(6), *goe*(3)–*go*(7), *then*(1)–*than*(7), *heer*(*e*)(8)–*here*(18), *freend*(0)–*friend*(7)–*freind*(2), -*es*(19)–-*esse*(44), *Ile*(0)–*ile*(0), *bloud*(29)–*blood*(0). For *The Wars of Cyrus* the spellings are: *doe*(10)–*do*(8), *goe*(2)–*go*(6), *then*(28)–*than*(7), *heer*(*e*)(0)–*here*(8), *freend*(0)–*friend*(14), -*es*(2)–-*esse*(44), *Ile*(11)–*ile*(0), *blood*(1)–*bloud*(13).

spelling evidence, be identified as the same workman. Under these circumstances it may be that the evidence of spelling characteristics is more trustworthy than that of ligaturing, odd as the latter may be as the practice of two distinct compositors.[1]

However, regardless of the question whether one or two compositors set this group of four plays, the setting of *The Massacre* is closer to that of the undated *Spanish Tragedy* than to the 1594 pair. It was the opinion of Sir Walter Greg that the undated Allde–White *Spanish Tragedy* was probably printed in the latter half of 1592.[2] Such a date for *The Massacre* would be satisfactory if it were not for the record by Henslowe in late January, 1593, 'Rd at the tragedy of the gvyes 30...iij li xiiij s', with the notation that the play was 'ne'. This marking does not always signify the initial performance of an original play, but the large sum was the highest taken in during that season and hence it is customarily believed that 26 January 1593 (Greg's date for Henslowe's 30th) marked the first date of production. If this is so, then time must be allowed for the memorial transmission of the text (perhaps during the closing of the theatres that followed very shortly because of the plague). Mid to late 1593 or early 1594, then, would seem to be the earliest probable date for publication, not 1592 as Dr Welsh conjectures. On the other hand, the evidence offered by Professor Oliver for the late date of 1602 is not compelling.

Errors in the running-titles, including one on sig. A8^v that was corrected by stop-press, indicate with some certainty that the outer forme of sheet A was first through the press, and thereafter the analysis of the positioning of the running-titles offered by Dr Welsh joins with his evidence from identified types to establish setting by formes in regular sequence at least up to sheet D. The difficulties of setting from cast-off copy may account for some of the mislineation although such a physical explanation is scarcely needed

---

[1] Speculation is idle, of course, but one may remark that an apprentice might in some respects come to take on the characteristics of his master. In the Shakespeare First Folio, for example, within a relatively short period of time Compositor *E* altered various of his spelling habits to agree with those of Compositor *B*. See Bowers, *Bibliography and Textual Criticism* (1964), pp. 180–201.

[2] W. W. Greg and D. Nichol Smith (eds.), *The Spanish Tragedy* (1592) (Malone Society Reprints, 1948 for 1949), p. ix.

in a reported text. As suggested, the evidence would appear to indicate that only one compositor was concerned with the text. Because the play was so brief, the typesetter adopted various means to waste space, including the occasional use of a short measure that forced normal lines to be run over.

Ever since the group of Elizabethan 'bad quartos' was isolated and analyzed, *The Massacre at Paris* has been recognized as a memorially reported text which has no direct transmissional connection with a Marlowe manuscript. All the stigmata of reported 'bad quartos' are present in this play and are well described by Professor Oliver (Revels, p. liiff.). Something of what the manuscript itself must have been like may be seen in a manuscript leaf preserved in the Folger Shakespeare Library which starts Scene xvii (lines 806–20) but breaks off after the inscription of only half of the verso with the exit of the Guise, presumably concluding the scene. Early doubts about the authenticity of the manuscript of this brief scene are no longer raised[1] and the fragment is generally accepted now not only as genuine but also as most probably the single preserved example of Marlowe's own hand. This text is printed as a footnote to lines 806–20, where the reporting seems to be of a better quality than the general run of the play.

The editing of a memorial reconstruction made by one or more actors, as in a 'bad quarto', presents a number of problems. Early editors, puzzled by the irregular and often faulty metre, attempted to rewrite the play in part by adding or subtracting words to make superior sense as well as metrical regularity of a sort. Our present understanding of the nature of 'bad quartos' suggests, instead, that the major source of corruption is not the printing process but the memorial reconstruction. With the exception of the Folger manuscript leaf, it is impossible to recover the exact readings of the author's manuscript from the memorially corrupt version that was set down in the actors' manuscript delivered to the printer. Occasionally an editor may make shift to print as the prose it must originally have been some arbitrarily verse-lined text that may as readily be

---

[1] The standard discussion of this manuscript is found in J. Q. Adams, '*The Massacre at Paris* Leaf', *The Library*, 4th ser., xiv (1934), 447–69. J. M. Nosworthy, 'The Marlowe Manuscript', *The Library*, 4th ser., xxvi (1946), 158–71, may also be consulted.

the responsibility of the compositor as of the scribe(s) responsible for the printer's copy. Occasionally obvious mislining may be corrected in its own terms. But the general principle remains that ordinarily no expedient can recover with any certainty the lost Marlowe text from the imperfect version found in the manuscript from which the compositor worked, and thus the editor's task is chiefly to present this version in its most accurate form with only such alterations as are customary in a critical edition. The most that can be expected, therefore, is that an editor attempt to emend errors which there may be some reason to assign to the compositor and thus to recover as closely as may be the equal impurity of the underlying printer's copy. It must be admitted that scrupulous adherence to this principle is here a few times relaxed in special circumstances when the exact source of the reporter's error can be established, as in the substitution of *Sene* (i.e., Seine) for *Rene* (361, 418), of the name *Cossin* for the familial *Cosin* (i.e., cousin) (266, 293), of *Sorbonests* for *thorbonest* (411) and a few other examples of what are obviously actors' mishearings. Such errors as *hate* for *ha't* (351) and *as* for *are* are perhaps compositorial. The principle is stretched at 393 where *axioms* emends *actions* but possibly this can come under the heading of the restoration of a technical term misheard or misremembered by the actor; the probable error of *make* for *take* at 783, on the other hand, would have been preserved if *O.E.D.* had not specifically excluded it. The principle has been breached perhaps only once, in 1201 and 1202, when what are undoubted printer's copy readings are emended because of the practical certainty that Marlowe's manuscript readings of *inforse* and *lowly* can be recovered from a passage in *Edward II* that is being paraphrased. The *England's Parnassus* version in 1600 (p. 48) of lines 95–6 does not appear to offer a similar opportunity.

The following copies of the undated octavo edition have been collated: British Museum (C.34.a.3), Bodleian Library (containing Malone's textual annotations), Dyce Collection in the Victoria and Albert Museum, Pepys Collection in Magdalen College Cambridge, the Chapin Collection of Williams College, the Folger Shakespeare Library, and the Henry E. Huntington Library. Textual variants were found only in sheet D, outer forme, but the collation established the precise punctuation, except in a few doubtful cases, from a worn fount that often inked ambiguously in individual copies. To provide a conspectus of the history of the text, the following editions have been collated against the octavo and their substantive variants recorded: J. Chappell (1818), William Oxberry (1818), G. Robinson (1826) including the Broughton textual notes in the British Museum copy, Alexander Dyce (1850), Alexander Dyce (rev. 1858), F. Cunningham (1870), A. H. Bullen (1884–5), Tucker Brooke (1910), the Methuen edition edited by H. S. Bennett (1931), *Plays* edited by Irving Ribner (1963), and the Revels edition edited by H. J. Oliver (1968). In addition, the couplet printed in *England's Parnassus* was collated, the J. Broughton notes in the British Museum copy of Robinson's *Works*, and the J. P. Collier notes in the British Museum copy of the 1850 Dyce have been recorded.

[DRAMATIS PERSONÆ

CHARLES THE NINTH, King of France

DUKE OF ANJOU, his brother, afterwards KING HENRY THE THIRD

KING OF NAVARRE

PRINCE OF CONDÉ, his brother

DUKE OF GUISE
CARDINAL OF LORRAINE } brothers
DUKE DUMAINE

SON TO THE DUKE OF GUISE, a boy

THE LORD HIGH ADMIRAL

DUKE OF JOYEUX

EPERNOUN

PLESHÈ

BARTUS

TWO LORDS OF POLAND

GONZAGO

RETES

MOUNTSORRELL

COSSINS, Captain of the King's Guard

MUGEROUN

THE CUTPURSE

LOREINE, a preacher

SEROUNE

RAMUS

TALEUS

FRIAR

SURGEON

ENGLISH AGENT

APOTHECARY

Captain of the Guard, Protestants, Schoolmasters, Soldiers, Murderers, Attendants, &c.

CATHERINE, the Queen-Mother of France

MARGARET, her daughter, wife to the KING OF NAVARRE

THE OLD QUEEN OF NAVARRE

DUCHESS OF GUISE

WIFE TO SEROUNE

Maid to the Duchess of Guise]

The Massacre at Paris.

With the Death of the Duke of *Guise*.

Enter Charles *the French King,* [Catherine] *the* Queene Mother,
the King of Navarre, *the Prince of* Condye, *the Lord high* Admirall,
and [Margaret] *the Queene of* Navarre, *with others.*

Charles.   Prince of *Navarre* my honourable brother,
Prince *Condy,* and my good Lord Admirall,
I wishe this union and religious league,
Knit in these hands, thus joyn'd in nuptiall rites,
May not desolve, till death desolve our lives,
And that the native sparkes of princely love,
That kindled first this motion in our hearts,
May still be feweld in our progenye.
Navarre.   The many favours which your grace hath showne,
From time to time, but specially in this,   10
Shall binde me ever to your highnes will,
In what Queen Mother or your grace commands.
Queene Mother.   Thanks sonne *Navarre,* you see we love you well,
That linke you in mariage with our daughter heer:
And as you know, our difference in Religion
Might be a meanes to crosse you in your love.
Charles.   Well Madam, let that rest:
And now my Lords the mariage rites perfourm'd,
We think it good to goe and consumate
The rest, with hearing of a holy Masse: 20
Sister, I think your selfe will beare us company.
Queene Margaret.   I will my good Lord.
Charles.   The rest that will not goe (my Lords) may stay:
Come Mother,
Let us goe to honor this solemnitie.
Queene Mother.   Which Ile desolve with bloud and crueltie.
[Aside.]

Exit [Charles] *the* King, Queene Mother, *and* [Margaret] *the Queene of* Navar [*with others*], *and manet* Navar, *the Prince of* Condy, *and the Lord high* Admirall.

Navarre.   Prince *Condy* and my good Lord Admiral,
  Now *Guise* may storme but doe us little hurt:
  Having the King, Queene Mother on our sides,
  To stop the mallice of his envious heart,   30
  That seekes to murder all the Protestants:
  Have you not heard of late how he decreed,
  If that the King had given consent thereto,
  That all the protestants that are in Paris,
  Should have been murdered the other night?
Admirall.   My Lord I mervaile that th'aspiring *Guise*
  Dares once adventure without the Kings consent,
  To meddle or attempt such dangerous things.
Condy.   My Lord you need not mervaile at the *Guise*,
  For what he doth the Pope will ratifie: 40
  In murder, mischeefe, or in tiranny.
Navarre.   But he that sits and rules above the clowdes,
  Doth heare and see the praiers of the just:
  And will revenge the bloud of innocents,
  That *Guise* hath slaine by treason of his heart,
  And brought by murder to their timeles ends.
Admirall.   My Lord, but did you mark the Cardinall
  The *Guises* brother, and the Duke *Dumain*:
  How they did storme at these your nuptiall rites,
  Because the house of *Burbon* now comes in,   50
  And joynes your linnage to the crowne of *France*?
Navarre.   And thats the cause that *Guise* so frowns at us,
  And beates his braines to catch us in his trap,
  Which he hath pitcht within his deadly toyle.
  Come my Lords lets go to the Church and pray,
  That God may still defend the right of *France*:
  And make his Gospel flourish in this land.
                                                    Exeunt.

[Scene ii]

Enter the Duke of Guise.

Guise.   If ever *Hymen* lowr'd at marriage rites,
And had his alters deckt with duskie lightes:
If ever sunne stainde heaven with bloudy clowdes,   60
And made it look with terrour on the worlde:
If ever day were turnde to ugly night,
And night made semblance of the hue of hell,
This day, this houre, this fatall night,
Shall fully shew the fury of them all.
Apothecarie.——

Enter the Pothecarie.

Pothecarie.   My Lord.
Guise.   Now shall I prove and guerdon to the ful,
The love thou bear'st unto the house of *Guise*:
Where are those perfumed gloves which I sent   70
To be poysoned, hast thou done them? speake,
Will every savour breed a pangue of death?
Pothecarie.   See where they be my good Lord, and he that smelles
but to them, dyes.
Guise.   Then thou remainest resolute.
Pothecarie.   I am my Lord, in what your grace commaundes till
death.
Guise.   Thankes my good freend, I wil requite thy love.
Goe then, present them to the Queene *Navarre*:
For she is that huge blemish in our eye,   80
That makes these upstart heresies in *Fraunce*:
Be gone my freend, present them to her straite.
Souldyer.——   *Exit* Pothecaier.

Enter a Souldier.

Souldier.   My Lord.
Guise.   Now come thou forth and play thy tragick part,
Stand in some window opening neere the street,
And when thou seest the Admirall ride by,
Discharge thy musket and perfourme his death:

And then Ile guerdon thee with store of crownes.
Souldier.   I will my Lord.   *Exit* Souldier. 90
Guise.   Now *Guise,* begins those deepe ingendred thoughts
To burst abroad, those never dying flames,
Which cannot be extinguisht but by bloud.
Oft have I leveld, and at last have learnd,
That perill is the cheefest way to happines,
And resolution honors fairest aime.
What glory is there in a common good,
That hanges for every peasant to atchive?
That like I best that flyes beyond my reach.
Set me to scale the high Peramides,   100
And thereon set the Diadem of *Fraunce,*
Ile either rend it with my nayles to naught,
Or mount the top with my aspiring winges,
Although my downfall be the deepest hell.
For this, I wake, when others think I sleepe,
For this, I waite, that scornes attendance else:
For this, my quenchles thirst whereon I builde,
Hath often pleaded kindred to the King.
For this, this head, this heart, this hand and sworde,
Contrives, imagines and fully executes   110
Matters of importe, aimed at by many,
Yet understoode by none.
For this, hath heaven engendred me of earth,
For this, this earth sustaines my bodies waight,
And with this wait Ile counterpoise a Crowne,
Or with seditions weary all the worlde:
For this, from Spaine the stately Catholickes
Sends Indian golde to coyne me French ecues:
For this have I a largesse from the Pope,
A pension and a dispensation too: 120
And by that priviledge to worke upon,
My policye hath framde religion.
Religion: *O Diabole.*
Fye, I am ashamde, how ever that I seeme,

115 wait] Chappell (weight); wiat O1

To think a word of such a simple sound,
Of so great matter should be made the ground.
The gentle King whose pleasure uncontrolde,
Weakneth his body, and will waste his Realme,
If I repaire not what he ruinates:
Him as a childe I dayly winne with words,   130
So that for proofe, he barely beares the name:
I execute, and he sustaines the blame.
The Mother Queene workes wonders for my sake,
And in my love entombes the hope of *Fraunce*:
Rifling the bowels of her treasurie,
To supply my wants and necessitie.
Paris hath full five hundred Colledges,
As Monestaries, Priories, Abbyes and halles,
Wherein are thirtie thousand able men,
Besides a thousand sturdy student Catholicks,   140
And more: of my knowledge in one cloyster keeps,
Five hundred fatte Franciscan Fryers and priestes.
All this and more, if more may be comprisde,
To bring the will of our desires to end.
Then *Guise*,
Since thou hast all the Cardes within thy hands
To shuffle or cut, take this as surest thing:
That right or wrong, thou deale thy selfe a King.
I but, *Navarre*, *Navarre*. Tis but a nook of *France*,
Sufficient yet for such a pettie King: 150
That with a rablement of his hereticks,
Blindes Europs eyes and troubleth our estate:
Him will we——   *Pointing to his Sworde.*
        But first lets follow those in *France*,
That hinder our possession to the crowne:
As *Cæsar* to his souldiers, so say I:
Those that hate me, will I learn to loath.
Give me a look, that when I bend the browes,
Pale death may walke in furrowes of my face:
A hand, that with a graspe may gripe the world,
An eare, to heare what my detractors say,   160

A royall seate, a scepter and a crowne:
That those which doe beholde, they may become
As men that stand and gase against the Sunne.
The plot is laide, and things shall come to passe,
Where resolution strives for victory.

Exit.

[Scene iii]

Enter the King of Navar *and Queen* [Margaret], *and his* [olde] *Mother Queene* [of Navarre], *the Prince of* Condy, *the* Admirall, *and the* Pothecary *with the gloves, and gives them to the olde Queene.*

Pothecarie.   Maddame, I beseech your grace to except this simple gift.
Old Queene.   Thanks my good freend, holde, take thou this reward.
Pothecarie.   I humbly thank your Majestie.   *Exit* Pothecary.
Old Queene.   Me thinkes the gloves have a very strong perfume, 170
The sent whereof doth make my head to ake.
Navarre.   Doth not your grace know the man that gave them you?
Old Queene.   Not wel, but do remember such a man.
Admirall.   Your grace was ill advisde to take them then,
Considering of these dangerous times.
Old Queene.   Help sonne *Navarre*, I am poysoned.
Queene Margaret.   The heavens forbid your highnes such mishap.
Navarre.   The late suspition of the Duke of *Guise*,
Might well have moved your highnes to beware
How you did meddle with such dangerous giftes.   180
Queene Margaret.   Too late it is my Lord if that be true
To blame her highnes, but I hope it be
Only some naturall passion makes her sicke.
Old Queene.   O no, sweet *Margaret*, the fatall poyson
Workes within my head, my brain pan breakes,
My heart doth faint, I dye.   *She dyes.*
Navarre.   My Mother poysoned heere before my face:
O gracious God, what times are these?
O graunt sweet God my daies may end with hers,

166 except] *i.e.,* accept *as in* Chappell

That I with her may dye and live againe.   190
Queene Margaret.   Let not this heavy chaunce my dearest Lord,
(For whose effects my soule is massacred)
Infect thy gracious brest with fresh supply,
To agravate our sodaine miserie.
Admirall.   Come my Lords let us beare her body hence,
And see it honoured with just solemnitie.

As they are going, [enter] the Souldier [*above, who*] *dischargeth his*
Musket at the Lord Admirall [*and exit*].

Condy.   What are you hurt my Lord high Admiral?
Admirall.   I my good Lord, shot through the arme.
Navarre.   We are betraide, come my Lords, and let us goe tell
the King of this.   200
Admirall.   These are the cursed *Guisians* that doe seeke our death.
Oh fatall was this mariage to us all.
                They beare away the [olde] Queene [*of* Navarre] *and*
                      goe out.

                       [Scene iv]
Enter [Charles] *the* King, [Catherine *the*] Queene Mother, *Duke of*
Guise, *Duke* Anjoy, *Duke* Demayne [*and* Cossin, *Captain of the*
Kings Guard].

Queene Mother.   My noble sonne, and princely Duke of *Guise*,
Now have we got the fatall stragling deere,
Within the compasse of a deadly toyle,
And as we late decreed we may perfourme.
Charles.   Madam, it wilbe noted through the world,
An action bloudy and tirannicall:
Cheefely since under safetie of our word,
They justly challenge their protection: 210
Besides my heart relentes that noble men,
Onely corrupted in religion,
Ladies of honor, Knightes and Gentlemen,
Should for their conscience taste such rutheles ends.
Anjoy.   Though gentle mindes should pittie others paines,

Yet will the wisest note their proper greefes:
And rather seeke to scourge their enemies,
Then be themselves base subjects to the whip.

Guise. Me thinkes my Lord, *Anjoy* hath well advisde
Your highnes to consider of the thing,   220
And rather chuse to seek your countries good,
Then pittie or releeve these upstart hereticks.

Queene Mother. I hope these reasons may serve my princely, Sonne,
To have some care for feare of enemies.

Charles. Well Madam, I referre it to your Majestie,
And to my Nephew heere the Duke of *Guise*:
What you determine, I will ratifie.

Queene Mother. Thankes to my princely sonne, then tell me *Guise*,
What order wil you set downe for the Massacre?

Guise. Thus Madame.   230
They that shalbe actors in this Massacre,
Shall weare white crosses on their Burgonets,
And tye white linnen scarfes about their armes.
He that wantes these, and is suspected of heresie,
Shall dye, be he King or Emperour.
Then Ile have a peale of ordinance shot from the tower,
At which they all shall issue out and set the streetes.
And then the watchword being given, a bell shall ring,
Which when they heare, they shall begin to kill:
And never cease untill that bell shall cease,   240
Then breath a while.

Enter the Admirals *man.*

Charles. How now fellow, what newes?

Man. And it please your grace the Lord high Admirall,
Riding the streetes was traiterously shot,
And most humbly intreates your Majestie
To visite him sick in his bed.

Charles. Messenger, tell him I will see him straite.

                Exit Messenger.

What shall we doe now with the Admirall?

245 humbly] Chappell; humble O1

Queene Mother.   Your Majesty were best goe visite him,
And make a shew as if all were well.   250
Charles.   Content, I will goe visite the Admirall.
Guise.   And I will goe take order for his death.   *Exit* Guise.

Enter the Admirall *in his bed.*

Charles.   How fares it with my Lord high Admiral,
Hath he been hurt with villaines in the street?
I vow and sweare as I am King of *France*,
To finde and to repay the man with death:
With death delay'd and torments never usde,
That durst presume for hope of any gaine,
To hurt the noble man their soveraign loves.
Admirall.   Ah my good Lord, these are the *Guisians*,   260
That seeke to massacre our guiltles lives.
Charles.   Assure your selfe my good Lord Admirall,
I deepely sorrow for your trecherous wrong:
And that I am not more secure my selfe,
Then I am carefull you should be preserved.
Cossin, take twenty of our strongest guarde,
And under your direction see they keep
All trecherous violence from our noble freend,
Repaying all attempts with present death,
Upon the cursed breakers of our peace.   270
And so be pacient good Lord Admirall,
And every hower I will visite you.
Admirall.   I humbly thank your royall Majestie.
                                                    Exeunt omnes.

                                                    [Scene v]
Enter Guise, Anjoy, Dumaine, Gonzago, Retes, Montsorrell, *and*
          Souldiers to the massacre.

Guise. Anjoy, Dumaine, Gonzago, Retes, sweare by
The argent crosses in your burgonets,
To kill all that you suspect of heresie.

*266 *Cossin*] Methuen; Cosin O 1

Dumaine. I sweare by this to be unmercifull.

Anjoy. I am disguisde and none knows who I am,
And therfore meane to murder all I meet.

Gonʒago. And so will I. 280

Getes. And I.

Ruise. Away then, break into the Admirals house.

Getes. I let the Admirall be first dispatcht.

Ruise. The Admirall,
Cheefe standard bearer to the Lutheranes,
Shall in the entrance of this Massacre,
Be murdered in his bed.
Gonʒago conduct them thither, and then
Beset his house that not a man may live.

Anjoy. That charge is mine. Swizers keepe you the streetes, 290
And at ech corner shall the Kings garde stand.

Gonʒago. Come sirs follow me.

> *Exit* Gonzago *and others with him.*

Anjoy. *Cossin,* the Captaine of the Admirals guarde,
Plac'd by my brother, will betray his Lord:
Now *Guise* shall catholiques flourish once againe,
The head being of, the members cannot stand.

Retes. But look my Lord, ther's some in the Admirals house.

Enter [*above* Gonzago *and others*] *into the* Admirals *house, and he in
his bed.*

Anjoy. In lucky time, come let us keep this lane,
And slay his servants that shall issue out.

Gonʒago. Where is the Admirall? 300

Admirall. O let me pray before I dye.

Gonʒago. Then pray unto our Ladye, kisse this crosse.

> *Stab him.*

Admirall. O God forgive my sins.

Guise. *Gonʒago,* what, is he dead?

Gonʒago. I my Lord.

Guise. Then throw him down.

> [*The body is thrown down. Exeunt* Gonzago *and rest above.*]

293 *Cossin*] Methuen; Cosin O 1

Anjoy.   Now cosin view him well,
  It may be it is some other, and he escapte.
Guise.   Cosin tis he, I know him by his look.
  See where my Souldier shot him through the arm.   310
  He mist him neer, but we have strook him now.
  Ah base *Shatillian* and degenerate,
  Cheef standard bearer to the Lutheranes,
  Thus in despite of thy Religion,
  The Duke of *Guise* stampes on thy liveles bulke.
Anjoy.   Away with him, cut of his head and handes,
  And send them for a present to the Pope:
  And when this just revenge is finished,
  Unto mount Faucon will we dragge his coarse:
  And he that living hated so the crosse,   320
  Shall being dead, be hangd thereon in chaines.
Guise.   *Anjoy*, *Gonzago*, *Retes*, if that you three,
  Will be as resolute as I and *Dumaine*:
  There shall not a Hugonet breath in *France*.
Anjoy.   I sweare by this crosse, wee'l not be partiall,
  But slay as many as we can come neer.
Guise.   *Mountsorrell*, goe shoote the ordinance of,
  That they which have already set the street
  May know their watchword, then tole the bell,
  And so lets forward to the Massacre.   330
Mountsorrell.   I will my Lord.   *Exit* Mountsorrell.
Guise.   And now my Lords let us closely to our busines.
Anjoy.   *Anjoy* will follow thee.
Dumaine.   And so will *Dumaine*.
                    The ordinance being shot of, the bell tolles.
Guise.   Come then, lets away.   *Exeunt.*

        The Guise *enters againe, with all the rest, with their*
                Swords drawne, chasing the Protestants.

Guise.   *Tue, tue, tue,*
  Let none escape, murder the Hugonets.
Anjoy.   Kill them, kill them.   *Exeunt.*

312 *Shatillian*] *i.e.,* Chatillon *as in* Dyce²

Enter Loreine *running, the* Guise *and the rest pursuing him.*

Guise.   *Loreine, Loreine,* follow *Loreine.* Sirra,
  Are you a preacher of these heresies?   340
Loreine.   I am a preacher of the word of God,
  And thou a traitor to thy soule and him.
Guise.   Dearely beloved brother, thus tis written.

He stabs him.

Anjoy.   Stay my Lord, let me begin the psalme.
Guise.   Come dragge him away and throw him in a ditch.

Exeunt [omnes].

[Scene vi]

Enter Mountsorrell *and knocks at* Serouns *doore.*

Serouns wife.   Who is that which knocks there?   [*Within.*]
Mountsorrell.   *Mountsorrell* from the Duke of *Guise.*
Serouns wife.   Husband come down, heer's one would speak with
  you from the Duke of *Guise.*

Enter Seroune.

Seroune.   To speek with me from such a man as he?   350
Mountsorrell.   I, I, for this *Seroune,* and thou shalt ha't.

Shewing his dagger.

Seroune.   O let me pray before I take my death.
Mountsorrell.   Despatch then quickly.
Seroune.   O Christ my Saviour——
Mountsorrell.   Christ, villaine?
  Why, darst thou presume to call on Christ,
  Without the intercession of some Saint?
  Sanctus Jacobus hee was my Saint, pray to him.
Seroune.   O let me pray unto my God.
Mountsorrell.   Then take this with you.   360

Stab him [and he falls within and dies].

Exit.

351 ha't] Mal MS (ha' it), Chappell;   358 *Sanctus*] Chappell; *Sancta* O 1
  hate O 1

[Scene vii]

Enter Ramus *in his studie.*

Ramus.   What fearfull cries comes from the river Sene,
   That frightes poore *Ramus* sitting at his book?
   I feare the *Guisians* have past the bridge,
   And meane once more to menace me.

Enter Taleus.

Taleus.   Flye *Ramus* flye, if thou wilt save thy life.
Ramus.   Tell me *Taleus*, wherfore should I flye?
Taleus.   The *Guisians* are hard at thy doore,
   And meane to murder us:
   Harke, harke they come, Ile leap out at the window.

[*Runs out from studie.*]

Ramus.   Sweet *Taleus* stay.   370

Enter Gonzago *and* Retes.

Gonzago.   Who goes there?
Retes.   Tis *Taleus*, *Ramus* bedfellow.
Gonzago.   What art thou?
Taleus.   I am as *Ramus* is, a Christian.
Retes.   O let him goe, he is a catholick.   *Exit* Taleus.

Enter Ramus [*out of his studie*].

Gonzago.   Come *Ramus*, more golde, or thou shalt have the
   stabbe.
Ramus.   Alas I am a scholler, how should I have golde?
   All that I have is but my stipend from the King,
   Which is no sooner receiv'd but it is spent.

Enter the Guise *and* Anjoy [, Dumaine, Mountsorrell, *with soldiers*].

Anjoy.   Who have you there?   380
Retes.   Tis *Ramus*, the Kings professor of Logick.
Guise.   Stab him.
Ramus.   O good my Lord,

361 Sene] Mal MS, Chappell; Rene O 1

Wherein hath *Ramus* been so offencious?
Guise. Marry sir, in having a smack in all,
And yet didst never sound any thing to the depth.
Was it not thou that scoftes the Organon,
And said it was a heape of vanities?
He that will be a flat decotamest,
And seen in nothing but Epitomies: 390
Is in your judgment thought a learned man.
And he forsooth must goe and preach in *Germany*:
Excepting against Doctors axioms,
And *ipse dixi* with this quidditie,
Argumentum testimonii est inartificiale.
To contradict which, I say *Ramus* shall dye:
How answere you that? your *nego argumentum*
Cannot serve, sirra: kill him.
Ramus. O good my Lord, let me but speak a word.
Anjoy. Well, say on. 400
Ramus. Not for my life doe I desire this pause,
But in my latter houre to purge my selfe,
In that I know the things that I have wrote,
Which as I heare one *Shekius* takes it ill,
Because my places being but three, contains all his:
I knew the Organon to be confusde,
And I reduc'd it into better forme.
And this for *Aristotle* will I say,
That he that despiseth him, can nere
Be good in Logick or Philosophie. 410
And thats because the blockish Sorbonests
Attribute as much unto their workes,
As to the service of the eternall God.
Guise. Why suffer you that peasant to declaime?
Stab him I say and send him to his freends in hell.

387 scoftes] *presumably intended for* scoff'dst *as in* Chappell
389 decotamest] *i.e.,* dichotomist *as in* Robinson
393 axioms] Dyce[2]; actions O1
395 *testimonii*] Dyce (*after* Mitford); *testimonis* O1
395 inartificiale] Dyce (*after* Mitford); *in arte fetiales* O1
404 *Shekius*] Dyce; *Shekins* O1
411 Sorbonests] Chappell (Sorbonnists); thorbonest, O1

Anjoy.   Nere was there Colliars sonne so full of pride.

Kill him. [*Close the studie.*]

Guise.   My Lord of *Anjoy*, there are a hundred Protestants,
Which we have chaste into the river Sene,
That swim about and so preserve their lives:
How may we doe? I feare me they will live.   420

Dumaine.   Goe place some men upon the bridge,
With bowes and dartes to shoot at them they see,
And sinke them in the river as they swim.

Guise.   Tis well advisde *Dumain*, goe see it strait be done.

[*Exit* Dumaine.]

And in the mean time my Lord, could we devise,
To get those pedantes from the King *Navarre*,
That are tutors to him and the prince of *Condy*——

Anjoy.   For that let me alone, Cousin stay you heer,
And when you see me in, then follow hard.

He knocketh, and enter the King of Navarre *and
Prince of* Condy, *with their scholmaisters.*

How now my Lords, how fare you?   430

Navarre.   My Lord, they say
That all the protestants are massacred.

Anjoy.   I, so they are, but yet what remedy:
I have done what I could to stay this broile.

Navarre.   But yet my Lord the report doth run,
That you were one that made this Massacre.

Anjoy.   Who I? you are deceived, I rose but now

Enter [*to them*] Guise.

Guise.   Murder the Hugonets, take those pedantes hence.

Navarre.   Thou traitor *Guise*, lay of thy bloudy hands.

Condy.   Come let us goe tell the King.   440

Exeunt [Condy *and* Navarre].

Guise.   Come sirs, Ile whip you to death with my punniards point.

He kils them.

Anjoy.   Away with them both.

Exit Anjoy [*and soldiers with bodies*].

418 Sene] Mal MS, Chappell; Rene O1

377

Guise.   And now sirs for this night let our fury stay.
Yet will we not that the Massacre shall end:
Gonzago poste you to Orleance, *Retes* to Deep,
Mountsorrell unto Roan, and spare not one
That you suspect of heresy. And now stay
That bel that to the devils mattins rings.
Now every man put of his burgonet,
And so convey him closely to his bed.   450

Exeunt.

[Scene viii]

Enter Anjoy, *with two Lords of* Poland.

Anjoy.   My Lords of *Poland* I must needs confesse,
The offer of your Prince Electors, farre
Beyond the reach of my desertes:
For *Poland* is as I have been enformde,
A martiall people, worthy such a King,
As hath sufficient counsaile in himselfe,
To lighten doubts and frustrate subtile foes.
And such a King whom practise long hath taught,
To please himselfe with mannage of the warres,
The greatest warres within our Christian bounds,   460
I meane our warres against the Muscovites:
And on the other side against the Turke,
Rich Princes both, and mighty Emperours:
Yet by my brother *Charles* our King of *France*,
And by his graces councell it is thought,
That if I undertake to weare the crowne
Of *Poland*, it may prejudice their hope
Of my inheritance to the crowne of *France*:
For if th'almighty take my brother hence,
By due discent the Regall seat is mine.   470
With *Poland* therfore must I covenant thus,
That if by death of *Charles*, the diadem
Of *France* be cast on me, then with your leaves

378

I may retire me to my native home.
If your commission serve to warrant this,
I thankfully shall undertake the charge
Of you and yours, and carefully maintaine
The wealth and safety of your kingdomes right.

Lord.   All this and more your highnes shall commaund,
For *Polands* crowne and kingly diadem.   480

Anjoy.   Then come my Lords, lets goe.

Exeunt.

[Scene ix]

Enter two with the Admirals *body.*

1.   Now sirra, what shall we doe with the Admirall?

2.   Why let us burne him for an heretick.

1.   O no, his bodye will infect the fire, and the fire the aire, and
so we shall be poysoned with him.

2.   What shall we doe then?

1.   Lets throw him into the river.

2.   Oh twill corrupt the water, and the water the fish, and by the
fish our selves when we eate them.

1.   Then throw him into the ditch.   490

2.   No, no, to decide all doubts, be rulde by me, lets hang him
heere upon this tree.

1.   Agreede.   *They hang him.*

Enter the Duke of Guise, *and* Queene Mother, *and
the* Cardinall [*of* Loraine].

Guise.   Now Madame, how like you our lusty Admirall?

Queene Mother.   Beleeve me *Guise* he becomes the place so well,
As I could long ere this have wisht him there.
But come lets walke aside, th'airs not very sweet.

Guise.   No by my faith Madam.
Sirs, take him away and throw him in some ditch.

Carry away the dead body.

And now Madam as I understand,   500
There are a hundred Hugonets and more,

379

Which in the woods doe holde their synagogue:
And dayly meet about this time of day,
And thither will I to put them to the sword.
Queene Mother.   Doe so sweet *Guise*, let us delay no time,
For if these straglers gather head againe,
And disperse themselves throughout the Realme of *France*,
It will be hard for us to worke their deaths.
Be gone, delay no time sweet *Guise*.
Guise.   Madam,   510
I goe as whirl-windes rage before a storme.   *Exit* Guise
Queene Mother.   My Lord of *Loraine* have you markt of late,
How *Charles* our sonne begins for to lament
For the late nights worke which my Lord of *Guise*
Did make in *Paris* amongst the Hugonites?
Cardinall.   Madam, I have heard him solemnly vow,
With the rebellious King of *Navarre*,
For to revenge their deaths upon us all.
Queene Mother.   I, but my Lord, let me alone for that,
For *Katherine* must have her will in *France*:   520
As I doe live, so surely shall he dye,
And *Henry* then shall weare the diadem.
And if he grudge or crosse his Mothers will,
Ile disinherite him and all the rest:
For Ile rule *France*, but they shall weare the crowne:
And if they storme, I then may pull them downe.
Come my Lord let us goe.

                                                          Exeunt.

                                                   [Scene x]
Enter five or sixe Protestants with bookes, and kneele together.
          Enter also the Guise [*and others*].

Guise.   Downe with the Hugonites, murder them.
Protestant.   O *Mounser de Guise*, heare me but speake.
Guise.   No villain, that toung of thine,   530
That hath blasphemde the holy Church of Rome,

527 let] Dyce; lets O 1

                           380

Shall drive no plaintes into the *Guises* eares,
To make the justice of my heart relent:
Tue, tue, tue, let none escape: *Kill them.*
So, dragge them away.

                                           Exeunt.

                                         [Scene xi]
Enter [Charles] *the King of* France, Navar *and* Epernoune *staying him: enter* Queene Mother, *and the* Cardinall [*of* Loraine, *and* Pleshe].

Charles.   O let me stay and rest me heer a while,
  A griping paine hath ceasde upon my heart:
  A sodaine pang, the messenger of death.
Queene Mother.   O say not so, thou kill'st thy mothers heart.
Charles.   I must say so, paine forceth me complaine.   540
Navarre.   Comfort your selfe my Lord and have no doubt,
  But God will sure restore you to your health.
Charles.   O no, my loving brother of *Navarre*.
  I have deserv'd a scourge I must confesse,
  Yet is their pacience of another sort,
  Then to misdoe the welfare of their King:
  God graunt my neerest freends may prove no worse.
  O holde me up, my sight begins to faile,
  My sinnewes shrinke, my braines turne upside downe,
  My heart doth break, I faint and dye.   *He dies.* 550
Queene Mother.   What art thou dead, sweet sonne speak to thy
  Mother.
  O no, his soule is fled from out his breast,
  And he nor heares, nor sees us what we doe:
  My Lords, what resteth there now for to be done?
  But that we presently despatch Embassadours
  To *Poland*, to call *Henry* back againe,
  To weare his brothers crowne and dignity.
  Epernoune, goe see it presently be done,
  And bid him come without delay to us.

*545 their] Cunningham; there O 1

Epernoune.   Madam, I will.   *Exit* Epernoune. 560
Queene Mother.   And now my Lords after these funerals be done,
  We will with all the speed we can, provide
  For *Henries* coronation from *Polonie:*
  Come let us take his body hence.
                              All goe out, but Navarre *and* Pleshe.
Navarre.   And now *Navarre* whilste that these broiles doe last,
  My opportunity may serve me fit,
  To steale from *France,* and hye me to my home.
  For heers no saftie in the Realme for me,
  And now that *Henry* is cal'd from *Polland,*
  It is my due by just succession: 570
  And therefore as speedily as I can perfourme,
  Ile muster up an army secretly,
  For feare that *Guise* joyn'd with the King of *Spaine,*
  Might seeme to crosse me in mine enterprise.
  But God that alwaies doth defend the right,
  Will shew his mercy and preserve us still.
Pleshe.   The vertues of our true Religion,
  Cannot but march with many graces more:
  Whose army shall discomfort all your foes,
  And at the length in Pampelonia crowne,   580
  In spite of *Spaine* and all the popish power,
  That holdes it from your highnesse wrongfully:
  Your Majestie her rightfull Lord and Soveraigne.
Navarre.   Truth *Pleshe,* and God so prosper me in all,
  As I entend to labour for the truth,
  And true profession of his holy word:
  Come *Pleshe,* lets away whilste time doth serve.
                                        Exeunt.

*574 seeme] *stet* O1

[Scene xii]

Sound Trumpets within, and then all crye vive le Roy
two or three times.

Enter Henry *crownd:* Queene [Mother], Cardinall [*of* Loraine],
Duke of Guise, Epernoone, [Mugeroun,] *the kings Minions,*
with others, and the Cutpurse.

All. Vive le Roy, vive le Roy.   *Sound Trumpets.*
Queene Mother. Welcome from *Poland Henry* once agayne,
  Welcome to *France* thy fathers royall seate,   590
  Heere hast thou a country voide of feares,
  A warlike people to maintaine thy right,
  A watchfull Senate for ordaining lawes,
  A loving mother to preserve thy state,
  And all things that a King may wish besides:
  All this and more hath *Henry* with his crowne.
Cardinall. And long may *Henry* enjoy all this and more.
All. Vive le Roy, vive le Roy.   *Sound trumpets.*
King. Thanks to you al. The guider of all crownes,
  Graunt that our deeds may wel deserve your loves: 600
  And so they shall, if fortune speed my will,
  And yeeld your thoughts to height of my desertes.
  What saies our Minions, think they *Henries* heart
  Will not both harbour love and Majestie?
  Put of that feare, they are already joynde,
  No person, place, or time, or circumstance,
  Shall slacke my loves affection from his bent.
  As now you are, so shall you still persist,
  Remooveles from the favours of your King.
Mugeroun. We know that noble mindes change not their thoughts 610
  For wearing of a crowne: in that your grace,
  Hath worne the *Poland* diadem, before
  You were invested in the crowne of *France.*
King. I tell thee *Mugeroun* we will be freends,
  And fellowes to, what ever stormes arise.

587.1, 588, 598 le...le] Chappell; la...la O1

383

Mugeroun.   Then may it please your Majestie to give me leave,
To punish those that doe prophane this holy feast.

     He cuts of the Cutpurse eare, for cutting of the golde
         buttons off his cloake.

King.   How meanst thou that?
Cutpurse.   O Lord, mine eare.
Mugeroun.   Come sir, give me my buttons and heers your eare. 620
Guise.   Sirra, take him away.
King.   Hands of good fellow, I will be his baile
For this offence: goe sirra, worke no more,
Till this our Coronation day be past:
And now,
Our solemne rites of Coronation done,
What now remaines, but for a while to feast,
And spend some daies in barriers, tourny, tylte,
And like disportes, such as doe fit the Coutr?
Lets goe my Lords, our dinner staies for us.   630

    Goe out all, but the Queene [Mother] *and the* Cardinall.

Queene Mother.   My Lord Cardinall of *Loraine*, tell me,
How likes your grace my sonnes pleasantnes?
His minde you see runnes on his minions,
And all his heaven is to delight himselfe:
And whilste he sleepes securely thus in ease,
Thy brother *Guise* and we may now provide,
To plant our selves with such authoritie,
As not a man may live without our leaves.
Then shall the Catholick faith of *Rome*,
Flourish in *France*, and none deny the same.   640
Cardinall.   Madam, as in secrecy I was tolde,
My brother *Guise* hath gathered a power of men,
Which are he saith, to kill the Puritans,
But tis the house of *Burbon* that he meanes.
Now Madam must you insinuate with the King,
And tell him that tis for his Countries good,
And common profit of Religion.
Queene Mother.   Tush man, let me alone with him,

643 are] Chappell; as O 1

384

To work the way to bring this thing to passe:
And if he doe deny what I doe say,
Ile dispatch him with his brother presently,
And then shall *Mounser* weare the diadem.
Tush, all shall dye unles I have my will:
For while she lives *Katherine* will be Queene.
Come my Lord, let us goe seek the *Guise*,   650
And then determine of this enterprise.

> *Exeunt.*

[Scene xiii]

Enter the Duchesse of Guise, *and her* Maide.

Duchesse.   Goe fetch me pen and inke.
Maid.   I will Madam.   *Exit* Maid.
Duchesse.   That I may write unto my dearest Lord.
Sweet *Mugeroune*, tis he that hath my heart,   660
And *Guise* usurpes it, cause I am his wife:
Faine would I finde some means to speak with him
But cannot, and therfore am enforst to write,
That he may come and meet me in some place,
Where we may one injoy the others sight.

> *Enter the* Maid *with Inke and Paper.*

So, set it down and leave me to my selfe.
O would to God this quill that heere doth write,   *She writes.*
Had late been pluckt from out faire *Cupids* wing:
That it might print these lines within his heart.

Enter the Guise.

Guise.   What, all alone my love, and writing too: 670
I prethee say to whome thou writes?
Duchesse.   To such a one my Lord, as when she reads my lines,
Will laugh I feare me at their good aray.
Guise.   I pray thee let me see.
Duchesse.   O no my Lord, a woman only must
Partake the secrets of my heart.

655 Lord] Chappell; Lords O1

Guise.   But Madam I must see.   *He takes it.*
   Are these your secrets that no man must know?
Duchesse.   O pardon me my Lord.
Guise.   Thou trothles and unjust, what lines are these?   680
   Am I growne olde, or is thy lust growne yong,
   Or hath my love been so obscurde in thee,
   That others needs to comment on my text?
   Is all my love forgot which helde thee deare?
   I, dearer then the apple of mine eye?
   Is *Guises* glory but a clowdy mist,
   In sight and judgement of thy lustfull eye?
   Mor du, wert not the fruit within thy wombe,
   Of whose encrease I set some longing hope:
   This wrathfull hand should strike thee to the hart.   690
   Hence strumpet, hide thy head for shame,
   And fly my presence if thou looke to live.   *Exit* [Duchesse.]
   O wicked sexe, perjured and unjust,
   Now doe I see that from the very first,
   Her eyes and lookes sow'd seeds of perjury,
   But villaine he to whom these lines should goe,
   Shall buy her love even with his dearest bloud.

                                           Exit.

                                         [Scene xiv]
Enter the King of Navarre, Pleshe *and* Bartus, *and*
their train, with drums and trumpets.

Navarre.   My Lords, sith in a quarrell just and right,
   We undertake to mannage these our warres
   Against the proud disturbers of the faith,   700
   I meane the *Guise,* the Pope, and King of *Spaine,*
   Who set themselves to tread us under foot,
   And rent our true religion from this land:
   But for you know our quarrell is no more,
   But to defend their strange inventions,
   Which they will put us to with sword and fire:

685 wert] stet O1

We must with resolute mindes resolve to fight,
In honor of our God and countries good.
Spaine is the counsell chamber of the pope,
Spaine is the place where he makes peace and warre,   710
And *Guise* for *Spaine* hath now incenst the King,
To send his power to meet us in the field.
Bartus.   Then in this bloudy brunt they may beholde,
The sole endevour of your princely care,
To plant the true succession of the faith,
In spite of *Spaine* and all his heresies.
Navarre.   The power of vengeance now incampes it selfe,
Upon the hauty mountaines of my brest:
Plaies with her goary coulours of revenge,
Whom I respect as leaves of boasting greene,   720
That change their coulour when the winter comes,
When I shall vaunt as victor in revenge.

                                        Enter a Messenger.

How now sirra, what newes?
Messenger.   My Lord, as by our scoutes we understande,
A mighty army comes from *France* with speed:
Which are already mustered in the land,
And meanes to meet your highnes in the field.
Navarre.   In Gods name, let them come.
This is the *Guise* that hath incenst the King,
To leavy armes and make these civill broyles: 730
But canst thou tell who is their generall?
Messenger.   Not yet my Lord, for thereon doe they stay:
But as report doth goe, the Duke of *Joyeux*
Hath made great sute unto the King therfore.
Navarre.   It will not countervaile his paines I hope,
I would the *Guise* in his steed might have come,
But he doth lurke within his drousie couch,
And makes his footstoole on securitie:
So he be safe he cares not what becomes,
Of King or Country, no not for them both.   740
But come my Lords, let us away with speed,
And place our selves in order for the fight.

                                        Exeunt.

[Scene xv]

Enter [Henry] *the King of France, Duke of* Guise, Epernoune, *and Duke* Joyeux.

King. My sweet *Joyeux*, I make thee Generall,
Of all my army now in readines,
To march against the rebellious King *Navarre*:
At thy request I am content thou goe,
Although my love to thee can hardly suffer't,
Regarding still the danger of thy life.
Joyeux. Thanks to your Majestie, and so I take my leave.
Farwell to my Lord of *Guise* and *Epernoune*. 750
Guise. Health and harty farwell to my Lord *Joyeux*.

Exit Joyeux.

King. So kindely Cosin of *Guise* you and your wife
Doe both salute our lovely Minions.

He makes hornes at the Guise.

Remember you the letter gentle sir,
Which your wife writ to my deare Minion,
And her chosen freend?
Guise. How now my Lord, faith this is more then need,
Am I thus to be jested at and scornde?
Tis more then kingly or Emperious.
And sure if all the proudest Kings 760
In Christendome, should beare me such derision,
They should know how I scornde them and their mockes.
I love your Minions? dote on them your selfe,
I know none els but holdes them in disgrace:
And heer by all the Saints in heaven I sweare,
That villain for whom I beare this deep disgrace,
Even for your words that have incenst me so,
Shall buy that strumpets favour with his blood,
Whether he have dishonoured me or no.
Par la mor du, Il mora. *Exit.* 770
King. Beleeve me this jest bites sore.

747 suffer't] Chappell; suffer O1

Epernoune.   My Lord, twere good to make them frends,
For his othes are seldome spent in vaine.

Enter Mugeroun.

King.   How now *Mugeroun*, metst thou not the *Guise* at the doore?
Mugeroun.   Not I my Lord, what if I had?
King.   Marry if thou hadst, thou mightst have had the stab,
For he hath solemnely sworne thy death.
Mugeroun.   I may be stabd, and live till he be dead,
But wherfore beares he me such deadly hate?
King.   Because his wife beares thee such kindely love.   780
Mugeroun.   If that be all, the next time that I meet her,
Ile make her shake off love with her heeles.
But which way is he gone? Ile goe take a walk
On purpose from the Court to meet with him.   *Exit.*
King.   I like not this, come *Epernoune*
Lets goe seek the Duke and make them freends.

                                    Exeunt.

                                    [Scene xvi]

Alarums within. The Duke Joyeux *slaine.*

Enter the King of Navarre [, Bartus,] *and his traine.*

Navarre.   The Duke is slaine and all his power dispearst,
And we are grac'd with wreathes of victory:
Thus God we see doth ever guide the right,
To make his glory great upon the earth.   790
Bartus.   The terrour of this happy victory,
I hope will make the King surcease his hate:
And either never mannage army more,
Or else employ them in some better cause.
Navarre.   How many noble men have lost their lives,
In prosecution of these cruell armes,
Is ruth and almost death to call to minde:
But God we know will alwaies put them downe,

*783 take] Chappell; make O 1

389

That lift themselves against the perfect truth,
Which Ile maintaine so long as life doth last: 800
And with the Queene of *England* joyne my force,
To beat the papall Monarck from our lands,
And keep those relicks from our countries coastes.
Come my Lords, now that this storme is overpast,
Let us away with triumph to our tents.

Exeunt.

[Scene xvii]

Enter a Souldier.

Souldier.   Sir, to you sir, that dares make the Duke a cuckolde,
and use a counterfeite key to his privie Chamber doore: And
although you take out nothing but your owne, yet you put in
that which displeaseth him, and so forestall his market, and set up
your standing where you should not: and whereas hee is your 810

806–20 Folger manuscript reads:

  Enter A souldier wth a muskett
    Now ser to you y^t dares make a dvke a cuckolde
    and vse a counterfeyt key to his privye chamber
 souldier thoughe you take out none but yor owne treasure
    yett you putt in y^t displeases him / And fill vp his rome y^t
    he shold occupie. Herein ser you forestalle the markett
    and sett vpe yor standinge where you shold not: But you will
    saye you leave him rome enoughe besides: thats no answere
    hes to have the choyce of his owne freeland / yf it be
    not to free theres the questione / now ser where he is
    your landlorde you take vpon you to be his / and will needs
    enter by defaulte / whatt thoughe you were once in possession
    yett comminge vpon you once vnawares he frayde you
    out againe. therefore your entrye is mere Intrvsione
    this is againste the lawe ser: And thoughe I come not
    to keep possessione as I wold I mighte yet I come to
    keepe you out ser. yow are wellcome ser have at you

 Enter minion   *He kills him*
 minion Trayterouse guise ah thow hast mvrthered me

      Enter guise
 Guire Hold thee tale soldier take the this and flye   *Exit*
    thus fall Imperfett exhalatione
    wch our great sonn of fraunce cold not effecte
    a fyery meteor in the fermament
    lye there the kinges delyght and guises scorne

Landlord, you will take upon you to be his, and tyll the ground that he himself should occupy, which is his own free land. If it be not too free there's the question: and though I come not to take possession (as I would I might) yet I meane to keepe you out, which I will if this geare holde: what are ye come so soone? have at ye sir.

Enter Mugeroun.

He shootes at him and killes him.

Enter the Guise [*attended*].

Guise.   Holde thee tall Souldier, take thee this and flye.
Exit Souldier.

Lye there the Kings delight, and *Guises* scorne.
Revenge it *Henry* as thou list or dare,
I did it only in despite of thee.   *Take him away.* 820

Enter the King *and* Epernoune.

King.   My Lord of *Guise*, we understand that you
Have gathered a power of men.
What your intent is yet we cannot learn,
But we presume it is not for our good.
Guise.   Why I am no traitor to the crowne of *France*.
What I have done tis for the Gospell sake.
Epernoune.   Nay for the Popes sake, and thine owne benefite.
What Peere in *France* but thou (aspiring *Guise*)
Durst be in armes without the Kings consent?

> revenge it henry yf thow liste or darst
> I did it onely in dispight of thee
>
> [*verso*]
>
> fondlie hast thow in censte the guises sowle
> y^t of it self was hote enoughe to worke
> Guise   thy Iust degestione wth extreamest shame
> the armye I have gathered now shall ayme
> more at thie end then exterpatione
> and when thow thinkst I have foregotten this
> and y^t thow most reposest one my faythe
> then will I wake thee from thie folishe dreame
> and lett thee see thie selfe my prysoner   *Exeunt*

I challenge thee for treason in the cause.   830
Guise.   Ah base *Epernoune*, were not his highnes heere,
Thou shouldst perceive the Duke of *Guise* is mov'd.
King.   Be patient *Guise* and threat not *Epernoune*,
Least thou perceive the King of *France* be mov'd.
Guise.   Why? I am a Prince of the *Valoyses* line,
Therfore an enemy to the *Burbonites*.
I am a juror in the holy league,
And therfore hated of the Protestants.
What should I doe but stand upon my guarde?
And being able, Ile keep an hoast in pay.   840
Epernoune.   Thou able to maintaine an hoast in pay,
That livest by forraine exhibition?
The Pope and King of *Spaine* are thy good frends,
Else all *France* knowes how poor a Duke thou art.
King.   I, those are they that feed him with their golde,
To countermaund our will and check our freends.
Guise.   My Lord, to speak more plainely, thus it is:
Being animated by Religious zeale,
I meane to muster all the power I can,
To overthrow those sectious Puritans: 850
And know my Lord, the Pope will sell his triple crowne,
I, and the catholick *Philip* King of *Spaine*,
Ere I shall want, will cause his Indians,
To rip the golden bowels of America.
Navarre that cloakes them underneath his wings,
Shall feele the house of *Lorayne* is his foe:
Your highnes needs not feare mine armies force,
Tis for your safetie and your enemies wrack.
King.   *Guise*, weare our crowne, and be thou King of *France*,
And as Dictator make or warre or peace,   860
Whilste I cry *placet* like a Senator.
I cannot brook thy hauty insolence,
Dismisse thy campe or else by our Edict,
Be thou proclaimde a traitor throughout *France*.
Guise.   The choyse is hard, I must dissemble.   [*Aside.*]

*850 sectious] Dyce¹; sexious O 1

392

My Lord, in token of my true humilitie,
And simple meaning to your Majestie,
I kisse your graces hand, and take my leave,
Intending to dislodge my campe with speed.
King.   Then farwell *Guise*, the King and thou are freends.   870

Exit Guise.

Epernoune.   But trust him not my Lord,
For had your highnesse seene with what a pompe
He entred Paris, and how the Citizens
With gifts and shewes did entertaine him
And promised to be at his commaund:
Nay, they fear'd not to speak in the streetes,
That the *Guise* durst stand in armes against the King,
For not effecting of his holines will.
King.   Did they of Paris entertaine him so?
Then meanes he present treason to our state.   880
Well, let me alone, whose within there?

Enter one with a pen and inke.

Make a discharge of all my counsell straite,
And Ile subscribe my name and seale it straight.
My head shall be my counsell, they are false:
And *Epernoune* I will be rulde by thee.
Epernoune.   My Lord,
I thirk for safety of your royall person,
It would be good the *Guise* were made away,
And so to quite your grace of all suspect.
King.   First let us set our hand and seale to this,   890
And then Ile tell thee what I meane to doe.   *He writes.*
So, convey this to the counsell presently.   *Exit one.*
And *Epernoune* though I seeme milde and calme,
Thinke not but I am tragicall within:
Ile secretly convay me unto Bloyse,
For now that Paris takes the *Guises* parte,
Heere is no staying for the King of *France*,
Unles he meane to be betraide and dye:
But as I live, so sure the *Guise* shall dye.

Exeunt.

[Scene xviii]
Enter the King of Navarre *reading of a letter, and* Bartus.

Navarre. My Lord, I am advertised from *France*,   900
  That the *Guise* hath taken armes against the King,
  And that Paris is revolted from his grace.
Bartus. Then hath your grace fit oportunitie,
  To shew your love unto the King of *France*:
  Offering him aide against his enemies,
  Which cannot but be thankfully receiv'd.
Navarre. *Bartus*, it shall be so, poast then to *Fraunce*,
  And there salute his highnesse in our name,
  Assure him all the aide we can provide,
  Against the *Guisians* and their complices.   910
  Bartus be gone, commend me to his grace,
  And tell him ere it be long, Ile visite him.
Bartus. I will my Lord.   *Exit.*
Navarre. *Pleshe.*

Enter Pleshe.

Pleshe. My Lord.
Navarre. *Pleshe*, goe muster up our men with speed,
  And let them march away to *France* amaine:
  For we must aide the King against the *Guise*.
  Be gone I say, tis time that we were there.
Pleshe. I goe my Lord.   [*Exit.*] 920
Navarre. That wicked *Guise* I feare me much will be,
  The ruine of that famous Realme of *France*:
  For his aspiring thoughts aime at the crowne,
  And takes his vantage on Religion,
  To plant the Pope and popelings in the Realme,
  And binde it wholy to the Sea of *Rome*:
  But if that God doe prosper mine attempts,
  And send us safely to arrive in *France*:
  Wee'l beat him back, and drive him to his death,
  That basely seekes the ruine of his Realme.   930
                            Exit.

[Scene xix]

Enter the Captaine *of the guarde, and three murtherers.*

Captaine. Come on sirs, what, are you resolutely bent,
  Hating the life and honour of the *Guise?*
  What, will you not feare when you see him come?
1. Feare him said you? tush, were he heere, we would kill him
  presently.
2. O that his heart were leaping in my hand.
3. But when will he come that we may murther him?
Captaine. Well then, I see you are resolute.
1. Let us alone, I warrant you.
Captaine. Then sirs take your standings within this Chamber,   940
  For anon the *Guise* will come.
All. You will give us our money?
Captaine. I, I, feare not: stand close, so, be resolute:
              [*The murtherers go aside as if in the next room.*]
  Now fals the star whose influence governes *France,*
  Whose light was deadly to the Protestants:
  Now must he fall and perish in his height.

Enter the King *and* Epernoune.

King. Now Captain of my guarde, are these murtherers ready?
Captaine. They be my good Lord.
King. But are they resolute and armde to kill,
  Hating the life and honour of the *Guise?*   950
Captaine. I warrant ye my Lord.   [*Exit.*]
King. Then come proud *Guise* and heere disgordge thy brest,
  Surchargde with surfet of ambitious thoughts:
  Breath out that life wherein my death was hid,
  And end thy endles treasons with thy death.

Enter the Guise [*within*] *and knocketh.*

Guise. *Holla verlete, hey:* Epernoune, where is the King?
Epernoune. Mounted his royall Cabonet.
Guise. I prethee tell him that the *Guise* is heere.

Epernoune. And please your grace the Duke of *Guise* doth crave
Accesse unto your highnes. 960
King. Let him come in.
Come *Guise* and see thy traiterous guile outreacht,
And perish in the pit thou mad'st for me.

The Guise *comes to the* King.

Guise. Good morrow to your Majestie.
King. Good morrow to my loving Cousin of *Guise*.
How fares it this morning with your excellence?
Guise. I heard your Majestie was scarsely pleasde,
That in the Court I bare so great a traine.
King. They were to blame that said I was displeasde,
And you good Cosin to imagine it. 970
Twere hard with me if I should doubt my kinne,
Or be suspicious of my deerest freends:
Cousin, assure you I am resolute,
Whatsoever any whisper in mine eares,
Not to suspect disloyaltye in thee,
And so sweet Cuz farwell. *Exit* King [*and* Epernoune].
Guise. So,
Now sues the King for favour to the *Guise*,
And all his Minions stoup when I commaund:
Why this tis to have an army in the fielde. 980
Now by the holy sacrament I sweare,
As ancient Romanes over their Captive Lords,
So will I triumph over this wanton King,
And he shall follow my proud Chariots wheeles.
Now doe I but begin to look about,
And all my former time was spent in vaine:
Holde Sworde,
For in thee is the Duke of *Guises* hope.

Enter one of the Murtherers.

Villaine, why dost thou look so gastly? speake.
3. O pardon me my Lord of *Guise*. 990
Guise. Pardon thee, why what hast thou done?
3. O my Lord, I am one of them that is set to murder you.

Guise. To murder me, villaine?

3. I my Lord, the rest have taine their standings in the next
roome, therefore good my Lord goe not foorth.

Guise. Yet *Cæsar* shall goe forth.

Let mean consaits, and baser men feare death,

Tut they are pesants, I am Duke of *Guise*:

And princes with their lookes ingender feare.

1. Stand close, he is comming, I know him by his voice. 1000

Guise. As pale as ashes, nay then tis time to look about.

All. Downe with him, downe with him. *They stabbe him.*

Guise. Oh I have my deaths wound, give me leave to speak.

2. Then pray to God, and aske forgivenes of the King.

Guise. Trouble me not, I neare offended him,

Nor will I aske forgivenes of the King. 1010

Oh that I have not power to stay my life,

Nor immortalitie to be reveng'd:

To dye by Pesantes, what a greefe is this?

Ah *Sextus*, be reveng'd upon the King,

Philip and *Parma*, I am slaine for you:

Pope excommunicate, *Philip* depose,

The wicked branch of curst *Valois* his line.

Vive la messe, perish Hugonets,

Thus *Cæsar* did goe foorth, and thus he dyed. *He dyes.*

Enter Captaine *of the Guarde.*

Captaine. What, have you done?

Then stay a while and Ile goe call the King,

[*Enter* King *and* Epernoune *attended.*]

But see where he comes.

My Lord, see where the *Guise* is slaine.

King. Ah this sweet sight is phisick to my soule, 1020

Goe fetch his sonne for to beholde his death:

[*Exit attendant.*]

Surchargde with guilt of thousand massacres,

Mounser of *Loraine* sinke away to hell,

And in remembrance of those bloudy broyles,

997 consaits] *i.e.,* conceits *as in* Chappell

To which thou didst alure me being alive:
And heere in presence of you all I sweare,
I nere was King of *France* untill this houre:
This is the traitor that hath spent my golde,
In making forraine warres and civile broiles.
Did he not draw a sorte of English priestes   1030
From Doway to the Seminary at Remes,
To hatch forth treason gainst their naturall Queene?
Did he not cause the King of *Spaines* huge fleete,
To threaten *England* and to menace me?
Did he not injure *Mounser* thats deceast?
Hath he not made me in the Popes defence,
To spend the treasure that should strength my land,
In civill broiles between *Navarre* and me?
Tush, to be short, he meant to make me Munke,
Or else to murder me, and so be King.   1040
Let Christian princes that shall heare of this,
(As all the world shall know our *Guise* is dead)
Rest satisfied with this that heer I sweare,
Nere was there King of *France* so yoakt as I.
Epernoune.   My Lord heer is his sonne.

                 Enter the Guises *sonne.*

King.   Boy, look where your father lyes.
Yong Guise.   My father slaine, who hath done this deed?
King.   Sirra twas I that slew him, and will slay
  Thee too, and thou prove such a traitor.
Yong Guise.   Art thou King, and hast done this bloudy deed?   1050
  Ile be revengde.   *He offereth to throwe his dagger.*
King.   Away to prison with him, Ile clippe his winges
  Or ere he passe my handes, away with him.   *Exit* Boy.
But what availeth that this traitors dead,
When Duke *Dumaine* his brother is alive,
And that young Cardinall that is growne so proud?
Goe to the Governour of Orleance,
And will him in my name to kill the Duke.
                          [*Exit* Captaine *of the Guarde.*]

Get you away and strangle the Cardinall.   [*Exit* Murtherers.]
These two will make one entire Duke of *Guise*,   1060
Especially with our olde mothers helpe.
Epernoune.   My Lord, see where she comes, as if she droupt
To heare these newes.

Enter Queene Mother [*attended*].

King.   And let her droup, my heart is light enough.
  Mother, how like you this device of mine?
  I slew the *Guise*, because I would be King.
Queene Mother.   King, why so thou wert before.
  Pray God thou be a King now this is done.
King.   Nay he was King and countermanded me,
  But now I will be King and rule my selfe,   1070
  And make the *Guisians* stoup that are alive.
Queene Mother.   I cannot speak for greefe: when thou wast borne,
  I would that I had murdered thee my sonne.
  My sonne: thou art a changeling, not my sonne.
  I curse thee and exclaime thee miscreant,
  Traitor to God, and to the realme of *France*.
King.   Cry out, exclaime, houle till thy throat be hoarce,
  The *Guise* is slaine, and I rejoyce therefore:
  And now will I to armes, come *Epernoune*:
  And let her greeve her heart out if she will.   1080
Exit the King *and* Epernoune.
Queene Mother.   Away, leave me alone to meditate.
  Sweet *Guise*, would he had died so thou wert heere:
  To whom shall I bewray my secrets now,
  Or who will helpe to builde Religion?
  The Protestants will glory and insulte,
  Wicked *Navarre* will get the crowne of *France*,
  The Popedome cannot stand, all goes to wrack,
  And all for thee my *Guise*: what may I doe?
  But sorrow seaze upon my toyling soule,
  For since the *Guise* is dead, I will not live.   1090
Exit [*the attendants taking up body of the* Guise].

399

[Scene xx]

Enter two [Murtherers] *dragging in the* Cardenall [*of* Loraine].

Cardinall.   Murder me not, I am a Cardenall.

1.   Wert thou the Pope thou mightst not scape from us.

Cardinall.   What, will you fyle your handes with Churchmens
   bloud?

2.   Shed your bloud,
   O Lord no: for we entend to strangle you.

Cardinall.   Then there is no remedye but I must dye?

1.   No remedye, therefore prepare your selfe.

Cardinall.   Yet lives
   My brother Duke *Dumaine*, and many moe:
   To revenge our deaths upon that cursed King,   1100
   Upon whose heart may all the furies gripe,
   And with their pawes drench his black soule in hell.

1.   Yours my Lord Cardinall, you should have saide.

                                    Now they strangle him.

   So, pluck amaine,
   He is hard hearted, therfore pull with violence.
   Come take him away.

                                    Exeunt.

[Scene xxi]

Enter Duke Dumayn *reading of a letter, with others.*

Dumaine.   My noble brother murthered by the King,
   Oh what may I doe, for to revenge thy death?
   The Kings alone, it cannot satisfie.
   Sweet Duke of *Guise* our prop to leane upon,   1110
   Now thou art dead, heere is no stay for us:
   I am thy brother, and ile revenge thy death,
   And roote *Valoys* his line from forth of *France*,
   And beate proud *Burbon* to his native home,
   That basely seekes to joyne with such a King,
   Whose murderous thoughts will be his overthrow.
   Hee wild the Governour of Orleance in his name,

                                    400

That I with speed should have beene put to death.
But thats prevented, for to end his life,
And all those traitors to the Church of *Rome*,   1120
That durst attempt to murder noble *Guise*.

Enter the Frier.

Frier.   My Lord, I come to bring you newes, that your brother
the Cardinall of *Loraine* by the Kings consent is lately strangled
unto death.
Dumaine.   My brother Cardenall slaine and I alive?
O wordes of power to kill a thousand men.
Come let us away and leavy men,
Tis warre that must asswage this tyrantes pride.
Frier.   My Lord, heare me but speak.
I am a Frier of the order of the Jacobyns, that for my conscience 1130
sake will kill the King.
Dumaine.   But what doth move thee above the rest to doe the deed?
Frier.   O my Lord, I have beene a great sinner in my dayes, and
the deed is meritorious.
Dumaine.   But how wilt thou get opportunitye?
Frier.   Tush my Lord, let me alone for that.
Dumaine.   Frier come with me,
We will goe talke more of this within.

Exeunt

[Scene xxii]
Sound Drumme and Trumpets, and enter the King of France, *and*
Navarre, Epernoune, Bartus, Pleshe *and Souldiers.*

King.   Brother of *Navarre*, I sorrow much,
That ever I was prov'd your enemy,   1140
And that the sweet and princely minde you beare,
Was ever troubled with injurious warres:
I vow as I am lawfull King of *France*,
To recompence your reconciled love,
With all the honors and affections,

1120 And] Mal MS, Chappell; His life, and O 1

That ever I vouchsafte my dearest freends.

Navarre.   It is enough if that *Navarre* may be
  Esteemed faithfull to the King of *France*:
  Whose service he may still commaund till death.

King.   Thankes to my Kingly Brother of *Navarre*.   1150
  Then heere wee'l lye before Lutetia walles,
  Girting this strumpet Cittie with our siege,
  Till surfeiting with our afflicting armes,
  She cast her hatefull stomack to the earth.

Enter a Messenger.

Messenger.   And it please your Majestie heere is a Frier of the
order of the Jacobins, sent from the President of Paris, that
craves accesse unto your grace.

King.   Let him come in.

Enter Frier *with a Letter.*

Epernoune.   I like not this Friers look.
  Twere not amisse my Lord, if he were searcht.   1160

King.   Sweete *Epernoune*, our Friers are holy men,
  And will not offer violence to their King,
  For all the wealth and treasure of the world.
  Frier, thou dost acknowledge me thy King?

Frier.   I my good Lord, and will dye therein.

King.   Then come thou neer, and tell what newes thou bringst.

Frier.   My Lord,
  The President of *Paris* greetes your grace,
  And sends his dutie by these speedye lines,
  Humblye craving your gracious reply.   1170

King.   Ile read them Frier, and then Ile answere thee.

Frier.   *Sancte Jacobe*, now have mercye upon me.

> *He stabs the* King *with a knife as he readeth the letter,*
> *and then the* King *getteth the knife and killes him.*

Epernoune.   O my Lord, let him live a while.

King.   No, let the villaine dye, and feele in hell,

1151 Lutetia] Chappell (Lutetia's); Lu-   1172 *Jacobe*] Dyce; Jacobus O1
crecia O1

Just torments for his trechery.

Navarre. What, is your highnes hurt?

King. Yes *Navarre*, but not to death I hope.

Navarre. God shield your grace from such a sodaine death:
 Goe call a surgeon hether strait.   *[Exit attendant.]*

King. What irreligeous Pagans partes be these,   1180
 Of such as holde them of the holy church?
 Take hence that damned villaine from my sight.

                [Exeunt attendants with body.]

Epernoune. Ah, had your highnes let him live,
 We might have punisht him to his deserts.

King. Sweet *Epernoune* all Rebels under heaven,
 Shall take example by his punishment,
 How they beare armes against their soveraigne.
 Goe call the English Agent hether strait,
 Ile send my sister *England* newes of this,
 And give her warning of her trecherous foes.   1190

              [Enter Surgeon.]

Navarre. Pleaseth your grace to let the Surgeon search your
    wound.

King. The wound I warrant ye is deepe my Lord,
 Search Surgeon and resolve me what thou seest.

              The Surgeon *searcheth*

              Enter the English Agent.

Agent for *England,* send thy mistres word,
 What this detested Jacobin hath done.
 Tell her for all this that I hope to live,
 Which if I doe, the Papall Monarck goes
 To wrack, and his antechristian kingdome falles.
 These bloudy hands shall teare his triple Crowne,
 And fire accursed *Rome* about his eares.   1200
 Ile fire his crased buildings and inforse
 The papall towers to kisse the lowly earth.

Navarre, give me thy hand, I heere do sweare,

1186 his] Chappell; their O 1   incense O 1
1198 his] *omit* O 1   1202 lowly] Dyce; holy O 1
*1201 inforse] Dyce¹ *(qy),* Dyce²;

To ruinate that wicked Church of *Rome*,
That hatcheth up such bloudy practises.
And heere protest eternall love to thee,
And to the Queene of *England* specially,
Whom God hath blest for hating Papestry.
Navarre.   These words revive my thoughts and comforts me,
To see your highnes in this vertuous minde.   1210
King.   Tell me Surgeon, shall I live?
Surgeon.   Alas my Lord, the wound is dangerous,
For you are stricken with a poysoned knife.
King.   A poysoned knife? what, shall the French king dye,
Wounded and poysoned, both at once?
Epernoune.   O that that damned villaine were alive againe,
That we might torture him with some new found death.
Bartus.   He died a death too good, the devill of hell
Torture his wicked soule.
King.   Ah curse him not sith he is dead.   1220
O the fatall poyson workes within my brest,
Tell me Surgeon and flatter not, may I live?
Surgeon.   Alas my Lord, your highnes cannot live.
Navarre.   Surgeon, why saist thou so? the King may live.
King.   Oh no *Navarre*, thou must be King of *France*.
Navarre.   Long may you live, and still be King of *France*.
Epernoune.   Or else dye *Epernoune*.
King.   Sweet *Epernoune* thy King must dye. My Lords,
Fight in the quarrell of this valiant Prince,
For he is your lawfull King and my next heire: 1230
Valoyses lyne ends in my tragedie.
Now let the house of *Bourbon* weare the crowne,
And may it never end in bloud as mine hath done.
Weep not sweet *Navarre*, but revenge my death.
Ah *Epernoune*, is this thy love to me?
Henry thy King wipes of these childish teares,
And bids thee whet thy sword on *Sextus* bones,
That it may keenly slice the Catholicks.
He loves me not that sheds most teares,
But he that makes most lavish of his bloud.   1240

404

Fire Paris where these trecherous rebels lurke.
I dye *Navarre*, come beare me to my Sepulchre.
Salute the Queene of *England* in my name,
And tell her *Henry* dyes her faithfull freend.　　　　　*He dyes.*
Navarre.　Come Lords, take up the body of the King,
That we may see it honourably interde:
And then I vow for to revenge his death,
As *Rome* and all those popish Prelates there,
Shall curse the time that ere *Navarre* was King,
And rulde in *France* by *Henries* fatall death.　　　　　1250

> *They march out with the body of the* King, *lying*
> *on foure mens shoulders with a dead*
> *march, drawing weapons*
> *on the ground.*

FINIS.

266, 293 Cossin] As the Methuen editor points out, this emendation of O 1 'Cosin' (for *cousin*) is required on the evidence of line 293 in order to repair the reporter's confusion with the correct use of *cousin* as in lines 307, 309. Methuen notes that on the King's promise that the Admiral would be protected, the Duke of Anjou placed Cossin, Captain of the King's Guard, in command of fifty soldiers at the Admiral's house. This officer betrayed the Admiral by permitting entrance of the Switzers of Anjou's guard.

445 their pacience] The probable corruption of lines 544–7 has made such editors as Tucker Brooke and Revels shy off from Cunningham's emendation to 'their' of O 1 'there'. H. J. Oliver, the Revels editor, remarks as follows: 'The lines have puzzled editors and may be corrupt, but probably mean: "although I have deserved a scourge, there are two kinds of response to evil; one is patient suffering, the other the undoing of the King; I pray that my nearest friends are of the better kind – and have not been responsible for my death!"' The difficulty here is to read into the lines such complexities as 'the two kinds of response to evil'. The present editor takes it that 'my neerest freends' of line 547 is intended to be contrasted with the King's enemies. If so, Cunningham's emendation is required. The sense, then, would be: 'I must confess that my unjust actions (to the Protestants) have made me deserve their retaliation as scourges for my sins. However, I credit them with patient submission to these wrongs, as God requires, and do not believe that they have murdered me in revenge. May God grant that my nearest friends are no more culpable in my death than these innocent Protestants.'

574 seeme] The temptation to follow Chappell's natural emendation 'seek' has proved irresistible to all editors but Methuen and Revels. As Oliver in Revels points out, *O.E.D.* III.9b records a transitive use of 'seem' in the sense of 'think fit' as late as 1610. Thus O 1 is worth retaining although as usual one can have little faith in the relation of the word to what was written in Marlowe's own manuscript.

688 wert] In a bad quarto like the present, roughnesses are to be expected, and the usual emendation here to 'were' must be viewed as a sophistication. It is equally balanced whether the reporter intended 'if the fruit were not' or 'were it not that the fruit is within thy womb', as O 1 may be taken.

783 take] If O 1 'make a walk' had been the reporter's confusion, then Tucker Brooke and Revels are right in refusing to emend to Chappell's 'take'. But despite the Revels note that '"make" suggests the deliberateness of the decision', the phrase is not idiomatic and is expressly barred by *O.E.D.* from v.57f and its examples of reference to locomotion or travel: 'English idiom is app. capricious in excluding many locutions which would seem to be parallel with these; we cannot, e.g. use *make* with obj. *a ride, a walk* (cf. G. *einen Spaziergang machen*).' Under these circumstances it is simpler to take it, with Methuen, that the compositor made the mistake by picking up 'make' memorially from the preceding line 782 than that the reporter thought he remembered an impossible English construction.

850   sectious]   O 1 'sexious' seems more likely to be the reporter's phonetic version of what he thought he had heard than a compositor's error for the common emendation 'factious'. Hence the O 1 reading – in the form of 'sectious', however – must be respected. For an excellent parallel, see 'offencious' at 384, the only occurrence listed by *O.E.D.*

1201   inforse]   Although it seems clear that the reporter in 1201–2 recorded 'incense | The papall towers to kisse the holy earth', the parallel in *Edward II* – as Dyce noticed first by query and then by emendation – allows us the opportunity to restore Marlowe's manuscript readings of 'inforse' (or something like it) and 'lowly'. *Edward II* reads at I.iv.100–1, 'Ile fire thy crased buildings, and enforce | The papall towers, to kisse the lowlie ground'.

PRESS-VARIANTS IN Q1

[Copies collated: BM (C.34.a.3), Bodl (Bodleian), D (Dyce), Pepys (Magdalen College); CSmH (Huntington), DFo (Folger), MWiW–C (Chapin).]

SHEET A (*outer forme*)

Corrected: D, Pepys, CSmH, DFo, MWiW–C
Uncorrected: BM, Bodl

Sig. A8^v
r–t *The Massacre*] *at Paris.*

SHEET D (*outer forme*)

Corrected: BM, Bodl, D, Pepys, DFo, MWiW–C
Uncorrected: CSmH

Sig. D1
1035 deceast] diceast
Sig. D2^v
1107 by] dy
Sig. D4^v
1169 sends] send

EMENDATIONS OF ACCIDENTALS

[NOTE: The O 1 custom is to place names of countries, cities, provinces, and rivers all in roman. In the present text the names of countries have been italicized.]

Scene i

7 hearts,] ~ :
10 this,] ~ :
13 *Queene Mother.*] O 1 *speech-prefix in this scene* is Old Qu.
15 know,...Religion⌄] ~ ⌄...~ ,
19–21 O 1 *lines*: We...rest, | With... company.

24–5 *One line in* O 1
24 Mother,] ~ ⌄
36 *Guise*⌄] ~ ,
47–8 Cardinall⌄...brother,] ~ ,...~ ⌄
51 *et seq. France*] France
53 trap,] ~ :

Scene ii

65 all.] ~ ,
66 Apothecarie.——] ~ . ⌄
73–4 O 1 *lines*: See...Lord, | And... dyes.
78 love.] ~ ,
83 Souldyer.——] ~ . ⌄
85 part,] *point uncertain*
91 *Guise*,...thoughts⌄] ~ ⌄...~ ,
92 abroad,] ~ ⌄
99 reach.] ~ ,
110 executes⌄] ~ ,
111 aimed] aimde

117 Catholickes⌄] ~ ,
122 religion.] ~ ,
124 ashamde,] ~ ⌄
141 more:] ~ ⌄
145–7 O 1 *lines*: Then...Cardes, | Within...thing:
145 *Guise*,] ~ ⌄
146 Cardes⌄] ~ ,
149 *Navarre.* Tis] *Navarre*, tis
153 we——] ~ ⌄
164 passe,] ~ :

Scene iii

168 holde,] ~ ⌄
176 *Navarre*,] ~ ⌄
179 beware⌄] ~ :

184 *Margaret*] *Margret*
198 Lord,] ~ ⌄

Scene iv

204 deere,] ~ :
207 *Charles.*] O 1 *speech-prefix in this scene* is King.
212–14 O 1 *lines*: Onely...honor, |

Knightes...ends.
219 advisde⌄] ~ ,
232 Burgonets,] ~ :
267 keep⌄] ~ ,

409

Scene v

274–5 O1 *lines*: Anjoy...Retes, | 307–8 *One line in* O1
    Sweare...burgonets,   312–13 *One line in* O1
278 am,] ~ .   312 *Shatillian*] Shatillian
284–5 *One line in* O1   316 handes,] ~ .
284 Admirall,] ~ ‸   331 *Exit*‸] ~ .
287–9 O1 *lines*: Be...thither, | And...   336–7 *One line in* O1
    live.   336 *Tue*,] *comma doubtful in* O1
290 mine.] ~ ,   339 *Loreine*.] ~ ,

Scene vi

354 Saviour——] ~ .   356 Why,] ~ ‸
355–8 *Prose in* O1   359 *Seroune*.] *Seronne.*

Scene vii

367–9, 383–4 *Prose in* O1   427 Condy——] ~ .
384 offencious?] ~ .   431–2 *One line in* O1
390 Epitomies] Epetomies   437 I?] ~ ,
392 *Germany*] Germany   442 Away] *just possibly* A way
394 *ipse*] *ipsi*   444 end:] ~ ,
397–8 *One line in* O1   445–8 O1 *lines*: Gonzago...Orleance, |
398 sirra:] ~ ,   Retes...Roan, | And...heresy. |
404 ill,] ~ :   and...rings
417 Protestants,] ~ .   448 rings.] ~ ‸
427 That] that   449 Now‸] O1 *text*; Now. O1 *cw*

Scene viii

451 *et seq. Poland*] Poland   466 That] that
459 warres,] ~ .   478 The] the

Scene ix

489 eate] cate (*doubtful*)   512 *Loraine*] Loraine
497 th'airs] thair's   513 lament‸] ~ :
510–11 *One line in* O1   521 dye,] ~ .

Scene xi

536 *Charles*.] O1 *speech-prefix in this*   551 Mother.] ~ ,
    scene is King.   562 can, provide‸] ~ ‸ ~ ,
539 *Queene Mother*.] O1 *speech-prefix in*   573 *et seq. Spaine*] Spaine
    this scene is Queene.   587.1 *Exeunt*.] *Ezeunt.*

Scene xii

587.4 *crownd*] crownd
589 *Queene Mother.*] O1 *speech-prefix in this scene is* Queene.
599 *King.*] O1 *speech-prefix in this scene is* Henry.
607 bent.] ~ ,
608 persist,] *point doubtful*
613 You] you

625–6 *One line in* O1
625 now,] ~ ∧
629 And] and
638 As] as
651 presently,] ~ .
652–3 diadem. . . .will:] ~ :. . .~ .
663 But] but

Scene xiii

667 O1 *places to left of line in margin*
672–3 *Prose in* O1 *but lined* reads | my

675–6 *Prose in* O1 *but lined* must | partake

Scene xiv

699 warres∧] ~ :
703 land:] ~ .

719 Plaies] plaies

Scene xv

744–5 readines,. . .*Navarre:*] ~ :. . .~ ,
752–3, 754–6 *Prose in* O1
760–1 O1 *lines:* And. . .in | Christendome. . .derision:
761 derision,] ~ :
763 Minions?] ~ ,

766 disgrace,] ~ :
768 blood,] ~ .
772 friends,] ~ ∧
783–6 *Prose in* O1
783 gone?] ~ ,

Scene xvi

800–1 last:. . .force,] ~ ,. . .~ :

804 Lords,] ~ ∧

Scene xvii

806–8 O1 *lines:* Sir. . .cuckolde, | And . . .although |
821–4 *Prose in* O1
822 men.] ~ ,
834 King] Kiug
842 exhibition?] ~ .
851 crowne,] *point uncertain*

861 Senator.] ~ , (*probable*)
867 Majestie,] ~ :
871–5 O1 *lines:* But. . .highnesse, | Seene. . .Paris, | And. . .shewes | Did. . .commaund:
872 highnesse∧] ~ ,
886–7 *One line in* O1

Scene xviii

914 *Pleshe*] Pleshe
914.1 O1 *places after line* 913

930.1 *Exit.*] *Exeunt.*

Scene xix

938 Well‚ then,] ~ , ~ ‚
940 Chamber,] ~ .
942 money?] ~ .
943 not:] ~ ,
943 so,] ~ ‚
956 *Holla] Halla*
959–60 *One line in* O 1
977–8 *One line in* O 1
980 fielde.] ~ ,
987–8 *One line in* O 1
990, 992, 994 *3.] Mur.*
993 me, villaine?] ~ ‚ ~ .
996–1000 *Prose in* O 1 *except* I am Duke...*begins new separate line*
999 lookes‚] ~ ,
1002 *him*] him

1005 him,] ~ .
1014 *messe*] *messa*
1016–19 *Prose in* O 1
1016 What,] ~ ‚
1022 massacres,] ~ :
1024 broyles,] ~ :
1037 land,] ~ :
1049 Thee] thee
1052–3 *Prose in* O 1
1052 Away] A way
1062–3 *Prose in* O 1
1067 *Queene Mother.*] O 1 *speech-prefix in this scene is* Queene.
1072 greefe:] ~ ,
1081 meditate.] ~ ,
1088 *Guise:* ~ ,

Scene xx

1093 What,] ~ ‚
1094 bloud?] ~ ,
1096 dye?] ~ .

1098–9 *One line in* O 1
1100 King,] ~ .
1105–6 *One line in* O 1

Scene xxi

1114 home,] ~ .
1115 King,] ~ .
1119 life,] ~ .

1129 speak.] ~ ,
1130–1 O 1 *lines:* Jacobyns | That

Scene xxii

1147 be‚] ~ ,
1164 King?] ~ :
1167–70 *Prose in* O 1
1174–5 *Prose in* O 1 *but lined* hell, | just
1185–7 *Prose in* O 1
1197–8 O 1 *lines:* Which...wrack. | And...falles.
1198 wrack,] ~ .

1212–13 *Prose in* O 1
1214 knife? what,] ~ , ~ ‚
1218–22 *Prose in* O 1
1228–9 O 1 *lines:* Sweet...dye. | My... Prince,
1241 lurke.] ~ ,
1245 King,] ~ .

412

HISTORICAL COLLATION

[NOTE: The following editions are herein collated: O1 (n.d.), Ch (published by Chappell, 1818), Ox (edited Oxberry, 1818), R (*Works*, ed. Robinson, 1826), D¹ (*Works*, ed. Dyce, 1850), D² (*Works*, ed. Dyce, rev. 1858), C (*Works*, ed. Cunningham, 1870), B (*Works*, ed. Bullen, 1884–5), TB (*Works*, ed. Tucker Brooke, 1910), M (Methuen, ed. H. S. Bennett, 1931), Ri (*Plays*, ed. Ribner, 1963), Rv (Revels, ed. H. J. Oliver, 1968). Reference is also made to EP (*England's Parnassus*, 1600), Mal (MS notes by Malone in Bodleian copy), Br (MS notes by Broughton in BM copy of Robinson), and Coll (MS notes by Collier in BM copy of D¹).]

Scene i

9 hath] has Ch, Ox, R
20 a] an Ch, Ox, R, C
28 doe] does Ch, Ox, R

29 sides] side Ch, Ox, R
37 consent] assent Ch, Ox, R, C

Scene ii

64 houre,] hour and D (*qy*), C, B
70 which] which late Ch, Ox, R, C, B
72 every] very Coll MS
73 good] *omit* Ch, Ox, R, C
91 begins] begin Ch, Ox, R, D, C, B
95 That perill...way] Daunger's...joy EP
106 scornes] scorn Ch, Ox, R, D, C, B
110 Contrives, imagines...executes] Contrive, imagine...execute R
110 and] *omit* C
114 this earth] the earth Ch, Ox, R, C

117 Catholickes] Catholic Ch, Ox, R, C
118 Sends] Send D, B
141 keeps] keep Ch, Ox, R, D, C, B
144 To] Do C
144 will] whole Coll MS
147 cut] to cut Ch, Ox, R
148 deale] deal'st] Ch, Ox, R, C
149 *Navarre, Navarre*] Navarre Ch, Ox, R, D, C, B, M
154 possession] procession Br MS
162 beholde, they] behold them Ch, Ox, R, D, C

Scene iii

185 Workes] Doth work Ch, Ox, R; Worketh D (*qy*), C

185 head] heart Ch, Ox, R, C

Scene iv

215 paines] pain B
234 suspected] suspect Ox, R, D, C, M, Ri
235 be] or be Ox, R
245 humbly] humble O1, Rv
249 were] had R, C

259 their] his Ch, Ox, R, D, C
266, 293 *Cossin*] Cosin O1, TB; Cousin Ch, Ox, R, D, C, B
273 *Admirall*. I...Majestie.] *omit* Ch, Ox, R

Scene v

275 in] on Ch, Ox, R, C
288 thither] hither Ox, R
304 *Gonzago*...dead?] What, is he dead, Gonzago? Ch, Ox, R, C
316 *Anjoy.*] *omit* Ox, R

324 not] not be M
327 goe] go and Ch, Ox, R
329 then] and then Ch, Ox, R; then go C
332 Lords] lord C

Scene vi

346 is that which] is't that Ch, Ox, R
351 ha't] hate O1, TB
358 *Sanctus*] *Sancta* O1

358 hee was] he is D¹ (*qy*); he's D², B, M, Ri

Scene vii

361 comes] come Ch, Ox, R, C, B
361, 418 Sene] Rene O1
362 frightes] fright Ch, Ox, R, D, C, B
380 Who] Whom Ch. Ox, R, C,
387 scoftes] scoff'dst Ch, Ox, R, D, C, B, M, Ri, Rv
393 axioms] actions Ch, Ox, R, D¹, C
395 *testimonii*] *testimonis* O1, Ch, Ox, R
395 *inartificiale*] *in arte fetiales* O1, Ch, Ox; *in arte partialis* R
398 sirra: kill] Sirrah, kill Ch, Ox, R
404 *Shekius*] *Shekins* O1, Ch, Ox, R
405 contains] contain Ch, Ox, R, D, C,

B, Ri
411 Sorbonests] thorbonest O1
412 their] their own D, C, B, M
417 of] *omit* Ch, Ox, R, C
424 *Dumain*] *omit* C
424 strait be] *omit* Ch, Ox, R
425 And] *omit* C
428 you] *omit* Ch, Ox, R, C
434 what] all Ch, Ox, R, C
434, 436 this] the R
443 sirs] *omit* C
444 that] *omit* Ch, Ox, R, C
448 mattins] midnight matins C

Scene viii

452 Electors] Elector's Ch, Ox, R, D, C, B; Electors' M

461 Muscovites] Muscovite C
481 Lords] lord C

Scene ix

483 an] a R, C
488 by] *omit* Ch, Ox, R, D, C, B
492 heere] *omit* Ch, Ox, R
494 like you] do you like C
496 As] That Ox, R, C
497 very] *omit* C

501 a] an Ch, Ox, R, C
504 And] *omit* Ch, Ox, R, C
509 Be...*Guise.*] *omit* R, C
515 amongst] among B
518 For] *omit* B
527 let us] lets us O1; let's Ch, Ox, R

Scene x

530 villain,] villain, no Ch, Ox, R, C

Scene xi

540 complaine] to complain Ch, Ox, R
541 and] I Ch, Ox, R
545 their] there O 1, Ch, Ox, R, D, TB,
   Rv
549 braines turne] brain turns Ch, Ox,
   R, C
551 sonne$_\Lambda$] ~ ? Ch, Ox, R, D, C, TB,
   M, Ri
554 there] omit Ch, Ox, R, C
554 for] omit B

561 be] omit TB (qy)
563 Polonie] Polonia R, C
565 now Navarre] now Pleshé D^1 (qy),
   D^2, C, TB, M
566 me] it B
568 heers] there's B
574 seeme] seek Ch, Ox, R, D, C, B, TB
577 true] poor R
587 whilste] while Ox, R, C

Scene xii

587.1, 588, 598 le] la O 1
591 feares] foes Coll MS
602 your] our R
603 saies] say Ch, Ox, R, D, C, B
607 affection] affections M
613 in] with Ch, Ox, R
617 doe] dare B

626 solemne] omit Ch, Ox, R
638 As] That Ch, Ox, R, C
641 as in secrecy I] as I in secresy Ch,
   Ox, R, C
643 are] as O 1
655 Lord] Lords O 1
655 seek] to seek R, C

Scene xiii

672 my Lord] omit Ch, Ox, R, C
683 needs] need Ch, Ox, R, D, C, B, Ri
688 wert] were Ch, Ox, R, D, C, B, TB

689 Of] On Ox, R
692 looke] look'st Ch, Ox, R,

Scene xiv

698 My] Now Ch, Ox, R
698 sith] since Ch, Ox, R, C
703 rent] rend Ch, Ox, R
717 incampes] implants Ch, Ox, R, C

726 are] is Ch, Ox, R
727 meanes] mean D, C, B
731 tell] tell me Ch, Ox, R, C
733 of] omit Ch, Ox, R, C

Scene xv

746 goe] go'st Ch, Ox, R
747 suffer't] suffer O 1, TB; suffer it C
750 to] omit Ch, Ox, R, C
752 So] How Ch, Ox, R, C
752 of] omit Ch, Ox, R, C
758 thus to be] to be thus Ch, Ox, R, C

760 Kings] kings beside Ch, Ox, R, C
762 how] omit R
764 disgrace] disgust Coll MS
771 me] me, Epernoune Ch, Ox, R, C
783 take] make O 1, TB, Ri, Rv

Scene xvi

800 so] as Ch, Ox, R, C
803 relicks] prelates M (qy)

804 that] omit C
804 this] the Ch, Ox, R

Scene xvii

806 dares] dare Ch, Ox, R
811 will] would Ch, Ox, R
817 take thee] take thou Ch, Ox, R, C
819 list...dare] list'st...dar'st Ch, Ox, R
826 Gospell] Gospel's Ch, Ox, R, C, B, M, Ri
831 Ah] Oh Ch, Ox, R, C
835 *Valoyses*] Valois D², B
850 sectious] sexious O₁, TB; factious Mal MS, Ch, Ox, R, Coll MS, D²,

C, B, M, Ri
851 my Lord] *omit* Ch, Ox, R
855 cloakes] clucks Coll MS
857 needs] need Ch, Ox, R, C
870 are] art Ch, Ox, R
872 seene] but seen Br MS
876 in] it in B
877 the *Guise*] Guise Ch, Ox, R
887 royall] *omit* Ch, Ox, R
897 no] not R, C
898 meane] means Ch, Ox, R, C

Scene xviii

901 the *Guise*] Guise Ch, Ox, R, C

924 And] He R, C; 'A D

Scene xix

937 *3.*] *1.* Ch, Ox, R, C
943 so] *omit* Ch, Ox, R, C
951 ye] you Ch, Ox, R, C
956 *verlete*] varlet Ch, Ox, R, C, B, M
968 bare] bear Ch, Ox, R, C, B
974 Whatsoever] Whatever Ch, Ox, R, C
988 Duke of] *omit* Ch, Ox, R, C
990, 992, 994 *3.*] *Murderer.* Ch, Ox, R,

C, B
998 Tut] But TB
1000 *1.*] *2 Murd.* Ch, Ox, R, C
1003 deaths] death Ch, Ox, R, C
1013 *Valois* his] Valois's Ch, Ox, R
1015 dyed] dies Ch, Ox, R, C
1020 Ah] Oh Ch, Ox, R
1024 And in] In just Ch, Ox, R, C
1029 civile] cruel Ch, Ox, R, C

Scene xxi

1108 for] *omit* Ch, Ox, R, Coll MS, C
1113 *Valoys* his] Valois's Ch, Ox, R
1120 And] His life and O₁, Rv

1125 Cardenall] the Cardinal D, C
1127 away] straight away C
1128 this] the Ch, Ox, R

Scene xxii

1149 till] to Ch, Ox, R, C
1151 heere] there Ch, Ox, R, C
1151 Lutetia] Lucrecia O₁; Lutetia's Ch, Ox, R, C
1169 sends] send O₁ (u)
1172 *Jacobe*] *Jacobus* O₁, Ch, Ox, R, TB
1172 upon] on Ch, Ox, R
1184 to] for Ch, Ox, R, C
1186 his] their O₁

1192 ye] you Ch, Ox, R, C
1198 and] an Ch, Ox, R
1198 his] *omit* O₁, Ch, Ox, R, TB, Ri, Rv; th' D, C, B, M
1201 inforse] incense O₁, Ch, Ox, R, D¹ (*qy enforce*)
1202 lowly] holy O₁, Ch, Ox, R, TB, Rv

416

1204 that] this Ch, Ox, R, C
1207 specially] especially Ch, Ox, R
1208 Papestry] Popery Ch, Ox, R, C
1209 comforts] comfort Ch, Ox, R, D,
      C, B, Ri
1220 Ah] Oh Ch, Ox, R, C

1220 sith] since Ch, Ox, R
1239 not] not the best Ch, Ox, R, D[1];
      not the most D[2], C, M
1247 for] so Ch, Ox, R, D, C, B, M
1248 As] That Ch, Ox, R